ISBN 978-1-332-81789-4
PIBN 10467378

1 MONTH OF
FREE
READING

at

www.ForgottenBooks.com

By purchasing this book you are eligible for one month membership to ForgottenBooks.com, giving you unlimited access to our entire collection of over 700,000 titles via our web site and mobile apps.

To claim your free month visit:

www.forgottenbooks.com/free467378

AGRICULTURE OF MAINE

ELEVENTH ANNUAL REPORT

OF THE

COMMISSIONER OF AGRICULTURE

OF THE

State of Maine

1912

SENTINEL PUBLISHING COMPANY

WATERVILLE, MAINE

1913

DEPARTMENT OF AGRICULTURE.

To His Excellency, Frederick W. Plaisted, Governor of Maine, and Council:

I hereby submit my second annual report as Commissioner of Agriculture of the State of Maine, for the year 1912, in compliance with chapter 204 of the Public Laws of 1901.

J. P. BUCKLEY, *Commissioner.*

Augusta, December 31, 1912.

ANNUAL REPORT OF THE COMMISSIONER OF AGRICULTURE.

The year 1912 has been a backward year for the farmer. The cold wet spring deprived him of the opportunity of putting in his crops when they should be put in, and he was obliged to change his plans and put in others that he did not intend to grow, crops that were not for his advantage, causing him a great loss in not growing those that will demand the best prices in the market. One of the most important outlooks for the State is the farm crop, and if the farmer does not succeed, it affects in a way the whole State; for we are called on more and more every year to reach out with our farm products and feed the large and increasing population of New England and other parts of the country. And the farmer must receive more for his crops in the future to enable him to cultivate more land to keep up with the increasing population of consumers. The past year most of the crops have fallen short of those of the two years previous. Though the heavy rains that fell the past season did interfere with the crop growing, it is a blessing that we had so much rain. It will surely assist us in the future. Still the rainfall, coming when it did, was a great drawback to all branches of agriculture in the State; but let us hope that we will get better conditions and better crops another year.

POTATOES.

The reports of the United States Department do not give us as large a yield of potatoes as last year. I believe that while in the northern part of the State the crop is not as large, the southern and central parts of the State have made quite a gain, so that our crop will be nearly as large as that of 1911,

making between twenty-seven and twenty-eight million bushels.
The price received this year will not'come up to that received
last year, but they will bring a good average price, and the coöperation of the Farmers' Exchange will enable the farmers to
secure better and surer prices. If the farmer could receive 50
cents per bushel delivered at the railroad station each year, he
could make a good profit on his crop. The demand for Maine
potatoes for seed is increasing in different parts of the country
and it would be well for the farmers that are a long distance
from the railroad to make an effort to grow good seed potatoes,
which would enable them to get better prices, and not sell their
potatoes for commercial use. The potato crop this year will
average the farmer about 60 cents per bushel. The State Exchange has been of great assistance to the farmers in putting
their potato crop on to the market in better shape and receiving
more uniform and better prices.

THE HAY CROP.

The hay crop is estimated at $25,420,000. That is not quite so
large as the estimate of the crop for 1911 but the quality is
superior to that of last year, making the value of the hay crop
for feeding purposes in the State as great, and on account of
the increase of all kinds of live stock (except horses), this will
be of great assistance in keeping up the fertility of our farms.
A large quantity of our hay is pressed and shipped out of the
State annually.

APPLES.

The apple crop this year has dropped off from that of last
year, being 2,400,000 bushels. It will bring on an average 50
cents per bushel to the growers. We hope the fruit growers
will continue to spray and care for their fruit trees and have
more apples that will be suitable for packing in boxes and get
better prices. I believe it is a mistake to allow apples from
outside our State to be shipped in and sold here when we have
the opportunity to grow splendid fruit, and the apples that are
shipped in, though they bring a very large price do not have
the delicious flavor of those grown in this State. The grower
must see that his fruit is properly packed and put on to the
market, so that it will be a credit to the grower and raise the
apple standard of our State.

THE OAT CROP.

The oat crop is estimated at $2,301,000. That is an increase from the crop of last year which is due in many cases to the fact that on account of the cold, wet spring the farmers could not put in the crop that they wished and were obliged to sow oats as this crop could be taken care of later in the season. On the whole the oat crop was a success, and it will enable the farmer to use more oats in connection with his other grain in feeding the dairy cow and other live stock.

SWEET CORN.

Our sweet corn crop was very poor this year, being only about 40 per cent of a regular crop on account of the cold wet spring of last year. This particular crop was more affected by the cold, wet weather than any other grown. Last year we had the largest crop that has ever been grown in the State, but the poor crop of this year was a great setback to many of our farmers and a loss to the packers. There were three new factories put in operation last year. That means that Maine sweet corn is coming to the front. Like our apples, it has the flavor that leads the country, and it is steadily gaining a fine market in different parts of the United States. Our farmers received in 1911 $1,025,000 for their crop, but this year they only received a small percentage on account of such a poor sweet corn season.

FIELD CORN.

The field corn crop was estimated at $480,000, which is a slight increase from that of last year. More of our farmers are growing corn and that is a great help to the State, as we have been sending too much of our money to the Middle West that might be kept at home by raising more corn, which can be raised with profit on our farms. We are keeping more beef cattle that can be fed corn meal to good advantage, so we can have our native beef which is of more value to the consumer than the cold storage beef shipped in from the West.

WHEAT.

The wheat crop has dropped off since last year, as the result of the condition of the weather in planting time. Some of the best wheat that can be raised in North America can be grown in this State, especially in Aroostook County, and I hope the farmers of that county will grow more wheat in the future and be able to supply those in the central and southern parts of the State with a large portion of the wheat that they now consume.

THE BARLEY CROP.

The barley crop has increased over last year, it being estimated at $115,000. This crop can be grown to good advantage in our State. It is a splendid grain for feed for all kinds of live stock and poultry and should receive more attention from the farmers as I believe it would be a very valuable crop to be raised in this State.

MISCELLANEOUS CROPS.

Our farmers are not paying attention enough to truck gardening, especially in the southern part of the State; as we are obliged to send to Massachusetts for a large portion of the garden truck to supply the hotels and summer homes of the people who spend their summers with us. This supply should be grown on our farms. We should not be obliged to send out of the State for what we can grow to such good advantage and supply to our visitors fresh from the farm. I hope this matter will be considered by the farmers in the southern part of the State, as I believe they have a great opportunity to take up this work. There are sections of the State where the farmers are raising large crops of squash and cabbage to good advantage, but this year the price of cabbage is very low and this crop will not bring the farmers very good returns.

THE MAINE ORCHARDS.

The orchards of this State are steadily on the increase. A number of new orchards were set out during the last year and old ones improved, and the fruit growers are taking better care of their orchards. I believe the demonstration work that has been conducted by our State Horticulturist and his Assistant in trimming, pruning and spraying has been of great assistance to the farmers for they did not realize the benefit from such work or know that it could be done with so little expense and labor. Many of the owners of orchards have purchased spray pumps and are taking the best of care of their orchards and will get good results in the future, which will enable them to demand and get better prices. And by growing better apples they can get a quality of fruit suitable for packing in boxes, and thus in many cases they can double the prices that they have been receiving in the past. The demonstrations of box packing that were given in different parts of the State by the men from this Department were very interesting to the fruit growers and impressed upon their minds that in order to put apples in boxes they must first grow the proper fruit, and to do this they must begin in the orchard by caring for their trees so that they will produce clean and better colored fruit.

BROWN-TAIL AND GYPSY MOTHS.

In many parts of the State the infestation of the brown-tail moth was very thick. A report circulated about the State that the brown-tails were all dead at the time the nests should be gathered did great damage in retarding the work. Many of the municipal officers and real estate owners neglected cutting the brown-tail nests from their trees and the result is that in most parts of the State there are more nests now than ever before. Many complaints have been entered in relation to cutting the branches from fruit trees. If the owners of orchards will spray at the proper time, it will take care of the brown-tail moth and benefit the trees in other ways. I was obliged to put a state crew into two different towns last spring on account of the failure of the selectmen to comply with the law in regard to removing the brown-tail moth nests from their fruit and shade trees.

The past season has been a favorable one for the gypsy as well as the brown-tail moth and the Field Agent in charge of the work reports that a large number of egg clusters have been located and destroyed. The infestation was much larger than in 1911. We had an appropriation of $15,000 for the work, and the greatest effort was made to prevent the spread of the moth in parts of the State not infested and to destroy all possible in the infested section, which is mostly in York and Cumberland Counties. The Federal Horticultural Board has

put a quarantine on different parts of the State for the brown-
tail and gypsy moths for interstate shipments, or shipments
from infested to uninfested sections of the State. And practically, in the case of the gypsy moth, no change has taken place
for in the past, inspection has been conducted by the United
States men or the state men, on all shipments of lumber, tele-
graph poles, railroad ties, etc. from the infested section of the
State.

THE DAIRY WORK.

The work done among the dairymen of the State has been
done by our State Dairy Instructor in different forms, and
especially with the cow test associations. These are of great
assistance to the dairyman in weeding out his poor cows, but
they do not give him the proper information as to the cost of
the production of milk; and the dairyman is in a large measure
to blame for this, as he is willing to sell his hay and other crops
for a much lower price than he could get in the market, and
does not expect to get a fair compensation for his labor and
the money invested. When the best authorities in the country
tell us that it costs from $100 to $147 per year to feed and
care for a cow it must be so, and it will take a very good cow
to give milk enough to pay her owner, at the price at which
many of our farmers are selling their dairy product. The
amount received for our dairy products for the past year is a
little more than that for 1911, which was $10,880,000. For
the last two years there has been an increase in the number of
cows kept in the State. Many dairy cows are being shipped
out of the State to the Middle West and many of them to
Massachusetts, and perhaps we can raise dairy cows and sell
them to good advantage in many parts of our State where the
hay will not bring a high price and the pastures are not of any
great value. I think in many cases it is better to raise our
dairy cattle and sell them when they mature at the present
prices than it is to feed them and sell the dairy product at the
prices we have been getting. The number of cows kept in the
State has increased for two years, from 132,339 in 1910 to
138,055 in 1912, a gain of 5,626 cows, and many are of beef
breeds which are taking the place of dairy cattle.

The State Dairy Conference was held at Saco and very much interest was manifested, it being the first dairy conference ever held in York Co.

SEED IMPROVEMENT WORK.

The field agent of this Department has been working among the farmers and has given them all the assistance possible, but many of our farmers do not realize the importance of selecting good seed and grading up their seed by careful selection. There is nothing that will reduce the yield of a crop more than poor seed. The coöperation of the Experiment Station and the Bureau of Plant and Animal Industry has been of great assistance, as they are continually demonstrating, especially on different kinds of grain, potatoes and other seeds. In many parts of our State the potato crop has been diminished in yield by the use of poor seed and the yield per acre is steadily dropping off, which is a great loss to the farmer.

POULTRY.

Our poultry industry is on the increase. The income from poultry in this State amounted to $4,500,000 for the past year. The assessors only give us the statistics on poultry every five years, the last being taken in 1908, at which time the number of hens was 1,907,656; turkeys, 2,836; ducks, 7,295; geese, 2,314. I believe we should have an appropriation for the interest of poultry in the State, for the work on poultry is sufficient to have a man along this line who would be well qualified to instruct the poultry keepers and thereby assist those that are engaged in this important industry; for I believe that fresh eggs and poultry are far better food than the beef and other meat products that the people now consume, and it is a well paying industry if it can receive the attention that it should. I think the poultrymen of the State should coöperate in putting their eggs and poultry on to the market in better shape and receive better prices.

SHEEP.

I am pleased to report an increase in the last two years in the number of sheep kept in the State. In 1910 we had 125,439 and in 1912 the State Assessors give us 133,702, making an increase of 8,263 in two years. If this rate of increase will continue, it will be of great assistance to the welfare of the State. There is much land in Maine suitable for sheep pasture that can be purchased for a very low price and it can be fenced properly without a great expense, and the State law will take care of the dogs. We have very good laws on the protection of sheep against the dog. The owner of sheep does not have to wait until the dog has killed his sheep, as the law states that if a dog worries the sheep he can take action against the owner of the dog, or if it is necessary he can kill the dog. And at the present time the high price of lamb and mutton for food and the profit on the wool makes the keeping of sheep a good paying investment. Sheep are easily cared for and sheltered in the winter and they will get their living in a pasture a large part of the year; and if our breeders would only raise a few more of their ewe lambs each year they would soon get where they would have large flocks that would pay a good profit. We have at our door one of the best markets in the world and we can demand high prices. The farmer that is a long distance from the railroad can raise sheep and they can be driven to the railroad station with very little expense compared with that of drawing many of our farm products a long distance to the railroads for shipment.

SWINE.

There has been an increase in the swine kept in this State the last two years, as the number in 1910 was 35,329 and in 1912, 50,675, making an increase of 15,346 in two years. I think this is a very good increase considering the large amount of hog cholera that has been found in the State. The keeper of swine should not let this disease interfere with his business, for by the use of hog cholera serum it can be prevented, and he will not take chances of losing his hogs. One keeping swine should be prepared to inoculate his hogs at any time there should be any indication of hog cholera, and he should be sure that there is no hog cholera in the herds from which he pur-chased his hogs for breeding purposes. There is not an animal that can be kept on the farm that will turn the waste products of the farm into money as well as the hog, and hogs will grow well and thrive in a pasture or orchard, and will improve both.

The high price of meat products has brought the price of pork where the farmer can sell his hogs to good advantage. He should give them good shelter in the winter and keep them comfortable and provide a chance for exercise. This will be a great prevention against any cholera or other trouble to which his hogs might be exposed.

FARMERS' INSTITUTES.

All of our institutes were held in connection with the granges in different parts of the State. Mr. W. F. McSparran of Furniss, Pa., talked on dairying and general farming and Mr. C. E. Embree on coöperation. With the men from this Department and Mr. McSparran and Mr. Embree, 90 institutes were held in different parts of the State from January 1st to May 15th and Mr. Embree was employed by the State until October 1st, holding meetings and organizing farmers' exchanges in different sections of the State. There is nothing in the line of agriculture that needed more attention than did the work of organizing the farmers to assist them to put their crops on the market in better shape and receive better prices, and to purchase the farm supplies.

This is one of the most important subjects that can be taken up with our farmers as the conditions that have existed in the State in the past have been a great drawback to the farmer. The farmer of this State has learned to raise large and good crops: he knows how to make cows give milk; he knows how to raise good live stock of all kinds; but what does all this amount to if he cannot receive a fair compensation for his money invested and his mental and physical labor? For it requires a man of good, sound judgment to manage a farm and do it as it should be done. What is more discouraging for a man of ability and energy than to put his time in on the hardest of all occupations, that obliges him to deal with the elements, the laws of nature in plant and animal life—for this is what a successful farmer has before him every day in the year —and not receive adequate returns for his labor? He has no iron clad rules to go by, for such do not exist in his line of work. He has different seasons, different kinds of soil, and different conditions in many ways to contend with. He never knows when he puts his seed into the ground what kind of a crop he will get or if he will get any crop. But he plants the seed, cares for and cultivates it, and harvests his crop and then he is ready for the market. Then the most important part for the farmer is to receive what he should for his crop, for his live stock and for all the products of the farm. As it has been in the past, the farmer would get what the dealer saw fit to give him, which is wrong. He does not object to the dealer's having a fair profit for handling his product, but he must stop the dishonest middlemen, so many of whom have been playing between the producer and the consumer. He must have control of the products that belong to him and not let them go into the hands of those who will not handle his products for his benefit and that of the consumer; and the consumer must assist in this work for it is for his benefit that many of the middlemen be eliminated.

CO-OPERATION BY THE FARMERS OF THIS STATE.

The following is a copy of the declaration of purposes of the Farmers' Exchanges, and the dates of incorporation and names of officers.

"The purposes of said corporation are the buying, selling and handling of produce, the inspection of all produce so sold or consigned, and the selling and consigning of produce as agent of the producer; the buying and selling of real estate, the buying and owning of stock in other associations, the owning or operating of storage warehouses, packing houses for produce, or other material, the building and maintaining of creameries, or fertilizer mixing plants, the mixing and selling of fertilizer, poisons, farm machinery and all such materials, articles or goods, as in the opinion of the Board of Directors can be conveniently and advantageously dealt in by the corporation."

FARMERS' UNION OF MAINE, BANGOR.

Incorporated July 15, 1912.

President—E. S. Crosby............................Bath
Vice-President—B. L. Batchelder...............East Dover
Secretary—W. C. Stetson ....Waterville, R. F. D. 37
Treasurer—W. S. Rogers.......................Cathance
General Manager—C. E. Embree...................Bangor
Directors—Wilbur E. Reynolds......................Unity
        C. R. Martin............................Dexter
        August Peterson...................New Sweden
        M. S. Lyons.............................Calais
        W. S. Rogers........................Cathance
Directors at Large—J. P. Buckley.................Augusta
        C. E. Embree.................Bangor

EXECUTIVE BOARD OF THE FARMERS' UNION OF MAINE.

President—E. S. Crosby.............................Bath
Vice-President—B. L. Batchelor................East Dover
Secretary—W. C. Stetson ....Waterville, R. F. D. 37
Treasurer—W. S. Rogers.......................Cathance
Directors at Large—J. P. Buckley..................Augusta
        C. E. Embree.................Bangor

THE NEW SWEDEN GRANGE PRODUCE COMPANY.

Incorporated June 29, 1911.

President—August Peterson...................New Sweden
Secretary—N. E. Ringdahl....................New Sweden
Treasurer—Andrew A. Olson................New Sweden
Directors—N. E. Ringdahl....................New Sweden
        Alfred Strobeck......................New Sweden
        August Peterson....................New Sweden
        C. E. Johanson....................New Sweden
        A. A. Olson......................New Sweden
        Olof Olander......................New Sweden
        Frank Anderson....................Woodland

Aroostook Potato Growers' Association, Presque Isle.

Incorporated August 18, 1911.

President—L. E. Tuttle.........................Presque Isle
Secretary—J. Frank Guiou.....................Presque Isle
Treasurer—Guy C. Porter..........................Houlton
Directors—L. E. Tuttle........................Presque Isle
       J. F. Guiou..........................Presque Isle
       Guy C. Porter..........................Houlton
       E. P. Titcomb..........................Littleton
       F. L. Leavitt.......................Island Falls
       D. W. Gilman.....................Presque Isle
       A. C. Stanley........................Monticello
       V. E. Wilder........................Washburn
       M. S. Rideout......................Bridgewater

Central Maine Co-operative Association, Dover.

Incorporated September 27, 1911.

President—E. W. Livermore...........................Sebec
Vice-President—C. R. Waugh..................Sangerville
Secretary—B. L. Batchelor.....................East Dover
Treasurer—H. J. Merrill...........................Dover
Directors—H. J. Merrill...........................Dover
       E. W. Livermore........................Sebec
       C. R. Waugh.......................Sangerville
       B. L. Batchelor.....................East Dover

Maine Central Potato Exchange, Brunswick.

Incorporated February 12, 1912.

President—W. T. Guptill.........................Topsham
Secretary—W. S. Rogers.........................Cathance
Treasurer—W. S. Rogers.........................Cathance
Directors—J. K. Estabrook......................Brunswick
       F. S. Adams.......................Bowdoinham
       L. H. Lamoreau..................Bowdoinham

MAINE CENTRAL POTATO EXCHANGE, DEXTER.

Incorporated May 9, 1912.

President—W. N. Eaton............................Dexter
Secretary—N. C. Bucknam........................Dexter
Treasurer—N. C. Bucknam........................Dexter
Directors—Walter N. Eaton.......................Dexter
          Joseph Bridge.............................Exeter
          C. R. Martin.............................Dexter
          F. L. Hutchinson...................Sangerville
          Almer M. Paul...........................Dexter

CENTRAL MAINE PRODUCE EXCHANGE, PITTSFIELD.

Incorporated June 18, 1912.

President—B. J. Slipp.............................Pittsfield
Secretary—Wm. M. Osborn.....................Pittsfield
Treasurer—A. B. Crawford.......................Pittsfield
Directors—B. J. Slipp.............................Pittsfield
          Wm. M. Osborn......................Pittsfield
          Isaiah Gould...........................Pittsfield
          A. B. Crawford.......................Pittsfield
          Ellery Jones...........................Pittsfield

CENTRAL MAINE FARMERS' EXCHANGE, WATERVILLE.

Incorporated July 20, 1912.

President—W. C. Stetson.............Waterville, R. F. D. 37
Secretary—J. Orrin Peck.............Waterville, R. F. D. 39
Treasurer—H. S. Howard.............Waterville, R. F. D. 39
Directors—W. C. Stetson.............Waterville, R. F. D. 37
          George E. Files............Waterville, R. F. D. 41
          J. O. Peck...............Waterville, R. F. D. 39
          H. S. Howard.............Waterville, R. F. D. 39
          George T. Jones..............Fairfield, R. F. D.
          J. H. Reed...........................Winslow

CUMBERLAND & OXFORD PRODUCE EXCHANGE, BRIDGTON.

Incorporated July 31, 1912.

President—B. W. Gibbs.........................Bridgton
Secretary—J. A. Chadbourne.....................Bridgton
Treasurer—J. A. Chadbourne.....................Bridgton
Directors—B. A. Whitney........................Bridgton
        O. B. Ingalls..........................Bridgton
        A. W. Sanborn.......................Bridgton
        A. E. Flint..........................Bridgton

MAINE CENTRAL PRODUCE EXCHANGE, FARMINGTON.

Incorporated August 8, 1912.

President—George H. Thomas.............Farmington Falls
Vice-President—E. V. Chapman...........Farmington Falls
Secretary—J. H. Merrill.................Farmington Falls
Treasurer—J. H. Merrill................Farmington Falls
Directors—V. C. Neal...................Farmington Falls
        T. C. Whittier................Farmington Falls
        F. H. Rollins.................Farmington Falls

AROOSTOOK FARMERS' EXCHANGE, FORT FAIRFIELD.

Incorporated August 17, 1912.

President—George F. Ashby...................Ft. Fairfield
Secretary—Enoch Patterson...................Ft. Fairfield
Treasurer—Stephen E. Ames.........Ft. Fairfield, R. F. D.
Directors—George H. Stone...................Ft. Fairfield
        Hiram Towle.....................Ft. Fairfield
        F. C. Cram......................Ft. Fairfield
        W. A. Harlow....................Ft. Fairfield
        F. H. Haines....................Ft. Fairfield
        Howard Kipp.....................Ft. Fairfield

THE NORTH PENOBSCOT PRODUCE EXCHANGE, SPRINGFIELD.

Incorporated September 9, 1912.

President—O. B. Abbott........................Springfield
Secretary—P. E. Averill...........................Prentiss
Treasurer—Jay D. Osgood.........................Prentiss
Directors—P. E. Averill...........................Prentiss
R. W. Barnes.............................Lee
C. E. Tolman...........................Carroll
B. H. Hanscom.....................Springfield
James A. Ham........................Lakeville
W. A. McKay.......................Drew Pla.

EASTERN MAINE CO-OPERATIVE ASSOCIATION, CALAIS.

Incorporated September 17, 1912.

President—M. S. Lyons............................Calais
Secretary—Jed Kelly............................ ...Calais
Treasurer—A. D. Lunn.........................Milltown
Directors—T. W. Edgerly........................Princeton
Harry Frost...........................Alexander
T. H. Tarbox.......................Red Beach
Ernest Brown.....................Robbinston
F. P. Washburn..........................Perry
Wm. A. Finch..........................Cooper
A. E. Lincoln......................Dennysville
F. T. Sprague.................Ayers, R. F. D.
T. A. Mahar.........................Topsfield

EASTERN MAINE PRODUCE EXCHANGE, DANFORTH.

Incorporated September 18, 1912.

President—B. E. Harding........................Danforth
Secretary—Lewis Huff............................Danforth
Treasurer—A. W. Gilpatrick...................Danforth
Directors—Horatio Spinney, Jr..................Danforth
Lewis Huff...........................Danforth
B. E. Harding........................Danforth

EASTON FARMERS' UNION, EASTON.

Incorporated September 20, 1912.

President—B. F. Cleaves.............................Easton
Secretary—Dura Stanchfield........................Easton
Treasurer—P. L. Herrick...........................Easton
Directors—E. L. Johnston..........................Easton
W. B. Fraser.............................Easton
Earl Kneeland...........................Easton
Robert Cleaves..........................Easton
F. J. Tuttle........................Presque Isle

ASHLAND MAINE FARMERS' UNION, ASHLAND.

Incorporated September 28, 1912.

President—C. C. Peterson..........................Ashland
Secretary—L. E. Young.............................Ashland
Treasurer—W. B. Hallett...........................Ashland
Directors—W. L. Colburn...........................Ashland
W. B. Hallett...........................Ashland
Whit Martin............................Ashland
L. K. Tilley...........................Garfield
Jasper Ellis...........................Castle Hill

FARMERS' UNION OF STOCKHOLM, STOCKHOLM.

Incorporated October 4, 1912.

President—A. W. Johnson...............Jemtland, R. F. D.
Secretary—J. E. Berquist.......................Stockholm
Treasurer—Carl Sandstrom.......................Stockholm
Directors—Hilmer Peterson......................Stockholm
John P. Sodergrin...................Jemtland
P. A. Carlstrom.....................Stockholm
Herbert Bergquist...................Stockholm
J. E. Soderstrom....................Stockholm

WALDO COUNTY FARMERS' UNION, UNITY.

Incorporated October 5, 1912.

President—Wilbur E. Reynolds..................Burnham
Secretary—Wilmot L. Gray.................Troy, R. F. D.
Treasurer—Chester A. Hall.....................Thorndike
Directors—D. E. Loveland.............................Unity
E. A. Twitchell......................Burnham
Wilmot L. Gray.................Troy, R. F. D.
H. C. McCorrison.....................Thorndike

WINDSOR'S FARMERS' UNION, WINDSOR.

Incorporated November 16, 1912.

President—F. D. Erskin......................Windsorville
Secretary—C. F. Donnell.........Week's Mills, R. F. D. 51
Treasurer—M. J. Mosher.....................Windsorville
Directors—A. H. Ware......................Windsorville
Edwin Bullock.....................Windsorville
J. A. McGrath...................Cooper's Mills

HAMPDEN PRODUCE EXCHANGE, HAMPDEN.

Incorporated November 22, 1912.

President—Chas. A. Nason............Hampden Highlands
Secretary—C. E. Carter..................Bangor, R. F. D. 2
Treasurer—Frank E. Emerson.............Bangor, R. F. D. 2
Directors—Leon J. Littlefield.............Bangor,R. F. D. 2
Melvin C. Patterson.........Hampden Highlands
Everett L. Hammond..........Bangor, R. F. D. 2
Charles H. Littlefield.................Hampden

CONTAGIOUS DISEASES OF ANIMALS.

The work of this Department on contagious and infectious diseases among animals has been given special attention, for the protection of the public, the state and the owner of animals. We have endeavored to stamp out tuberculosis in cattle, especially in cows giving milk that is consumed by the public and cattle killed for beef or intended for food and found tuberculous. The checking of the spread of the disease among cattle is a great expense to the State and a great loss to the owner. We have also tried to stamp out glanders among horses that is so contagious to man and horse and can be spread so rapidly. It cannot be controlled when once contracted by man or horse. There is no medical assistance for a man who contracts this terrible disease, and in a horse there is no way of checking it after he once contracts it, except by destroying the animal. This disease can be spread very rapidly by a diseased horse, endangering many valuable horses that come in contact with him, and it can be spread rapidly by drinking fountains in public streets which so many horses visit daily and in the stables where glandered horses come in contact with others.

We have also cared for many sheep and hogs that have been found to be tuberculous when killed for food, thereby preventing the chance of the carcass being offered for food.

This work was done by Mr. Van W. Carll as Live Stock Sanitary Commissioner. Mr. Carll was practically Field Agent, covering nearly all sections of the State where animals were reported as being diseased and his report can be found in another part of this book, giving the number of animals condemned and the expense of conducting the work.

WEIGHTS AND MEASURES.

The work of State Sealer of Weights and Measures was added to this Department without any appropriation, and the Governor and Council gave me an order for $2,000 of unexpended money in this Department in order to purchase a set of state standards. After purchasing we were obliged to send them to Washington to have them compared and sealed by the United States standards, and on account of many other states in the Union taking up this work there were many state standards to be certified and we were delayed sometime in receiving our standards. We now have one of the best state outfits in the country, for doing the work of state sealing, but without an appropriation and not being able to put a man on the work, very little could be accomplished. As soon as our standards were complete I sent notices to the twenty cities of the State, asking them to send in their city standards of weights and measures to be sealed. Nine cities responded, and out of all that were sent in from the nine cities one could not get a complete outfit that would be sufficient for taking up the work of a sealer of weights and measures. This will give an idea of the condition of the weights and measures of the cities of the State.

I also sent out a recommendation to the towns, giving them a list of what would be required to make a complete outfit for a town in order to seal the weights and measures and to do the work correctly. I also advised the towns to coöperate, by four or five towns getting together to purchase a set of standards and having one man do the sealing, so that each town would not be obliged to go to the expense of purchasing an outfit, as many of the towns have only a few places where measures and scales are used.

There was an interesting exhibit of condemned weights and measures and a splendid lecture given by Mr. A. S. K. Clark, a deputy state sealer of Massachusetts, at our Dairy Meeting held in Saco December 12th, which can be seen in another part of this report.

I hope the coming legislature will make an appropriation so that a man can be put on this important work, to protect the honest dealer and the consumer, as well as the farmer who sells the product of the farm to the dealer.

ACKNOWLEDGMENTS.

In consideration of the splendid assistance that has been rendered me as Commissioner of Agriculture, I wish to acknowledge my appreciation as follows:

To the Governor and Council for their approval and support in so many different branches of my work that are for the benefit of those interested in agriculture as well as the State and her people.

To the Attorney General, Hon. W. R. Pattangall, who has rendered me such valuable assistance in the interpretation and the enforcement of the laws of this State which must be carried out in the different branches of this Department.

To the State Auditor, Hon. Lamont A. Stevens, to whom all accounts must be rendered for approval before going to the Governor and Council for the drawing of warrants. All business has been done in harmony.

To the United States Department of Agriculture at Washington, especially the Bureau of Animal Industry and the United States inspectors in different parts of this State who have assisted this Department in the work relating to contagious and infectious diseases among animals; and to the Dairy Division of the United States Department for the assistance they have given me.

To Dr. Robert J. Aley, president of the University of Maine, for the assistance he has rendered us personally.

To Dr. Chas. D. Woods, Director of our Experiment Station, for the assistance rendered by him and his professors at the Station, especially in the line of entomological work, and for the annual report of his Station and that of Highmoor Farm.

To Prof. Henry D. Evans, in charge of our State Laboratory of Hygiene, for the assistance he has given our state chemist in prosecutions for violations of the dairy laws.

To the Pomona and subordinate granges in different parts of the State for their able assistance in conducting our Farmers' Institutes by furnishing halls and entertaining the speakers that were sent from this Department.

To the Maine Central and Bangor and Aroostook Railroads for the assistance rendered by giving passes to men in the institute work from out of the State, giving a chance to do much more work with the money appropriated, and the assistance rendered the Farmers' Union, giving the Farmers' Exchange the preference and assisting those representing the exchanges in different parts of the State.

To the men in this Department for the able support they have given me in the different branches of the work; also, to those who have assisted us in the institute work conducted by the Department the past year, and to my chief clerk and her assistants, who are always ready and willing to assist me.

REPORT OF STATE DAIRY INSTRUCTOR.

To the Commissioner of Agriculture:

I have the honor to hand you herewith my first annual report as dairy instructor.

I was appointed to this office on Dec. 16, 1911, and at that time was ignorant of the details of its manifold duties which up to this time so far as I, at least, was concerned, had been enshrouded with a mantle of authority beneath which burned a lamp of mystery. I immediately began to familiarize myself with the workings of this branch of the Department.

My first duty was to take the place of an institute speaker who had been called home suddenly, which continued until the end of the year. The middle of January. when Mr. Embree was again brought into the State in response to the very general demand for him to talk about coöperative exchanges, it was thought fit that I accompany him as a representative of the Department. I have since thought many times what good fortune this was, for had I been left to my own inclinations I should have visited those localities where only the most promising herds were kept and in sections where dairying was an acknowledged industry. I knew quite a lot about these sections to begin with and had it not been for this trip with Mr. Embree into those sections of Maine where cows are kept for family convenience and not as a branch of farming, this report would certainly have been much more glowing about our live stock industry, for on this trip I saw and had an opportunity to study dairy conditions at their worst.

I discovered at once that while a fur cap might keep one's head warm, it would not save a man from perishing if his hands and feet and body were exposed to a drifting storm in zero weather. Nor would glowing reports of what dairymen in Auburn, or Gorham, or Turner, or Paris, or Farmington, our

five towns of largest cow population, were doing, save the
dairy industry in Maine.

We had tried the glowing report business and every year
from 1904 to the time you assumed the duties of Commissioner
of Agriculture, Jan. 1, 1911, there was a continuous and alarming drop in the number of cows, one year right after another,
until it had amounted to nearly 35,000. Back in 1897 there
were cows enough, had they been equally divided among all of
the farms in Maine, to have had three for every farm, yet in
1910 there were only 2 1-5 for each farm. Perhaps you would
be pleased to figure it for yourself. Here are the figures as
taken from the state assessors' report of 1910,—132,339 cows
to be divided among 60,000 farms in the State.

1910 was the low water mark for the number of cows in
Maine for a good number of years; in 1911 and 1912 the
number increased almost 6,000.

Perhaps it was a fear of this very thing that caused the
gentlemen who had regaled themselves for the last decade upon
the authority and honor which naturally follow the Department
positions, to make such a fearful noise when they started out
to pursue you. A fine bunch!

This institute work lasted almost without interruption until
the middle of May. Soon after this I began inspection of
creameries.

CREAMERY INSPECTION.

Before I started out from the office I was handed some blanks
in the nature of a score card to fill out upon my visit to each
creamery. They contained questions that could be easily put
under one of three heads: Does this creamery take measures
to keep its buildings and machinery clean and sanitary? Does
it handle its goods properly in the making? Does this building
need to be destroyed together with its equipment and a new
plant established in its place?

I used this form for some time and tried, while using it, to
get the view point of the men who run the creameries and I
have to report that with few exceptions they were not only courteous, but I believe were also conscientious and painstaking

about their work. Some of the buildings have been built for sometime and never were of the most approved model, but I should have considered myself suffering from a surfeit of good dinner and a lack of sawing wood, had I recommended their destruction without an adequate compensation from some source, being returned.

At several places that I called during the rush hours, things did not look exactly as they should. I did not make my identity known, but sometime afterward would call and see them clean up at night for the beginning of the next day. These places were all right in the morning to begin with and I was unable to see how they could improve conditions during their rush hours and still maintain a working basis.

BREEDERS' MEETINGS.

I visited each of the three Holstein Breeders' Associations and the Aroostook Jersey Breeders' Association. At these meetings I found some very intelligent men working seriously on breeding problems, but the continual cry came to me from each of them, "How can we sell our surplus stock for big money?" It is needless to say that I did not consider this any part of the work which devolved upon me from my position as a state officer except indirectly; that is,—as we want to see all farmers, whether thoroughbred breeders or not, prosper. The fact is, when cows are dropping off at more than 5,000 a year, it immediately becomes evident that more people are selling than buying, whereas if the reverse were true and more people were buying than selling a stronger market is at once established for all grades, and when the condition becomes acute thoroughbred stock of high quality brings fancy prices readily. And yet the man who raises fancy stock to prosper must add to his ability as a good breeder, that other quality fully as rare, good salesmanship, a quality that is recognized and paid high prices for in all commercial lines.

FAIRS.

In this connection I may as well say that I visited the large fairs at Lewiston and Waterville and the county fairs of

Presque Isle, South Paris, Skowhegan, Readfield, Madison and New Gloucester, all of which draw stipends from the State. At Lewiston and Waterville, also at South Paris and Presque Isle, the exhibit of stock was large and of a satisfactory character. The competition in many classes was sufficiently hot so that not only individual merit but also the knowledge of proper development cut its figure. Such contests are of actual benefit to the contestant and to the observer, but where classes are only half filled, the money and time are thrown away and the State can ill afford to pay stipends to such fairs. They simply furnish an excuse and an opportunity for a lot of fakirs to get together and jointly soak the crowd for all they can.

COW TESTING ASSOCIATIONS.

At the time of my assuming the duties of this office, I found in existence four active cow testing associations and four that had been in existence but were then dormant. These associations had been very much exploited in the public press and especially in the agricultural press and I turned to them with a great deal of interest every spare moment of my time in order to determine for my own satisfaction of just how much importance they were.

After a careful study of them, I am prepared to endorse some of the things that have been said about them and any community that is so situated as to have a commercial outlet for their product at a profit may essentially increase that profit by an association. If it has not a profitable commercial outlet a cow testing association will not of its own accord make one. The proper attitude for dairymen to take is that ordinary dairymen with ordinary cows are entitled to make a living and that a superior dairyman with superior cows ought to make big money. Superiority in any other calling is rewarded. In law, in medicine, in business, in baseball, the man who accomplishes things beyond the ordinary is richly rewarded for his accomplishment but in dairying if a man complains, "I am not making a living," his agricultural instructors at once say, "The fault is entirely yours," yet no one ever hears of a doctor that is not making a living or a lawyer, even though every patient he looks at dies and every case in court is lost.

The motto in the past has been "Keep more cows," and whoever dared add to this motto so it should read "Keep more cows if they pay," has been a heretic.

Dairymen must talk more in the future about profitable outlets for their products and about actual money made in the business and demand good money for average ability.

Crackerjack cows and crackerjack feeders have been worked over hours in the past and the crackerjack knowledge is cornered in our agricultural schools by men who know nothing actually of getting a living from a farm and do not intend to as long as a good salary holds out, or even if it does not hold out.

Those associations that were dormant were dormant only because they could not get suitable testers at figures they could afford to pay.

W. T. GUPTILL,
State Dairy Instructor.

REPORT OF STATE DAIRY INSPECTOR.

To Hon. J. P. Buckley, Commissioner of Agriculture:

I respectfully present my report as Dairy Inspector for the year 1912.

During the past year I have given much of my time to the inspection of milk in many cities and towns visited. There has been a total of 1294 inspections relative to protecting the public from unsanitary or below standard dairy products. During the year I have secured from dealers 528 samples of milk, 45 samples of cream and 177 samples of butter and butter substitutes.

Grocery stores, bakeries, restaurants and drug stores visited and inspected for their care and method of selling dairy products number 210, and examinations of milk wagons and of milk for sediment without a sample being taken, number over 165.

I have visited 65 city milk rooms and dairies where milk from farmers, shipped over the railroad, is mixed and bottled for city use, offering suggestions for sanitary improvements when it was possible. Score cards were used when practical.

During the year, 85 milk producing farms have been visited for the purpose of offering, if possible, some suggestions for sanitary and economic improvement, rather than for the purpose of criticising.

In coöperation with the Experiment Station at Orono, I have visited and inspected 21 creameries in nearly every section of the State. Special note of the sanitary conditions was made and reported with decided resulting changes for the better in many instances. A Bulletin issued by the Experiment Station contains these reports.

An effort has been made to stop the general practice of shipping or returning unclean cans or other receptacles. I have noted 152 cases of unclean cans being present at stations or in possession of express companies and in coöperation with the several creameries lists have been made and copies of Chapter 60 of the Laws of 1911 have been sent to all violators with the statement that they will be prosecuted for future violations.

Of the milk and cream samples secured the following table shows the results better, perhaps, than in any other way:

SAMPLES.	Above Standard and Clean.	Below Standard in Solids.	Below Standard in Butter Fat.	Skimmed.	Containing Visible Sediment.	Containing Added Water.
573	82	46	†4	6	370	65

The following table shows the results of complaints made for 69 samples reported below standard in butter fat or adulterated with water. Because several samples were secured in some cases, the actual number of violators becomes 57, of whom 35 were convicted, 5 appealing to a higher court.

Pleaded guilty and fined.....................................12

Pleaded not guilty. Found guilty and fined...................... 6

Pleaded nolo contendere. Found guilty and fined............... 4

Nol prossed because sample was traced back.....................19

Convicted in cases traced back................................ 8

Nol prossed: Failure to convict because of unsealed cans........11

Cases appealed from convictions............................... 5

When we see that out of 573 samples of milk and cream only 82 are above standard and clean, we stop to wonder why this is true. Certainly there is a great chance for improvement along this line of the milk business and if any city contemplates making a standard for the number of bacteria in milk it would do well to first see that all visible dirt is removed.

Under the present state law the burden of proof seems to be too heavy for a conviction for dirt in milk. A statute bearing definitely on this point should be in our dairy laws, if convictions and improvement in this matter are desired.

Milk showing visible sediment was also a common occurrence in the 165 instances where no sample was taken and I have often suggested that before asking the consumer to pay more

† One sample of cream below standard delivered to ice cream maker whose product had consequently been below standard.

for his milk the producer take a little more precaution as regards the entrance of dirt.

The advocating of the covered or hooded pail has had but little effect as very few have adopted it. Those who have tried it know well the results, but there are many who try and do not keep clean cows at the same time, so no improvement results and the improved pail is condemned by them.

It has been interesting to follow the bacteria counts in milk and cream sent to our Fairs and Dairy Meetings and the relation of the number to the method used. In nearly every instance where the lowest counts were secured, a covered or a hooded pail, as well as clean cows, were used.

As a means of knowing their actual efficiency as producers of sanitary milk and cream, I know of no better way for city milk dealers than to patronize all milk and cream scoring contests possible. As a basis for determining the exact quality of their product, no better way is open. It would seem to be a sane proposition to sell according to quality and that more milk dealers are not so doing is rather surprising.

None of our cities have as yet required milk of a known bacteria content to be sold and very few, if any, milkmen who buy from farmers pasteurize their milk. The creameries of the State pasteurize all of the milk and cream received to insure as uniform a product as possible going out.

It is a common practice for milkmen to buy skim-milk and heavy cream in the short season from creameries and to standardize to 4 per cent milk or less. This is a very variable product in many instances after it is handled in the city, for it is a well known fact that when pasteurized milk, devoid of souring bacteria, becomes slightly aged, it may be a very dangerous liquid even though it may not be sour. In a few states the mixing of skim-milk and cream in this way is prohibited by statute and if such a practice becomes obnoxious in this State we must seek new statutes for regulation.

Many complaints are received from time to time in certain sections from a product known as homogenized cream, because of its lack of whipping qualities. This is cream increased in bulk but as it contains the per cent of butter fat required by law nothing can be done. It is possible to make cream by this process from skim-milk and butter and a rigorous inspection of these constituents must be practiced because of the possibility of substitutes for butter being used.

During the extremely hot weather in July, milk became a very scarce article and in quite a few instances samples containing added water were secured. By your advice prosecution was withheld and an effort made to trace the poor milk back to its source. Accordingly letters stating that help would be given were sent to ten Portland violators who purchase most of their milk. With a little help on their part I was able to trace 8 of the 10 cases to the places where they received it from the express companies. Being assured that a prosecution was possible, I brought complaint against the farmers who shipped the milk.

Unfortunately for all concerned, the cans in which the milk was shipped were not sealed, making it possible for the milk to be changed after it left the farmer and before it was received by the dealers. As the express company from whom the milk was taken were not agents for the farmer, it is plainly seen that the poor milk could not be traced to the producer.

Unwarranted criticism appeared at the time in the Portland papers but as it was based upon direct misstatements and contained no signature, I did not deem it necessary to reply other than to state my position and to correct the misstatements made.

It has been proven to my satisfaction that milk dealers are at the mercy of farmers and others selling them milk during the short season. It also has been proven that there is a decided lack of activity on the part of the milk dealers to find out for themselves just what they are receiving and if they do find out they will not inform this office that they wish help. Their excuse is that they must have milk and that if trouble comes to the producer he will cut them off. In the past year requests for help have been received from eight wholesale receivers of milk in Pittsfield, Skowhegan, Newport, Saco, Scarboro, South Portland and Portland, and in each instance the poor milk was traced to its source with resulting prosecutions. It is the intention of this Department to help all dealers who suspect that they are buying watered or otherwise impure milk, but unless the dealer shows activity in his own behalf and sends a request

for help, it is difficult to understand just why he believes himself exempt from prosecution when found selling below standard milk.

If sealed cans were used by farmers and dealers when shipping milk, the responsibility would then be on the shipper and
greater protection would result.

Under the present system of shipping in unsealed cans, a
large number of agents are necessary to secure samples of milk
from the many farmers shipping from many different stations,
but if dealers in cities will patronize the local inspector, some
idea of what they are receiving can be obtained and then a
request to this office will bring further help.

Conditions under which milk, butter and butter substitutes
are sold in grocery stores and bakeries have been noted and
many changes brought about. Grocerymen are rapidly learning
the unsanitary aspects of handling and selling milk from cans.
That milkmen usually sell their poorest milk in cans to stores
is a well known fact and when this is exposed to dust as well
as to odors of the meat room or ice chest, it becomes an undesirable product. Then, too, the quart measure is a source of
contamination from dust and flies. It has been a common
sight to find a milk measure on the end of a meat bench or
hanging on a nail literally swarmed with flies and in some
instances curdled milk has been found in the measure. It is
not always possible to thoroughly mix milk in cans and to
protect themselves from prosecution for selling below standard
milk or for unsanitary conditions, grocerymen and others
should insist on having bottled milk left with them.

In restaurants and lunch rooms the milk dip tank is in very
common use. I have condemned a number for being old and
patched and while much dust is liable to enter and a variable test
for butter fat results from uneven mixture, the fact that the
milk is kept cold detracts from the other objections to quite a
degree.

In drug stores I have found milk being stored in cans, pitch-
ers, bottles and iced or vacuum tanks for use in drinks of many
descriptions. I have criticised when this milk has been found
exposed or not kept cold and in many cases where a dirty
bottle and milk soaked cap are used, I have suggested remedies.

The safest and most sanitary way to dispense milk in restaurants and drug stores is to install iced tanks or vacuum tanks which assure cleaner milk at a low temperature and better satisfaction to all concerned.

That many dealers have been lax in regard to the laws relating to the sale of renovated butter and oleomargarine was evident from samples secured. In each instance a request for butter was made, a package was received and paid for by your agent without his identity being known. Actual conditions under which an average purchaser is subject were wanted because of the extreme prices demanded for butter and the possibility of substitutes being sold to the dependent consumer and a resulting big gain to the dealer.

Accordingly 177 samples from six cities and four towns were secured and inspected for marks or labels on the outside of the package. The contents were then analyzed to determine what was actually secured and to establish a proof for prosecution.

The following table shows the variable results and when we keep in mind that butter was asked for in each instance, it is plain to see that the public either through carelessness or willfulness on the dealer's part were being imposed upon.

SAMPLES.	Butter.	Stamped Renovated Butter.	Not Stamped Renovated Butter.	Stamped Butterine.	Stamped Oleomargarine.	Not Stamped Oleomargarine.
177	64	67	31	6	7	2

Results of complaints brought against violators are as follows:

	Complaint withdrawn, or nol prossed, identity of clerk uncertain.	Found Guilty.	Found guilty and Appealed.	Found not Guilty.
Selling renovated butter in unmarked pk.	4	23	4	1
Selling oleomargarine in unmarked pk .	–	2	–	–

In the City of Portland where 20 of the cases were tried there was an effort on the part of opposing counsel to have the prosecutions stayed, it being thought that because of carelessness on the part of some of their clients, the giving of a criminal record for first offence was too severe. Several conferences were held with the seven opposing attorneys and the cases were continued at their wish until finally disposed of. I regret that I could not reward them for their courteous treatment during this time but the law could not be changed and the prosecutions were finally made.

In visiting many stores where samples of butter were not purchased I noted the sanitary conditions under which butter and its substitutes were kept and I found a general lack of knowledge or disregard of proper labeling and covering, especially for renovated tub butter. It was commonly exposed to dust and flies and no covering placed over it during sweeping time. This method is very unsanitary and wasteful to the dealer and from criticisms made, many have seen the wisdom of selling butter substitutes in sealed, plainly marked packages not less than one-half pound in weight, as they come from the wholesaler.

Many complaints have been made to me personally about poor butter being sold by large butter concerns, but as far as I have been able to learn these concerns are far from violating any dairy laws even though their product may be very inferior in taste.

It is a common and legitimate practice for large creameries to buy surplus butter from smaller concerns in the flush season and to ship that butter to cold storage until the supply runs short. Then this bought-up butter is brought back to the creamery and worked in with fresh made butter and sold under its stamp. Poor quality butter when sold to the general public does not benefit the reputation of the concern under whose stamp it is sold, but in some sections the demand is great enough so that the public must accept or go without.

Rather than make their own cream into butter of a known quantity some of the creameries ship sweet cream to Boston in summer and prefer to sell poor quality butter brought from cold storage or from the western states in winter, worked over and bearing their stamp.

It is surely a slight imposition on the public to supply their demands with poor grade butter and in every section there is a big premium on homemade butter of known quality, making butter making on the farms near our cities a profitable industry.

During my visits to cities I have, in a few instances, written articles for the local papers endeavoring to enlighten the consumer in some degree relative to the local milk supply and the care that milk should receive after it is delivered. Articles have been prepared and printed in papers in Bangor, Waterville, Lewiston, Biddeford and Portland, touching on the local milk situations in those cities. With the object in mind of finding out as near as possible the conditions and extent of local milk inspection, I sent letters of inquiry to the local inspectors in our cities. From replies received from ten cities, I found

1. That all the inspectors were severely handicapped by lack of ordinances and equipment to work with.

2. That very small funds, or none at all, were allowed for the work.

3. That political preference caused frequent changes and lack of time for competent men to become familiar with the office and to do efficient service to the community.

4. That in a few instances the inspector was appointed simply because the law required it and not because there was need for one.

5. That the work of inspection had been left for the State to carry out, in cities where no local inspector was appointed.

An effort has been made to coöperate as much as possible with local inspectors in my work and whenever I have come in contact with these men, I have found them always anxious to assist.

The Quarterly Bulletins containing analyses of all samples secured and results of prosecution of violations have been edited. In addition to these lists, articles have been written in the Bulletin with the aim of placing before the consuming public suggestions and information relative to more sanitary conditions and better and cleaner milk. The articles include "The Fly and Sanitary Dairy Products," "Extra Cost of Producing Clean Milk," "Sanitary Suggestions for the Consumer," "Sanitary Suggestions for the Producer," "The Improvement of Our Milk Situation," "The Oleomargarine Controversy."

"The Sale of Renovated Butter in Maine," and "The Food Value of Clean Milk."

The object of these Quarterly Bulletins is to place before the consuming public some data and information about dairy products that are being sold, and, as a means for dairymen to advertise the quality of their product, it serves well.

The principal receivers of the Bulletins at present are the milkmen themselves, but our present mailing list of 4500 names shows an increase over last year and that more actual users of dairy products are availing themselves of the opportunity offered.

It was my privilege to be in attendance and to address Grange meetings at East Vassalboro, Hiram and Thorne's Corner, on some phase of the clean milk question. At East Vassalboro considerable interest was taken in a milk, cream and butter scoring contest suggested by this Department and worthy of attention by other Granges as a means of determining the efficiency of their dairymen as producers of products of high quality.

I was in attendance at the Maine State Fair and Central Maine Fair in charge of the exhibits of dairy products and of the competitve contests for milk and butter fat production.

At the Maine State Fair some effort was made to give a clean milk exhibit by showing growing bacteria and their relation to dirty milk. Prepared slides of stained bacteria were shown through a microscope, and suggestions relative to clean milk were given to many interested people.

At your request I was in attendance at the Androscoggin County Fair at Livermore Falls, the Monroe Fair and the Bristol Fair, where exhibits and conditions were noted.

I was in attendance at the Dairy Meeting in Portland and assisted in computing scores of milk and cream.

At the Dairy Meeting at Saco I was in charge of the exhibit of dairy products and assisted in scoring the same. At this meeting I delivered an address entitled "Our Present Economic Dairy Situation and its Relation to Consumer and Producer."

In the December Quarterly Bulletin issued from your office, I was privileged to include an article entitled "Sanitary Remodeling of Dairy Barns." This article contained practical suggestions that have seemed possible on many of the dairy farms that I have visited.

Near the close of the year, I was pleased to be of assistance in comparing and adjusting with the new corrected state standards, weights and measures from nine cities. From this experience it is plain to see that new standards must be secured in a number of cities if efficient work is to result. This should be an important matter to the consuming public and for their future protection new state statutes and regulations must be made and strictly enforced.

I desire at this time to thank you for the help given and courtesies shown in my endeavor to carry out my duties.

The clerical force of the Department, the newspapers of the State, Boards of Health and local inspectors have rendered valuable assistance.

I am indebted to Henry D. Evans, our State Chemist, and to his assistants for aid in prosecuting violations and to Charles D. Woods, Director of the Experiment Station at Orono, for assistance and results in inspection of creameries and dairies.

Court officials and prosecuting attorneys have at all times rendered proper decisions and help in my efforts to carry out the law.

Respectfully submitted,

RUSSELL S. SMITH,
State Dairy Inspector.

REPORT OF FIELD AGENT, SEED IMPROVEMENT WORK.

To the Hon. J. P. Buckley, Commissioner of Agriculture, Augusta, Me.

I respectfully submit herewith my first annual report as Field Agent of the Plant and Seed Improvement Division of the Maine State Department of Agriculture.

When I assumed my duties on the 17th of June, the work of this Division was in rather bad shape. The first thing to do was to get things straightened out and find out just what should be done.

With this end in view I began at once to visit those farmers interested in seed improvement and learn what they were doing, had done and wanted to do. I called on 160 farmers at their farms and of these I called on 36 a second time.

In these visits I tried in every case to assist the farmers as much as possible with advice and suggestions, on all lines and kinds of farm work. As it was too late to do any real work in seed selection I tried to bring to their attention the great value of good seed and hope that I shall see the result of my visits next year when the crop is put in.

In the months of October and November, I made my second visits to 36 of the farmers. I also attended the New England Fruit Show at Portland where I saw several men interested in the seed improvement work. At the New England Corn Show in Boston I had the pleasure of meeting and getting acquainted with several of the men interested in the question of seed improvement in other states of New England.

December was taken up very largely with the meeting of the Seed Improvement Association, the Maine State Grange and the State Dairy Conference. The time in between was spent in attending Grange meetings and the writing of reports, or other office work.

During my visits to the farmers this summer, the following points became apparent to me:

First. The average farmer does not know the value of pure, strong, selected seed of one variety.

Second. Very few farmers know where to obtain such seed and if they do know where to obtain it, they are not willing to pay the necessary price.

Third. The average farmer will go to some expense and much labor to prepare his land for a crop and then he will plant as seed anything he can not sell. He does not know that if he should use the best seed he could obtain, he would increase the value of his crop 15 per cent to 75 per cent.

Fourth. The ordinary farmer does not know how to select his seed so as to increase and improve his crop.

Fifth. The principles ordinarily applied to business are used on the farm in only a very few cases, and as a result the farmers do not know how much a crop costs them or how much it is worth and in some cases they do not even know how much they are getting. This is not business and as a result of such methods the farmers very often lose when by a little care, bookkeeping, and inquiring, they could turn to a profit what is now a loss.

THE VALUE OF HOME GROWN SEED.

The value of growing their own seed is not understood by many farmers. If the seed is grown at home, any danger of bringing in new diseases is avoided and in the potato crop this is worthy of much consideration. The seed becomes accustomed to the climate and soil and larger and better crops will result. This is especially true of corn. Seed grown at home can be kept free from all weed seeds and seeds of other crops, and varieties of the same crop. This is of great value in the small grains and potatoes.

Before seed should be grown at home, however, it is most necessary to obtain a sort that is good.

Good seed may be defined as *seed that is of one variety and is superior in the following points:*

1. *Suitability for the conditions under which it is to be grown.* That is, seed should be adapted to the climate and soil

conditions.   If the farmer does not know what seed is best suited to his conditions, it will certainly pay him to find out. That is what the Experiment Station and Department of Agriculture are for.

2. *Yielding power.*   Seed that is of any value should yield at a high average rate.   A large number of varieties of oats, wheat, barley and even some potatoes are not yielding as high as other varieties that are bringing just as high a price.   Yet many of the farmers persist in raising the less desirable and less profitable varieties.

3. *Purity.*   No seed is of any value as seed unless it is pure.   It must be free from all weed seeds and also from seeds of all other varieties of the same crop or other crops.

The value of having it all of one variety is that it will all ripen at the same time and the yield will accordingly be increased and the quality of the seed will be much better than if there were several varieties and some would not be ripe when the rest was harvested.

4. *Quality of the product for marketing and feeding purposes.*   The quality should be such that there will be no difficulty in selling it on the open market or to a private trade.

5. *Hardiness.*   This means the strength and vitality of the seed.   The seed that has good vitality is more able to resist poor weather conditions and inequalities in the character of the soil.   It will also be less easily affected by changes in temperature.

6. *Strength of stalk or straw.*   This applies largely to grains. Some varieties of grain will not lodge on a sandy soil, but on a rich loam they will lodge.   There are also varieties that will not lodge on the rich loam.   The grower should get the variety that is best suited to his conditions.

7. *Ability to resist disease.*   This will apply to a greater or less extent to all crops.   It is one of the points that should be more carefully considered than at present.   If, for instance, a variety of potatoes can be secured that will not rust, about one-sixth of the cost of production will be avoided.

Agreeing that the above mentioned points must be had to obtain good seed and get good crops, the points at issue are first, to obtain desirable seed, and second, to keep it pure and in good condition.

The best way to obtain a good quality of good seed is to make inquiries either at the Department of Agriculture, or the Experiment Station at Orono, as to the varieties best suited to your conditions. If you know the best varieties by experimentation, that is sufficient, because even the best judgment will not always be able to tell the right varieties to use from a mere description of your conditions.

When a farmer buys his seed from either the Experiment Station or some reliable western seed house, he should demand that he get the percentage of germination and purity; also, if possible, the yield per acre. The yield serves as an indication as to what he may expect. The cost of this seed will be more than that of the ordinary seed, but it is worth more.

After he once obtains a good variety of seed, he should take all the precautions necessary to keep it pure and all of one variety. *Keep the weed seeds out; keep the seeds of other varieties and cultivated crops out.* Unless this is done, the product of this good seed is not fit to use for seed again.

A good fanning mill is one of the necessary implements where grain is being raised. The farmer should not try to raise grain seed without using one, but should clean the crop thoroughly and get every weed seed out. He should raise only one variety of that crop on the farm, excepting potatoes and apples, and be careful to keep that absolutely pure. If this is done he will be able to get a larger yield per acre and get more money per bushel for his product.

The only times it is advisable to change seed are:

1.   When seed of a better and more serviceable variety than that now being used can be obtained.

2.   When one variety becomes mixed with other varieties.

3.   When a crop becomes seriously damaged by reason of unfavorable weather or other agencies.

4.   When seed is damaged by threshing or defective storing methods.

5.   When suitable machinery is not available for cleaning the seed properly. That means a fanning mill.

Unless some of these conditions prevail it is not advisable to change the seed, but keep the quality up to standard by careful selection.

There are a few points to observe in the selection of some of the crops. What will apply to one of the small grains will serve for all. When it is time to harvest the crop, walk through the field and select an armful of about 500 of the best heads. Later on in the winter thresh them out and put them through a fanning mill, being careful to keep them pure. The next year plant them in a small plot and thresh the product of that plot separately; clean it and plant it in a larger plot the year following. By keeping up this method of selection every year a high standard can be maintained and it is quite possible that it can be increased.

To get the best results with corn, select, while the crop is yet in the field, those ears that are best filled out and show the largest per cent of corn to the cob. This is indicated by the depth of kernel, the lack of space between the kernels and the rows, and a well and closely covered butt and tip.

Potatoes should be selected by hand digging, before the general crop is dug. Select those hills that have the largest number of marketable potatoes, are free from diseases of all kinds and are known to be of one variety. It is quite desirable, if possible, to select the potatoes so that one good tuber is finally discovered, the product is increased and the final result is that the whole field is from one potato. If that one was a good one, the grower has something to sell and can get a good price for it.

The chief point in selection of any kind of seed stock is to get an ideal fixed in the mind and then use one's head to select the seed that is most likely to produce that ideal.

The following paragraphs will show why better seed and methods should be used. Note the low average yields of some of the crops. Also observe the low average acreage. In some cases there is not enough land in any one crop to make it worth while. Machinery can not be employed and the cost of production is increased. Raise enough of one crop so that it will be necessary to take care of it to live.

In November the Department sent out 850 post cards in an endeavor to learn the amount of land cultivated, the yield of the different crops and the amount of land in pasture and wood lot.

Of the 850 cards sent out, 159 were returned, a very small number; from that 159 the following figures have been compiled:

THE CROP.	Average No. Acres.	Average Yield per Acre.		No. Farms Reporting.
Potatoes................................	24.80	230.83	bu.	159
Sweet Corn.............................	3.91	$64.38		55
Yellow Corn............................	4.65	62.94	bu.	75
Hay....................................	125.28	1.30	tons	159
Oats...................................	37.85	37.61	bu.	117
Apple Orchards.........................	11.26	33.59	bbls.	89
Tillable...............................	151.13	–		159
Woodland..............................	435.64	–		132
Pasture...............................	116.19	–		140
Wheat.................................	29.85	21.00	bu.	10
Barley.................................	5.70	33.00	bu.	14
Buckwheat.............................	27.31	28.00	bu.	7
Beans..................................	1.34	22.10	bu.	7
India Wheat............................	1.04	31.00	bu.	5
Oats and Peas..........................	8.00	5.00	tons	5
Hungarian.............................	7.40	1.95	tons	6
Turnips................................	.50	275.00	bu.	1
Cabbage...............................	.50	4.00	tons	1
Green Peas.............................	1.00	34.00	bu.	1

While these figures are not as correct as they would have been if 800 farms had responded instead of only 159, still this will show in a brief way the low yields that many farmers are getting and the slight variety of crops that are raised in Maine.

If good seed were used and reasonable farm management employed, there is no reason why the acreage of some crops could not be doubled and the acreage of several crops greatly increased. This is especially true of the hay, barley, wheat and bean crops.

Seed improvement and better farm management will increase the yields and profits of the average Maine farm very materially.

I wish at this time to express my thanks and appreciation for the kind assistance rendered by the Maine Experiment Station. I wish also to express my gratitude and appreciation for the assistance and freedom of action allowed me by you.

Respectfully yours,

AUSTIN W. JONES,

Field Agent.

REPORT OF STATE HORTICULTURIST.

To the Hon. J. P. Buckley, Commissioner of Agriculture:

I herewith submit my second annual report as State Horticulturist for the year 1912.

Early in the year Mr. G. A. Yeaton, the Assistant Horticulturist, resigned to accept another position, and much difficulty was experienced in obtaining a capable man for the position which he had so ably filled. Mr. H. P. Sweetser of Cumberland Center was finally chosen and has proven a very valuable man in the work. To each of these men I wish to extend my warm appreciation for their hearty coöperation at all times.

The results from this season's work are very encouraging and the interest and enthusiasm manifested in many sections argue well for the rapid improvement in our fruit. The number of growers who have sprayed their trees is much larger than heretofore, and, while there remains a great deal to be accomplished along this line, the prejudice is being overcome by results shown. More realize the absolute necessity of applying the spray mixtures at certain times and within limited periods, if good results are to be obtained.

Lime-sulphur has been used more than any other fungicide and has given good satisfaction. Bordeaux Mixture has been used sparingly, mainly for the scab spray, and has not been a successful material when used later in the season. Arsenate of lead has been found to burn the foliage somewhat this year, but has not done serious damage, and is still the most satisfactory insecticide.

The unsprayed fruit was not as good as during the previous season, mainly because of climatic conditions. It was much subject to scab, fruit spot and other diseases. This is also true of the sprayed fruit where the regular scab spray was omitted. The red varieties, after a spring two weeks late, and a damp, rather cloudy summer, did not mature as early as they did the

Portion of Exhibit at American Land and Irrigation Exposition, New York City, November 3-11, 1911.

season of 1911, nor did they attain the brilliant coloring then produced.

The fruit has averaged somewhat smaller than last year, especially the Ben Davis, and has been selling at a smaller price. Much was sold in the orchard at $1.50 per barrel, which did not leave a great profit when costs of picking, packing and transportation to railroad stations were taken out. Barrels were rather high this season and averaged over 35 cents apiece throughout the State.

Some of the growers obtained prices as good as last year, especially on some of the fancy varieties. In one section the Gravenstein netted $4.00 per barrel and in another the Mc-Intosh, $3.75, Kings as high as $3.25 and Baldwins, $2.80.

The associations received on an average much better prices than the surrounding growers, showing that coöperation is a very important factor, not only in disposing of the fruit, but also in raising the standard and maintaining a strict pack.

Three new associations were formed this year,—The Kineo Fruit Growers of Foxcroft, the Auburn Fruit Growers of Auburn and the Norway Fruit Growers at Norway. Maine. Each has an attractive label and has put out a pack that will go a long ways toward making them known on the market. In three other localities the movement is started and should come to a head next year.

The importance of storage plants was never more noticeable than it has been this fall. Quantities of clean fruit have been sold for a song on account of lack of storage, and the grower was left absolutely at the mercy of the buyer. So much fruit on the market of course made a depression, but it does not seem as if this condition would last, as the amount of fruit is not greatly in excess of the 1911 crop.

ORCHARD INSPECTION.

It was not possible to devote as much time to orchard inspection as was desired, as other work was pressing. We did a great deal in connection with other work, however, and have kept in touch with many orchards during the year.

As has been said, many are spraying their trees; some but once, others as many as four or even five times. Cultivation is being practiced more and more, especially as the fruit has been somewhat smaller in size than is desirable. A few prefer the mulch system and some beautiful fruit has been produced by this method.

Only a few thin their fruit, but those that have done this are enthusiastic over the results they have obtained and will do more of it from now on.

Renovation is being carried on steadily and is rendering land more and more valuable. Fewer varieties are being planted and the growing of fruit is being put upon a more business-like basis.

INSECTS OF THE ORCHARD.

Green Aphis. In point of numbers the green aphis has been our worst pest. On the tender shoots of young trees they have been particularly abundant, checking and sometimes completely killing back the growth of the season; on the older trees, especially those that have been trimmed heavily, the tender growth has been badly infested and hard to treat effectively.

On the fruit itself, evidence of their work has been discovered, it being slightly misshapen and presenting a stung appearance. Undoubtedly the lime-sulphur, as the dormant spray, killed many of the eggs and aided greatly in controlling the pest. Summer sprays, kerosene emulsion, tobacco infusion, soap solutions, etc., have been both satisfactory and unsatisfactory in places used; kerosene has tended to injure the foliage to a greater extent than the other materials, but this has been due to lack of care in preparing and to too concentrated solutions. Ivory soap, 1 pound to 10 gallons of water, was used on some orchards and proved very effective. It has been found that these sprays are all more effective when used in damp weather, or in the late afternoon, than when applied on warm sunshiny days; this may be due to the rapid evaporation, but is certainly true. Under unfavorable weather conditions the twigs were partially infested, even after being completely immersed a short time in properly made solutions. Greater care must be exercised in the future if we are to successfully control this pest.

Blister Mite. The rapidity with which this orchard mite is increasing in numbers is alarming the orchardists through the

State. Most varieties, and particularly the Baldwin, were seriously handicapped by the infestation of this insect. It will not be surprising if the trees show a lack in vigor next year as the leaves have had a poor opportunity of fulfilling their regular functions.

On examination these spots first show darker color than the remainder of the leaf; this color changing to a dark brown on the apple and a reddish brown on the pear, as the season advances. Many times these spots merge and cover a large portion of the leaf, often causing it to fall prematurely.

Lime-sulphur has proven the best material for control, but whether fall or spring applications are best, it is impossible to say, as little fall spraying has been practiced. A medium time in the spring gave the best results; not so early that there was little life in the tree and not so late that the mites had a chance to enter the opening leaf tips. As these insects live through the winter in the folds of the leaf buds, it would seem that the fall application would be more effective.

Bud Moth. More or less damage is done each year by this pest, but it is hardly ever a serious menace to the crops. The lead in the spray for scab has controlled it sufficiently to insure a good set of fruit.

Woolly Aphis. This pest has been found from time to time in the abrasions of the bark and is easily noticed because of its whitish, cottonlike covering. Only a very few of the root infesting forms have been seen on the nursery stock this year.

Codling Moth. The results obtained by growers in spraying for the codling moth were particularly gratifying and the percentage of wormy fruit was greatly reduced. One grower, spraying for the first time, had but two wormy apples from a tree that bore six barrels of fruit. Its control depends largely upon thoroughness and applying the spray within a limited period after the blossoms fall. In some varieties this year, the calyces had closed too much at the end of six days to warrant effective work. This seemed to be especially true of the varieties that are most susceptible to the attacks of this pest.

Arsenate of lead gave better satisfaction than any of the other materials when everything is considered, although it is somewhat more expensive than some. Both the dry powder and the paste forms were used and seemed to give about the same results, though the powder form has not been tried sufficiently for a fair test as yet.

Trees that were well pruned were much easier to spray and gave much more satisfactory results.

In the unsprayed orchards the percentage of wormy fruit was not quite as large as for the previous season, but must have been in the vicinity of 40 per cent, varying quite a lot in different sections.

Railroad Worm. As this insect is not controlled by spraying, it is much harder to check its injury. Only conscientious picking up of the windfalls, deep, early spring plowing, or sufficient sheep or swine to eat all the drops, seem to affect the amount of fruit infested. It has been demonstrated in various sections, however, that these methods aid greatly and that if each grower would do his own share this pest might be entirely controlled.

Curculio. The work done by this pest does not seem to have been as great as last season. Its occurrence on some varieties is so common as to lead to the impression that it is a marking of that particular fruit. This marking is due to the failure of the egg to hatch, leaving the russet spot as a surface blemish.

Best results have been obtained where the orchard is cultivated until about the first of August.

Spraying aids greatly in the destruction of the adult beetle and the destroying of the fallen fruit removes many eggs and larvæ.   .

Cultivation aims at the destruction of the pupae which are very sensitive to light and air and which are invariably at a depth of less than two inches.

Orchard Tent. These caterpillars were first seen April 26th and became very much in evidence later. In fact, the cherry and neglected apple trees were soon defoliated, presenting a very unsightly appearance along the roadside.

In the orchards they were easily controlled by spraying with arsenate of lead in May. When spraying was not carried on, the nests were either burned or neglected, the branches being seriously injured in either case.

Smaller infestations of tussock moths, canker worms, forest

tent caterpillars, red-humped, tiger moths, case bearers, leaf rollers and fall web-worms were found, but not in sufficient numbers to do a great amount of damage.

Scale Insects. On February 28th, San Jose scale was found on some four-year-old trees in Wells. This infestation was introduced through nursery stock. Two trees were condemned and burned and the remainder are being watched to see if there is any further spread of the pest.

On February 29th, some plum trees at Crowley's Junction were found to be slightly infested. They were sprayed late with dormant strength (1-8) lime-sulphur and the scale is apparently exterminated; a watch will also be kept upon these trees.

Those, as far as we know, are all the new infestations, though undoubtedly there are a few more. The appearance on nursery stock is not common as the various state nursery inspection laws are fairly rigid and the nurseries carefully watched. If any scale is present in the orchard, it should be sent to the Department or to the Experiment Station for identification at the earliest opportunity.

Great quantities of European fruit scale have been found this year, especially in Oxford, Androscoggin, Cumberland and York Counties. It resembles San Jose in appearance, but is not as destructive, having but one brood a year. It had impaired the vigor of the trees in Mere Point very seriously and in other places has done more or less harm. The lime-sulphur (1-8) removed the greater part this spring and will undoubtedly control this scale in another season. This spraying is rendered much more effective if the trees are scraped beforehand, thus exposing the insects to the ready access of the material. It is very difficult to reach them through heavy, loose bark.

The oyster-shell bark-louse continues on unsprayed trees to some extent, but seldom enough to cause death. A vigorous tree is seldom badly infested, though young trees may be. We have obtained twigs from neglected orchards that are completely covered with the scale and are in a dying condition because of them. This has not been the case in an orchard that is well taken care of.

The lime-sulphur and kerosene emulsion have both proven effective in their control.

Scurfy Scale. The first of these scales were found in Buckfield this spring, but they were not very numerous. Since then they have been found in various other sections in small numbers. They have been controlled by the same methods as have the other scale insects.

Limb Borers. These borers are beginning to appear in different parts of the State. In the vicinity of Greene, in particular, their work is noticeable and many trees are threatened seriously by their attacks. In Franklin County also they have infested many trees and have killed some outright.

Many infested limbs were removed and burned and the remainder treated with lime-sulphur.

Round Headed Borer. These continue to worry the growers, in young trees, and are most successfully controlled at present by carefully watching the trees and cutting them out when found.

Repellent washes have aided in keeping them away, but have not proved entirely efficient as a protection. Wire, that is used for protection from mice, also aids in preventing their egg deposits, provided it does not rub against the tree at any point.

DISEASES OF THE ORCHARD.

Scab. There has been, together with great quantities of other fungous diseases, a vast amount of scab; it has been very prevalent on fruit, foliage, and even on the small twigs.

Climatic conditions have been particularly favorable to its development, the weather being damp and cloudy with insufficient sunshine to check its growth. At a conservative estimate fully 45 per cent of the crop has been affected, and this amount will increase upon that fruit which has been put into storage.

Although the foliage of the Baldwin has been more or less affected, the fruit itself has seemed more resistant than most of the other varieties. The McIntosh, Stark, Spy, Rhode Island Greening, Fameuse, Ben Davis and numerous others have suffered severely from its attack.

As the previous season was practically free from this disease, but few of the growers sprayed at the proper time to insure its control, and depended upon the codling moth spray to check it. In these cases it was proven conclusively that spraying at this time is not effective and that an earlier application must be put on.

The spores of this disease live through the winter in the leaves under the trees and are liberated during the moist weather of early summer. When set free into the air they are carried to the foliage and start growth at once.

The summer spores are soon produced and spread rapidly under favorable weather conditions. The lower leaves are usually infected first, then all parts of the foliage and fruit.

Because of this rapid development and dissemination, it is necessary to spray two or three times during the season, to effectually control it.

In the fruit the fungus grows between the skin and the underlying tissue, causing the diseased regions to grow more slowly than the other parts of the fruit. Occurring on the stem it cuts off the supply of nourishment from the young fruit and causes it to fall early. On the stem of the leaf it also shuts off the supply of food and often causes it to fall prematurely. As the fruit grows larger, scab, if abundant, causes one side to become dwarfed and cracked, presenting a lopsided appearance.

In storage the disease spreads rapidly, and renders worthless much of that fruit which was clean when put in.

Other diseases such as pink rot, blue mold, etc., gain an entrance in the scab spots and cause rapid decay.

Its importance has been greatly underestimated and it is time that we appreciated the amount of damage it is capable of doing. Trees whose foliage has been badly infected, are certain to be less vigorous the following season, as the disease has interfered with the proper accumulation of nourishment. Sometimes the entire failure of a crop is due to the presence of this fungus.

In treating this disease the first application should be made just before the blossoms open, when the buds are showing pink. Either Bordeau mixture 4-4-50 or lime sulphur 1—20 may be used, together with 2 1-2 lbs. of arsenate of lead.

Lime-sulphur should be used for the second and third sprayings at the rate of 1—40 with 2 1-2 lbs. of arsenate of lead, applied directly after the blossoms fall and again about ten days or two weeks later if the season is such as to warrant its development.

Sufficient apparatus should be at hand to insure the application before it is too late to be effective.

The dormant spray for the leaves under the trees, should be applied as soon as the leaves have fallen, using lime-sulphur 1—11. If possible select a time when the ground is hard so that the wheels will not injure the roots. Early spring plowing will aid in burying the leaves so that the disease will decay and be rendered harmless.

Fruit Spot. Here is a disease that we are neglecting to notice as carefully as we should. As it has been considered a regular marking of certain varieties by many growers, it has escaped the attention which would otherwise have been bestowed upon it. Showing as dark red spots on red varieties and as red and carmine spots on yellow varieties, it is very noticeable and easy to detect. It has been confused with San Jose scale and resembles it to some extent upon casual examination; on close inspection it is easily identified, however. It is also confused with the Baldwin spot.

In the sprayed orchards there has been but little of this spotting, but on unsprayed trees of varieties such as Bellflower, Greening, etc., it has been very abundant.

Leaf Spot. When it is understood that this disease is produced by the same spores that produce canker, it is not surprising that we have been troubled greatly by its prevalence this year. It has occurred abundantly on the foliage of unsprayed trees and to some extent on those where spraying had been done.

Canker. The growers are realizing the necessity of controlling canker if they are to save their older trees. The methods of controlling and the necessary precautions to prevent further infection are generally known and are being more widely practiced this year than ever before. Each orchard, however, is usually more or less affected and we must improve in thoroughness and carefulness in our work.

Wounds, either from pruning saws or other causes, should be treated with some efficient dressing that will remain on a long time and act as a protection to the raw wood.

Cankers are the worst enemies we have at present; let us keep the fact in mind.

INSECTS INFESTING SHADE TREES.

Borers. During the year the following borers have been received at the office for identification:—Hickory bark borer, *Scolytus quadrispinosus* (Say.), mottled willow borer, *Cryptorhynchus lapathi* (Linn.), elm borer, *Saperda tradentata* (Oliv.), sugar maple borer, *Plagionotus speciosus* (Say.), pine bark beetle, *Tomicus pini* (Say.).

The elm borer and maple borer have damaged great numbers of our best shade trees and appear to increase greatly each year. The badly infested trees should be cut and burned; the remainder thoroughly inspected and larvae killed where found. It is shameful to lose our elms which are as beautiful as any in the country and which go so far towards making our towns attractive.

Elm-leaf Aphid. Numbers of complaints were received from the southern parts of the State during July, because of the dampening of sidewalks under elm trees. This was due to the work of the leaf aphid, occurring in large numbers. Both the winged and wingless forms are very similar in color to the leaves, making it difficult to distinguish them; they cling to the leaves a considerable time, unless heavy rains occur. It is hard to spray for them on large trees, but kerosene emulsion has given good satisfaction on smaller ones.

Elm-leaf Beetle. Even more damage was done to the elm trees by this pest than during the previous season. The infestation is greatest in York and Cumberland Counties, but is increasing in the surrounding counties of Androscoggin, Sagadahoc and Oxford. The defoliation of the tree in midsummer is a serious thing, preventing as it does the proper function of the leaves. Occurring for a period of years, such defoliation will cause death to the tree, and loss in vigor when occurring occasionally. We have tried to impress upon the owners of shade trees the importance of controlling this pest before it has become so abundant as to weaken or destroy a majority of the elms. Arsenate of lead has controlled it when applied to the foliage early in the spring. Care should be taken to spray the top of the tree, as the attack usually begins with the upper and more tender leaves.

The disinclination of this insect to fly a great distance is encouraging to the man who sprays his own trees, as it reduces the chances of new infestation from uncared for trees nearby.

The natural enemies do not as a general thing greatly reduce the numbers of this pest.

Spruce Bud Worm. This pest has been characterized as the most destructive enemy of the spruce in certain portions of Maine, by Dr. Packard. It certainly has been this season and the damage has been exceptionally great. The terminal shoots of the spruce began to turn brown about the middle of June and some looked as if fire had run through them.· The larvae fed on the needles of both the first year's and the previous year's growth in most places. The adults were first noticed the first week in July and were very numerous.

Valuable trees should be sprayed early next season with arsenate of lead.

Brown-tail Moth. The situation as regards this pest is somewhat peculiar. While there were numerous nests and much defoliating in the fall of 1911, there was comparatively little damage during the present season. Only a part of the caterpillars were alive this spring, a fact due to climate and parasites both, it would appear. Many nests were torn open evidently by birds, so that the caterpillars were exposed directly to the weather and were not hardy enough to endure it. Many parasitic flies were found living through the winter in the nests of the brown-tail.

This season the moths have extended their boundaries somewhat, but not to any great extent. The flight was very large considering the comparatively small number of larvae and there are more nests at present than there were last year. After more parasites have been acclimated and generally disseminated the work of cutting the nests will be greatly reduced, but until that happy time arrives we must push the work with unabated vigor and determination. The success or failure to control the pest rests mainly upon the authorities of the cities and towns, so let all do their share and keep the damage as small as is possible.

The Quarantine Act is given in toto elsewhere in the report.

THE WHITE PINE BLISTER RUST.

This disease has been introduced through foreign nursery stock, and unless carefully guarded against will work havoc with our white pine.

As far as we know, there are no infested trees in this State, but the nature and importance of this disease should be known so as to guard against future introduction.

It does not show on the white pine for some time, usually a year or more, and then on three-year-olds or those older. The bark swells usually near the lower branches, tapering in either direction so as to resemble a spindle, more or less. The swelling may be irregular and extend into the branches. The growth begins to look stunted and the trees do not branch freely.

Usually in May or June yellow bunches are discernible on the eruptions of the swollen parts and when mature set free orange colored spores which are carried to other plants.

This disease can not live on pine alone, but requires a second host plant for a part of its life history. This second host must be the currant or gooseberry, and unless the spores liberated from the pine reach one of these plants, they cannot develop. After reaching the leaves of one of these plants they start growth and soon develop so-called summer spores on the under sides of the leaves. These spread to other plants and so are rapidly increased. After a month or so these cease to form and other "winter" spores are developed. These spores will not start growth again on the currant or gooseberry but must be blown to a white pine. Thus the disease alternates from pine to the groseilles and back to pine and so on.

Young pines are usually killed with the development of the first spores, ultimately at any rate.

Older trees lose their new growth and may be killed outright.

Should this disease reach our white pine, it would be about impossible to save them and thousands of dollars worth of timber would be destroyed.

If anything suspicious is noted on this kind of tree, notify the Department at the earliest moment.

SMALL FRUITS.

Strawberries. Because of its adaptability to various soil and climatic conditions, the strawberry has found favor throughout the State. Each locality finds one or more varieties that do well. Each garden has a few plants for home use and some growers have large commercial plantings. The labor problem seems to be the main obstacle in the way of commercial berry growing and applies to other small fruits as well as to the strawberry. There is not at present sufficient cheap labor to handle large crops.

The Senator Dunlap, Glen Mary, Abington and Sample are the leading varieties in the State, although new varieties are pressing closely on their heels. The Lyons seems to be a fine producing berry and is doing exceptionally well in some places. The Brandywine and Stevens' Late Champion have been planted a good deal, but vary greatly in results. Of the newer varieties recommended in Experiment Stations, the Early Ozark and Battenburg are very productive and the Parcell Early is very early.

Insect pests have troubled the berry but little.

There has been quite a lot of leaf blight because of the season and the results from spraying have varied.

Bordeaux is generally regarded as a little better than lime-sulphur as a fungicide for strawberries and has given favorable results where properly applied.

Not enough care has been paid to the fertilizing of the fruit as is seen by the condition and quantity produced. A 3-9-7 fertilizer seems to give excellent results, but this will vary in different soils. It is very hard to give specific directions in cultivating for this reason.

All of the above varieties are apparently sufficiently hardy for our climate.

Better care should be taken in picking and grading and marketing. The berries are too often bruised in picking: too much poor fruit is put into the boxes; boxes are apt to be a little slack when offered for sale and are often second hand so that they present an unattractive appearance. New boxes pay for themselves.

Raspberries. Although the canes in many localities were badly winter-killed, the crop in general was good. The cane borer was prevalent in all sections and did a good deal of damage.

One of the things that has been neglected is pruning. A grower in Auburn cut back all his canes to 18 inches and obtained better results than ever before. The plants are more stalky, easier to pick, and have a much greater bearing surface. Too many canes are left in the hill oftentimes, 3 to 5 giving better results than a larger number. The Cuthbert is easily the most popular variety, but there are more or less Herberts, Kings, Loudons, Eatons and Clines.

Neither the purple nor the black raspberry is gaining favor rapidly at present; of the former, Columbia and Shaffer are leaders and of the latter, Cumberland, Black Diamond, Palmer, Eureka and Gregg.

Blackberries and Loganberries. This season has been very favorable to the growth of the blackberry and the crop in general has been excellent. The climatic condition was very favorable and in almost any soil they did well. The canes were badly infested with cane borers which may cause less vigorous growth next year, although the actual damage done this year did not appear to be great. There was little winter-killing of canes, except in cases where new varieties were being tried.

Agawam, Eldorado and Snyder are all hardy and have many advantages. The Snyder is the best all-round berry, although the fruit is somewhat smaller than that of the other varieties.

The loganberry which has such a reputation in the West has been tried on a small scale and appears to be hardy.

Gooseberries and Currants. Only a comparatively small amount of gooseberries and currants were raised commercially this year, although each garden usually had a few plants. The hot weather in July again caused many of the gooseberries to drop and there didn't seem to be much difference in varieties. Perhaps the Downing dropped a little less, but not noticeably so.

The currants were quite free from disease and insect pests; were abundant and of good quality. Some growers are highly recommending the Pomona and it is certainly a high quality fruit. Fay's Prolific and Wilder are set more than other varieties and are giving fine results.

THE BLUEBERRY CANNING BUSINESS OF
WASHINGTON COUNTY.

Among the industries of this State of which the general public knows very little is the blueberry business of Washington County. This industry rightfully belongs to our most eastern county for there it had its origin and there today is the seat of the canning operations. This industry, returning some $250,-000.00 to the county annually, rightfully deserves a place in this Agricultural Report.

The great areas once covered with pine and oak forest were cleared and for many years were burned over at intervals. These acres thus kept barren proved to be natural blueberry territory.

The soil for the greater part is a light sandy loam and on the "barrens" stretches for miles with little to obstruct the view. Old settlers tell us that the area originally covered with oak is the most valuable for the blueberry culture, although the pine areas are very good. These barrens are for the most part comparatively level territory and are located chiefly in the southwestern to the central northern portion of the county. The last few years show that much of the more hilly country is also adapted to the growth of the berries, especially for the early crop, so it is hard to say definitely how many acres of blueberry territory there are in Washington County, but different estimates give an average of about 250,000 acres.

The land although very easily and inexpensively operated is valued at $45.00 to $50.00 per acre. A large portion of the barrens is owned by the men who operate the canneries, although other individuals own large tracts and share the profits of the crop with the canners. The ease with which a crop can be produced is remarkable, for the most advanced methods, as yet, consist of the simple method of burning over the area once in three years. Only the more particular owners cut the large bushes of birch, etc., in the fall, so that the territory will be perfectly clean after the burn, for many do not even go to that small expense, allowing the fire to kill the larger bushes if it will.

The burn is an interesting operation in its simplicity. The person in charge selects the area and in the morning after the material on the ground is dry enough to burn, he arms himself with a long torch constructed of a pipe which is filled with oil and a sort of wick attached to the end in such a way as to be supplied with only enough oil to burn freely. Starting on the side from which the wind blows he then travels along, lighting many fires as he walks. The wind carries this fire onward across the plains until night falls. The damp evening air is usually sufficient to check the fire enough so that it will die out before morning. Thus a single man is able to burn a large area in a day.

This work is done in the spring as soon as the fire will run, usually in the month of May, and there is of course some danger in a dry season of losing control of the fire, but this does not occur often on territory properly cared for, because the burn is made once in three years and in that period hardly material enough will collect to make a disastrous fire. Too heavy burns destroy many of the roots so that the crop is materially affected. For this reason little burning is attempted in unusually dry seasons.

Of course there is no crop to harvest the first year, but the following two years are the ones which the owners depend on for their returns. Sometimes three seasons' crops are picked before the process is repeated.

The land owners usually divide their territory into three portions, so that two parts will be yielding a crop and the other will be burned and ready to produce the next year.

The fertilizing problem has received little or no attention for this is virgin soil and all that seems to be necessary for fertilizer is the ashes from the cover of berry vines and bushes.

In the summer when the berries are about ready to pick, the land is leased to pickers who are ready to go on to the work as soon as word is given. Usually one person gets the lease permission to pick on a specified staked territory, and he will furnish pickers enough to gather that area while he himself will attend to the hauling to the cannery. Usually one picking will gather the entire crop and this year it took just about five weeks, which is an average season's picking. The berries are usually picked only when the vines are dry so that dull weather sometimes lengthens the season.

The early berries are rushed to market in crates and from one station alone over 1000 bushels of fruit were shipped this season to all parts of New England and more distant markets. Of course these berries bring a good price, averaging 10c to 12c per quart, which for the county will probably total some over $8,000.00 this year.

At the cannery the land owner receives so much per quart stumpage. This year the price was 1 1-2c to 2c per quart. This means that all the berries are accounted for as they arrive at the cannery and credited to the tract on which they were grown.

The average yield is estimated to be about 60 bushels per acre, although with a little care and a favorable season that amount is often increased considerably. This means that the owner receives from $25.00 to $35.00 per acre every two years out of three, and his only expense is that of burning, taxes, and the small expense of leasing the plots to the pickers.

The most interesting scene is that presented on the barrens at the time of picking when the territory gives the appearance of an army in camp. It is the custom as soon as the berries are ready to pick for men with their entire families to go to the barrens and live in tents or small shacks until the crop is harvested. All go into the fields except the smallest children and pick what they can. Each person uses a berry rake which is constructed of small wooden teeth with a flattish tray to catch the berries. These rakes cost from $1.50 to $3.00. The rake is swung forward with an upward lifting motion, which collects the berries very rapidly. When the tray of the rake has been well filled, the contents are emptied into pails and carried to the winnowing machine. Here each person usually empties his berries into the machine, which turns by hand, and blows out all of the leaves and light waste which have been collected with the berries. They are then poured into half bushel boxes and hauled to the factory. Sometimes the berries are hauled 30 to 40 miles to the cannery.

Pickers working for a wager have been known to pick, or rather rake, 11 bushels of berries in a single day. This of course is way above the average for many small children do good work at this employment. For this reason large families make a fine wage during the berry season. The average daily picking must be about 2 1-2 to 3 bushels per person. The total crop for this season is estimated as 80,000 bushels, so that there must be somewhere between 1200 and 1500 people on the barrens during the picking season of five weeks.

The pickers are paid in many cases this year 56c per bushel, while some dry seasons, approaching the last of the picking, they get as high as $1.00 a bushel. This year something like $45,000.00 must have been paid to the pickers alone.

At the factory the work of canning is practically the same in all of the towns. The teams drive up to a raised platform where the boxes are unloaded and the berries passed directly through another winnowing machine or fanning mill. They are then poured on to tables where they are carefully inspected by women who stand on either side of the table and pick out all foreign material. Next the berries are emptied into the cookers, which are very similar to the corn cookers used in the corn canning plants. The one which is claimed to do the best work is a long steam jacketed cylinder about eight inches in diameter, within which is a long rod having the shape of a screw. This screw turns as the berries are poured in and keeps them in motion until they drop out the other end of the cylinder. The temperature within this cooker is kept up to 175° F to 200° F and it is estimated that the berries do not remain in it over 3 to 4 minutes when all is going well.

From the cooker the material is run into large vats so constructed that men can work on either side and dip the berries into cans and in the act of dipping keep the material of a uniform quality as far as proportion of berries and juice is concerned. These cans are passed along as soon as filled through a groove where they are brushed clean and presented to the machine which caps and seals them the same as is done in corn canneries. The hot cans are immediately transferred to the cooling platform where they are piled in tiers and washed down with cold water.

They are allowed to dry and then are labeled and packed in boxes ready for shipment. In some canneries sugar is added to the berries as they are canned and where this is done it is used at the rate of about 4 ounces to the two-pound can. Two-pound and ten-pound cans are used in this work and about 36 two-pound cans are put up from a bushel of berries. The shipping cases contain two dozen small cans and either 6 or 12 of the large cans to each, and practically all of the carload shipments are made up of both sizes of cans.

The cannery of Charles Stewart, Cherryfield, this year employed 30 hands and packed a total of about 10,000 bushels. This is one of the newest and best equipped plants and in a day they packed 700 to 800 bushels with their two cookers in operation. Of this crew about half were men and the other half women and boys who do the lighter work, such as picking over the berries, placing caps on the cans, labelling the cans, etc. The canneries work only a nine hour day for the most part. The average wage is $2.00 for the men and $1.25 for the women and boys.

The other factories work about the same crews. The three canneries of Jasper Wyman and Son employed about 80 hands and put out a daily total of 1400 bushels in the best of the season. In the county there are the following canneries in operation:

Charles Stewart & Co........ Cherryfield.
Jasper Wyman & Son....... Cherryfield, Columbia and Machias.
Acme Canning Co.......... Ayers Jct.
A. & R. Logie............. Columbia Falls.
Frank & Hall.............. Columbia Falls.
Gillis Bros................ East Machias.

There may be also a few small canneries but the total crew must have been about 300 hands and the total output is estimated as about 80,000 bushels, which is considerably more than last year.

The canned product is sold all over the United States. Concerns in Cherryfield shipped to Florida and California, this year, showing the extensive demand for the product.

SUMMARY OF STATISTICS.

Total acreage, 250,000 acres.

Valuation at $50.00 an acre is $1,250,000.

Total crop canned 85,000 bushels, which means about 3,060,-000 two-pound cans.

Average cost per bushel to the canners, $2.50.

Total cost to the canners for berries	$212,500.00
Total wage, 150 men at $2.00 for six weeks	10,800.00
Total wage, 150 women and boys, $1.25 six weeks	6,750.00

Total amount returned to the county not including amounts paid for supplies, boxes, teaming, loading, etc.	$230,050.00
The crop of crated fresh berries will add about 1500 bushels at $3.50	5,250.00
Total	$235,300.00

GREGORY ORCHARDS.

Some of the Gregory orchards were not visited during the past season, because of the pressure of other duties. The number neglected was very small however, and such growers will surely be visited next year.

Twenty-four failed to send in reports for 1911. As yet, some of the remainder have not sent in reports but it is expected that they will all do so at an early date.

Poor stock to start with, and various other unfavorable conditions caused many of the growers to lose their enthusiasm, but on the whole the orchards are doing well and are a credit to the growers as well as to the State. Many are exceptionally fine and present a striking example of what is possible with young trees properly cared for.

Fruit was produced on some of the trees, especially on the Wealthy and Yellow Transparent.

From the reports sent in, some 115 in number, some tabulations have been made and some interesting data obtained.

The finish of the contest is beginning to draw near and even greater efforts should be made to have one of the prize orchards. About $900.00 will be available for the prizes, making it worth while to put in one's best efforts to be a winner.

Now is the time to think of the next contest also. Have the ground for it fixed in mind and make preparations to have that ground in fine physical condition when it is time to get the trees. Plan on getting first-class trees and on having orders in early, so as to obtain the desired variety or varieties. A good start is half a victory.

STATISTICS.

VARIETY AS PER LAST YEAR'S REPORT.

Stark	51
McIntosh	46
Baldwin	27
Wolf River	18
Wealthy	16
Spy	16
Tallman Sweet	12
King	10
Gano	10
Gravenstein	7
Delicious	6

Rest very scattering.

PRUNING—115 ORCHARDS TO DATE.

High open top	32
High center stalk	20
Low open top	28
Low center stalk	8
Not mentioned	27

SPRAYING.

	1.	2.	3.	4.
Lime-sulphur used	20	9	3	–
Arsenate of Lead	13	11	–	–
Pyrox	5	4	2	–
Bordeaux Mixture	5	1	–	–
Kerosene	2	–	1	3
Tobacco	6	–	–	1
Soap	2	1	–	–
Bordo Lead	1	–	–	–
Bug Death	1	–	–	–

CULTIVATION.

Clean cultivation	8
Dug around	17
Crop	59
Sod	22
Clover	111
Mulch	11
Grain	14

FERTILIZER.

Manure	46
Commercial	62

Trees Reset.

Winter-killing	48
Mice	70
Snow	3
Deer	26
Drouth	13
Canker	10
Lack of vigor	9

Insect Pests.

Green aphis	39
Brown-tail moth	31
Tent caterpillar	6
Gypsy moth	111
Borers	5
Red-humped	2
Woolly aphis	4
Fall web-worm	3

Mice Protection.

Veneer	5
Tarred paper	22
Wire	26
Paint	3
Pure tar	1
Sheath paper	1
Sand paper	1
Slats	3

Borer Protection.

Knife	57
Wire	26
Paper	7
Paint	3
Tobacco	1
Soap	1
Lime-sulphur	1

COSTS PER ACRE.

Pruning.

Highest	$7 50
Lowest	10
Average	1 20
Popular—18 growers	1 00

Spraying.

Highest	$4 00
Lowest	25
Average	1 60
Popular—13 growers	1 00

FERTILIZER.

Highest	$12 00
Lowest	.25
Average	3.25
Popular—11 growers	2.00

CULTIVATING.

Highest	$10 00
Lowest	35
Average	2 80
Popular—9 growers	3 00

MULCH.

Highest	$5 00
Lowest	60
Average	2 38
Popular—5 growers	1 00

COST OF INSECT PROTECTION OTHER THAN BY SPRAYING.

Highest	$15 00
Lowest	15
Average	1 11
Popular—16 growers	50

NURSERY INSPECTION.

Chapter 176 of the Public laws of 1911 provides that all nurseries or places where trees, shrubs, vines and plants are grown or offered for sale shall be inspected at least once a year by the State Horticulturist or by some person by him deemed competent. In accordance with this law the several nurseries in the State were visited and a careful inspection made.

The law provides that a certificate shall be issued to the nurseryman and a copy of the form follows:

No................

State of Maine.

DEPARTMENT OF AGRICULTURE.

Certificate of Inspection of Nursery Stock.

This is to certify that the nursery stock of ....
growing at .... State of Maine,
was examined .... 19 , , in compliance with the
provisions of Chapter 15 of the Public Laws of 1907, as
amended, and found to be apparently free from San Jose scale
and other injurious insects or diseases.

This certificate expires June 30, 19 .

....
Commissioner of Agriculture.

Augusta, Me., ...19 .

. The table printed below gives the tabulated result of the
inspection.

ANDROSCOGGIN COUNTY.

Nurseries.	Address.	Date of inspection.	Acres.	Apples.	Pears, peaches.	Cherries, plums.	Raspberry.	Currant.	Gooseberry.	Blackberry.	Miscellaneous.	Conifers.	Hardwood.	Ornamental shrubs.	Total.	Number condemned.
Chaput, J. P.	Auburn	June 27	3	–	–	–	3,000	–	–	100	–	–	–	–	3,100	–
Lapham, E. A.	Auburn	July 23	1/3	–	–	–	1,500	–	–	100	–	–	–	–	1,600	–
Merrill, C. A.	Auburn	July 24	1	–	–	–	2,050	–	–	450	–	–	–	–	2,500	–
Roak, Geo. M. Co.	Auburn	July 24	1/4	–	–	–	–	–	–	–	–	–	–	350	350	–

CUMBERLAND COUNTY.

Nurseries.	Address.	Date of inspection.	Acres.	Apples.	Pears, peaches.	Cherries, plums.	Raspberry.	Currant.	Gooseberry.	Blackberry.	Miscellaneous.	Conifers.	Hardwood.	Ornamental shrubs.	Total.	Number condemned.
[illegible]e, J. A.	Bridgton	June 26	1/4	–	–	–	800	–	–	–	–	–	–	–	800	–
Goddard, L. C.	Woodfords	June 25	1/2	–	–	–	25	–	–	25	–	15	30	525	620	2
Gould, C. E.	Woodfords	June 26	1/4	–	–	–	200	–	–	–	–	–	–	–	200	–
Casco Bay Nursery Co.	Yarmouth	July 20	1/2	–	–	–	–	–	–	–	–	4,825	–	220	5,045	3
Jackson, H. A.	[illegible]	June 26	5	–	–	–	–	–	–	–	–	750,000	100	500	750,600	–
Macomber, E. R.	Woodfords	June 25	1/3	10	–	6	20	–	–	–	48	1	10	–	95	1
Minot, J. W.	So. Portland	June 26	1/4	–	–	–	–	–	–	–	200	–	–	–	200	3
Ramsey, W. A.	Woodfords	June 25	1/4	–	–	1	65	18	8	–	–	–	–	73	165	–
Smith, G. W.	Woodfords	July 17	1/2	–	–	–	1,200	–	–	–	–	–	–	–	1,200	–
Soule, [illegible]	Freeport	Aug. 20	1/2	–	–	–	1,000	12	–	–	10	–	–	–	1,022	–

HANCOCK COUNTY.

Nurseries.	Address.	Date of inspection.	Acres.	Apples.	Pears, peaches.	Cherries, plums.	Raspberry.	Currant.	Gooseberry.	Blackberry.	Miscellaneous.	Conifers.	Hardwood.	Ornamental shrubs.	Total.	Number condemned.
Ball, H. A.	Hancock	July 5	1/4	–	–	6	200	100	50	–	–	–	–	–	356	6
Ball & Son	Hancock	July 5	1	–	–	–	300	110	100	–	–	–	–	–	510	–
Hancock Nursery Co.	Surry	July 5	1/2	2,500	30	50	100	–	–	–	–	–	–	–	2,680	10
Mt. Desert Nursery	Bar Harbor	July 1	20	800	60	50	300	475	30	–	175,000	100,000	7,500	10,750	294,965	16
Mt. Desert Nursery	Northeast Harbor	July 2	2	20	3	22	50	25	30	–	1,000	2,650	1,350	800	5,950	21
Penney, C. A.	Hancock	July 5	1/8	–	–	–	900	150	–	–	–	–	–	–	1,050	–
Phillips, W. H.	Nicolin	July 5	1	–	–	–	800	–	–	300	–	–	–	–	1,100	–
Wooster, E. W.	Hancock	July 27	1 1/2	–	–	–	3,000	–	–	–	–	–	–	–	3,000	–

KENNEBEC COUNTY.

Nurseries	Address	Date of inspection	Acres	Apples	Pears, peaches	Cherries, plums	Raspberry	Currant	Gooseberry	Blackberry	Miscellaneous	Conifers	Hardwood	Ornamental shrubs	Total	Number condemned
Elm Brook Farm Co..	Augusta	July 23	1¼	76	17	60	1,100	70	115	—	—	7	50	150	1,645	20
Hussey, J. C.	Oakland	July 8	¼	—	—	—	300	—	—	—	—	100	—	3,000	3,400	—
Mitchell & Co.	Waterville	July 31	15	100,000	—	1,100	—	—	—	—	—	—	3,000	4,500	108,600	—
Perley, C. A.	Winthrop	July 8	¾	8,000	—	—	—	—	—	—	—	10	—	200	8,210	—
Twitchell, Dr. G. M.	Monmouth	Aug. 15	1⅛	—	—	—	100	—	—	—	—	—	—	—	100	—

KNOX COUNTY.

Nurseries	Address	Date of inspection	Acres	Apples	Pears, peaches	Cherries, plums	Raspberry	Currant	Gooseberry	Blackberry	Miscellaneous	Conifers	Hardwood	Ornamental shrubs	Total	Number condemned
Glaentzel, Geo.	Camden	June 21	1	—	—	—	—	200	100	—	100	—	100	150	650	—
Lufkin, W. T.	Glen Cove	June 21	1	—	—	—	1,000	—	—	—	—	—	—	—	1,000	—

OXFORD COUNTY.

Nurseries	Address	Date of inspection	Acres	Apples	Pears, peaches	Cherries, plums	Raspberry	Currant	Gooseberry	Blackberry	Miscellaneous	Conifers	Hardwood	Ornamental shrubs	Total	Number condemned
Chase, Homer	Buckfield	Aug. 14	¼	10,000	—	—	—	—	—	—	—	—	—	—	10,000	—
Conant, C. A.	Hebron	July 17	1	—	—	—	2,000	—	—	—	—	—	—	—	2,000	—

PENOBSCOT COUNTY.

Nurseries	Address	Date of inspection	Acres	Apples	Pears, peaches	Cherries, plums	Raspberry	Currant	Gooseberry	Blackberry	Miscellaneous	Conifers	Hardwood	Ornamental shrubs	Total	Number condemned
Bodge, A. R.	Dexter	July 25	1	—	—	—	1,000	1,000	200	—	—	—	—	—	2,200	—
Eastman, A. A.	Dexter	July 25	2¼	—	—	—	1,000	2,000	2,000	—	—	—	—	—	5,000	—
Hoyt, Wm.	Dexter	July 26	1	—	—	—	—	—	—	—	Gin seng.	—	—	—	—	—

WALDO COUNTY.

Nurseries.	Address.	Date of inspection.	Acres.	Apples.	Pears, peaches.	Cherries, plums.	Raspberry.	Currant.	Gooseberry.	Blackberry.	Miscellaneous.	Conifers.	Hardwood.	Ornamental, shrubs.	Total.	Number condemned.
Smith, Chas	Thorndike	July 25	⅛	—	—	—	—	—	—	500	—	—	—	—	500	—

WASHINGTON COUNTY.

Nurseries.	Address.	Date of inspection.	Acres.	Apples.	Pears, peaches.	Cherries, plums.	Raspberry.	Currant.	Gooseberry.	Blackberry.	Miscellaneous.	Conifers.	Hardwood.	Ornamental, shrubs.	Total.	Number condemned.
McCabe, John	Machiasport	July 3	¼	—	16	—	L	—	—	—	—	—	650	200	866	6

YORK COUNTY.

Nurseries.	Address.	Date of inspection.	Acres.	Apples.	Pears, peaches.	Cherries, plums.	Raspberry.	Currant.	Gooseberry.	Blackberry.	Miscellaneous.	Conifers.	Hardwood.	Ornamental, shrubs.	Total.	Number condemned.
Fernald, Linwood	Eliot	June 24	2	—	—	—	1,200	125	5	500	300	156	—	755	3,041	1,700
Mahoney, Geo. L	Saco	June 25	1¼	—	—	—	—	—	—	—	—	100,000	—	100	100,100	—
Smith, T. A. W	Biddeford	June 21	1¼	—	—	—	—	5	—	—	—	—	3	150	158	—
Strout's Nursery Co	Biddeford	June 21	1½	—	—	—	—	—	—	—	—	—	—	200	200	—
			69 17-24	121,406	126	1,295	23,210	4,290	2,638	1,975	176,658	957,764	12,793	22,623	1,324,778	1,788

It will be noted in the above table that 86 trees and shrubs were condemned and 1700 raspberry and blackberry plants held in quarantine until treatment should be applied and the pest controlled. The canes of these plants at Eliot were seriously infected with scale insect commonly known as the rose scale (aulacaspis rosae.) This scale is easily controlled by the use of kerosene emulsion, repeated at intervals, and the certificate was withheld until the pest should be entirely controlled. Untreated, the pest is certain to materially affect the growth and production of fruit and new canes.

The trees and shrubs which were condemned were destroyed at once. The cause of condemning was in nearly every case lack of vigor, caused by oyster-shell scale, borers, canker, or general neglect.

Other pests discovered in this inspection work include the raspberry cane borer. These were found to be very abundant in many localities and while not serious enough to make it necessary to quarantine the plants, a circular letter was sent to each of the growers outlining the method of control. This consists of the simple operation of picking and destroying the tips of the canes as soon as the drooping leaves indicate the presence of the borer.

Red rust on blackberry plants was located in some places. This disease, while as yet not common; should be destroyed as soon as discovered. It is a fungous disease attacking the under side of the leaves, and the canes to some extent, forming a waxy growth, reddish in color, and causing the foliage to turn yellow. Spraying with fungicides helps to prevent its appearance but does not control it when once established. All infected plants should be burned.

The pine tip moth borer was found to be doing some damage in nurseries of the white pine. Its presence is indicated by the dying of the tender terminal shoots. Examination shows the little borer working in the wood under the bark. The infested portion should be cut off and burned. Of course the affected tree is made worthless for ornamental purposes so that a close watch should be kept to prevent the spread of this pest.

The caterpillars of the mourning cloak were found in many of the nurseries of poplar and willow trees. The arsenical sprays will control this trouble if applied at the time the cater-pillars make their appearance.

Green aphis, brown-tail moth, rose chafers, trunk borers, and such common pests were all present to some extent but they need only mention in this part of the report.

Special attention of all freight and express agents was called to Section 5, Chapter 15, Public Laws of 1907, which specifies that all packages and boxes of nursery stock transported within the State must have attached an unexpired official certificate of inspection. No cases of violation of this law had to be prosecuted.

INSPECTION OF IMPORTED NURSERY STOCK.

In compliance with an act approved by the President on August 20th, 1912, entitled, "An act to regulate the importation of nursery stock and other plants and plant products, etc.," Mr. Marlatt, Chairman Federal Horticultural Board, is making a strenuous campaign against the introduction of any destructive pest on imported stock.

As soon as a case of imported stock arrives notice is sent to the State Horticulturist and an inspection of each plant is made as soon as possible following the arrival of the shipment at its destination.

Inspection under this Act has been made as follows:

Kennebec Greenhouses	Bath, Me.	Oct. 23, 1912	Azaleas.
E. Saunders	Lewiston	Oct. 25,	Azaleas and palms.
T. G. Danforth	Skowhegan	Nov. 1,	Azaleas.
L. C. Goddard	Portland	Nov. 5,	Azaleas.
R. Stoble	Waterville	Nov. 20,	Roses.
L. C. Goddard	Portland	Nov. 23,	Azaleas and shrubs.
J. W. Minot	So. Portland	Nov. 23,	Shrubs.
E. Saunders	Lewiston	Dec. 11,	Shrubs.

GIPSY AND BROWN-TAIL MOTH QUARANTINE.

The nursery men and florists as well as the farmers and lumbermen are affected by the passing of the "Plant Quarantine Act." This step taken by the Federal Government is a radical one but made absolutely necessary by the existing conditions. It should receive the hearty support of all concerned if the spread of these injurious insects is to be held in check.

"NOTICE OF QUARANTINE NO. 4 (DOMESTIC),

WITH REGULATIONS.
(Effective on and after November 25, 1912.)

GIPSY MOTH AND BROWN-TAIL MOTH.

The fact has been determined by the Acting Secretary of
Agriculture, and notice is hereby given, that two injurious
insects new to and not heretofore widely distributed within and
throughout the United States, exist in parts of the following
States, to wit: The gipsy moth (*Porthetria dispar*), in the
States of Maine, New Hampshire, Massachusetts, and Rhode
Island; and the brown-tail moth (*Euproctis chrysorrhœa*), in
Maine, Vermont, New Hampshire, Massachusetts, Connecticut,
and Rhode Island.

Now, therefore, I, Willet M. Hays, Acting Secretary of
Agriculture, under the authority conferred by section 8 of the
act approved August 20, 1912, known as "The Plant Quarantine Act," do hereby quarantine the area hereinafter described as
infested by the brown-tail moth and the area hereafter described
as infested by the gipsy moth, and do order by this Notice of
Quarantine No. 4, under the authority and discretion conferred
on the Secretary of Agriculture by said section 8 of the act of
Congress approved August 20, 1912, that the interstate movement of (1) coniferous trees such as spruce, fir, hemlock, pine,
juniper (cedar), and arbor-vitæ (white cedar), known and
described as "Christmas trees," and parts thereof, and decorative plants such as holly and laurel, known and described as
"Christmas greens or greenery," and (2) forest plant products,
including logs, tan bark, posts, poles, railroad ties, cordwood,
and lumber, and field-grown florist's stock, trees, shrubs, vines,
cuttings, and other plants and plant products for planting or
propagation, excepting buds, fruit pits, seeds of fruit and orna-

mental trees and shrubs, field, vegetable, and flower seeds, bedding plants, and other herbaceous plants and roots, from any point in the areas herein quarantined to any point not located in said quarantined areas shall be made only in accordance with the rules and regulations hereinafter prescribed and amendments thereto.

The following territory is quarantined for the brown-tail moth:

All towns between the Atlantic Ocean and including Robbinston, Charlotte, Cooper, Plantation XIX, Wesley, Plantation XXXI, Plantation XXX, Devereaux, Plantations XXVIII, XXXIII, and XXXII, Milford, Alton, Bradford. Atkinson, Dover, Sangerville, Parkman, Wellington, Brighton, Solon, Embden, Anson, New Vineyard, Farmington, Temple, Wilton, Carthage, Mexico, Rumford, Newry, Riley, *Maine;* Shelburne, Gorham, Randolph, Jefferson, Whitefield, Dalton, Littleton, and Monroe, *New Hampshire;* Ryegate, Newbury, Bradford, Fairlee, Thetford, Norwich, Hartford, Hartland, Windsor, Weathersfield, Springfield, Rockingham, Westminster, Putney, Dummerston, Brattleboro, and Guilford, *Vermont;* Leyden, Greenfield, Deerfield, Whately, Hatfield, Northampton, Easthampton, Holyoke, West Springfield, Springfield, Longmeadow, East Longmeadow, and Hampden, *Massachusetts;* Stafford, Union, Woodstock, Pomfret, and Killingly, *Connecticut;* Foster, Coventry, West Greenwich, East Greenwich, and North Kingstown, *Rhode Island.* In addition to these the towns of North Adams and Clarksburg, *Massachusetts,* are also infested and are included in the quarantine area.

The following territory is quarantined for gipsy moth:

All the territory between (and including) the towns named and the Atlantic Ocean, as follows: Georgetown, Westport, Edgecomb, Damariscotta, Nobleborough, Newcastle, Alna, Whitefield, Chelsea, Pittston, Dresden, Richmond, Bowdoin, Webster, Lewiston, Auburn, Poland, Casco, Raymond, Windham, Standish, Limington, Cornish, and Porter, *Maine;* Freedom, Ossipee, Tuftonborough, Meredith, New Hampton, Hill, Danbury, Wilmot, Salisbury, Warner, Henniker, Hillsborough, Antrim, Hancock, Dublin, Troy, Richmond, and Winchester, *New Hampshire;* Warwick, Orange, Athol, Petersham, Barre,

Oakham, Spencer, Sturbridge, Charlton, Dudley, and Webster, *Massachusetts;* Burrillville, Gloucester, Johnston, Cranston, Warwick, and North Kingstown, *Rhode Island;* excepting the towns of Newport, Tiverton, and Little Compton, *Rhode Island;* Westport, Fall River, Somerset, Dighton, Freetown, Dartmouth, Fairhaven, and Mattapoisett, *Massachusetts.*

GIPSY MOTH REGULATIONS.

Coniferous trees of the area quarantined for the gipsy moth, such as spruce, fir, hemlock, pine, juniper (cedar), and arbor-vitæ (white cedar), known and described as "Christmas trees," and parts thereof, and decorative plants of the area quarantined for the gipsy moth, such as holly and laurel, known and described as "Christmas greens or greenery," shall not be moved or allowed to move interstate to points outside the quarantined area.

Forest plant products of the area quarantined for the gipsy moth, including logs, tan bark, posts, poles, railroad ties, cordwood, and lumber, and field-grown florist's stock, trees, shrubs, vines, cuttings, and other plants and plant products for planting or propagation, of the area quarantined for the gipsy moth, excepting buds, fruit pits, seeds of fruit, and ornamental trees and shrubs, field, vegetable and flower seeds, bedding plants and other herbaceous plants and roots shall not be moved or allowed to move interstate to any point outside the quarantined area unless and until such plants and plant products have been inspected by the United States Department of Agriculture and pronounced free from the gipsy moth.

BROWN-TAIL MOTH REGULATIONS.

Deciduous trees or shrubs of the area quarantined for the brown-tail moth, or parts thereof, including all deciduous field-grown florist's stock, vines, cuttings, grafts, and scions shall not be moved or allowed to move interstate to points outside the quarantined area, unless and until such plants and plant products have been inspected by the United States Department of Agriculture and pronounced to be free from the brown-tail moth.

GENERAL REGULATIONS.

(1) Every car, box, bale, or other container of plants and plant products of which inspection is required by these regulations shall be plainly marked with the name and address of the consignor and the name and address of the consignee, and shall bear a certificate showing that the contents have been inspected by the United States Department of Agriculture and found to be free from moth infestation.

(2) Carload and other bulk shipments of plants and plant products for which inspection is required by these regulations shall not be transported or offered for transportation interstate by cars, boats, and other vehicles, unless each shipment is accompanied by a certificate showing that the plants and plant products have been inspected by the United States Department of Agriculture and pronounced to be free from moth infestation. The inspection certificate shall accompany the waybills, conductors' manifests, memoranda, or bills of lading pertaining to such shipments made by cars or boats.

(3) Certificates of inspection will issue only for plants and plant products which have been actually inspected by the United States Department of Agriculture, and the use of such certificates in connection with plants and plant products which have not been so inspected is prohibited.

(4) Where inspection and certification are required by these regulations, inspection and certification by an inspector or other agent of the Federal Horticultural Board are meant, and such inspection and certification will be furnished without the payment of fees or charges of any nature.

(5) Plants and plant products, of which the interstate movement is prohibited or restricted by these regulations and which are grown outside the areas quarantined for the gipsy moth or the brown-tail moth, may be shipped interstate from points within the quarantined areas to points outside the quarantined areas under permit from the Secretary of Agriculture. Permits will issue only for plants and plant products which are not infested with the gipsy moth or brown-tail moth and transportation companies shall not accept or move interstate from within the quarantined areas such plants and plant products grown outside the quarantined areas, unless each shipment is

accompanied by a permit issued by the superintendent of moth work[1] at Boston, Mass.

(6) Persons intending to move or allow to be moved interstate plants and plant products for which certificates of inspection or permits are required by these regulations, will make application therefor as far as possible in advance of the probable date of shipment. Applications should show the nature and quantity of the plants or plant products it is proposed to move, together with their exact location and, if practicable, the contemplated date of shipment. Applicants for inspection will be required to place the articles to be inspected so that they can be readily examined. If not so placed inspection will be refused.

(7) The interstate movement of all classes of plants and plant products entirely within the area quarantined for the gipsy moth and the brown-tail moth will be permitted without restrictions, other than those which may be imposed by state officials at points of destination.

On and after November 25, 1912, and until further notice, by virtue of said section 8 of the act of Congress approved August 20, 1912, it shall be unlawful to move in interstate commerce any of the above-described plants or plant products from the areas herein quarantined, except in accordance with these regulations and amendments thereto.

Done at Washington this 5th day of November, 1912.

Witness my hand and the seal of the United States Department of Agriculture.

(Seal.)

WILLET M. HAYS,
Acting Secretary of Agriculture."

---

[1] Blanks on which to make application for inspection or for permits will be furnished upon request by the United States Department of Agriculture, Bureau of Entomology, 6 Beacon Street, Boston, Mass.

Part of a Twelve Acre Patch of Raspberries on Farm of H. F. Maxim, Locke's Mills.

LAW RELATING TO NURSERY AGENTS.

"Section 6. (As amended by P. L. 1909, c. 34, and P. L. 1911, c. 84 and c. 176.) Agents or other parties excepting growers who wish to sell nursery stock shall make application for an agent's license and shall file with the state horticulturist the names and addresses of nurseries or parties from whom they purchase their stock. Such application shall be accompanied by a fee of ten dollars. On receipt of such application the state horticulturist shall issue an agent's license valid for one year in such form and with such provisions as the commissioner of agriculture may prescribe. Such license may be revoked at any time for failure to report names and addresses of nurseries from which stock is purchased or for such other causes as may in the opinion of the commissioner of agriculture be deemed sufficient. Any violation of this requirement shall be punishable by a fine of not less than ten nor more than fifty dollars for each offense.

For the purpose of this act the term nursery stock is hereby applied to all fruit and ornamental trees, shrubs, and vines, and includes currant, gooseberry, blackberry and raspberry bushes."

That this law should not be overlooked, a statement explaining it was sent to all the licensed agents in the State in August, 1911. January 1, 1912, fifty agents had been licensed according to the new law, which took effect July 1, 1911, but some were selling without any license. This, of course, made a lot of complaint from the licensed men and demanded some immediate action.

Two cases were carried to court March 29th, in Franklin county, and found guilty. They were fined ten dollars and costs of court. All of the other cases that were reported to the office up to the 1st of May were attended to as soon as possible. Only two other cases were prosecuted, both in York County.

The American Association of Nurserymen did not believe the law constitutional and persuaded the agents to carry the cases to court. This was done, Thaxter & Holt of Portland being employed by the defense. The case of Staples waived an examination in the Biddeford municipal court July 17th and was carried to the Supreme Court at Alfred, September 27th. From here it was carried to the Law Court on a statement of

6

facts.   The December term of the Law Court took up the case, and on December 16th, the case was argued in the court before the full bench judges.   Thaxter & Holt of Portland and Satterlee of Rochester, N. Y. appeared for the nurserymen, and County Attorney Walker of York, (Biddeford) presented a brief for the State.   Twenty days were allowed the State to reply to the arguments presented by the gentleman from Rochester.   At the end of the year 1912, the decision had not been handed down from the court.

The agent's license is valid for but one year and the following list shows the number of licenses that have not been renewed Dec. 31, 1912, but have been in operation this past summer:

NAME.	Address.	License Expired.
Bolton, F. O.	Portland	August 14, 1912.
Bowie, G. A.	Intervale	December 3, "
Cannon, S. F.	Augusta	August 17, "
Cole, J. E.	Union	December 19, "
Dearborn, D. P.	Dexter	August 28, "
Dudley, F. H.	Auburn	August 22, "
Fowler, W. B.	Monmouth	August 12, "
Fox, A. N.	So. Berwick	August 28, "
Gay, W. R.	Gardiner	November 20, "
Gould, R. D.	So. Paris	October 5, "
Gove, G. W.	Dexter	September 5, "
Green, Melvin A.	Parkman	July 18, "
Hersey, G. L.	East Corinth	October 11, "
Hobbs, J. C.	Turner	August 15, "
Kimball, Geo. E.	Pittsfield	July 10, "
Littlefield, S. L.	Minot Corner	October 24, "
Merrick, W. S.	Unity	October 31, "
Merrill, A. J.	Bangor	July 29, "
Miller, Geo. D.	Pembroke	July 25, "
Patten, L. P.	Carmel	August 28, "
Phillips, W. H.	Hancock Pt.	July 10, "
Purrington, James	No. Berwick	July 10, "
Reynolds, Geo. L.	Graniteville, Vt.	July 22, "
Sherman, Chester E.	Whitefield	August 28, "
Small, Ernest B.	Lisbon Falls	November 9, "
Smith, Alfred J.	Gardiner	July 5, "
Small, Fred A.	Searsport	September 5, "
Spaulding, Geo. E.	Orono	August 30, "
Sullivan, D. Y.	Waterville	September 8, "
Woodman, F. D.	Winterport	July 18, "
Wright, F. W.	Wilton	July 31, "

List of agents licensed by the State Horticulturist from July 1, 1912 to Dec. 31, 1912.

Name.	Address.	License Expires.
Atwood, W. H.	Lisbon	August 13, 1913.
Barker, George.	Presque Isle	May 21, "
Daggett, Lee.	Strong	July 2, "
Dakin, E. J.	Wilton	December 26, "
Davis, Albert C.	Sq. Paris	August 20, "
Earle, C. H.	Richmond	September 4, "
Eaton, S. H.	Oxford	June 29, "
Ellingwood, A. P.	Monroe	September 25, "
Farnum, Mark.	Wells	August 14, "
Huntress, Sarah L.	Sq. Berwick	September 5, "
Jellison, E. L.	Biddeford	August 17, "
McCabe, Geo. L.	Bangor	July 8, "
McCabe, John C.	Bangor	August 6, "
Merrill, James.	Augusta	June 3, "
Norton, A. D.	Farmington	August 30, "
Prescott, Emery.	Etna	July 1, "
Purinton, W. S.	Augusta	September 17, "
Roberts, James A.	Waterboro	July 20, "
Savage, J. A.	Skowhegan	April 9, "
Sawyer, C. L.	Westbrook	October 22, "
Small, Harry E.	Vassalboro	May 7, "
Smith, Joseph C.	Bridgewater	April 24, "
Stevens, Bion P.	Kingfield	June 18, "
Stevens, Lillian E.	Kingfield	July 8, "
Tash, George W.	New Vineyard	April 22, "
Victory, O. W.	Houlton	June 3, "
Wallace, C. W.	Berwick	March 13, "
White, Albert K.	Portland	August 17, "
White, James W.	Ludlow	May 31, "
Whitney, Geo. M.	Falmouth	April 16, "
Wiggin, Clarence S.	Waterford	November 25, "
Williams, Fairfield.	Athens	July 31, "
Wood, E. L.	Unity	September 3, "

SPRAYING DEMONSTRATIONS.

In March the following notice was sent to the subordinate granges throughout the state and put in the local papers:—
"Dear Sir:—

"If any member of your Grange wishes to have a demonstration in spraying or pruning on his orchard, will he please communicate with the Department at his earliest convenience, in order to arrange the date. The work will begin soon and it is desirable to do as much as possible in the limited time. We furnish the pump, material and power; all we ask is, invite some of the neighbors and ask questions.

We must raise cleaner fruit and we must spray. Let us help you in selecting material, pumps, etc., and give any information we may have on the subjects of spraying and pruning. No matter what section you are in, write us."

The result was most encouraging inasmuch as over one hundred and fifty growers immediately applied for such a demonstration. One hundred or more had to be refused for this season, as fifty meetings were all that we could handle and this number only by taking all possible advantage of climatic conditions in different parts of the State.

The requests were granted according to their arrival in the office and fortunately covered nearly every fruit section of the State, Franklin County being the only one not represented.

The demonstrations were held with the following orchardists:—

DORMANT SPRAY.

Date.		Owner.	Address.
April	1	M. M. Pearson.....................	Cumberland Ctr.
"	2	†Geo. A. Murch....................	Old Orchard.
"	3	†Philip H. Wiggin.................	No. Baldwin.
"	4	H. A. Shorey & Son...............	Bridgton.
"	6	Moses P. Adams..................	Woodfords, 47 Grafton St.
"	8	John B. Skolfield................	Brunswick.
"	9	Henry Snow......................	Lisbon Falls.
"	10	A. N. Leonard...................	Lewiston, Bates College.
"	11	W. J. Crooker...................	Mechanic Falls.
"	12	N. E. Morrill....................	Buckfield.
"	13	Frank Fortier....................	Turner Ctr.
"	15	†Dr. W. T. Merrill...............	West Auburn.
"	16	A. T. Giddinge & Sons...........	Auburn, R. F. D. 6.
"	17	James W. Morrill................	Hallowell, R. F. D. 8.
"	18	†E. P. Ham......................	Lewiston, 206 Main St.
"	19	†Harry L. Mitchell..............	Bath, 22 Lincoln St.
"	23	J. H. Holmes....................	So. China.
"	24	L. W. Mason	Augusta, R. F. D. 6.
"	25	C. F. Donnell...................	Week's Mills, R. F. D. 51.
"	26	L. R. Bucklin...................	So. Warren.
"	29	H. L. Seekins...................	Belfast, R. F. D. 3.
"	30	Ernest A. Foy...................	Thorndike, R. F. D. 2.
May	1	H. D. Littlefield	Newport.
"	2	D. C. Boyd......................	East Newport.
"	3	Mrs. J. S. Rogers...............	Carmel, R. F. D. 3.
"	4	C. A. York & Sons...............	Bangor, Cram Road.
"	6	L. E. Colomy....................	Bucksport.
"	7	Chas. Clements..................	Winterport.
"	8	Orlando W. Foss................	Hancock.
"	14	H. B. Crawford.................	Houlton.
"	15	Fred S. Wiggin.................	Maysville Ctr.
"	17	W. Y. Johnson.................	Perry.

† Water used instead of spray material.

CODLING MOTH SPRAY.

Date.		Owner.	Address.
June	3	Joseph B. Clark.................	Ogunquit.
"	4	Geo. T. Libby...................	Scarboro Beach.
"	5	W. H. Briggs...................	Harrison, R. F. D. 3.
"	6	E. S. Douglas..................	Douglass Hill.
"	7	G. E. Elwell...................	West Buxton.
"	8	Harry A. Goss..................	Greene.
"	13	H. L. Hayes....................	Augusta, R. F. D. 2.
"	14	Albert P. Small................	West Bowdoin.
"	15	H. H. Payson..................	Hope.
"	17	B. L. Mitchell.................	Appleton.
"	18	Fred A. Gleason...............	Union, R. F. D. 3.
"	19	U. H. Heald...................	Paris.

The demonstrations consisted of pruning in the forenoon and spraying in the afternoon. The pruning was confined largely to old trees; thinning, heading, dehorning, and cutting out canker. Together with this work we showed how to bud and how and when to use the different forms of grafting. Up-to-date pruning tools were used and only those which were essential and best adapted to the various needs of the work. Only a limited amount of spraying could be done and we used only

material enough to make a creditable showing.   Generally one
barrelful of material was used; otherwise two.   We used lime-
sulphur, Pyrox, and atomic sulphur,—the Pyrox being a gift
of the Bowker Insecticide Company, to whom we wish to
extend our appreciation at this time for the spirit of coöperation which they manifested.

While applying the mixture, different nozzles were used,
showing their advantages and disadvantages.   A talk was given
in connection with the work, discussing the various phases of
orchard management.   Sheets, containing condensed notes on
spraying, were given out at each meeting.   The following is
a copy of same.

MAINE DEPARTMENT OF AGRICULTURE.

SPRAYING DEMONSTRATIONS.

"Why We Spray.

Insects and diseases destroy over 60 per cent of otherwise fancy fruit in the State. $26,000,000 worth of fruit was rendered worthless last year in the United States, because of the San Jose scale and Codling moth. We have great numbers of Codling moths and the San Jose scale is rapidly gaining entrance. *All* insects except the Railroad worm can be controlled by thorough spraying.

When We Spray.

In the spring before the buds swell for (1) San Jose scale, (2) Oyster-shell scale, (3) Eggs of Green Aphis, (4) Canker, (5) Blister Mite. Before blossoming for (1) Bud moth, (2) Canker worm, (3) Scab. As the petals fall for (1) Codling moth, (2) Curculio, (3) Scab, (4) Lesser Apple-worm, etc. Last of July for (1) Brown-tail moth, (2) Fall Web-worm, (3) Fungus on fruit, etc.

WHAT TO SPRAY WITH.

Dormant spray............	Lime-sulphur..............	1 — 10	
Before blossoming........	Lime-sulphur.............	1 — 20	
	Arsenate of Lead..........	2 — 50	
After petals fall..........	Arsenate of Lead..........	2½ — 50	
	Lime-sulphur..............	1 — 40	
Last of July.............	Lime-sulphur.............	1 — 40	
	Arsenate of Lead..........	2½ — 50	
For Green Aphis..........	Kerosene Emulsion........	2 gals. kerosene, 1 gal. water, 1 lb. soap, diluted 12-15 times.	
	Or Tobacco...............	2 lbs. to 4 gals. water.	

Spray Outfits.

1. Have a brass lined pump. (It does not corrode as much.)

2. Have a good agitator. (The spray will be uniform.)

3. Have nozzles that do not clog readily and do not catch in the foliage.

4. Have a good sized air chamber, so as to allow even pressure.

5. Use a strainer and have a good one.

6. Have good hose, long enough to work easily; have long couplings.

7. Bamboo extension rods are cleaner and lighter to handle.

8. Use a Beaumé hydrometer with lime-sulphur.

Points In Spraying.

1. Don't hurry.

2. Be thorough.

3. Get there ahead of the pest.

4. Clean out the barrel thoroughly when through using.

5. Keep a business account and know how much spraying is costing you."

CONCLUSIONS DRAWN FROM DEMONSTRATIONS THIS SPRING.

In this work the total number of meetings	32
Total number of spraying demonstrations	27
Total attendance	837
Average attendance	26
Total number of trees sprayed	965
Average number of gallons per tree, dormant spray	1.8
Average cost of lime-sulphur for dormant spray (dilution 1-11) per tree	2.8c.
Maximum cost of lime-sulphur for dormant spray	4.7c.
Minimum cost of lime-sulphur for dormant spray	2c.
Average cost of lime-sulphur for the Bud moth spray	1.3c.
Average cost arsenate of lead	.43c.
Average cost of the combination of lime-sulphur with lead	1.7c.
Average cost of Pyrox for the same work	2.2c.

The largest meeting was at Buckfield, in the orchard of N. E. Morrill; the attendance was seventy.

In regard to this Bud moth spray, it should be stated that only about 200 trees were sprayed, so that the averages given here are not large enough to be of great practical value, but it does show the difference in expense for the early Bud moth spray between lime-sulphur and lead and Pyrox.

CODLING MOTH SPRAY.

12 meetings,	
Total attendance...	262
Total number of trees sprayed...................................	216
Total number of gallons applied.................................	540
Average attendance...	22 5-6
Average cost...	$ .025
Average number of gallons per tree..............................	2½
Maximum expense per tree.......................................	$ .05
Lowest cost per tree..	.01½
Highest attendance...	70

That is the lime-sulphur and lead spray and for the atomic sulphur the average cost per tree was seven cents on thirteen trees; three different days.

BOX PACKING DEMONSTRATIONS.

The existing market conditions, with boxed apples bringing the top prices and certain of our own growers obtaining favorable results from packing fruit in boxes, has been an interesting topic for several years. This fall it seemed expedient that the methods employed in box packing apples should be brought to the attention of more of the growers. Consequently, the following notice was published in the newspapers of Androscoggin, Franklin, Kennebec, Oxford, Somerset and Waldo Counties:—

"The Department of Agriculture at Augusta is planning to give a limited number of box packing demonstrations this fall and will be pleased to hear from growers that desire such a meeting in their orchard.

The Department will furnish press, packing table, boxes and paper so that no expense will be incurred by the grower other than transportation from the nearest railroad station.

The increased number of orchardists that are spraying and giving good care to their trees, must necessarily increase the amount of fruit fit for box pack and it seems important at this time to demonstrate the different packs and manner of packing so that better work along this line may be accomplished.

Individuals or Granges that are interested will receive prompt attention by writing the Department at the earliest opportunity."

As a result demonstrations of box packing of apples were conducted at the following places during the period from September 5th to October 21st:—

Mrs. Fanny S. Swain	Newfield.
C. E. Felch	Limerick.
B. W. Gibbs	Bridgton.
Herbert S. Hill	Wells.
Chas. H. Berry, Jr	Hartford.
J. Willis Jordan	Farmington.
L. W. Mason	Augusta.
F. A. Gleason	Union.
A. E. Brumberg	Camden.
Walter E. Cunningham	Belfast.
W. N. Foy	Montville.
J. Otto	Richmond.

In each case the person named above had charge of the work and furnished the apples. Boxes, paper, etc., were furnished by the Department, and we carried with us packing table, nailing-press and sorting board to demonstrate their use.

At each demonstration we graded the fruit and on an average packed about six boxes, showing the different styles of packs, as far as we could, with the fruit at hand. It usually happened in each place that one or two boxes were left, so that those interested might have a chance to practice the different packs when time permitted·

A total of 337 attended the demonstrations, the largest meetings being at Wells, Hartford and Belfast. The average attendance of twelve at this busy season shows that there is considerable interest in this work, although not as much as was apparent at the spraying demonstrations in the spring.

The actual expense of the box demonstration is itemized as follows:—

For a box containing 175 apples, 4½ tier pack:

12 ounces Manila wrapping paper, 8″ x 8″ at 4 cents per lb	$0.03
1 oz. Continental White at 6 cents per lb	.003½
6 sheets Manila Tag Board	.015
. Total expense of paper, approximately	$0.05
Box in shook	.15½
Expense of nailing and nails	.01½
Packing, 15 minutes at 20 cents an hour	.05
Making a total of	$0.27

These statements and schedules were circulated at each meeting for reference.

Advantage of box over barrel.

1. More attractive and neater.
2. Successful in places where extensively used·
3. Supplies the demand of a certain class of trade.
4. Actual number of apples known.
5. Fruit less liable to damage.
6. Only fine apples can be used.

Oregon standard box.

Dimensions, 10 1-2 in. x 11 1-2 in. x 18 in.

Capacity, 2173.5 cu. in.   Standard bushel, 2150.41 cu. in.

Ends, 3-4 in· Sides, 3-8 in. Tops and bottoms, 1-4 in.

Material, White Spruce.   Cost, $.11 to $.20 in shooks.

Lining paper.

Side lining, 17 3-4 in. x 26 in.   Grade news, $.03 per lb.

Layer paper, 17 1-2 in. x 11 in.   Manila tag board, $7.50 per M·

Wrapping paper, 10 x 10, 8 x 10 and 9 x 9.   O. B. Manila, $.045 per lb.   Wrapping paper causes apples to pack easier, makes the pack firmer, prevents the spread of decay and makes it more attractive.

Packing.

Grade according to size to 1-4 in.   Grade according to shape and color.

Sorting board.

Holes 2 3-8 in. for 5-tier.   2 5-8 for 4 1-2-tier·   2 7-8 for 4-tier.   3 1-8 for 4-tier.   3 3-8 for 3 1-2-tier.   3 5-8 for 3-tier.

Packs.

1. Diagonal.   Most used in box packing as each apple fits on four under it, making less danger of bruising; only disadvantage is that in some sizes holes are left in the pack.

2. Straight.   Each apple fits directly on the one under it, so this pack is used only where the diagonal is not effective·

3. Off-set.   Leaves too many holes.

4. Riff-raff.   Good for making a tight pack for large apples of certain shapes.

APPLE PACKING SCHEDULE FOR STANDARD BOX.

Group Size.	No. in Box.	Style of Pack.			No. in Rows.	No. in Layers.
3-tier..................	45	Cheek	Straight	3	5	3
3-tier..................	54	"	"	3	6	3
3-tier..................	56	"	Diagonal ..	2–2	3–4	4
3½-tier................	64	End	" ..	2–2	4–4	4
3½-tier................	72	"	" ..	2–2	4–5	4
3½-tier................	80	"	" ..	2–2	5–5	4
3½-tier................	88	Cheek	" ..	2–2	5–6	4
4-tier.................	96	"	" ..	2–2	6–6	4
4-tier.................	100	"	" ..	3–2	4–4	5
4-tier.................	104	"	" ..	2–2	6–7	4
4-tier.................	112	"	" ..	2–2	7–7	4
4-tier.................	113	End	" ..	3–2	4–5	5
4-tier.................	125	"	" ..	3–2	5–5	5
4-tier.................	128	"	Straight	4	8	4
4½-tier................	138	"	Diagonal ...	3–2	5–6	5
4½-tier................	150	"	" ...	3–2	6–6	5
4½-tier................	163	"	" ...	3–2	6–7	5
4½-tier................	175	"	" ...	3–2	7–7	5
5-tier.................	188	"	" ...	3–2	7–8	5
5-tier.................	200	"	" ...	3–2	8–8	5
5-tier.................	200	"	Straight.....	5	8	5

CONCLUSION.

From the condition of the fruit presented it is evident that we must do more spraying and cultivating to increase the percentage of fancy grades.

The common objection expressed in relation to the necessary close grading for size and freedom from blemishes shows the necessity of greater publicity of results obtained by careful grading.

PACKING AND GRADING LAW.

For several years it has been the desire of those persons most interested in the welfare of the orchardists to enact some law which would regulate the grading and packing of apples. Our own state law of 1909 has not been an efficient regulation and little attempt has been made to enforce it.

However, the Federal Government has taken hold of the matter and July 1st, 1913, the so-called Sulzer Bill goes into effect, which is as follows:—

AN ACT to establish a standard barrel and standard grades for apples when packed in barrels, and for other purposes.

Be it enacted by the Senate and House of Representatives of the United States of America in Congress assembled, That the standard barrel for apples shall be of the following dimensions when measured without distention of its parts: Length of stave, twenty-eight and one-half inches; diameter of head, seventeen and one-eighth inches; distance between heads, twenty-six inches; circumference of bulge, sixty-four inches outside measurement, representing as nearly as possible seven thousand and fifty-six cubic inches: *Provided,* That steel barrels containing the interior dimensions provided for in this section shall be construed as a compliance therewith.

SEC. 2. That the standard grades for apples when packed in barrels which shall be shipped or delivered for shipment in interstate or foreign commerce, or which shall be sold or offered for sale within the District of Columbia or the Territories of the United States shall be as follows: Apples of one variety, which are well-grown specimens, hand picked, of good color for the variety, normal shape, practically free from insect and fungous injury, bruises, and other defects, except such as are necessarily caused in the operation of packing, or apples of one variety which are not more than ten per centum below the foregoing specifications shall be "Standard grade minimum size two and one-half inches," if the minimum size of the apples is two and one-half inches in transverse diameter; "Standard grade minimum size two and one-fourth inches," if the minimum size of the apples is two and one-fourth inches in transverse diameter; or "Standard grade minimum size two inches," if the minimum size of the apples is two inches in transverse diameter.

SEC. 3. That the barrels in which apples are packed in accordance with the provision of this Act may be branded in accordance with section two of this Act.

SEC. 4. That all barrels packed with apples shall be deemed to be below standard if the barrel bears any statement, design, or device indicating that the barrel is a standard barrel of apples, as herein defined, and the capacity of the barrel is less than the capacity prescribed by section one of this Act, unless the barrel shall be plainly marked on end and side with words or figures showing the fractional relation which the actual capacity of the barrel bears to the capacity prescribed by section one of this Act. The marking required by this paragraph shall be in block letters of size not less than seventy-two point one-inch gothic.

SEC. 5. That barrels packed with apples shall be deemed to be misbranded within the meaning of this Act—

First. If the barrel bears any statement, design, or device indicating that the apples contained therein are "Standard" grade and the apples when packed do not conform to the requirements prescribed by section two of this Act.

Second. If the barrel bears any statement, design, or device indicating that the apples contained therein are "Standard" grade and the barrel fails to bear also a statement of the name of the variety, the name of the locality where grown, and the name of the packer or the person by whose authority the apples were packed and the barrel marked.

SEC. 6. That any person, firm or corporation, or association who shall knowingly pack or cause to be packed apples in barrels or who shall knowingly sell or offer for sale such barrels in violation of the provisions of this Act shall be liable to a penalty of one dollar and costs for each such barrel so sold or offered for sale, to be recovered at the suit of the United States in any court of the United States having jurisdiction.

SEC. 7. That this Act shall be in force and effect from and after the first day of July, nineteen hundred and thirteen.

Approved, August 3, 1912.

CROP REPORT.

Cards were sent out just before the end of the month, during the fall, to find out as definitely as possible the conditions of the crops in the State and to further find out the conditions throughout the country.

Inquiries were sent to the various Bureaus in the fruit producing states to obtain their estimates and reports. In this way we hoped to get an accurate and unprejudiced estimate and to put it out so the orchardists in the State might benefit by it in disposing of their fruit.

The following card was sent to as many active growers as were interested enough to send in prompt answers and who were scattered throughout the fruit sections:

"Dear Sir:—

It is the aim of the Department to obtain data regarding the apple crop in monthly periods, and publish this data in the papers as soon as it is received in the office. We hope to obtain estimates from other states also, and in this way aid the grower in disposing of his crop. Please answer the following questions, on attached card, and mail as soon as possible.

1. Per cent of full crop?
2. Per cent of last year?
3. Estimated number of barrels of No. Ones?
4. Total number of barrels?
5. Percentage of last year in your vicinity?
6. Estimated crop in barrels in your vicinity?
7. Principal varieties?"

By these returns we established our crop reports and put them in the various papers. The following is the first September report:—

REPORT ON APPLE CROP.

After communicating with different states and different sections of this State. the Department wishes to make the following estimates:

As compared with crop of last year,

Androscoggin County	85%
Cumberland County	85
Franklin County	75
Kennebec County	65
Knox County	70
Oxford County	75
Penobscot County	60
Piscataquis County	70
Somerset County	70
Waldo County	85
York County	100
Relative average	75%

Reports from the different States, show figures as follows: Percentage of full crop.

Vermont	75%
Massachusetts	60
Rhode Island	75
Connecticut	50
New York	70
Pennsylvania	50
Virginia	59
West Virginia	70
Ohio	50
Iowa	50
Illinois	55
Nebraska	80
Mississippi	66
Wisconsin	60
Kansas	71
Delaware	70
Idaho	75
Oregon	80
Washington	75
Canada	75

Average in United States, 72%. 4% increase over last year. Great Britain, average crop."

Some corrections should be made in the form of these cards but the idea seems to be working out all right and can be made very profitable to the growers and to the Department.

Only the three State Fairs were attended this year with the exhibit of insects and diseases of the orchard. At each a good location was furnished and much interest shown in the display. The large number of fairs in the State cut into the attendance of the State Fairs, so that the interest in each is not increasing as rapidly as it should. A smaller number would be a benefit to all.

The exhibit consisted of the various orchard insects and wood infected with a large number of diseases, together with bottles and jars of spraying material and literature covering the methods of control or prevention.

During the year we have published a Bulletin entitled "Orcharding in Maine," which covers apple growing up to the point of picking. The cuts were all from pictures taken by the Department.

We have spoken at two Farmers' Institutes, fifteen Grange meetings, fifty-six demonstration meetings, one Fruit Growers' Field Day and at the Pomological Meeting.

Respectfully submitted,

A. K. GARDNER,

State Horticulturist.

Burlapping Crew in Wells, 1912.   Gypsy Moth Work.

REPORT OF FIELD AGENT, GYPSY MOTH WORK.

Hon. J. P. Buckley, Commissioner of Agriculture:

I hereby submit a report of my work as Field Agent of the Gipsy moth force during the year of 1912.

Scouting operations were continued from January first, 1912, until June first, except from January 17th to January 22nd, during which time the work was discontinued on account of the deep snow. During the first five months of the year, however, the force was reduced in numbers since it seemed expedient to save the greater part of our appropriation for the fall scouting. On June 1st scouting was discontinued and the summer work began.

Lack of funds made it impossible to engage in extensive summer work in all the territory. Accordingly I persuaded three of the worst infested towns to raise money for summer work in those towns, with the understanding that whatever amount was raised, an equal amount would be placed with it by the State and the entire amount expended in the town making the appropriation. York raised $500.00, Wells, an equal amount, and South Berwick, $300.00. The work in these three towns during the summer consisted of spraying and burlapping. During a part of the month of June, the badly infested woodlands were sprayed with Lead Arsenate and in the neighborhood of seventy-five acres were thus covered. In these woodlands, the trees were swarming with Gipsy moth larvæ and were in danger of immediate defoliation. The spraying was effective as usual and killed practically all the larvæ. Our force was not large enough, however, to cover all the infested woodlands and consequently in some places defoliation occurred. During the remainder of the summer until August 9th, the infested trees were burlapped and inspected by the men as often as possible. 75,000 trees were thus burlapped and hundreds of thousands of caterpillars were destroyed. The entire force was laid off from August 9th until September 3d. This is the period in which the female moth is depositing her eggs and during this time work in the field is not productive of good results.

The fall scout began on September 3d. Thirty-three men were placed in the field and about this average number of men have been employed up to December 14th. Our efforts have resulted in the destruction of thousands of Gipsy moth egg clusters. Operations have been carried on in twenty towns and I give below the number of egg clusters destroyed in each town, and, in comparison, the number destroyed in some of the same towns during the year previous:

Town.	Number of Egg Clusters Destroyed.	
	In 1911.	In 1912.
York	30,096	77,484
Eliot	16,176	53,720
Wells	15,639	33,651
Kittery	15,384	†22,574
South Berwick	9,588	22,311
Berwick	4,031	24,249
Lebanon	2,129	14,980
Kennebunkport	1,449	†733
Kennebunk	399	3,383
Acton	315	8,899
Sanford	271	†4,715
Portland	–	1,244
Newfield	–	1,483
Shapleigh	–	8,436
Brunswick	–	4,188
Waterboro	–	431
Falmouth	–	63
Alfred	–	564
Biddeford	–	1,482
Saco	–	1,441

† Town not finished Dec. 31, 1912.

It will be noted from the preceding figures that there has been a large increase in the number of egg clusters destroyed in 1912 over the number for 1911.

PRESENT EXTENT OF INFESTED AREA.

The total number of infested towns a year ago was 66. In addition to these, nineteen more infested towns have been found during 1912. The total list of infested towns to Jan. 1st, 1913 is as follows:

Acton	Durham	Lisbon	Sebago
Alfred	Edgecomb	Litchfield	Shapleigh
Alna	Eliot	Lyman	South Berwick
Arrowsic	Falmouth	Minot	South Portland
Auburn	Farmingdale	Monmouth	Standish
Augusta	Freeport	Newcastle	Topsham
Baldwin	Fryeburg	Newfield	Turner
Bath	Gardiner	New Gloucester	Waterboro
Berwick	Georgetown	North Berwick	Webster
Biddeford	Gorham	North Yarmouth	Wells
Bowdoin	Harpswell	Otisfield	West Bath
Bowdoinham	Hiram	Oxford	Westbrook
Brownfield	Hollis	Parsonsfield	West Gardiner
Brunswick	Kennebunk	Phippsburg	Westport
Buxton	Kennebunkport	Pittston	Whitefield
Cape Elizabeth	Kittery	Portland	Windham
Chelsea	Lebanon	Pownal	Winthrop
Cornish	Leeds	Richmond	Wiscasset
Cumberland	Lewiston	Saco	Woolwich
Damariscotta	Limerick	Sanford	Yarmouth
Dayton	Limington	Scarboro	York
Dresden			

The total number of towns known to be infested with the Gipsy moth is at present, eighty-five. This area comprises territory in seven counties. A straight line drawn on a map of Maine from Damariscotta to Augusta and from there west to Fryeburg represents approximately the present northern border of infested territory. The entire area south of these two lines is infested with the Gipsy moth and it is very likely that the limit has not been reached.

That branch of our work which consists of scouting new towns along the border of infested territory has been conducted by the United States Government force. There has been during the past year and is at present a force of about forty men working under the direction of the government in an effort to prevent further spread by the moth into the interior of the State.

In view of the warnings issued by this Department in years past, it should surprise no one to learn that the Gipsy moth is now beginning to destroy woodland growth in York County. During the past summer, I have noticed several cases of defoliation in Wells, South Berwick and York. The most serious of these was in the vicinity of Mount Agamenticus in the town of York. Here, about twenty acres of oak growth were stripped of foliage. No work was done there this year on account of lack of funds.

In the early fall a woodland infestation was discovered on the bank of the New Meadows river in the town of Brunswick. The selectmen proceeded to furnish $150.00 and this with an equal amount from the State was expended in placing this infestation under control. Our work there resulted in the destruction of over 4,000 egg clusters. In addition, this woodland was thinned out and all dead wood and slash were burned so that a little effort each year will now handle it satisfactorily. Finding an infestation of this size so far towards the interior of the State is unusual and alarming, since it is probable that there are others in that vicinity or even farther up the State.

In addition to the field work, considerable correspondence has been carried on by the Field Agent in connection with inquiries concerning the Gipsy moth. Many reported infestations have been investigated and several new ones located in that way.

A set of lantern slides has been prepared during the year for the use of the Department and is now available for lecture work, showing the Gipsy moth in all its stages and the methods used for its suppression. These pictures were shown for the first time by the Field Agent at the State Dairy Meeting at Saco, Dec. 13th.

In consideration of the rapid increase of the Gipsy moth and our inability to hold it in check during the past two years, there seem to be two courses left to pursue,—either to appropriate a sum of money sufficient to make the present methods effective or to adopt a new policy. I believe that the first course is not feasible inasmuch as the amount of money requisite for carrying on present methods effectively over all the extent of infested territory would be an excessive sum for the State to raise for this work. Although the work conducted during the past six

years has not been wholly barren of good results, I am convinced now that to carry on our present methods with *small*
appropriations is not feasible. It will require much larger appropriations than any previous ones to come anywhere near
holding this pest in check. From my experience on this work,
I have come to the conclusion that instead of the State trying to
check the moth by mechanical methods, we should show the
property owner. by educational methods, how to do this. I
believe that the best service can be rendered to the citizens of
this State by teaching them how to best protect their shade
trees, orchards, and woodlands from the ravages of this insect.
The real Gipsy moth problem does not concern the orchards,
nor the shade trees. This class of trees has been and still
can be protected by the State, if necessary, but the better
plan would be to show the owner how to protect them himself.
The real Gipsy moth problem is in the woodlands. Never,
since the work began in Maine has this insect been under control
in the woodlands. There have been a few instances where
certain woodland infestations have been checked temporarily,
but while this was being done, other woodlands were all the
time becoming more dangerously infested. I recommend that
no more work be done in woodlands along present or past methods. I believe, however, that by practicing methods of judi-
cious cutting out of certain kinds of trees along forestry lines,
most of the danger from the Gipsy moth can be eliminated.
The State should investigate this matter and see that property
owners are informed as to how these methods should be pur-
sued in order to safe-guard as far as possible the shade trees,
orchards and woodlands from the dangers of this destructive
pest.

If we are ever to get any relief from this pest, it will be
afforded eventually by the parasites. Even if a large sum of
money were raised—large enough to check the increase of the
Gipsy moth in all infested woodland—it is a question whether
such a policy would be a good one, since by keeping the pest
reduced in numbers, we would at the same time be checking
the development of its parasites and perhaps postponing our
eventual relief.

I believe that the work has been done faithfully and conscientiously by the men in the field during the past year. The one discouraging feature has been that we have had to work in twenty towns with an appropriation sufficient to handle only three towns satisfactorily. I wish at this time to thank the foremen and men for their faithful service and coöperation. I feel under deep obligation to Mr. D. M. Rogers of Boston, Superintendent of the U. S. Government Gipsy moth force, for his continued assistance throughout the year.

In closing, permit me to express to you my gratitude for the encouragement and assistance given me during my service under you.

Respectfully,

A. O. PIKE,
Field Agent.

Pine Tree on Mt. Agamenticus, Town of York, showing defoliation by gypsy moth caterpillars.   Taken in July, 1912.

REPORT OF LIVE STOCK SANITARY COMMISSIONER.

To His Excellency, Frederick W. Plaisted, Governor of Maine:

I herewith submit the report of the Live Stock Sanitary Commissioner from May 1, 1911, to December 31, 1912, containing an account of the cattle, horses, sheep and hogs condemned and ·destroyed under the provisions of Chapter 195 of the Public Laws of 1911, relating to contagious diseases among cattle, horses, sheep and swine.

I have personally killed and held post mortems on 147 cattle that have reacted to the tuberculin test and have found but very few that did not show marked signs of tuberculosis to the naked eye. The tuberculin test is no longer an experiment, but has proved itself to be a very reliable test for tuberculosis. More farmers are being convinced of this fact every year and are trying to clean up their herds. The value of cattle has increased fully 20 per cent during the past two years, and as the limit of appraisals is now $50 on grades, $100 on registered animals and $100 on horses, the appraisals must necessarily be higher than ever before. The farmers have paid for their own testing, under the new rules, which some object to, but I think the farmer should have some of the responsibility, for when he has no responsibility he loses all interest in the matter. The old law provided that the State should pay for the testing of pure bred cattle, and if the State paid for the testing of any cattle it should be the grades, the poor farmer's cow.

A great many of the condemned cattle have been killed under United States inspection and the meat has been sold. For these carcasses and hides the State has received $5,577.83.

I have done a great deal of disinfecting of stables personally. Where I have not done it myself the owners have done the work under my instructions as well as possible, which has made the expense of disinfecting much less than ever before. No state in the Union is paying as much as Maine to stamp out tuberculosis and keep its herds healthy and no state allows such a large appraisal for cattle that are condemned. And if the State, the farmers and the veterinarians will continue to coöperate in the work, the disease can be practically stamped out. In sections where the testing has been followed up, the percentage of diseased animals has decreased very much, but in sections where testing has not been done in many herds a large number of reactors are found and destroyed; but on the whole there are few, if any, states that have as low a percentage of tuberculous cattle as has this State.

It has been impossible to get the exact percentage of cows condemned to the total number tested, as the veterinarians have neglected to send in reports of animals that passed the test.

The following figures show the amount of business done from May 1st, 1911, to Dec. 31, 1912:

FINANCIAL STATEMENT.

May 1, to December 31, 1911.

Appropriation for 1911	$25,000 00	
Received from sale of hides and carcasses........	1,486 18	
		$26,486 18
Paid for condemned animals *$18,224 47		
Salary and expenses of Live Stock Sanitary Com-		
missioner	1,755 37	
Disinfecting	171 75	
Other services and expenses of assistants.........	*417 42	
Clerical work	253 00	
Printing and binding	84 87	
Hog cholera serum	115 00	
Express, telephone and telegraph.................	110 23	
Miscellaneous supplies and incidental expenses....	*447 95	
Balance reverting to State Treasury..............	4,906 12	
		$26,486 18

* Amounts increased by bills received after report of 1911 to Commissioner of Agriculture. .

STATISTICS OF CONDEMNED ANIMALS.

May 1 to December 31, 1911.

	No.	Amount.	Average Amt. per Animal.
Pure bred cattle condemned for tuberculosis..	9	$800 00	$88 88
Grade cattle condemned for tuberculosis.....	322	*12,301 50	38 20
Cattle killed for beef and found diseased with tuberculosis	27	734 10	27 19
Cattle condemned for lump jaw.............	4	120 00	30 00
Pure bred cattle condemned at Brighton, Mass. for tuberculosis	3	159 20	53 07
Grade cattle condemned at Brighton, Mass. for tuberculosis	94	*2,910 67	30 96
Total appraisals of cattle killed at Brighton, $4,375.00; amount received for hides and carcasses, $1,305.13.			
Horses condemned for glanders	29	999 00	34 45
Horses condemned for cerebro-spinal meningitis	4	200 00	50 00
	492	$18,224 47	$37 04

FINANCIAL STATEMENT, 1912.

Appropriation for 1912	$25,000 00	
Received from sale of hides and carcasses.......	4,091 65	
		$29,091 65
Paid for condemned animals.....................	24,438 81	
Salary and expenses of Live Stock Sanitary Commissioner	2,668 95	
Disinfecting	349 51	
Other services and expenses of assistants........	411 69	
Clerical work	583 98	
Printing and binding	35 38	
Hog cholera serum.............................	70 00	
Express, telephone and telegraph...............	136 06	
Miscellaneous supplies and incidental expenses...	397 27	
		$29,091 65
Amount due for condemned animals (deficiency)		7,741 10
Total business for the year		$36,832 75

* Amounts increased by bills received after report of 1911 to Commissioner of Agriculture.

STATISTICS OF CONDEMNED ANIMALS, 1912.

	No.	Amount.	Average Amt. per Animal.
Pure bred cattle, condemned for tuberculosis.	41	$3,610 00	$88 05
Grade cattle condemned for tuberculosis......	463	18,195 50	39 30
Cattle killed for beef and found diseased with tuberculosis	110	3,272 39	29 75
Pure bred cattle condemed at Brighton, Mass., for tuberculosis	1	58 23	58 23
Grade cattle condemned at Brighton, Mass., for tuberculosis	107	3,249 44	30 37
Total appraisals of cattle killed at Brighton, $5,269 00; amount received for hides and carcasses, $1,961.33.			
Horses condemned for glanders.............	73	3,017 50	41 33
Hogs condemned for tuberculosis	16	167 85	10 49
Sheep condemned for tuberculosis	223	609 00	· 2 73
	1,034	$32,179 91	$31 12

ADDRESSES DELIVERED AT STATE DAIRY CON-
FERENCE, SACO, DECEMBER 12 AND 13, 1912.

ADDRESS OF WELCOME.

By Mayor F. L. Palmer.

It is customary to ask the Mayor to say a few words on occasions like this and I am very glad to do so, and to extend to you in behalf of the City, a hearty welcome. I feel that we ought to appreciate what has been done in bringing this Conference to York County. As has been said by the Chairman. this is the first time that we have had this opportunity. This Conference has never been held here before and of course a great many do not realize the value of it. I hope that as a result of this meeting we will be able to awaken public interest in the dairy industry. There are a great many engaged in the dairying business in this section, and there is an opportunity for more. There is an opportunity for us to adopt business principles in the conduct of our dairying, which will no doubt make it more profitable so that it will appeal to us more than it does at the present time.

To those who are visitors to Saco I will say that I am very sorry that as a result of our fire last Monday morning we cannot offer you the hotel accommodations that we expected to and would like to very much, but we will do our best. In behalf of the City I extend to you a welcome and assure you that anything we can do to help make this Conference a success we shall be only too pleased to do.

FALSE WEIGHTS AND MEASURES.

By A. S. K. Clark, Boston, Mass., Deputy Sealer of Weights and Measures.

In addressing this audience upon the subject of *"False Weights and Measures"* I am, of course, taking it for granted that the same conditions exist in the State of Maine as are now found elsewhere.

I feel that I am safe in predicting that should a thorough investigation of the weights and measures conditions be made in your State you would find the same conditions as prevailed in Massachusetts within a few years past,—and again I do not wish to lead you to think that such evils have been eliminated in Massachusetts, for such is not the case.

As long as commodities are bartered and exchanged, just so long will false weights and measures be found and false and insufficient weight and measure be given.

This evil can be kept in check by energetic work on the part of the officials appointed for the purpose of seeing that measuring devices are kept in order and that they are properly used. The motto of such officials should be "Eternal Vigilance."

Previous to 1907 Massachusetts had no distinct State Department of Weights and Measures and the supervision of the use, by the trade, of weights and measures, was performed wholly by the local town and city officials.

Many of these officials were political appointees and in many instances men wholly unfitted for the work they should have performed. They were also very poorly paid and were not expected to do much.

In 1907 a separate State Department of Weights and Measures was established by the Legislature and placed in charge of a Commissioner, with power to appoint four Inspectors. This force has been increased to six Inspectors, all of whom are on the Civil Service List.

The Sealers of Weights and Measures in all cities, and of all towns of 10,000 inhabitants, or over, are now under Civil Service and in case of new appointments, such appointments are made from the Civil Service List, made up of those who have passed the examination prepared by the Civil Service Commission.

This examination covers all details a Sealer should have knowledge of, so that no man in Massachusetts is now appointed to the important position of Sealer until he has demonstrated his fitness, both mentally and physically.

In the United States we have taken great care to regulate the money but we have not even attempted to regulate a uniform or even an honest standard of weights and measures, and in this latter subject conditions are as chaotic as could well be imagined.

The regulation of the weights and measures and the weighing and measuring of commodities, and a control of the manner of sale of commodities is a crying need to-day. The grower, without assurance of the honesty of standards, cannot obtain equitable value for his product, nor the manufacturer, who must needs meet one or more competitors who can under sell him by making the apparent cost of his commodity less by cutting off, here and there, on the quantity delivered. The distributor welcomes an honest standard and efficient regulation thereof, because the honest dealer cannot possibly compete with the one that gives short weight or measure.

As an illustration, I will cite an actual occurrence:—When the retail price of apples was 70 cents per peck, a peddler approached a housekeeper, offering apples at 35 cents a peck. This housekeeper had a set of certified standards, and after examining the apples and seeing that they were of good quality offered to buy a peck. Said peddler, his measure heaping full, poured the apples into the standard. Lo! It filled not quite half full. It took two and a fraction of his measure to make a peck. His remark, after receiving the 35 cents and looking at the housekeeper and then at the standard, was characteristic,— "Madam, I will never come here again. Thank God, they are not all as wise as you are."

What honest dealer had a possible chance against such competition? How many housekeepers were easily deceived?

This furthermore illustrates that if an efficient inspection of weights and measures had existed the peddler could not have used a short, double-bottom measure, and the consumer would have been protected. The above easily shows that the peddler got more than the market price,—in short, the consumer's cost of living was increased.

The short weight and measure evil exists in three forms,—first, faulty apparatus to determine the quantity; second, faulty use of correct apparatus; third, the goods put up in packages with no indication of the quantity of contents. Let us look at these three evils.

Included among false scales are the peddler's and ragman's spring scales with sliding fronts, adjustable springs, bent points, that will show whatever the thumb and index finger of the manipulator desires; computing scales with false computations; weights made lighter by every possible means; dry measures with adjustable bottoms, false bottoms, raised bottoms, with sides cut down or relapped, false bottoms and sides, ice cream pails from five to fifteen per cent short, short milk bottles; "fake" milk dippers; "short," "snide" and "shallow" berry boxes; liquid measures with holes in the side, etc.

These are but samples and many are still in use, daily defrauding the poor—daily committing moral crimes worse than picking pockets.

The second form of evil is the one where the dealer uses heavy wrapping paper on the polished glass scale pan for "sanitary reasons" and incidentally to have the customer pay for two ounces of paper, a brine-soaked or heavy butter tray at the price per pound of the meat or butter. Here also we find the butcher who weighs his thumb or knife by quickly but steadily and stealthily prying under the weight side of the scale, thereby assisting the hard-earned cents and dollars out of the hands of the widow washerwoman. Everyone who has observed rush hour trading has noticed the trick of throwing the meat on the spring scale and reading the pointer to the graduation to which it bounds instead of waiting for a steady reading.

The case of trimmings may be mentioned here. I will mention an extreme case. Seven lbs. of lamb chops were bought and paid for; the butcher delivered 3 3-4 lbs.; remonstrance brought forth the usual excuse—"trimmings". 3 1-4 lbs. of trimmings out of 7,—verily, it was trimming. The trimmings were sold at another profit to the rendering works.

A grain merchant, selling three car-loads of grain per week at $1.60 per hundred weight, if he includes the bag, weighing one pound for every one hundred pounds of grain sold, sells these bags for, or gains an illegal profit on the bags of over $1,000.00 per year; in other words, gains illegally $1,000.00 per year over a competitor in the same town selling grain at the same price per pound and delivering net 100 lbs. If the bag weighs more, and I think some do, the loss to the consumers is more, for a pound-and-a-half bag would give such a dealer $1,500.00 per year illegal profit.

I believe that the above figures of output sold annually by an ordinary grist mill are not excessive.

In the case of fertilizer, if you are paying for bags at fertilizer price the loss to you will aggregate quite a sum in a short time.

The merchant selling meat at 30 cents per lb. and averaging one ounce of wrapper and string with each pound sold, on a sale of 300 lbs. per day, would receive in the course of a year, a profit not belonging to him amounting to over $1400.00, and at the small amount of 1-2 ounce to a pound, for wrappers, etc., it would mean an unjust profit of $700.00.

In the case of butter it has been demonstrated in my own State of Massachusetts, what a just demand may accomplish. Five years ago it was no uncommon occurrence to find the five-pound boxes, sold as such, which were 1-4 lb., and sometimes more, short.

One-pound prints weighed, sometimes, less than 15 ounces. It is a rare instance to-day to find such extreme shortages, although I cannot say but that short butter may be found. It is not a universal custom.

Now it may be claimed by some dairymen that the consumer pays for it. Yes, that is so, but he knows what he is paying for and the manufacturer knows that his competitors are required to deliver full weight and that competition in quantity is not a feature of his business.

Then again, take for instance, the advantage of a good reputation in the line of full weight. A large amount of the butter sold in Massachusetts comes from the State of Vermont, and a few years ago it was discovered that short weight butter was being delivered from that State. Steps were at once taken to stop that practice,—and let me say here, that in most cases it was found that shortage was not intentional for upon investigation the scales used by the creamery were at fault, or the moulds were to blame, and in the case of 5 lb. boxes it was often found that the paddle used to press the butter into the box and smooth it over, had become worn so deep at the notch where it fits over the top edge of the box that it scraped deeper than it should have, causing shortage.

As soon as Vermont established its State Department this butter shortage in its State was called to its attention and the Department was soon in touch with the creameries and faulty conditions were remedied.

Now, if we in Massachusetts have a complaint that any certain creamery in Vermont is sending short butter, our commissioner notifies the Vermont commissioner and the creamery is called to account.

This supervision is working to the benefit of the dairymen in Vermont, for the merchants in Massachusetts, at least, feel assured that the Vermont creamery will deliver full weight, and with this assurance they feel disposed to favor the Vermont trade.

Like conditions should exist in all states and just as soon as your State Commissioner is given the essentials to carry on his work, the better it will be for all.

The third form of the evil is a direct result of the short-comings of the National Pure Food and Drugs Act. This Act, as is well known, was a compromise measure and only by allowing the clause which would have required the branding of the net contents on the outside of the package to be stricken out, could even so powerful a champion as Congressman Mann succeed in getting this magnificent piece of legislation enacted.

Packages have been constantly shrinking in size and content.

No technical violation,—merely a loophole, merely a study of how gradually the visual perception of the people can be destroyed.

A single illustration will suffice. "Quaker Oats", the package that had the big "2" on it, the one that we associate with the picture of the sturdy Quaker and "Sold by all Grocers in 2-pound packages," advertised thus before 1906 in magazines, proclaimed so from bill boards, contains now only 1 lb. 5 ounces. How long will it take the public to realize that this now costs them 100 per cent more than the bulk rolled oats?

One more instance, quoted from a letter of a reputable manufacturer of syrup:—"We must frankly and regretfully say that in the molasses business there has been, and is still, some of the worst sort of deception. For instance, it is a common practice to put into a quart can the contents of a No. 2 1-2 can.

There is nothing on the label referring to the size, but the customer is deceived by the appearance. We deplore this because we would like to see the whole molasses business conducted on a clean, honest basis."

There is no reasonable excuse for not marking the contents in terms of weight, measure or numerical count on the outside of every package or every can. A simple analysis of the arguments of the opponents,—and, by the way, look at the composition of the ranks of the opponents,—shows the misleading statements and shows the utter disregard of the rights of the consumer.

In North Dakota a law was passed requiring the contents to be marked on containers, and Commissioner Ladd officially reports that there resulted an increase of contents in canned goods of from 17 to 21 per cent without an increase in cost.

Time does not permit me to call your attention to the specific instances of picture cord, 19 feet short in 25 yards; thread and yarn, 25 per cent short; braid, ribbon and tape, from 5 to 10 per cent short; toilet paper of less than 500 sheets when sold as 1000 sheets; wall paper, from 5 to 10 per cent short; writing pads, 10 per cent short; some flavoring extracts 25 per cent short; flour when you pay for the bag that cannot be made into bread, at the price of flour; butter prints from 5 to 25

8

per cent short of a pound; butter in crocks, 10 to 30 per cent short; lard sold in No. 3, No. 5 and No. 10 pails, *but not* 3, 5 or 10 lbs.; coal sold to the poor at $13.50 per ton; wood in the stacked barrels, and kindling in short bundles; matches sold to the consumer as boxes of 500 and not holding 400; paints and oils shy in quality and quantity; the list could be extended ad infinitum through the whole list of articles that are put into our bodies, on our bodies, over, under or on the side of us, indeed whether it be for ourselves, our dogs, horses or cows or for our stoves, furnaces, or our streets.

What are the causes of these three evils? The faulty apparatus or false use of correct scales, weights and measures, is due to ignorance, negligence, acquired dishonesty or inherent dishonesty.

The first three can be overcome and the last three should be and can be eliminated by effective legislation, providing for intelligent inspection.

Results of the three evils are evident. We pay for things we do not get, and though many of the shortages violate no statute, and as in the case of package goods are only taking advantage of the fact that we have an exceedingly poor visual concept of quantity, though few realize it or are even willing to admit it, yet the purchasing power of a dollar is reduced. The poor, the very ones who need the fullest protection, suffer most.

Whatever other causes may contribute to the high cost of living, one evident cause is shortage in weight and measure of the commodity purchased. We need Federal Legislation giving to some Bureau, power to regulate and pass upon the types of scales, weights and measures that can be manufactured and used.

We shall have in force a National Standard Apple Barrel Law next July,—why not the same for other commodities? Why should we not have a standard caliper and a uniform measurement of lumber? Why should we not have a standard shingle and an authorized bundle? We are receiving many complaints regarding the measurement of shingles and lumber.

Bundle hay is received in my state that will not weigh up to the markings on the bale. A correct tolerance for hay should be established to allow for reasonable shrinkage to be used in adjusting the sale of this commodity. The subject of marked weights on bales of hay was investigated in 1911 by the sealer in one of our largest cities and he reported that from one shipment he weighed up 18 bales billed as 1886 pounds, and the shortage was 266 pounds, a little over 14 per cent. At $25.00 per ton this would have caused a loss to the purchaser of about $3.30. In Massachusetts the seller was liable to prosecution. The maximum for the first offence would be $50.00; second offence not more than $200.00, and for a subsequent offence, a fine of $50.00 and imprisonment for not less than thirty days nor more than ninety days. (Chapter 163, Acts of 1911.)

We need a National Net Container Law framed to be equitable alike to the producer and consumer. Few of us stop to think, when purchasing package goods, what quantity we are receiving for our money. Our Commissioner made a limited investigation in this line for the high cost of living commission and I will give you a few illustrations of the cost of goods when purchased in package form.

Please compare them with the prices in bulk for like articles.

	Package.	At the Rate per Pound.
Beachnut Bacon	18c.	57.6c.
Rex Sliced Bacon	15c.	43 c.
Tuxedo Currants, 14 6-16 oz	12c.	13.3c.
Velveteen Currants, 14 11-16 oz	14c.	15.2c.
Baking Powders		
Cleveland, 8 oz	20c.	40 c.
Congress, 6 1-32 oz	18c.	35.8c.
Queen, 7 11-16 oz	13c.	27 c.
Royal, 8 2-16 oz	23c.	45.2c.
Rumford, 8 3-16 oz	15c.	29.2c.
Crackers		
Cheese Biscuit, 8 oz	15c.	30 c.
Graham, 8 7-8 oz	10c.	18 c.
Oysterettes, 5 4-16 oz	5c.	15.2c.
Oatmeal, 9 7-8 oz	10c.	16.2c.
Uneeda, 5 17-32 oz	5c.	14.4c.
Zu Zu, 4¼ oz	5c.	18.7c.
Breakfast Cereals		
Corn Flakes, 11 3-16 oz	10c.	14.3c.
Cream of Wheat, 1 lb., 12 7-16 oz	15c.	8.4c.
Force, 10 10-16 oz	12c.	18 c.
H. O., 1 lb., 8 1-16 oz	14c.	9.3c.
Hecker's Cream Hominy, 2 lbs., 14 3-16 oz	12c.	4.1c.
Malto, 1 lb., 15 7-16 oz	14c.	7.1c.
Maple Flake, 10 11-16 oz	15c.	22.4c.
Beck's Rolled Oats, 1 lb., 13 9-16 oz	10c.	5.4c.
Quaker Oats (Pure), 21½ oz	10c.	7.5c.
Quaker Oats (White), 1 lb., 4 9-16 oz	10c.	7.7c.
Puffed Rice, 6¾ oz	13c.	31.4c.
Cook's Flaked Rice, 9 15-16 oz	14c.	22.7c.
Cook's Malto, 10 7-16 oz	15c.	22.9c.

Don't wait for National Legislation, for I believe that those interests that are advising State Legislative Committees not to pass a "Net Container Bill", but to wait for such action by Congress, are doing so for the purpose of delay, and also to be able to make their opposition felt all at one point.

Massachusetts did not wait for action by Congress before placing a Pure Food Act upon the Statute Book.

If the states will follow the examples of Connecticut and New York and put in force a "Net Container Law" I believe that we will then have the assistance of these same selfish interests to pass a National Law, and that such a law will the sooner be obtained.

The importance of uniform laws throughout the United States cannot be overestimated, but if we cannot attain that then let each state see to it that its own citizens are protected.

I know from what I have seen in the State of Maine, in passing through to the place where I spend my vacation, that there is need of energetic work on the part of your officials.

In one store I visited I noticed a two-pound weight was kept on the scale all the time, and force of habit prompted me to investigate. Upon removing the weight, the pan or scoop, where the goods are placed while being weighed, dropped to down weight although nothing was in the scoop. I found that the dealer was obtaining 2 ounces that did not belong to him every time he used the scale.

In returning through this same town, from my outing, I was anxious to learn how much I had gained in weight during my vacation and was much pleased to find that the Maine air and a good rest had increased my weight by 8 pounds, in one month, but I was somewhat disappointed upon weighing again at my office in Massachusetts the next day to find that I had lost 5 pounds of that apparent gain of 8.

The Massachusetts scale was correct but the Maine scale had deceived me to the extent of 5 pounds.

Our Ex-Governor Guild fittingly said, in referring to the weights and measures situation, a few years ago:—"Good citizenship is benefited by the enforcement by statute of common honesty in everyday dealings of one man with another in every walk of life.

Some reforms only touch the average citizen once in a life-time, but the enforcement of honest weights and measures touches every human being at every moment of the day."

I hope, Gentlemen, that you will take a hand with Mr. Buckley before your legislature and see that he is furnished with sufficient funds to carry on this work. We are interested in your weights and measures laws, and that is the reason I came here today. We have a selfish interest for Maine and New Hampshire to wake up in this matter. Vermont has waked up, and if Maine and New Hampshire will wake up and get things in their states in better condition, you will help us and you will help your own people.

I asked a man who carries most of the butter that goes into the Boston market from the State of Maine if he had any trouble about weights. He said he had considerable trouble. He got prints from Maine the other day and it took three half-pound prints to make a pound. It may not have been the fault of the Maine man; it may have been the fault of the scales. I am connected with a club where we buy large quantities of goods preserved down here in Maine, and I believe that firm is honest but their scales had not been under the supervision of a man who had sufficient test weights. You have standards here in Maine but your Commissioner has told you that it was 20 years since they had been adjusted. Those standards should go to Washington at least once in five years. I think our standards are sent oftener than that,—every two or three years, because we use them a great deal. Every city in the State of Massachusetts has been furnished with a set of standards which is very exact, down to one-fifteenth of an ounce avoirdupois. Those are sent into our office once every five years, and we take them and adjust them. They are corrected once in two or three years, but come to our office once in five years. One man does the adjusting, and another man goes through the same work, and he must make the weights agree so that we know a 50 pound weight is within two grains of a correct weight. Those are sent to the towns, and the sealer has a duplicate set of those standards. He tests up his working weights with the standard that we have furnished him and then he goes out among the stores and adjusts all the weights he finds

in the stores every year; he is supposed to do this. If you had
that inspection in Maine the places where I have found a broken
scale with a pound weight kept on it and where I found a 125
pound scale five pounds out of the way, in your State, would
have been found by the sealer. I inquired if they had a sealer.
They said yes, but they did not know who he was. You have
not sufficient supervision of your weights and measures. It is
going to cost money, but the money is coming back to you two
fold because you are going to have honest weights and measures if you have the right officials. Be sure that you appoint
your officials and I hope you will not attempt to put a sealer
into every single little town, but will have a district of towns.
We have a sealer in every town and some of them haven't work
enough to do to keep the rust off from their weights. They
get $5.00 a year and they do not do a thing. If you are going
to start in Maine, start right. If you put a group of towns
into the hands of one man he will have something to do and
you can afford to pay him something for doing it.

THE VALUE OF FEEDING STUFFS FOR THE DAIRY COW.

By Prof. J. M. Bartlett.

When asked to give a paper or talk on feeds for the dairy cow at this annual meeting of dairymen, I took down my set of Commissioner's reports and looked through them to learn what had been given previously on this important subject. I found that at nearly every meeting for the past 15 years feeds for dairy cows had been very ably and thoroughly discussed by both practical dairymen and scientific investigators; consequently there is practically nothing new to be presented; and it seems like threshing over old straw to attempt to say anything on the subject. There is one consolation, however, in the fact that if there is not much new to say there are always some new listeners and, if we do have to use old material, there are always some in the audience who have not heard it before, and I expect one reason why our Commissioners get new speakers to come to these meetings and speak on these old subjects, "chestnuts" if you choose to call them, is because the new man presents his ideas with more enthusiasm under the delusion that he is presenting something new to his audience. Notwithstanding how stale the subject is, it is, nevertheless, an important one to the dairyman and must be studied and discussed as long as the business of dairying continues, otherwise we will not progress and the business will deteriorate.

THE PRINCIPAL COMPONENTS OF THE ANIMAL BODY.

In order to know the essentials and value of feeds, or foods, for animals we should first know of what the animal body and its products are composed and what is needed to sustain them.

The working parts or the machinery of the body, although containing a great variety of substances, differing but slightly in chemical composition, may for our purpose be grouped under three heads,—water, ash and protein. Water is rarely less than half and sometimes is three-fourths the entire weight. The proportion is greatest in young or lean animals and decreases as they become more mature or fatter. Ash or mineral matter is the portion left after the animal is burned. It is principally in the bones, or framework, but is found in all parts of the body and is just as essential as water. Protein is the name given to a highly important group of substances of which white of egg, lean meat, the casein or curd of milk and the gluten of flour are familiar examples. They are composed of the chemical elements nitrogen, carbon, hydrogen and sulphur. This group of substances differs from others principally in containing nitrogen, which is an important element in both feeds and fertilizers. Protein is the basis of the living tissues of the body, the so-called protoplasm, and is the substance through which life manifests itself. Besides the working parts, the body contains a store of reserve materials in the form of fat, which is stored up when food is abundant and drawn on when food is scarce. The per cent of fat in farm animals varies greatly, seldom going below six per cent, or rising above 30 per cent. In addition to fat the animal also contains a small amount of carbohydrates (sugar) called glycogen. Neither of these substances contain nitrogen.

THE COMPONENTS OF FEEDING STUFFS.

The vegetable feeding stuffs which nourish the animal, like it, are made up of a wide variety of substances but for our purpose here may be classified in a few groups which are the same as those found in the animal, namely water, ash, protein, fat and carbohydrates. The proportions of these ingredients in the plants are widely different from what they are in the animal kingdom. Protein is the predominant ingredient, aside from water, in animals; also a large amount of reserve force is stored up in fat with a very small amount of carbohydrates. Protein is also present in all plants, but the predominating ingredient is the carbohydrates which are found as sugar or starch in the cells or crude fiber in the cell walls. A few plants like cotton and flax store up fat or oil in their seeds instead of starch, also large amounts of protein. We, therefore, see that the component parts of plants are the same as those of the animal body and furnish the material necessary to sustain it.

The animal body is often spoken of as a machine and the plant the natural fuel to run it. The body is certainly a most wonderful machine. It might be likened to a gas engine which supplies power to move itself and other bodies from power developed by burning the fuel within its cylinders or body walls. The animal body is more wonderful than the engine inasmuch as when furnished with material it does its own repairing. In one respect it differs from the artificial machine in that it cannot be stopped and started again at will.

NUTRIENTS.

The component parts of plants of which we have been speaking, viz.: water, protein, ash, carbohydrates and fat, are called nutrients, a term with which you are probably all familiar. Now what is the special office of these different substances? Water is essential as a food but may be disregarded in this discussion. The ash supplies the mineral portion of the bone and serves to replace the constant waste of mineral matter in the system. The protein differs from the other nutrients, as has already been pointed out, in that it contains nitrogen and sulphur. Its primary office is that of building tissue. It is the sole source whence may be made good the loss of proteids from the body. The protein of the body or other nitrogenous material like wool, hair or flesh, cannot be made in the animal except from protein of the food. We, therefore, see that a sufficient supply of protein is absolutely necessary in the food. Protein also if fed in excess of the needs for repair or growth can be and is used as a fat former or heat producer, or, in other words, as fuel to run the engine, but this is not an economical use to make of it as it is the most costly nutrient in foods.

The carbohydrates and fat are so similar in their offices in feeding that they may be considered in this connection as one.

Their functions in the body are many, namely, the production of heat and energy, the formation of body fat, the protection of the flesh of the body from too rapid breaking down as a result of vital processes, the manufacture of non-nitrogenous organic milk constituents, i. e., sugar and fat. These nutrients are more directly comparable to the fuel which is used to run the engine. They are burned in the body not only to keep it warm but also to produce energy used in muscular motion and in the vital activities of the body. If an excess of these materials is fed over what is needed for immediate use in keeping up the temperature and producing energy it is stored away in the form of body fat for future use. For the purpose of making energy or producing heat there is a difference between these materials we are considering together, that is, it has been found by actual experiment, by actual burning, that fat will on the average produce two and one-fourth times as much heat as the same weight of carbohydrates, and this fact has to be taken into consideration when considering the value of these materials.

You will pardon me for considering somewhat in detail in a more technical way than is desirable perhaps at a meeting of this kind, the component parts of feeding stuffs, but it seemed necessary in order to present what I wish to consider farther on.

TERMS USED IN MAKING UP RATIONS.

Having considered briefly the nutrients contained in feeds and fodders there are terms which are used in connection with making up rations which may be familiar to you all as they have been used for more than twenty-five years in the literature on the subject.

Digestible dry matter is a term applied to that portion of the total dry matter of the food which is dissolved out by the digestive fluids in the alimentary tract of the animal and becomes available as food. The digestible nutrients are likewise that portion of the nutrients that are available as food.

Digestion coefficients are the percentages of the various nutrients in foods found to be digestible by actual experiments with animals, and these factors are used to calculate the amounts of the various nutrients digestible in the different foods.

Nutritive ratio is a term you have often heard used and maybe most of you know what it means and how it is obtained, but I think perhaps, although many of you have seen and used the term, you may not know its full significance. A "nutritive ratio" is simply an expression of the amount of digestible carbohydrates and fat, or energy material, in a feed or a ration to one part of digestible protein. That is, a nutritive ratio of 1:6 means that there are six pounds of digestible carbohydrates and fat to every pound of digestible protein. To illustrate, suppose that a ration or feed is used that contains two pounds of digestible protein and twelve pounds of digestible carbohydrates and fat (the per cent of fat is multiplied by 2 1-4 and added to the carbohydrates), the proportion ratio would be as 2 is to 12, which is equal to a nutritive ratio of 1 to 6 or one part of protein to six of carbohydrate and fat material. Nutritive ratios are termed wide, medium or narrow, depending on the proportion of protein to the other materials. 1 to 3 ɪs a narrow ratio; 1 to 6 medium; 1 to 10 a rather wide ratio for rations for dairy purposes.

PRACTICAL FEEDING.

You may have become wearied somewhat from the more or less technical part of this paper I have given and wonder of what practical benefit it can be to you. You have probably all heard many times of a balanced ration and perhaps you may all know how to figure one out, but at any rate there are some people in the State, if none are in this audience, who are not yet familiar with the method as letters very frequently come to the Station, with a list of feeds, asking how to mix them to make a balanced ration.

There is ample opportunity now with all the tables and literature in books on agriculture, station bulletins, etc., that have been published on the subject, for anyone who has a knowledge of common school arithmetic to easily figure rations for himself and it is for this reason I have called your attention to the subject. Some one may inquire what is a balanced ration? It is one having a correct nutritive ratio or the right amount of protein as compared with the carbohydrates and fat for the purpose for which it is intended. All balanced rations are not alike. A quite different nutritive ratio would be given to a fattening animal than to a milch cow. The fattening animal should have more of the fat forming material, carbohydrates,— a wider ration. But our discussion today is in the interest of dairymen and we, therefore, should confine ourselves to discussing rations for the dairy cow. The old German standard worked out by Wolff called for a somewhat narrow ration with 2 1-2 lbs. of digestible protein in a day for a 1000 lb. cow in full flow of milk. Practice, however, has proven, and experiments have been made with hundreds of cows showing that a wider ration with two pounds or less of digestible protein per day, is more profitable in this country, particularly when the welfare of the cow is considered, as experience has shown that a cow will last much longer when fed a fairly wide ration.

In making up rations no hard and fast rules can be followed. The standard ration can only be used as a guide and must be varied to suit each case. The variations in foods of the same class, the condition of the animal, period of lactation, milk flow, etc., must all be taken into consideration. A rule which is followed by some feeders is to feed rough fodder enough to support the cow if giving no milk—a maintenance ration— and then feed one pound of grain mixture for every 3 or 4 pounds, depending on its richness, of milk given. Then a cow giving about 30 lbs. of 4 per cent fat milk would receive a grain ration of 8 lbs. of a proper grain mixture.

HOW CAN WE FEED WITH PROFIT?

Having learned the ration best adapted to his purpose the practical feeder is most interested in learning what method he can follow in obtaining feeds to yield him the most profit.

There are two classes of dairymen in the State today, that are making money. To the one belongs the man who is conveniently located to markets or means of transportation, is making a gilt edge product and selling it at a high price. He may or may not buy all his grain, but he is selling his product enough above the market price to yield a good profit. To the second class belongs the man who is not so favorably located, is obliged to sell his product at market price, but is growing most of his own feed and thereby saving, a great outlay of money. Outside of these two classes mentioned is a third class, and I regret to say much the largest, to which belongs the men who are selling their product at market prices and buying most of their feed. The men who belong to this last class are the ones who most need to improve their methods because they are making little or no money at the business unless they are fortunate enough to have cows far above the average as producers. These men cannot perhaps easily change their location or obtain a better market, but what they can do in most instances is to grow more feed. Every dairyman should have a silo well filled with mature corn. There is nothing that we can grow that will furnish so much digestible dry matter to the acre at the same cost. It will grow on almost all kinds of soils and does not need heavy fertilization and when preserved in a silo it is not an expensive crop to handle and furnishes succulent food at low cost. It is important that the corn be well matured and carry a plentiful supply of well glazed ears. Green corn stalks carry much sugar in their juices which ferments and makes a much sourer and less nutritious silage than mature stalks and corn in which the sugar has changed to starch and remains permanent in the silo. Experiments have been made showing that 100 lbs. of good well matured corn silage contains as much nutrients as 180 lbs. of silage made from green southern corn stalks.

Clover should be grown much more extensively than it commonly is for hay. Early cut, well cured clover has nearly the same feed value as wheat bran, which costs $26 per ton, and aside from furnishing a nutritious fodder leaves the soil in better condition than it found it. We are inclined to mourn because we cannot grow alfalfa but I am inclined to believe that in our short summer season clover is more valuable for us. Hungarian can be easily grown and produces a large amount of green fodder late in the season when the pastures are getting short. Mixed early cut English hay is also good fodder for cows, but pure timothy is better to sell to the Boston market than to feed.

Large acreage of peas and oats should be grown and threshed · for grain as is the custom of the Canadian farmers who buy very little feed for their cows. No better balanced ration can be found than one carrying 40 lbs. well matured corn silage, 7 lbs. clover hay and 8 lbs. oats and peas ground together. This is sufficient for a thousand pound cow producing 30 lbs. of milk. I would most strongly urge the home growing of feeds as much as possible and firmly believe it is the only salvation for the average dairyman. In most sections of the State the soil is good and productive and with the large amount of valuable manure from dairy stock one ought at least to grow all the carbohydrates and a part of the protein needed.

COMMERCIAL FEEDS.

Notwithstanding the desirability of growing all feeds on the farm circumstances will not always permit this to be done and many farmers will continue to buy from the markets. As briefly as possible I will, therefore, take up and discuss the value of the various feeds found upon our markets today for the dairy cow. For convenience we may divide them into three classes.

Class 1. Those rich in protein.

Class 2. Those medium in protein.

Class 3. Those poor in protein and rich in carbohydrates.

Under the first class we have the oil meals, the most prominent among which is cottonseed meal. This meal is the richest in and cheapest source of protein of any of the feeds offered. It is, however, somewhat constipating and should be fed with laxative foods as silage, bran, etc. There are two grades on the market, namely, choice, guaranteed 41 per cent protein; and prime, guaranteed 38.50 per cent protein. The choice is usually the cheaper meal to buy as the lower grade is made by adding ground hulls which have little feeding value. The better grades of meals run well up to their guaranties.

Linseed oil meal is the next in order of the seed meals. They usually carry about 36 per cent protein and are laxative in their effect, particularly the old process meal that contains quite a high percentage of oil. This is a safer feed than cottonseed meal but the protein costs more. These meals are better to use with dry, coarse fodders on account of their laxative properties.

Distillers' grains come next in order of richness in protein, carrying about 31 per cent, and they also carry about 11 per cent oil. It is a bulky feed and is very desirable to feed with a heavy material like corn meal.

Gluten feed is a by-product which is produced in the manufacture of corn starch. It is quite bulky and for that reason is a good grain to feed alone. The protein is guaranteed 23 per cent but usually runs higher. As a source of protein alone these feeds are more expensive than those going before, but they contain more carbohydrates.

Under class 2 we have the wheat offals, including wheat bran, mixed feed, and middlings. These materials carry from 14 to 18 per cent protein, but contain large amounts of carbohydrates and are rich in ash materials which makes them valuable for growing animals. As a source of protein, however, now they are expensive at present prices on account of their low digestibility. Their bulkiness makes them desirable to feed with heavy grains. Some of the mixed feeds are adulterated with corn cobs and sold under special names. These adulterated mixed feeds are reduced in value about one-fourth and sell at nearly the same price as the straight goods. The corn cobs with which they are adulterated have practically no feeding value. Under the inspection laws they are obliged to mark them as carrying corn cobs.

Under Class 3 would come the oat feeds, hominy feed and corn meal. The oat feeds are a cheap class of feeds and at the present time we are finding very few of them in the State. No one can afford to buy them as they are largely made up of oat hulls that have no more feeding value than oat straw. Under this class corn meal is the most concentrated and valuable feed, but, as you know, carries so little protein that it can only be fed profitably with other material rich in this ingredient.

We have on the market some other feeds which I have not mentioned under the classes given. Among them are the molasses feeds so-called, sold under varying names. Feeding experiments with these goods have shown them to be fairly economical. They should not, however, be purchased as a source of protein as they carry only about as much as mixed feed—15 to 16 per cent. Feeders who find it necessary to purchase nearly all their feed may find these molasses feeds economical to use in place of bran or mixed feed. The chief objection to them is found in the material which is used to absorb the molasses, namely, screenings and elevator chaff which contains large amounts of weed seeds. The best manufacturers now claim to kill all the seeds by heat before mixing. Malt sprouts, cottonseed meal and other concentrates are used to bring up the protein.

Some other ready mixed rations like the Union Grains or Biles Ready Ration are on the market, but are not sold very extensively. These feeds are well balanced and made of good material but cost more than the unmixed goods usually.

WHAT CONCENTRATED FEEDS ARE MOST ECONOMICAL TO BUY?

Having considered briefly the nature of the concentrated feeds on the market we now come to the practical side of the question which most interests the dairyman—What are the most economical feeds to purchase?

As a general rule the most concentrated feeds furnish the various nutrients for the least money. That is, to illustrate, if one is buying protein it will cost in cottonseed meal at present prices about 4 cents per pound, in linseed meal 4.5 cents per pound, in distillers' grains about 5.6 cents, in wheat bran about 8.5 cents. In these you see we can get protein in cottonseed meal and linseed meal for about half what it costs in wheat bran.

This same is true in the case of carbohydrate material. Corn meal, which is the richest feed in this class of nutrients, carrying about 72 per cent, furnishes them most cheaply, even at its present high price, of any of the grains. If we are feeding growing animals and ash material is wanted we should look to the grain that carries the most good ash, wheat bran. Individually, however, this is a question every man must decide for himself after taking into consideration what he has on hand for home grown fodders. If he has silage made from well matured corn, and mixed English hay, he has a good supply of carbohydrates and needs to buy little else than protein. This can be most cheaply supplied in cottonseed meal, but such a concentrated grain cannot safely be fed alone and a little bran should be added for bulkiness, also to supply ash materials. If the silage is not well supplied with ears of corn (as it is likely not to be after a cold summer like the one just past) some corn meal should be added to the grain ration. I am not specifying absolute amounts as that is something the feeder must determine with each animal, but would not feed over 3 1-2 lbs. cottonseed per day in any case. If more protein is needed it can be supplied by adding distillers' grains or gluten feed to the grain mixture. For a general guide I would suggest a very satisfactory ration for a 1000 lb. cow giving 30 lbs. of milk containing 4 per cent fat would be:

```
35   lbs.  corn silage (ears glazed)
 7½   "    mixed hay
 3    "    cottonseed meal
 2    "    corn meal
 2    "    bran
```

This will give a ration carrying 2 lbs. digestible protein and 13 lbs. digestible carbohydrates, fats included, and gives nutritive ratio of 1:6.5. If the silage is made from immature corn and carries few or no ears then the corn meal should be increased at least one pound.

I regret to say many of our farmers have no silos and depend wholly on dry fodder for roughage. If no succulent food is fed then we must be more careful in our grain mixture, and it is better to use mixtures that are somewhat laxative and some of the cottonseed meal should be replaced by oil meal. Bran is also laxative but is expensive at present prices. For a grain ration in such cases I would suggest the following mixture:

```
Cottonseed meal..............................  2
Oil meal.....................................  1
Gluten feed..................................  1
Corn meal....................................  2
Bran.........................................  2
```

This mixture fed with 20 lbs. hay gives 2.1 lbs. digestible protein and a nutritive ratio of 1:6.3.

In closing I would again urge our dairy farmers to grow
more feed. Grow corn, roots, hungarian and hay for a supply
of carbohydrate material; also grow peas and oats, clover and
the vetches for a part, at least, of the protein supply. Then
shall we check to some extent, the immense volume of money
that is now going out of the State to enrich the South and
West, and grow not quite so poor ourselves, if we do not grow
rich, but not until then.

COST OF MILK PRODUCTION.

Prof. j. M. Trueman, Storrs, Conn.

Mr. Chairman, Ladies and Gentlemen:

The cost of producing milk varies in different states, and even in different parts of the same state. This afternoon I intend to tell you how we figure in Connecticut, and you can apply the same methods to your conditions in Maine.

In the first place, we believe that money invested in the dairy business should draw interest, so we must determine as accurately as possible the amount invested.

We found by keeping careful records that it costs us at least $75.00 to raise a heifer from birth to the milking age. It costs about the same amount to buy a good cow, and we therefore allow $75.00 as the capital invested in each cow. The other item of fixed capital is for barn room. We estimate that it will cost not less than $1200.00 to build a bare stable for 20 cows. This means $60.00 per cow. This added to the $75.00 invested in the cow, gives us a total amount of $135.00. Allowing 5 per cent interest on this amount, gives us $6.75.

Unfortunately the amount of money invested in the cow must be replaced on the average every four or five years. The cow gives out, and will not sell for as much as it cost to raise her. As a rule, she will not sell for more than $25.00 and she cost $75.00. Here is $50.00 gone, and on the average, it is gone in less than five years. We found at the Connecticut Agricultural College that the cost of keeping up our herd was a little over $13.00 per year, per cow.

We found that bedding cost us $5.00 per year per cow, and that it cost $3.00 per cow to keep a bull for a herd of 25 cows. Taxes on cow and barn amounted to $1.25 and insurance to 40 cents. Sundries including light, medicine, veterinary bills, etc., cost $2.00.

The two other large items are labor and feed. We found at the College that our yearly labor bill per cow, amounted to $33.60. A study of several other herds in Connecticut showed a labor cost of from $27.00 to $40.00 per year per cow. To be on the safe side, that is, not to charge too much, we will allow an average of $30.00 per year. This seems high, but if you will consider the fact that the cow must be milked about 320 days every year and that it cannot be done for less than 4 cents per day, you will see that milking alone accounts for nearly half of the $30.00. Besides this, the cow must be fed, the barn cleaned out, the cow cleaned off, the utensils washed, the milk cooled, and a large number of small chores attended to. All this takes time and means money, so that $30.00 is not too much to allow for labor.

The cost of feeding a cow is not difficult to obtain. Of course there is a great difference in the amount fed among dairymen. We find in Connecticut that a cow that will produce over 6000 pounds of milk, requires about the following amount of feed in one year.

Corn silage, 4 tons at $4.00	$16 00
Hay, 1¼ tons at $16.00.... ....:	20 00
Grain, 1½ tons at $30.00.....	37 50
Pasture (5 months)...............................	10 00
	$83 50

This calls for a daily ration during the winter months, 220 days, as follows:

Daily ration,	35	lbs.	Silage
	12	"	Hay
	2	"	Wheat Bran
	2	"	Corn Meal
	2	"	Gluten Feed
	2	"	Cottonseed Meal

The total cost of keeping a good cow well fed and cared for, for one year is therefore as follows:

Interest on Investment..............................	$6 75
Depreciation in value of cow...	13 00
Bedding..	5 00
Bull..	3 00
Taxes...	1 25
Sundries (light, medicine, utensils, etc.)	2 00
Insurance........................	40
Labor...	30 00
Feed..	83 50
	$144 90

The total amounts to practically $145.00. Of course cows can be kept for less money, but it is a well established fact in these days that it does not pay to keep poor cows, or to feed any cows poorly.

We are now ready to consider the other side of the account. What can we reasonably expect to get from this cow in one year? She ought to give 6500 pounds of milk, or practically 3000 quarts. The credit account would stand as follows:

3,000 quarts milk at 4 cents........................	$120 00
1 calf at $3.00....................................	3 00
1 year's manure...................................	10 00
	$133 00

The total income is only $133.00 to offset an expense of $145.00. Clearly 4 cents per quart will not pay for producing milk under these conditions. If we allow 4 1-2 cents per quart, the half cent will add $15.00 to the income, which will make the total $148.00. This amount balances the account and leaves $3.00 of net profit. We therefore consider that under Connecticut conditions, we cannot afford to sell milk for less than 4 1-2 cents at the farmer's dairy house.

When the expense account of $145.00 has been paid, the dairyman may be considered to be doing a safe business. All his expenses have been paid and he has received interest on his investment, and wages for his work. Anything above $145.00, is net profit and should be credited to expert management.

You should note, however, that in my items of expense I have allowed nothing for management of the business. The breeding up of a dairy herd to the point where it will produce 6500 pounds of milk per year, per cow, calls for a lot of thought, time and skill in selecting, breeding, and caring for animals, in buying and raising feeds, and in many other activities that are not represented by mere laborers' wages.

All things considered, the farmer living on medium or high priced land and subject to modern demands for clean milk production, cannot afford to sell his milk for less than 5 cents per quart at his dairy house.

MARKET GARDENING.

By H. C. Thompson, Asst. Horticulturist, U. S. Dept. of Agriculture, Washington, D. C.

No section in the United States has as good home gardens as New England and in no section is the market garden industry better developed than in parts of New England. The people of this region have learned the value of vegetables as articles of food, and as a commercial crop. In many sections vegetables are produced for distant markets and the local markets are neglected. These local markets must either do without the products or get them from a distance. It is for the purpose of interesting you in supplying your own needs and the local demand that I am making this talk to you today. I am told that the vegetables used by the summer hotels in this region are shipped in from other sections and other states. This is wrong, for you are sending money out of the community that should be kept at home. No part of the farm pays as well as the vegetable garden. In fact, according to the census reports, an acre in vegetables brings in as much money as 10 acres of common farm crops. I do not mean that the profit will be ten times as great per acre, but the gross returns will be that much, and no doubt the profit is several times greater, under good management.

Before anyone should go into a new line of business he should make a study of it and he should have a love for it. A man who has no love for plants could not make a success of market gardening. The market gardener needs to be more than a grower to be successful. He must be a good business man for he will have to be his own salesman, and to sell the products to good advantage he must be a good salesman. Many gardeners make a success of growing the crops and still fail in their business because they do not use business methods in disposing of the product. In addition to this he should be somewhat of an artist, so that he can pack his goods in such a way that they are attractive to the eye for it is appearance that sells a commodity. The prospective market gardener should study the soil and the plants he is to grow, their peculiarities and needs. Only by systematic study of the requirements of different crops and their adaptation to soils and other conditions will the grower be able to make a success. In addition to studying these factors the grower should study the subject of fertilizers, manures, methods of culture, diseases and insects, and methods of grading and packing his products.

In selecting a location for a garden we should consider slope, topography, soil and drainage. In a general way the land should be level or nearly so, or in case it is slightly rolling it should slope to the South or East. The soil best adapted to most vegetables is a sandy or sandy loam, because this type of soil responds readily to fertilizers and manures and is a warm soil or what gardeners call an early soil. Early soil is very important because the earliest crops are nearly always the most profitable.

Vegetable growing is the most intensive kind of farming and it pays to do the work on the most intensive scale. Here is where we use the largest quantities of manures and fertilizers, and, while I am thoroughly convinced that some growers use too much commercial fertilizers, what would be considered excessive amounts for general farm crops will be profitable for vegetables. We often find gardeners who apply a ton of high grade fertilizer per acre and in some cases as high as two tons. This latter figure is too high for the best interest of the grower and his soil. By heavy application of commercial fertilizers without the addition of humus in some form we find that the soil becomes what is commonly called "fertilizer sick." Continuous clean culture with use of commercial fertilizers account for this trouble.

For growing vegetables no fertilizer or manure is as good as barnyard or stable manure, but for best results a combination of commercial fertilizers and barnyard manure should be used. To supply sufficient plant food in barnyard manure would require such a large amount that it would be practically impossible to secure it. The best way to use manure is as a compost and market gardeners almost always have a compost heap and allow the manure to thoroughly decompose before using it. In making the compost heap a long time in advance of using it the manure not only decays but weed seeds are destroyed. The most common method of making compost is to pile the manure and waste material, as old hay, straw, leaves, &c., in alternate layers with soil. The soil will absorb the nitrogen liberated as ammonia, thereby saving the most valuable element in the manure. Three inches of soil to a foot of manure will be sufficient to absorb the ammonia and to keep the manure from heating. Many gardeners apply ground rock phosphate or acid phosphate to the compost heap. This is a very good practice and should be encouraged. Diseased plants should never be thrown on the manure pile, for many of the common diseases live over winter and are distributed to the soil in the manure. Where the manure is well rotted it should be applied to the soil after plowing, and thoroughly disked and harrowed in. For some crops like melons the manure is often applied in the furrow and mixed with soil, or the soil bedded back over the manure.

Where barnyard manure is not available commercial fertilizers will have to be used, but these will not be at all satisfactory after a few years unless used in connection with humus. By plowing under clover, beans or other leguminous crops not only will humus be supplied but also the most expensive fertilizing element—nitrogen. Any kind of vegetables will supply the humus but legumes are best because of the addition of nitrogen. Even where barnyard manure is used it is desirable to use commercial fertilizers to supplement the manure. Commercial fertilizers are more readily available than animal manures so are important in starting the crop to growing and hastening maturity.

In using commercial fertilizers there are three elements of plant food to be supplied—nitrogen, potash and phosphorous. The nitrogen can be secured from nitrate of soda, cottonseed meal, fish scrap, tankage, etc. The most readily available nitrogenous fertilizer is nitrate of soda and it is as cheap per pound of nitrogen as any of the others. Potash can be secured in the form of kainit, muriate and sulphate of potash—the last two being the preferred as kainit is a low grade potash fertilizer. Phosphoric acid comes in the form of acid phosphate, phosphate rock, bone meal, basic slag and from other sources. Raw rock should not be used except where there is plenty of humus. The most common phosphate fertilizers used by gardeners are acid phosphate and steamed bone meal, because they are more readily available than the others. These fertilizers can be bought ready mixed in any proportion desired, but the plant food can be secured at less cost per pound by buying the different kinds separately and mixing them at home. The dealers or mixers charge from five to eight dollars per ton for mixing, and, besides, the farmers have to pay freight on worthless filler. For most garden crops a high grade fertilizer is used and some gardeners use practically the same kind for all crops. This is not a good practice for different classes of crops require different amounts and proportion of plant food. For example, foliage crops like cabbage require relatively larger quantities of nitrogen than root or seed crops. Root crops such as potatoes, turnips, parsnips, beets, etc., require more potash and seed crops relatively more phosphorous than the other two classes.

Many gardeners hesitate to mix their own fertilizer because they think there are scientific mysteries involved. It is very simple when once explained. Take a formula 8-4-8 and see what it means. It means simply that each one hundred pounds of the mixture contains eight pounds of phosphoric acid, four pounds of nitrogen and eight pounds of potash. In a ton there would be twenty times this much or one hundred and sixty pounds of phosphoric acid, eighty pounds of nitrogen and one hundred and sixty pounds of potash. To secure one hundred and sixty pounds of phosphate from acid phosphate containing sixteen per cent phosphorous, we would need one thousand pounds. To find the amount needed, divide the amount of each element required by the per cent in the source used, and multiply by 100. To get eighty pounds of nitrogen from nitrate of soda which contains fifteen per cent nitrogen, divide eighty pounds by fifteen and multiply by one hundred. This would give us five hundred and thirty-three and one-third pounds nitrate of soda. In muriate of potash there is about fifty per cent potash so that one hundred and sixty pounds would be secured in three hundred and twenty pounds of the muriate. This would give us only one thousand eight hundred and fifty pounds, but it has the same plant food, that is, in one ton of 8-4-8 goods. The dealer or mixer would simply add one hundred fifty pounds of dirt as filler. You can do the same, but this is unnecessary for the food is what you want, and the dirt as filler would only add to the cost of handling. By buying and mixing your own fertilizer you know what you are getting. Dealers often use cheap materials to supply the elements.

PREPARATION OF SOIL.

The soil should be plowed deep and thoroughly pulverized by harrowing, disking and dragging. Nothing is more important than a good seed bed and the only way to get it is thorough preparation. By deep plowing the soil will hold more water so that heavy rains will not do as much damage and the dry weather will not have as bad effect on the crops. The deeper the soil the larger the water storage reservoir, and the longer the crops can withstand dry weather.

CULTIVATION.

In cultivation we have in mind three objects—conservation of moisture, killing weeds, and soil aeration. The first is probably the most important. The method that will best serve these three objects is the one to use, and this is frequent shallow cultivation. This leaves a fine dust mulch. By cultivating often the weeds are killed before they get a foothold and hand labor is thereby reduced. Cultivation should be given each crop after each rain or whenever the soil becomes packed. Hand hoeing is necessary to some extent for most garden crops, but this should be reduced to the minimum for hand work adds greatly to the cost of production.

STARTING PLANTS.

As already mentioned earliness is of prime importance and in many cases this can be secured by starting plants in hotbeds and cold frames. Such plants as cabbage, cauliflower, eggplant, peppers and tomatoes should always be started in this way. By this method the gardener can have large plants ready to transplant out-of-doors by the time it would be safe to plant the seed outside. In many cases the seeds are sown in hotbeds and the plants transplanted to cold frames or other hotbeds. This is a very good method to follow because stocky, well-rooted plants can be secured in this way, and then hardened off for outdoor planting where cold frames are used. Some growers start beets, onions, cucumbers, and melons in hotbeds. The two last named are usually planted in plant bands and set into the open ground without the soil around the plants being disturbed, when all danger of frost is past.

Time for planting garden seeds. In a general way vegetables can be grouped into about three classes in regard to time of planting. Such plants as onions, peas, potatoes, and cabbage can be planted as soon as the soil can be gotten in good condition. Beets, radishes, lettuce, turnips, kale, spinach, and parsnips may be planted as soon as danger of hard frosts is over. Such crops as tomatoes, eggplants, peppers, cucumbers, melons and beans, should not be planted until all danger of frost is over and the soil is warm. Since earliness is of prime importance it will pay to take a little risk by planting early. Should frost kill first planting, a second one could be made.

CROPS TO BE GROWN.

The market gardener should grow a large number of crops so as to supply his customers with vegetables of some kind through the season. Of course, the standard crops would take up most of the space, because these crops are eaten by more people and with more regularity. Among the standard crops are potatoes, cabbage, cucumbers, corn, beans, peas, and tomatoes. Other crops that should be grown on a small scale are asparagus, cauliflower, lettuce, spinach, kale, mustard, turnips, beets, parsnips, carrots, salsify, melons, squash and parsley.

ROTATION OF CROPS.

Rotation is just as important in the garden as on the farm. In planning a rotation we should consider the following points:

1. Avoid having closely related plants follow each other, such as tomato and eggplant, or cabbage and cauliflower, because the same pests that affect cabbage also affect cauliflower. This is true of all closely related plants.

2. We should rotate our crops so that plants having different food requirements follow each other, as root crops following those grown for their foliage, or those grown for their seeds or fruit, shallow or surface rooted plants followed by deep or tap rooted plants.

In planning a rotation the gardener should bear in mind the humus requirement of the soil and whenever it is practical a crop should be plowed under. A suggestive rotation is somewhat as follows, bearing in mind the two factors mentioned. Beans or peas followed by cabbage or potatoes; potatoes followed by cabbage or other foliage crop and this in turn followed by a seed crop like peas or beans. Each gardener will have to work out his own rotation to fit in with his general plan.

Closely associated with rotation is intercropping and succession of crops. By intercropping is meant growing two or more crops on the same land at the same time by interplanting. This can often be done by planting quick maturing crops like radishes, lettuce, snap beans, etc., between rows of long season crops like celery, cabbage, etc. Succession of crops means following one crop with another the same season. For example, early lettuce, onions, or other crops may be followed by a crop of late potatoes, cabbage, beans or peas. Intercropping and succesion are very important because on high priced land it is necessary to get large yields per acre. Specific advice cannot be given along these lines for each farm will need separate treatment to suit local condition and needs.

DISEASES AND INSECTS.

I have not time to go into detail in regard to diseases and insects, but unless the grower studies them he will not make a success. There is a continuous struggle for existence in nature and if man lets up on his warfare against the enemies of plants the enemies will survive and the grower fail. You will find it necessary to spray for many diseases and insects, and for this purpose an outfit of some kind will be necessary. On a garden of two or three acres some form of power sprayer will be most economical while for a smaller garden a good barrel pump will serve the purpose.

In treating most diseases Bordeaux mixture is the best material to use and in treating all biting insects, or those that actually eat the part attacked either paris green or arsenate of lead is used. By writing to your Experiment Station you can secure bulletins which will give you detailed information how to make and apply these mixtures. I could give you the formulæ, but you would not remember the figures any longer than it takes me to give them.

HARVESTING, PACKING AND MARKETING.

When you are supplying a local market the vegetables should be allowed to mature before harvesting. Gather vegetables the same day they are to be sold, if possible, and pack them in neat attractive packages for most products are sold by appearance. It is very important that the grower grade his product and give a uniform, honest pack, so that the goods are their own advertisements. The grower should strive to have such a uniform pack and good quality that consumers who once buy his goods will always be his customers.

OUR PRESENT ECONOMIC DAIRY SITUATION AND ITS RELATION TO THE CONSUMER AND PRODUCER.

By R. S. Smith.

In almost any business its success other than the esthetic phase must depend on whether it is continuously profitable or not. Testing and keeping records of the individual cows have been preached and will continue to be preached to dairymen until they realize the folly of feeding high cost grain to dairy animals without receiving milk or manure enough to balance the cost of that grain.

A dairy cow is a complex machine constructed to convert food into milk and the best economy and surest profit consist in employing the most efficient machines and men able to handle them.

The price of dairy products has advanced to the consuming public but not in proportion to the advance in the prices of land values, building material, grains and other farm products.

As this article deals with the dairy side of farming, it will be interesting for consumers to note just where the products of the dairy farm compare with other farm products and whether the dairyman of to-day is receiving his just due.

The following has been taken from the Congressional Record, May 27, 1910, with the advance in retail milk prices in Maine added.

"While the prices of practically all commodities have shown some advance during the past few years, the products of the farm show a much greater advance than do the prices of the products of mines and factories.

Farm land itself has advanced in value rapidly and everything produced on the farm has also advanced materially. The financial condition of the grain raiser of the Northwest, the general farmer of the Middle West, the cotton planter of the South, is better than ever before. Instead of having to market the grain as soon as harvested and the cotton as soon as picked the producer is now in a position to hold his crop and market it to the best possible advantage. Financially the farmer has become independent. The rural free delivery and the telephone have placed him in touch with the world, and he is as familiar with current events as is the city dweller."

The average prices of the principal farm products in March, 1910, and in March, 1896, show in a striking manner the farmer's condition at the present time as compared with his condition in 1896. All prices used in the following tables are taken from Bulletin No. 39 and Bulletin No. 87 of the United States Bureau of Labor.

PRODUCT.	1910, March.	1896, March.	ADVANCE SINCE MARCH, 1896.	
			Actual Advance.	Per Cent.
Corn, per bushel	$0.624	$0.285	$0.338	118.4
Wheat, per bushel	1.187	.631	.556	88.1
Cotton, per pound.	.150	.078	.072	92.2
Oats, per bushel.	.447	.192	.254	132.2
Rye, per bushel..	.791	.364	.426	117.1
Barley, per bushel.	.693	.305	.387	126.8
Hay, timothy, per ton	17.050	11.400	5.650	49.5
Hops, per pound	.330	.075	.255	340.0
Potatoes, per bushel	.321	.185	.136	73.7
Flaxseed, per bushel	2.145	.885	1.260	142.4
Cattle, choice to extra steers, per 100 lbs .	8.190	4.250	3.940	92.7
Hogs, heavy, per 100 lbs.	10.615	3.902	6.712	172.0
Butter, dairy, per pound	.311	.198	.112	57.3
Eggs, per dozen	.257	.124	.133	107.3
Milk	.070	.050	.020	40.0

The price of these farm products practically doubled.

Corn advanced 118.4 per cent.
Wheat advanced 88.1 per cent.
Cotton advanced 92 2 per cent.
Hay advanced 49.5 per cent.
Hops advanced 340 per cent.
Potatoes advanced 73.7 per cent.
Flaxseed advanced 142.4 per cent.
Milk advanced 40 per cent.

Oats advanced 132.2 per cent.
Rye advanced 117.1 per cent.
Barley advanced 126 8 per cent.
Fat cattle advanced 92.7 per cent.
Fat hogs advanced 172 per cent.
Dairy butter advanced 57.3 per cent.
Eggs advanced 107.3 per cent.

It must not be forgotten that the milk industry is a gigantic industry, yet it received the smallest advance. "In the United States the production of dairy farms ranks third in value, and is exceeded only by corn and beef."

Just why there has been no rapid increase in price of milk and why it now becomes an economic problem for a man of brains to produce milk with profit is easily understood. We know that lack of method and hit-or-miss slack dairying have been practiced from the beginning on the majority of dairy farms.

Lack of attention to details, without any thought of the future, has been the condition of our dairy industry until only a few years ago. Now that there is more demand for a clean, wholesome product that cannot be produced with profit under the past slack methodless way, we find men left with a herd of cows on their hands which are losing them money, but who continue selling their milk sometimes at 3 1-2 to 4 1-2 cents a quart at wholesale for want of a better occupation; trusting to the other products of the farm to bring them an existence.

Undoubtedly dairy conditions would have continued under the old regime if it were not for competition of substitutes and it is to these that we must owe in a certain degree the lack of advance in milk. Prices were suppressed at the beginning by careless, slack attention to an all important product, resulting in no corresponding advance in price as with other farm products and we now find the dairyman's problem confronting him and the grain farmers of the Middle West prosperous.

Many dairymen are at a loss to know why the consuming public does not readily yield to their demand for higher wages. City people who have paid from 6 to 7 cents a quart for the past dozen or more years fail to understand and wonder why such a demand is made. The excuse usually is that "Grain is higher." That is very true, as a reference to the advance in prices of farm products will confirm.

The number of oleomargarine dealers is 704 in Maine, 234 in New Hampshire, and 19 in Vermont.

The evaporated milk output of the United States increased 154 per cent and the condensed milk output 6 per cent during the five years 1905-1910, showing that these products are being used in a large degree.

Only a few years ago grain was comparatively cheap and dairymen drifted into the extravagant method of feeding dairy cows on a ration composed largely of concentrates. Higher prices of grain without higher prices for the product has caused a realization that a ration composed largely of roughage is now most economical.

An American grain farmer has been continually increasing his production at an increase in price but when that grain leaves the farm much fertility goes with it. Some of this fertility must be put back to insure continuous production. If we are to maintain the highest type of permanent agriculture for Maine, dairying should be a prominent economic feature. As a proof let us look to Denmark and Holland where dairying is the specialty of prosperous farmers.

The Danish farmers are feeding products of our soil to their dairy cows and selling their butter on the British market in competition with ours.

The American grain farmer growing corn, oats, wheat and clover and plowing under the clover for nitrogen, then selling the grain from the soil, loses the following amount of fertilizer in four years.

CROP.	Yield per Acre.	MARKET VALUE.		Total.
		Phosphorus.	Potassium.	
Corn..........................	55 bu.	$1.12	$0.63	$1.75
Oats..........................	50 bu.	.66	.48	1.14
Wheat.........................	25 bu.	.72	.39	1.11
		2.50	1.50	4.00

A dairy farmer selling whole milk will reduce his fertility only one-fourth as fast as the grain farmer provided he takes proper care of his manure, for nearly 75 per cent of fertilizer value of feed consumed comes back. When butter fat is sold from the farm and all the skim-milk retained, more fertility is kept.

"On a well conducted dairy farm, 70 pounds of butter may be produced per acre which would contain 42-100 of a cent's worth of phosphorus and potassium. In other words, it would take the dairy farmer, selling nothing but butter, 238 years to remove as much value in fertility as the grain farmer would remove in one year, selling an average grain crop."

This shows what we do when we export grain to Denmark and Holland. Which is better economy for American agriculture, to lose this prosperity, or convert it ourselves into butter containing little or no fertility at 25 or more times the price per pound?

At the beginning of this article you have read how prosperous and independent the cotton planter, general farmer and grain raiser in different sections have become. But what of the dairy farmer of whom no mention was made?

The Dane is the best farmer in the world according to some authorities and the secret of his success is intensive dairy farming. Denmark changed in thirty years from the lowest to the highest agricultural country when she changed from excessive grain farming to dairying. Now within only a few years she is considered the most prosperous agricultural country in the world and is exporting butter to England, South America and the Philippines, her butter receipts increasing over 17 fold in thirty years. She sold in 1912 $40,000,000 worth of dairy products to Great Britain alone.

If this is the prosperity we here in New England wish for, then live stock farming and especially dairying should form an important part.

A problem faces the dairyman of this State and to solve it he must be a close student of all the principles of dairying. He must understand that dairying is an occupation requiring brains, thought and skill; that he must have efficient cows, economically fed, and well cared for, that he must practice a definite system of improvement.

Milk production is like a vast chain made up of many links and the final result is no stronger than the weakest links which limit the profits.

The chief obstacle to progressive dairying is carrying it on in a slipshod manner without a well balanced, intensive method needed in producing milk profitably. Many dairymen attempt to make money without the application of business principles. It would be unwise for any man to conduct a losing business when fully aware of what he is doing yet men can be found trying to support a family with a herd of cows utterly unable to return them a profit. That this is a universal fact is shown by the average annual production of the cows in the United States which is only 150 lbs. of butter fat, resulting in a profit of about $1.40 to the owner.

The reader may ask, "How can it be true that the average production is so low and at a loss?" The answer is, "Most dairy farmers do not weigh and test their milk so as to know, in some degree, whether their cows are profitable or not."

They are losing money and are not aware of the fact. Usually they continue in the business, getting an existence by having the rest of the family do a large amount of work without pay. Those men think they know what they are doing, but such an existence and its influence on growing children is worse than failure and a disgrace to the dairy industry.

"There are over 2,000,000 people milking about 18,000,000 cows twice a day in the United States, yet about one-third of this energy is wasted as there are 6,000,000 cows that never did anything to help sustain the farm, and never can or will." Such a waste of energy is appalling. Maine has a total of 138,000 cows averaging less than $26 apiece in valuation.

Lack of intelligence is the only reason why these scrubs and boarder cows are continually bred. Trained and intelligent judgment, based on sound theory and practice, is the factor needed in every dairy community.

The food supply of any people and its cost, are of course one of its most important questions. Since the dairy cow is the most economical producer of human food, of all of our domestic animals, and as she can live and produce milk on a ration composed entirely of roughage, why is she not the animal we will resort to in order to convert half of the energy of our common crops, which are otherwise unavailable, into human food.

The following quotation from Dean Davenport is well worth attention here:

"The population is beginning to overtake production in this country. We have doubled our population four times in a century. By twenty-five years from now at this rate, there will be as many people living at one time and asking for food as have now lived up to this time since America was discovered. In fifty years from now we shall have the population of China in this country, unless something goes wrong, and it is the business of Agriculture to learn how to feed them, and feed them well. We have never gone up against such numbers as are just ahead. There is to be in the very near future a struggle for land and the food it will produce, such as the world has never yet beheld. He who knows where and how to look can see it coming. For us, there are no more new worlds. For us there is no more 'Out West'."

It would seem then, that from now on our problem is how to develop our own agricultural possibilities from the land we now possess. There is no better way to do this than by devoting a part of it to dairy farming.

SUMMARY.

The American dairyman should wake up to a full realization of·his natural advantages, of climate, transportation and good markets with a source of stock food near at hand.

The production of clean milk is what every dairyman must come to before high-standard dairy products can be attained.

The first essential in money making in dairying is to climinate every animal that loses money and work on a system of improvement that may be continued through generations. This does not necessarily mean that pure bred herds must be had.

There must be great opportunities ahead if the dairymen of Denmark can profitably feed our grain and maintain, through dairy exports, her place as one of the most thrifty nations of the world.

When conditions resembling those of Denmark can be found among Maine farmers who now pretend to be dairymen, there will be less wasting of human energy and capital in years of weary unprofitable toil.

If our Middle West can produce grain for Danish farmers and they can feed with profit, there is no reason why Maine dairymen cannot do likewise with even greater profit.

The advance in price of milk has been hampered by the slack methods first employed and the failure at the very beginning to recognize milk according to its real value as a food. Introduction of substitutes has helped to stop any material advance, and so the present problem of producing milk with profit confronts the dairy farmer.

The failure of the consuming public to pay the dairy farmer what he now justly deserves for his product means his failure sooner or later.

A reference table of increase in prices for farm products has been submitted and is worthy the study of all fair minded consumers. Admitting mistakes on the dairyman's part in the past, at present he must have support in his problem. Why is he not entitled to advances in proportion to the advance in prices of other farm products?

It is only when he receives his just due that better dairy farm conditions and better dairy products will result.

MILK; ITS PRODUCTION, CARE AND USE.

By S. C. Thompson, Dairy Division, U. S. Department of Agriculture, Washington, D. C.

Milk is said to constitute 16 per cent of the food of the average American family and it is estimated that an average of 30 gallons are consumed per year by each person. Since milk is used largely in the raw state by infants and invalids as well as by the healthy and robust, it is necessary that it be clean, pure and wholesome. The production and distribution of milk is an industry which has assumed large proportions and represents a large amount of capital, therefore, the subject is of importance to both the consumer and the producer of this product. The producer of milk is interested because he is required to furnish an article that is clean and wholesome; also one that contains the required amount of fat and solids not fat, to meet the standards imposed. He is further interested because he must be able to produce such a product at a profit. The consumer of milk is interested because he must have an article that is pure and wholesome and safe for use in its raw state, regardless of the cost. Both, then, have a common interest in this matter and each should consider the rights of the other.

At the present time there seems to be some misunderstanding on the part of both the producer and the consumer. The producer feels that the consumer is not willing to pay a sufficient price to enable him to produce a satisfactory milk profitably, and the consumer has in some way got the impression that he is forced to pay unnecessarily high prices for milk. Since this product is indispensable to the consumer it seems to me that the claims of each should receive careful consideration from the other with a view of adjusting the differences. It is true that the cost of producing milk has been greatly increased during the last decade. This increase has been brought about by a general advance in the prices which go to make up the cost of production. The cost has also been increased by a general demand for a cleaner and more wholesome article produced under more sanitary conditions. The first item has only kept pace with a general advance in food products while the second item has been found necessary as a protection to the public health, in which the consumer has received the benefits. It is perhaps unfortunate that modern health regulations have imposed additional burdens on the producer of milk at a time when a general advance in the price of his product was necessary since it has tended to further increase this advance. At the same time consumers of milk are receiving a just protection from such regulations and they should be willing to pay the extra cost for producing milk under such superior conditions. It can not be denied that the requirements of health boards have increased the cost of production but they have undoubtedly increased the actual value of the milk from a hygienic standpoint many times over. Therefore, it seems to me that consumers of milk should give careful consideration to the cost of providing for this protection and if it can be proven, as I believe it can, that the producer is not getting an unreasonable price for a safe product, that there should be no objection on their part to the increase which has been asked.

Competent men who have studied milk production have found that it costs about 4 1-2 cents per quart to produce milk that meets the usual requirements with a herd of average cows. Distributors of milk have shown that the cost of transporting, bottling and delivering a quart of milk in our large cities is practically the same amount. On this basis then the cost of producing, handling and marketing milk in the centers of population amounts to about 9 cents per quart for milk of usual quality. An investigation made by the Department of Agriculture the last week in June, 1910, showed that the average price paid by the consumer of milk in 78 of the large cities and towns of the United States was almost exactly 8 cents per quart. In the Northern Atlantic and Northern Central states it was 7.5 cents; in the Western states 8.9 cents; in the Southern Central states 9.1 cents and in the South Atlantic states 9.3

cents. The same investigation showed that the producer received approximately 50 per cent; that the railroads received about 7 per cent and that the retailer received 43 per cent of the consumers' price. If these reports are correct, as I presume they are, then it is evident that consumers in our cities should not expect to buy ordinary milk for less than 9 cents per quart and if they expect a product of unusual quality they should be willing to pay more. If the retailers' price of 8 cents per quart, as shown by this report, is correct, and it actually costs as much or more to produce and distribute the milk, then it is very evident that the producer is not receiving a profitable price for his product provided he is producing a milk of standard quality under proper sanitary methods. It has been estimated by competent authority that the cost of producing milk to meet the requirements of health boards has been increased approximately one cent per quart on a 15 cow dairy for the improved methods and equipment. If the producer is required to sell milk for less than it actually costs him to produce it, he must either reduce the cost of production or go out of business. The figures quoted then show, first, that it costs approximately 9 cents per quart to produce and distribute milk of usual quality in our larger cities; second, that the price paid by consumers is no more than equal to the cost of production; third, that the increase in cost of producing milk to meet health board requirements is approximately one cent per quart. Therefore, we must conclude that either the producer must frequently sell milk of inferior quality or else sell it at a loss. There is no one who can deny that the requirements of health boards regarding milk are a necessary protection to the health of consumers, but if it costs the producer more to raise milk which meets these requirements then they should be willing to pay for this improvement. .

PRODUCTION OF MILK.

The production of milk is one of the most highly specialized branches of agriculture and the successful producer must have a good knowledge of the various branches of farm operation. He must understand handling crops which will give him the greatest amount of desirable feed at all seasons, including roughage, pasture, green feed with which to supplement his pasture during the summer, succulent food for winter and a part at least of the grain used. He also must understand the selection, breeding and care of dairy animals and must know the proper methods for securing clean milk and caring for the same while it remains in his care. A successful producer of milk must be a good judge of dairy cattle in order to secure animals that will produce at a profit. He must understand how to provide stables which can be kept clean with the least amount of labor. He must be able to instruct milkers how to secure milk with the least possible chance of contamination and have suitable facilities for cooling the product and holding it at a low temperature until it leaves the farm and he must provide means for properly washing and sterilizing the utensils used. The work is confining, for if he expects to get good results the milking, feeding and cleaning must be done regularly every day. All of these items represent a considerable outlay of money on which a fair return of interest must be realized, and altogether, such a man must receive a profit if he is to remain in the buisness and make the necessary advancement in his work.

The man who is not making a profit lacks interest and is quite likely to become slack in his habits with the result that he produces an article of poor quality and is finally forced out of business. There was a time when farmers could keep a few cows without paying any special attention to their care. They could sell milk at a price which seemed satisfactory but at the present time with the high cost of feed and labor and with the sanitary requirements to be met, he must select animals capable of producing at a profit, then study their needs to secure the maximum of production consistent with the cost entailed. It is a fact which must not be forgotten that many animals are being kept which do not produce enough milk to pay for their feed and the cost of caring for them. The up-to-date farmer now realizes this and he is striving to weed out the boarders and to keep only those that are capable of producing at a profit. At the time when farmers were satisfied to milk their cows for six months and allow them to go dry the other six months, they figured that what they received was practically all profit as they milked them while they were at pasture and fed them coarse, inexpensive fodder during the winter. Modern dairying has shown that this is not the most profitable way to handle animals and while the modern methods require more skill and increased cost there is no question that with proper animals, under skilled management, a greater profit can now be secured. The increase in the price of milk and other dairy products has made the profitable dairy cow more valuable than ever before and on the other hand the increased price of feed and labor has made the unprofitable animal more worthless than before. If it costs $100 a year to feed and care for a cow producing 2000 quarts of milk, which sells for 4 cents a quart, and there are plenty of such cows in existence, it is plain to see that a loss of $20 has been sustained; but if a cow produces 3500 quarts of milk, which sells at 4 cents, at a cost of $125, and it is possible to breed such animals, a clean profit of $15 per cow is shown. It is, therefore, evident that if milk is to be produced at a profit with the present prices prevailing it is necessary to keep only such cows as will produce at a profit and to discard all others. All dairymen must sooner or later realize this fact or they will be forced out of business. The ordinary cow is no longer profitable and a better class of animals must be secured by careful and scientific selection, breeding, feeding and care. Conditions today make it necessary for successful dairymen to be better equipped with both practical and scientific knowledge and to apply business principles to their work. The time is past when dairying, or any other business for that matter, can be profitably done in an unsystematic slipshod manner. But the man who is thoroughly equipped for this work can make a good profit out of dairying and have a most interesting and attractive business.

CARE AND USE OF MILK.

The purity and wholesomeness of milk depend almost entirely on the care it receives after being drawn from the cow. Milk when drawn from a healthy cow is practically sterile and is in its best condition for feeding and other purposes. It is, however, impossible to deliver it to the consumer immediately after it is milked.   It is usually contaminated during the various processes of handling and proper care is necessary to reduce this contamination to the minimum.   In an up-to-date dairy the flanks and udder of the cows are brushed before milking and wiped with a damp cloth to remove any loose particles of dirt that may be there.   The hands of the milkers are clean and are kept dry during the milking process.   Precautions are taken to prevent dust from circulating in the air during the period of milking and the utensils used are thoroughly cleaned, sterilized and properly aired before being used.   As soon as the milk is drawn from the cow it is taken at once from the stable and immediately cooled, then either put in bottles for delivery to customers or placed in cans preparatory to shipping to the distributing plant in the city.   If it is to be kept over night on the farm, it is usually placed in a tank of ice water to keep it cold and is protected from all contaminating influences. If milk is shipped in cans to the distributor in the city it should be carefully examined when received, and unless it was produced under conditions known to be safe it should be thoroughly pasteurized in order to retard souring and to kill any pathogenic germs which may be present.   After being heated it should be thoroughly cooled, then bottled for delivery.   If the producer and the distributor have done their work properly then the customer receives each morning a bottle of clean, cold, pure milk but this does not necessarily insure a wholesome product when it is consumed, since it may become contaminated after being opened by the consumer.   Very often the housewife has no ice or other means of cooling the milk and occasionally it is allowed to undergo changes before being used, which render it unwholesome.   Often it is placed in a refrigerator used for other foods which impart a disagreeable flavor and while it may not be rendered unwholesome it does become unpalatable.   Probably flies are the most dangerous source of contamination of milk in the home as they often make it unsafe for use, especially for children.   Milk should be placed where it will keep cool immediately after delivery and it should never be allowed to set where the rays of the sun will strike it.   If placed in a refrigerator it should be in a compartment directly under the ice as cold air settles.   Milk which has been exposed to the air and allowed to warm up should not be returned to the vessel from which it was taken as such a practice is likely to cause rapid deterioration. Empty bottles should be thoroughly cleaned before being returned to the dealer. This is best done by first rinsing in lukewarm water, then thoroughly washing and scalding. Dealers should always rewash the bottles before refilling but washing at the home is necessary in order that they may not be returned in a filthy condition. Milk, as a rule, should be used within 24 hours of the time of its delivery as changes take place which render old milk undesirable to use even though it is still sweet. If proper precautions are taken in handling milk at the farm, in the distributing plant, and in the home, the product is a very wholesome and desirable article of food. Milk of average quality contains about 87 per cent of water, 3.7 per cent of fat and 9.3 per cent of solids not fat, although the composition of milk varies considerably, depending largely upon the breed of cows and the period of lactation; but as nearly every city has a standard for milk the, consumer is usually protected against an abnormally low food value. A quart of milk is said to contain as much nutritive value as three-fourths of a pound of average beef or eight eggs and even at ten cents per quart is usually cheaper than either of these commodities. There is no doubt that a freer use of milk would often provide a more satisfactory diet at less cost than is now generally obtained. This economy, however, would be secured by serving it in the place of other foods instead of using it as a beverage. The following extract from a publication on the food value of milk by Caroline L. Hunt presents some ideas on the use of milk which may be used to advantage in many homes:

"*****It is very often economical to serve milk in place of other foods, but extravagant to add it to a meal which from the point of view of nourishment is already adequate. The following menu is given, which may be called a 'milkless' bill of fare, as no milk is supplied, except in so far as it enters into the composition of the cake or other dishes:

Breakfast.—Oranges, eggs on toast, coffee with cream.
Luncheon.—Cold lamb, potato salad, tea, bread and butter, preserves, and plain cake.
Dinner.—Sirloin steak, potatoes, asparagus, bread and butter, strawberry shortcake.

The nourishment in such a bill of fare, which has been selected not because it is any more desirable than a thousand others which might have been chosen, but merely to give something to discuss, would of course depend on the size of the portions served. For the purpose of giving some idea of how large the portions should be, let us imagine that the family being served consists of a man, a woman, a boy of 15, and a girl of 12. It is quite generally agreed that this family would usually eat and would, in fact, need about 3.3 as much food as one man would need. Without going into all the figures, it may be considered that such a family would get enough nourishment from the above bill of fare, if the amounts of foods used per day were 2 pounds of meat, 1 1-2 pounds of flour, 3-4 pound of butter (or of butter and other fats, oil, or drippings), 1 pint of cream, 6 eggs, 3-4 pound of sugar, 4 oranges, 2 pounds of potatoes, 1 bunch of asparagus, 1 box of berries and 1 pint of canned fruit. These materials would supply the required fuel and would give 11 1-2 ounces of proteids, the amount usually considered to be needed each day by the family of the size given above. The cost of food materials, in case meat is 20 cents a pound, butter 40 cents, eggs 24 cents a dozen, coffee 35 cents a pound, cream 20 cents a pint, oranges 30 cents a dozen, potatoes $1 a bushel, asparagus 15 cents a bunch, and strawberries 15 cents a box, would be not far from $1.60.

If milk were taken as a beverage in addition to the other materials in this bill of fare, every quart so used would increase the proteids unnecessarily by more than an ounce. When it is considered that the entire allowance for the 4 people per day is only 11 1-2 ounces, it will be seen that this addition is quite significant. The addition of a quart of milk would raise the cost of the food by 8 or 9 cents. A glass of milk taken as a beverage at each meal by every person, amounting to 3 quarts per day, would add 3 1-2 ounces of proteids to the daily diet and 27 cents to the cost of the food materials for the entire family.

But if, instead of adding the milk to the other foods, it were substituted for some of them, and 3 quarts of milk were purchased instead of half a pint of cream, it could either be used as a beverage or it would supply one-half pint of cream for tea and coffee, 1 pint of half milk and half cream for use on cereals or puddings, and 2 1-4 quarts of skimmed milk for cooking. A bill of fare which would utilize this milk is as follows:

Breakfast.—Oranges, oatmeal with half milk and half cream, coffee with cream.
Luncheon.—Eggs on toast, lettuce, bread and butter, tea, old-fashioned rice pudding (1 quart of milk, ¼ cup sugar, ¼ cup of rice, flavoring.)
Dinner.—Cream of tomato soup, sirloin steak, creamed potatoes, strawberry shortcake

So far as the nutritive value is concerned, the milk with the addition of the small amounts of oatmeal and the rice contained in this bill of fare would take the place of the cream, part of the potatoes, 1 pound of meat, the preserves, and the cake of the first bill of fare. Using the same sort of data with respect to food prices, the computed cost of the second bill of fare would be about 23 cents less than that of the first.

The above is one specific example taken merely for purposes of illustration of the way in which milk may be substituted for other foods. In general, in making this substitution, the fact given on another page that a quart of milk is equal in nutritive value to three-fourths of a pound of beef or 8 eggs should be kept in mind. Or, to give the equivalent in smaller amounts, a cup of milk is equal to 3 ounces of lean beef or 2 eggs in total nourishment."

Let me urge upon consumers of milk to carefully investigate the source of their supply and if they find it to be pure, wholesome and of standard quality to increase the quantity used in the interest of economy; also not to question a reasonable price for a desirable article. I would urge upon producers of milk that they furnish a product of high grade and that they insist on reasonable prices for the same; also that they study the question of milk production in order to improve their conditions and to increase their profits to a reasonable degree. If this advice is followed more satisfaction will result to all.

There has been a tendency on the part of the producers to estimate the cost of production too low. For that reason I think the farmer should get away from what I believe is a mistaken idea that he can produce milk for 2 or 2 1-2 cents a quart, by producing the feed and giving the benefit of the feed that he produces to the cow and in that way figuring the cost

of production. One of the reasons why the average farmer in
this country has not succeeded better is because he does not know
absolutely what it costs him. He figures that he had so much
money at the beginning of the year, that he fed and clothed
himself and his family, perhaps he sent some of his children
away to school, he may have put $50 or $100 into the bank, and
he feels that he was prosperous and that he was making some
money because he has done this and at the end of the year
he has his herd of cows and his buildings are kept up. Now
a man ought to be able to earn his living and a living for his
family and get more than $50 or $100. That is where the
farmer, I believe, has made a mistake. He has been contented
with getting a living and a small margin of profit, without
considering the actual value that has been put into the production of his crops and his milk. I think our weak point today
is the fact that we are not applying business principles, and by
business principles I mean an absolute record of the money that
we receive and that we pay out and what it costs us to produce
potatoes per acre and milk per quart, and such other operations as go to make up our farm operations. If we did that we
would be surprised at the results, and would be on our guard,
and I believe it would make us better business men and make
us more prosperous.

MR. GUPTILL—I coincide with Mr. Thompson in his belief in
this respect to quite an extent. For instance, I introduced the
subject here for the consideration of this audience, of business
principles in selling exactly what the law demanded and no
more. I did it to see how the audience would take it. As a
matter of fact, the farmers of this State do not make the laws.
Somebody else makes the laws and sets up the standards. I
cannot see that the farmer can afford to sell milk which is
above standard unless he gets extra pay for it. Yet Mr. Thompson said in his address that you should produce extra nice milk
and try to teach the people to come up to it. If a man drives a
milk route in a city, working night and day to make a living,
it is a different proposition.

MR. THOMPSON—My idea of a first class, high grade product
is not necessarily a milk rich in fat, but it is a milk that is pure
and wholesome. I agree with you to a certain extent on this

standard proposition, but the other point I wanted to make was this,—that a man who feels that he is producing a high grade product is in a position to charge more money for it, and I would consider that a more satisfactory business than dealing in a low grade product.

MR. GUPTILL—I think that the proposition as far as producing a clean wholesome product from healthy, vigorous cows is concerned, is all right, but it is the economic feature that I wanted to bring out. In regard to Mr. Thompson's statement about farmers being business men and conducting their business on business principles, of course we know that every man who has a farm worth $3.500 has got it stocked with a pair of horses which cost him $500,. we will say, and if he is in the milk business to a certain extent—and every man ought to be to the extent of ten cows—within bounds there is $500 for the cows. His horses and cows cost him $1,000, and if he has a riding wagon, express wagon and market wagon, as well as harnesses and tools, he has another thousand invested. He has his furniture in his house and his dairy appliances, which will cost him from $500 to $750, making $2750, which added to the price of the farm. $3,500, would make $6,250 invested in his farm. Those horses and tools are losing in value every day. As a matter of fact we do not enter into these things. We ought to demand as good a showing as a man who has $6,500 invested in a store. The farmers are not insistent enough in their demand. People will say to us that we should get up a little earlier and work a little harder and we will make a little more money. As a matter of fact, that is not a proposition for us to consider. We should work only eight hours, the same as the man who works in the mill, the carpenter shop, or the blacksmith shop and when food supplies become short something will happen. But we hang to the 15 hour system instead of the 8 hour, and labor becomes scarcer and scarcer. There is no use in producing food at a loss. If you are doing business, do it on business principles, and insist that you get what should come to you.

MR. SMITH—Granting the statement that a man who is selling milk for a business should not sell milk much above the state standard, I find in my inspection work that the majority of the men who are selling milk do not know exactly what the milk tests, and they have no knowledge of the sanitary quality. In times gone by we have tried to point out to the average milkman that it is for his interest to patronize meetings such as we have here, with milk contests, and to the dairymen who are making butter and cheese that they should patronize these places and find out the exact quality of their product and learn their efficiency as producers of sanitary butter, milk, cream and cheese. The majority of them do not have the interest in the business that they should. Why is it uot a safe and sane proposition for a milkman to know the exact quality of his milk, the exact per cent of fat, and then demand from the consuming public a price which will compensate him for its production, on a definite basis. There are so many now who do not know what they are selling. They know they are selling milk, and the consumer takes it for granted that the milk is of ordinary quality. And when a milkman in a city undertakes to increase the price of milk, he has got to show to the consuming public that the quality is better. The dairyman should patronize the dairy shows or the milk contests where milk and cream are scored for quality, and find out definitely the quality of his product and then he is in a position to demand from the public a corresponding price.

MR. THOMPSON—I believe there should be a standard for the bacteria, and then the milk should be paid for according to the amount of butter fat.

MARKETING FARM PRODUCTS AND PURCHASING FARM SUPPLIES CO-OPERATIVELY.

By C. E. Embree.

We are met to discuss the question of marketing and while my remarks will be entirely out of the usual methods of treating the subject, I will, nevertheless, enter into the very foundation of marketing and point the way whereby the producer shall realize more for his product.

I believe we have reached an era in the history of farm praetices when business methods are more important than even the coming together of the dairymen of the State to discuss conditions affecting the business in which they are engaged.

You are met here to gather information from the experience and investigations of the individual in the hope that you will be able to carry back to your homes these experiences which others have found profitable and apply them for the betterment of your individual dairy.

For years you have had your Experimental Stations, your Agricultural Colleges or Universities and the Institute meetings, and from all these sources scientific knowledge has been sent abroad, reaching every farming community it mattered not how isolated.

Because of these Colleges and other valuable sources of information the farmer has now a very thorough knowledge of soil conditions and is able to treat these conditions both scientifically and practically. He knows the principal elements of plant food and their relations to the various plants; he now knows the meaning of the analyses on the bags of fertilizer and if informed as to the cost of the ingredients that enter into the make-up of a complete fertilizer, he can figure the money value of the mixture. In fact, from a scientific standpoint the farmer is well equipped to farm along correct lines, in that he is able to get from the soil the last pound it is capable of producing. If I am asked what more is required, my answer would be prompt and to the point,—"Better business methods in the conduct of the farm and strict attention to marketing methods."

If the farming population of the State of Maine realized the importance of better business methods, before another month had passed away meetings would be called from one end of the State to the other and the farmers would act as a unit in adopting some method which had proved the salvation of other farming communities. In the past the farmers of this and other countries have stood in the background with hands outstretched asking for government aid. Instead of doing this and waiting for others to act for them, they should have taken the initiative and forced themselves to enter into the busy marts of trade on an equality with the man of the town or city.

The first thing for the farmer to overcome is his lack of confidence not only in himself but in his fellow farmer. In order to overcome this unfortunate condition he must first consider his importance to the country and how far he has entered into the building and maintaining of this great and prosperous Nation. He must remember that it was the farmer army who gained the independence of the Colonies and brought forth upon this continent a new Nation conceived in liberty and dedicated to the proposition that all men are created free and equal. He must remember that at the close of the struggle he became the advance guard at the outposts of civilization where he prepared the way for others to follow. At the breaking out of the war with Mexico, and Indian uprising, to further convince the Mother country that America was determined to be free he again appeared in the ranks with his musket, but when peace was declared he again returned to the business of feeding the Nation. For six score and sixteen years he has tilled the soil under a free government right here in the State of Maine and carried on his business in a way that has not brought to him more than 50 per cent of what was rightly his. He has seen the bright boys of the farm go to the city and there become millionaires in some cases, and these boys left the farm for the reason that their fathers could not show them a profit on the farm.

Up to a very short time ago the farmer gloried in the prosperity of the city and was willing to toil on without receiving sufficient to maintain him except in a very ordinary way. In the past he has depended upon others instead of relying upon himself. He has stood in the markets and asked "How much will you take? How much will you give?" Thousands who never sow or reap have become wealthy from what the farmer produces. He has bought his fertilizer on November payment, paying 24 per cent interest for the use of the money and in this way annually sends out of the State nearly 300,000 dollars to enrich other states, while the banks of his own State have not sufficient funds to finance even the business men of the city.

It is useless to point out undesirable conditions without suggesting a remedy. This remedy could have been applied years ago but the farmers of Maine have not until recently realized what others have accomplished along the lines of progress. I feel that I cannot too urgently impress upon the farmers of the State the importance of the movement started by the Agricultural Department one year ago. In the years to come when the history of the Farmers' Union of Maine is written due credit will be given the present Commissioner for his effort to better farm conditions by opening the way for the farmer to become a business man.

At this time perhaps it might be well to outline the objects and purposes of the Farmers' Union of Maine and its relations to the seventeen or eighteen auxiliaries, or rather their relations to the "Farmers' Union."

The plan at the start was to first lay the foundation at the farm, to place the farmer in control at the loading station, to have him control the business methods of the "Farmers' Union" and also the salesman in the city.

In accordance with this plan local organizations were formed in most of the important producing centers and these organizations were formed under the laws of Maine. Most of these corporations were incorporated with $10,000 capital stock and the shares placed at from $10.00 to $20.00.

Each organization elected a full corps, including from three to five directors and the business was placed in their hands between the annual meetings. The first cost of organizing amounts to $25.00 which goes to various State Departments. In every case the local affiliated with the Farmers' Union of Maine by purchasing 5 shares of stock at $10.00 per share. The 'Farmers' Union" was organized in June last by representatives from the locals. All the officers are members of some local and the general board of management is made up of one director from each of the locals, therefore the business of the Farmers' Union is in the hands of the locals or the farmers themselves. The Farmers' Union is what might be called a selling and buying agency for the locals. The Manager of the Farmers' Union transacts the business in accordance with the instructions of the Board and does not handle a dollar of the funds of the loeals and in fact depends upon the locals for all sources of revenue with which to meet expenses. When the locals or an individual stockholder desires to ship a car of his product he notifies the Manager of the Farmers' Union who secures a bid and if the bid is satisfactory to the loader he ships the car with draft attached to bill of lading and collects back every cent the car was sold for. The only cost is a cent and a half per bushel for potatoes, which the loader pays the Farmers' Union to meet the expenses locally and in the market center.

If at the end of the year the money received is more than sufficient to meet the running expenses it is paid back to the locals in the way of a dividend. It will thus be noted that the responsibility rests with the farmer. Again, the farmer's organization places him in a position to buy his supplies at the lowest market price and wholesale prices. In my opening remarks I stated that I would go to the foundation of marketing and now let us see if I have made good that statement.

The market to day is 70 cents per bushel for potatoes delivered at N. Y. City. If the car is to go to thirty-third street from Maine Central points the rate is 23 cents per hundred which is about 14 cents per bushel and the Heater charges are 3 1-2 cents per bushel which makes 17 1-2 per bushel and this together with cost of selling amounts to 19 cents, therefore the farmer has received 51 cents per bushel.

The cost for freight and Heater charges and all other costs amount to 19 cents, leaving a balance of 51 cents. Therefore it will be understood that the farmer has received every cent the stock was sold for, less the expense of sending it to the market. This in my estimation is the very foundation of marketing for the farmer. In this way he gets as near the market as it is possible under present conditions.

There is a movement that has gained considerable headway in New York and other large cities in the way of the consumers' coöperative stores, and these stores propose to buy direct from the producer. Even if they do buy direct it is doubtful if higher prices can be obtained from them than can be obtained from the dealers who sell the grocers.

The selling of the product of the farm is only one part of the benefits that the farmers will secure through organization. As a rule the farmer gives more attention to selling than to buying and on this account thousands of dollars are being paid out every year that can be saved through organizing. The Farmers' Union is now buying grain, flour and stable goods and soon will be furnishing the exchanges with practically everything required at wholesale prices. The rural problem which interests our government. our colleges and many public spirited citizens will never be solved by these agencies.

The future of the farmer rests with him and him only. The American farmer is not a serf. He must have adequate remuneration for his labor. The popular cry, "Back to the farm!" will prove a passing hobby unless it can be demonstrated that farming is not only a profitable occupation, but that the farmer can be surrounded by the comforts and conveniences of modern life.

The individual farmer may study scientific methods of farming with pleasure and profit, but the vital question of marketing must be solved, if solved at all, by the coöperation of individuals.

COST OF MILK PRODUCTION.

Compiled from the South Lyndeboro Cow Test Association,
and from other sources.

By Fred Rasmussen, Professor of Dairying, New Hampshire
College.

INTRODUCTION.

The South Lyndeboro Cow Test Association began operations January 15, 1911, with Mr. B. C. Higgins as official tester.
Mr. Higgins made a visit to each farm once a month, weighed
and tested the milk produced, and weighed and figured the feed
consumed and profit made by each cow during the twenty-four
hours, which was used as a basis for the month's record. The
results were entered in the farmer's herd book, which is always
in the possession of the farmer and in the Association Record
Book which is kept by the tester. At the end of the year each
farmer was given a complete record of the production of individual cows and a herd summary.

CONDITION OF HERDS.

Through the South Lyndeboro Cow Test Association data
were collected on the feed cost of milk production from twenty-
six herds comprising 325 cows. Of these 288 or 88.4 were
grades or cows of mixed breeding, 37 or 11.6 per cent were
pure bred cows. The conditions for an economic production
from these herds is a great deal better than the average New
Hampshire conditions (1) because the cows are above the
average as found in the State. The United States Department
of Agriculture in a field survey in coöperation with the New

Hampshire Experiment Station found the average production to be 5062 pounds per cow, while the average of the above mentioned herds was 6463.2 pounds. (2) Because the farmers during the year had the opportunity of monthly receiving expert advice on the feeding and other factors entering into economic production of milk. Also the discussions at the monthly meetings showed that the majority of the farmers fed liberally and studied the whole proposition of economic production. (3) The fact that 103 cows were sold before the end of the year, most of them because they were found unprofitable, tends to show a higher production and a higher profit per cow, than if they had been kept for the whole year.

VALUATION OF FEED AND PRODUCT.

Grain is charged at the actual price paid. The price for cottonseed meal ranged from $32 to $36; bran $27 to $30; gluten $27 to $35; corn meal $22 to $33; mixed feed $30 to $33; and Ajax $31.60 to $35; dried beet pulp $27 to $28 per ton.

Hay raised on the farm is charged at the price the farmer could obtain in his barn. The price per ton is as follows: Timothy hay, $15 to $20: mixed hay, $15 to $18; meadow hay, $8 to $12. Corn silage is charged at $3.00 and green millet and green fodder at $2.50 per ton.

The price charged for hay was determined by the owner and the tester, taking into consideration the market price and quality of the hay.

Silage and green feeds are not quoted on the market and are, therefore, the most difficult product upon which to place a price. Possibly a fair method of determining the value of silage when considering the cost of milk production on a particular farm, would be to figure the land rent upon which the silage is grown and all the actual expense of raising the corn and placing it in the silo. In this case it was agreed upon and seemed the best to place the price at $3.00 per ton.

The pasture was charged at from $.25 to $1.00 per month. Anyone acquainted with New Hampshire conditions and the dry summers can easily understand this wide variation. In figuring money value of product the actual market price for milk the farmer obtained was used.

HERD SUMMARY.

Table I shows the production of milk and butter fat; feed cost of production; profit above feed cost; returns for $1.00 worth of food consumed; and the cost of producing 100 lbs. of milk.

Herd.	Average No. of cows.	Lbs. of milk.	Lbs. of butterfat.	Milk value.	Cost feed.	Profit.	Returns, $1.00.	Milk cost, 100 lbs.
1	5.0	5,282.3	218.39	$81 26	$62 44	$18 82	$1 30	$1 18
2	6.3	6,393.9	250.00	113 83	68 77	44 06	1 65	1 07
3	15.9	6,398.4	219.51	116 07	67 18	48 87	1 73	1 05
4	8.9	7,025.9	261.09	95 85	71 96	23 77	1 33	1 02
5	14.6	5,047.5	185.59	84 13	52 12	38 83	1 61	1 03
6	10	5,669.6	208.78	104 70	55 29	49 45	1 89	97
7	17.7	6,587.4	242.68	116 77	78 56	38 21	1 49	1 19
8	4.5	7,110.3	271.43	130 12	71 52	58 60	1 82	1 00
9	4	4,981.7	222.35	76 33	48 93	27 40	1 56	98
10	5.5	7,341.4	280.36	130 57	86 45	44 12	1 51	1 18
11	7.8	7,605.6	281.38	140 00	69 54	70 46	2 01	91
12	20.8	7,929.8	308.43	148 38	87 63	60 85	1 69	1 10
13	62.7	6,157.1	237.39	113 35	82 46	30 94	1 37	1 34
14	21	7,662.6	316.33	140 33	87 25	53 08	1 61	1 14
15	6.2	5,575.9	209.15	97 13	62 74	34 69	1 55	1 12
16	38.9	5,697.2	212.07	104 61	68 82	35 79	1 52	1 21
17	10.1	7,379.9	270.04	140 40	81 54	58 86	1 72	1 10
18	10	6,315.5	225.96	117 46	73 50	43 96	1 59	1 16
19	5.8	5,930.8	224.24	108 72	65 09	43 63	1 67	1 10
20	9.9	5,645.8	216.95	104 00	52 90	51 10	1 97	95
21	10.2	5,247.7	199.01	92 93	49 08	43 85	1 89	93
22	8.6	6,406.7	221.74	111 70	59 70	52 00	1 87	93
23	9.7	8,079.3	266.33	145 99	83 98	62 02	1 74	1 04
24	10	8,444.0	300.90	152 28	80 74	71 54	1 89	96
Av.	325.1	6,463.2	243.6	$116 42	$73 03	$43 77	$1 59	$1 13

The average per cent of fat from the milk of all the cows is 3.76 per cent. The average cost of feed per can (18 pounds) is 20.3 cents or $1.13 per 100 pounds.

All of the above herds may be compared on the basis of production, cost of feed, and cost of producing milk, as the results for all herds are figured the same.

Although the product from the greater number of the herds was sold as milk, in a few cases it was sold as cream and comparison can not therefore be made of all of the herds on the money value received for the product.

COWS COMPLETING A YEAR'S WORK.

Of the 325 cows in the Association 103 were sold during the year, seven died, five were killed and the records of seven for other reasons cannot be considered when making comparisons, leaving 203 cows only with absolute complete records for the year.

TABLE 2. SUMMARY OF AVERAGES.

No.—Amount.	Lbs. of Milk.	Lbs. of fat.	Total cost.	Profit above feed cost	Roughage.	Grain.	Milk cost of 100 lbs.	Cost of 1 lb. B. F.	Returns, $1.00.
Highest Producer...	12,275	463.50	$106 80	$119 23	48.56	58.24	$ 87	$ 228	$2 12
8—10,000-over....	10,875	380 3	$88 59	$106 82	37.33	51.26	$0 81	$0.2328	$2 21
14—9,000-10,000....	9,396	343.4	88 25	79 18	38.23	50.02	93	.2592	1 90
26—8,000-9,000.....	8,434	301.3	83 46	63 86	38.29	45.17	98	.2729	1 77
41—7,000-8,000.....	7,381	277.1	81 18	52 11	38.47	42.72	1 10	.2929	1 64
40—6,000-7,000.....	6,499	239.6	73 59	43 65	37 50	36.09	1 13	.3071	1 59
39—5,000-6,000.....	5,540	209 3	65 91	34 56	33.76	32.14	1 19	.3147	1 52
25—4,000-5,000.....	4,605	176.0	56 61	27 20	29.58	27.02	1 23	.3216	1 48
10—4,000-less......	3,061	117.4	57 22	-4 25	36 62	20.61	1 86	.4874	93
Average of whole	7,094	262.3	$83 04	$49 48	38.17	39.66	$ 87	-	$1 59

Table No. 2 shows the production, cost of production, and profit above feed cost of 203 cows completing a year's work. The cows are classified in order of the amount of milk produced.

Table No. 2 is exceedingly striking and interesting. It shows a decrease in profit with a decrease in production. The eight highest producers gave an average profit of $106.82 above feed cost while the ten lowest producers failed to pay for their feed, losing on an average of $4.25. The return for $1.00 worth of food consumed varied from $2.21 to $.93; the cost of producing 100 pounds of milk from $.81 to $1.86.

Cows that produced less than 4000 pounds of milk per year did not give enough milk to pay for their feed. The cows here recorded only returned $.93 for every dollar's worth of food consumed. In addition there was no return for labor or housing or interest on investment on such cows.

The columns "Profit above feed cost of producing 100 lbs. of milk" and "Returns for $1.00 worth of feed" show clearly that the largest producers on the average are the most profitable.

The average feed cost for the eight cows producing over 10,000 pounds of milk is quite low, due to the fact that four of the eight cows were fed heavily on silage, as high as 45 pounds per day, with meadow hay and oat hay as roughage.

In the case of one of these cows the value of roughage was
recorded at $28.22 while the grain bill was $61.21. The cows
calved late in the fall and were fed some grain on pasture.

In comparing the cost of roughage with that of grain with
cows producing 7000 pounds of milk or over, the cost of grain
exceeded that of roughage; while with cows giving below 7000
pounds of milk the cost of roughage exceeded that of grain.

It was found that in every herd were some good and some
poor cows. It is interesting to note that the herd having the
highest producer and the most profitable of all the cows in the
association also had the lowest producer and the least profitable
cow.

The following table shows the highest and lowest producer in
three respective herds :—

	Milk.	Fat.	Feed Cost.	Profit.	Cost, 100 Lbs. Milk.	Cost, 1 Lb. Fat.	Return, $1.00.
1...............	12,275	463.5	$106 80	$119 00	$ 87	$ 23	$2 12
2...............	1,540	60.4	44 73	−15 38	2 90	74	66
3...............	9,773	351.2	96.21	76 88	98	27	1 80
4...............	3,824	155.3	69.28	−5 15	1 81	45	92
5...............	8,410	307.3	83.58	65 11	99	27	1 78
6...............	4,845	227.3	73 83	16 44	1 52	32	1 22

Cow No. 1 equals 7 like No. 6 in profit.
Cow No. 5 equals 4 like No. 6 in profit.

These cows had the same care and treatment. The difference
in production and profit represents the difference in milking ability and capacity of the individual cows.

Cow No. 6 represents about the average production in the
State of New Hampshire. No. 1 therefore would be equal in
profits to seven average cows of the State.

A comparison of No. 5 and No. 6 should be especially interesting as a great many farmers would have just such a case.
Although No. 5 gave 3565 lbs. more than No. 6 it cost only $9.75
more to feed No. 5 than No. 6. No. 6 gave a profit above feed
cost of $16.44 while No. 5 gave a profit of $65.11 or four times
as great. One of the main reasons for the small difference in

cost of feed and the large difference in profit is this: It takes from 35 to 60 per cent of all a cow can eat for her maintenance ration. A cow of limited capacity to consume food frequently does not eat enough in addition to her maintenance ration to produce enough product to pay for all the food consumed. This type is illustrated by No. 2 and No. 4.

Some cases like No. 6 produced enough milk to pay for the maintenance ration and the food utilized for production, but the percentage of food available for milk production is still small and consequently the profit is small.

Good cows like Nos. 1, 3, and 5 use a smaller portion of all food consumed for maintenance and hence more food is available for production, resulting in larger profits; the profit generally increasing with an increase in quantity of food consumed.

Capacity, although not the only factor to be considered in connection with a large production, is absolutely necessary in a good dairy cow.

Cows Nos. 1, 3, and 5 represent the hope and the future of the dairy business, while Nos. 2, 4, and 6 represent the present despair. Cows of the former type are a source of pleasure and profit while those of the latter are a source of discontent, drudgery and loss.

Cows of the type of No. 2 and No. 4 are not the greatest danger to the profits and to the future of the dairy business as they are so poor that even the least observing dairyman will realize they are unprofitable and will dispose of them. Cow No. 6 is a greater danger. The man who does not keep records of his cows assumes that such a cow is profitable and he not only keeps her but often breeds her to an inferior bull and raises heifers of the same limited capacity for production and for profits.

These figures like those in table No. 2, emphasize that the larger the yield of milk the greater the profit.

COST OF KEEPING COW PER YEAR.

In considering the cost of milk production the cost of feed is only one factor; in fact it is sometimes less than one-half the expense of keeping a cow.

Most of the following figures on cost of milk production are obtained from records of the South Lyndeboro Cow Test Association; others are from records obtained from other farms. It is fully believed, however, that the figures are a conservative estimate on the yearly expenses entering into the production of milk on a dairy farm in New Hampshire.

SUMMARY OF COST.

Debit.

Cost of feed	$73	03
Labor	32	33
Delivery	7	18
Housing	9	05
Depreciation on cow	8	83
Bedding	4	00
Bull	3	79
Taxes, interest	4	55
Ice, coal and wood for heating	2	17
Veterinarian		87
Tools, utensils, salt		53
Cow Test Association expenses per cow	1	40
	$147	73

Credit.

Manure	$15	00	
Calf	3	00	18 00
			$129 73

ITEMIZED STATEMENT OF COST OF KEEPING A COW.

The following will explain methods of deriving at the above figures :—

COST OF FEED.

The figures on the cost of feed are from records of twenty-five herds comprising 325 cows, obtained by B. C. Higgins in charge of the South Lyndeboro Cow Test Association.

LABOR.

From a number of inquiries it was found that the average wage paid hired men on dairy farms varied from $20 to $30 a month with board and room, and from $40 to $55 without. Nearly every New Hampshire farmer whether in the business on a small or a large scale takes an active part in the dairy work and since no charge is made for manager's services one dollar and fifty cents per day is a moderate wage.

On a number of specialized dairy farms where the men taking care of the cattle are not required to do other work each man takes care of 15 cows. The cost of labor under those conditions would be $36.00 per cow per year.

Milking.

Wages per day	$1 50
Wages per hour	15
Average No. of cows 1 man can milk per hour	7
Cost of milking 1 cow	.021
Cost per day of milking one cow	.042
300 days at .042	$12 60

At first thought seven cows per hour looks like a small number and no doubt there are farmers who average more. On farms where poor cows are kept and where no preparations are made before milking, and where no records are kept, and the milker empties the milk pail only for every three cows milked, the number sometimes reaches nine or ten. However, these figures are based upon weighing and recording each cow's milk, and considering also the many factors such as unusually hard milkers, inflamed udder, teat troubles, and flies in the summer time, which all tend to decrease the average. On many farms the average is only six cows per hour, which will increase the cost of milking from $12.60 to $15.00 per cow per year.

Handling milk and cleaning Utensils. The handling of the milk, the icing, including the removal of ice from the ice house, and the cleaning of the utensils twice a day will take on the average one hour per day.

365 days at $.15, per cow $2 73

Care of Cow. The care of the cow, feeding, preparing feed, cleaning cow, and barn at 15 cts. per hour, $17.00

DELIVERY.

The cost of delivering milk from the farm to the station varies from two to three cents per can. In most cases the milk is delivered for two cents a can. If the dairyman delivers his own milk to the station it will cost more. Especially is this true when hauling small quantities long distances. Also the cost of delivery when based on the number of cans of milk produced will vary with the amount of milk produced by each cow. Taking the average production per cow as found in South Lyndeboro Cow Test Association, 6463.2 pounds of milk or 359 cans.

359 cans at two cents $7 18

HOUSING.

Under housing is considered the cow barn, barn for storing feed, silo, and places for handling and storing of the milk. From estimate of buildings of members of South Lyndeboro Cow Test Association this part of the equipment was valued at $2000 for twenty cows. The buildings for 10 to 20 cows will cost almost as much, while for a larger number, as 20 to 30 or more, the cost per cow will be considerably less.

The tax rate of $1.59 used for this figure is the average tax rate for the State for 1913 as reported by the Tax Commission.

Repairs and depreciation are rated at 3 per cent on the capital invested. On new buildings this rate is high, but with the age of a barn the repairs will increase. When the repairs on the buildings exceed the interest on the investment they should be rebuilt. By that time the amount of money set aside each year for depreciations and repairs over the actual cost and not used when placed at interest should have accumulated to a sum sufficient to build new buildings.

Estimated value of buildings for 20 cows $2,000
Interest on $2,000 at 5 per cent...... $100 00
Taxes, assessed value of buildings
$1,000 at 1.59 per cent 15 90

Insurance, $1,500—1 per cent for 3
    years; per year $5 00
Repairs, depreciation, 3 per cent to-
    tal value; per year 60 00
Housing per cow $9 05

DEPRECIATION OF COW.

During the last two years dairy cows have increased considerably in value. This year on the Brighton market, Mass., good grade cows of good size having the appearance of being able to produce from 6000 to 8000 lbs of milk have found a ready market at from $100 to $135 and in a few cases even higher. According to the last census the average value per cow in the State is given at $38.67. No doubt this is lower than actual value. In the section from which these figures are taken the average value is estimated at $75.00.

The depreciation per cow is a most difficult factor to determine as it varies with the value of the cow. A poor dairy cow is worth almost as much for beef as for dairy purposes; in reality she is worth more as she often is a source of loss to the dairy. The depreciation per cow per year will increase with an increase in the value of the cow as a milk producer. Many cows sold today for from $60 to $80, are worth as much for beef at the end of their period of usefulness as milk producers, as cows worth $120 to $135. In the case of high priced pure bred cows the depreciation is still greater.

There are many factors influencing the depreciation of cows, such as death, age, udder troubles, failure to breed, abortion and minor accidents. The greatest depreciation is not from death, but from depreciation from cows sold for beef. Estimating the average value of the cows in the Association at $75.00 and their value when disposed of for various causes for beef at $40, the average depreciation for two years is $8.83 per cow per year or 11.8 per cent. The death rate was 1.5 per cent and the disposal due to other causes 22 per cent. At this rate the life of a cow in the herd would be a little over four years. 35 per cent of the cows were disposed of during the first year compared with 13 per cent for the second. This very large

12

difference is undoubtedly due to the fact that during the first
year in many of the herds records were kept for the first time
which revealed a large number of unprofitable cows. If all
the herds had been tested for tuberculosis and reacting animals
removed the depreciation no doubt would have been still greater.
It is probably fair to estimate that under normal conditions the
average life of a cow in a dairy herd is about six years.

Dairymen engaged in the milk business who do not raise
heifers but depend entirely upon buying cows to replenish the
herd, if they buy cows of good dairy type at present prices will
have a depreciation often as high as 15 per cent.

Depreciation per cow $8 83

COST OF KEEPING OF BULL.

The many poor bulls are here as elsewhere chiefly responsible
for the large number of unprofitable cows found. The fact that
the number of cows per farm is small makes the question of
having the use of a good bull one of the most serious problems
confronting the dairy farmers of New Hampshire. To accept
the offer of the free service of a poor bull would be "penny
wise and pound foolish," while it might be wisdom and prove
profitable to pay as much as five or even fifty dollars for the
service of a hull of good breeding. A full grown bull can easily
serve from 75 to 100 cows if they are distributed throughout
the year. In herds of fifteen cows or less, it is cheaper to pay
five dollars for service per cow than it is to keep a bull. If a
number of farmers having an aggregate of 50 cows to be
served bought a $200 bull, interest, taxes, depreciation and feed
would average 106.59 or the cost of keeping a $200 bull per
cow would be $2.15.

A good bull should be kept and used until danger from inbreeding is anticipated. The time will vary according to the
quality of the bull and the type of cows kept. Ordinarily a bull
can be kept from four to five years.

According to the last census the average number of cows
per farm in the State of New Hampshire is five It is impossible for the thousands of small farmers as individuals to
keep a bull of sufficient merit to improve the cattle. But it is
possible, practical and economical for them to coöperate in the

keeping of bulls. In fact it is the only method which will assure a rapid improvement of the dairy cows in New Hampshire.

The cost of keeping a bull valued at $100 would be as follows:—

Value of Bull		$100
Interest on $100, 5 per cent	$5 00	
Taxes, valuation $50 at 1.59 per cent	80	
Value after 4 yrs. service $60		
Depreciation on bull per yr........	10 00	
Feed	60 00	
Cost of keeping a bull for 20 cows	$75 80	
Cost per cow		3 79

TAXES AND INTEREST ON COWS.

Value per cow $75		
Appraised value $50		
Taxes on $50 at 1.59 per cent....	$ 80	
Interest on $75 at 5 per cent	3 75	
Taxes and Interest per cow		$4 55

VETERINARIAN AND MEDICINE.

There are veterinary expenses on every herd of cattle kept, either as direct service of a veterinarian or for medicine or equipment for home treatment. These expenses will increase with the value of the cows kept. It hardly pays to spend a great deal of money on a cow worth about $40 often kept at a direct loss to the owner of from $10 to $25 yearly. It generally pays, however, to secure the services of a veterinarian when cows valued from $100 to $500 are sick. Although in many cases the veterinarian can be of little assistance, he is called because the farmer is then satisfied of having done all it is possible for him to do. Every dairy barn ought to be thoroughly disinfected once a year whether there is even the slightest suspicion of disease or not. By so doing many disease bacteria may be destroyed and dangerous infectious diseases prevented from spreading to the cattle.

Many farmers use special tonics for their cattle throughout the year which should be charged to the account of medicine.

An estimate of the veterinary expenses on 20 cows on a dairy farm would be as follows:

Veterinarian and veterinary equipment..	$12 00
5 gal. disinfectant	3 25
10 lbs. Epsom salts	1 00
Vaseline	40
3 qts. of linseed oil	66
Total for 20 cows	$17 31
Cost per cow ....$.87	

BEDDING.

Bedding costs the Farm Department of New Hampshire College on an average of two cents per bushel, 1-2 cent per bushel for the sawdust and 1 1-2 cents for hauling. The amount used averages 200 bushels per cow. When shavings were used, figuring one bale of shavings for 20 cows it cost the New Jersey Experiment Station $5.30 per year.

Cost of bedding per cow, 200 bushels sawdust at 2 cts...................	$4 00

ICE, COAL OR WOOD.

Even in New Hampshire it is necessary to use ice from five to seven months during the year and in some cases ice is used for cooling the milk for even a longer period. According to circulars sent out by milk contractors to the producers for cooling 50 quarts of milk 50 pounds of ice per day is required. Waste in ice house and elsewhere is 100 per cent. In other words two tons of ice should be harvested for each cow. Figuring the ice for cooling each cow's milk in the South Lyndeboro Association based on actual production the cost would be as follows:—

1 lb. ice will cool 155 lbs. milk 1° F
Amount of milk per cow, 6463.2 lbs.

Ice used only 1-2 the year

3231.6 ÷ 155 = 20.85 lbs. ice to cool 3231.6 lbs. of milk 1° F.

Necessary to cool milk from 90° to 50° or 40°

20.85 × 40 = 834 lbs. ice to cool 3231.6 lbs. milk to temperature below 50°

Waste in ice house in handling and during cooling 100% or 834.

834 + 834 = 1668 lbs. ice to cool one-half of one cow's milk

Value of ice 10 cts. per 100 lbs.

1668 × 10 .... $1 67 per cow

Coal or wood for heating water for utensils and for cows at time of calving .... 50 per cow

Total per cow $2 17

PERISHABLE TOOLS, UTENSILS, SALT.

3	pails, strainer, forks, and shovels	$4 50 pr. yr.
50	yds. strainer cloth	1 50
2	scales (good for 5 yrs.)	1 00
2	brushes	1 00
2	curry combs	50
2	cards	15
2	bbls. salt	2 00

$10 65

53 pr. cow

No two localities are exactly alike or are the conditions on any two farms exactly alike. It is impossible ever to get figures on the cost of keeping a cow per year that in every particular will fit the conditions of every farmer. No doubt that some may find one item too low, some may find another item too high, depending upon conditions and locality. The figures very nearly represent the average cost of keeping a cow for milk production in the section covered by the South Lyndeboro Association. Every farmer must solve his own problem. By making use of the above items each individual can determine almost exactly the cost of keeping a cow on his farm.

PROFIT AND LOSS ON 203 COWS.

The following table gives the return above feed cost of 203 cows that completed a year's work, arranged in order of profit above feed cost.

Cows.	Profit.	Cows.	Profit.
7 made	$100 to $126 27	37 made	$40 to $50
2 "	90 " 100 00	35 "	30 " 40
9 "	80 " 90 00	19 "	20 " 30
17 "	70 " 80 00	17 "	10 " 20
18 "	60 " 70 00	3 "	1 " 10
31 "	50 " 60 00	8 "	-16 " 1

Crediting the cows with $18.00, the value of the calf and the manure, and arranging them in order of profit the results are as follows.

Cows.	Profit.	Cows.	Profit.
15 made	$100 to $144 27	25 made	$50 to $56 70
17 "	90 " 100 00	19 "	40 " 50 00
16 "	80 " 90 00	19 "	30 " 40 00
29 "	70 " 80 00	5 "	20 " 30 00
30 "	60 " 70 00	8 "	10 " 20 00
18 "	56 " 60 00	2 "	0 " 10 00

$56.70 represents the expense of keeping a cow above feed cost, when she has been credited with the calf and manure.

139.5 cows or 68.5 per cent of the cows paid a profit, while 64 or 31.5 per cent were kept at a loss. For reasons already stated these figures represent conditions considerably above the average. Of the 103 cows nearly all were sold because they were found to be unprofitable. This would indicate that one-half of the cows in the Association more than paid for all the expenses entering into the cost of production.

It does not follow that every cow which failed to return $56.70 above feed cost was kept at a loss. Some food such as pasture and certain kinds of roughage raised on the farm has been marketed which otherwise might have had little or no value.

Under average farm conditions it is almost impossible to figure the profit of the dairy separate from the rest of the farm. A farmer may figure a loss on his dairy and a profit on the farm. He has, however, marketed his crops through the dairy, which may be largely responsible for making a net income on the farm as a whole.

PRODUCTION NECESSARY FOR PROFIT.

If the income from the cow outside of the income from the calf and the manure is $129.73, the question arises how many pounds or cans of milk must a cow produce at the New Hampshire price of milk to equal this amount. As the the average price for milk in the different zones varies, the following table will make it possible to make comparisons for any price.

PRODUCTION NECESSARY FOR PROFIT.

Average Price per Can.	Amount.	No. of Cans.	No. Pounds of Milk.
$.34	$129 73	381.5	6,867.0
.33	129 73	390.1	7,021.8
.32	129 73	405.7	7,302.6
.31	129 73	418.5	7,533.0
.30	129 73	432.4	7,783.2
.29	129 73	447.3	8,051.4
.28	129 73	463.0	8,334.0
.27	129 73	479.3	8,627.4
.26	129 73	498.9	8,980.2

THE PRODUCTION OF CLEAN MILK.

By Prof. H. D. Evans, State Laboratory of Hygiene.

In these days of comparative enlightenment it hardly would seem necessary to speak of the importance of clean milk. The experience of all, who have had to do with the control of our milk supplies, does, however, show a very real need of more knowledge and care on the part of our milk producers. Thus it is not out of place this evening to call to the attention of both producers and consumers the need of cleanliness in milk and its products; and to briefly indicate both what this dirty milk means from a health standpoint, and how the condition can be remedied, at least to a large extent.

The dictionary tells us that "any foreign substance in, or on a material" is *"dirt."* This is a broad definition, and, under it. watered, colored or preserved milk would have to be considered as dirty. The word dirt calls to our minds some such thing as mud, sand, or organic refuse, and dirty milk is generally thought of as contaminated with such substances. In this discussion I shall not consider as "dirt" substances deliberately added to milk, as water, coloring matters and preservatives, but shall confine the consideration to the visible earthy and organic matters, together with the invisible dirt attached to it. For this discussion we may class dirt into *physical dirt* and *bacterial dirt.*

Physical dirt, which we find in milk, is such as is visible to the eye. It consists of earthy matters, straw, dust, hair, and manure flakes. It is derived from the cow's body as in the case of hair, dandruff and manure flakes; from the dirt in the stable, as in the case of straw, hay and some of the earthy materials; and from the air, as in the case of dust. In addition there is the possibility of all kinds of physical dirt entering the milk in the milk room, from dirty utensils. dirty shelves, and being shaken off from dirty employes.

This kind of dirt is never present in the milk as it comes from the cow's udder. It is derived entirely from outside sources. The amount of organic and earthy matters thus introduced into the milk are, *in themselves,* harmless. The quantities· present in even a very dirty milk would not cause disease to follow its use. If such dirt as this were all that entered the milk the only objection to its presence would be the esthetic one of poor appearance. The real cause for objection to the presence of this physical dirt is that it carries, attached to it at all times, bacterial dirt, or swarming myriads of bacteria of various kinds. The real objection, then, to physical dirt is that it forms the vehicle for the transmission of the harmful bacterial dirt, which not only causes economic loss to the producer, but also often results in disease among the users of the resulting milk. Physical dirt is thus to be considered an indicator of the bacterial condition of the milk in which it occurs.

As you all know "bacteria" are minute vegetable organisms, which multiply with great rapidity in favorable environment and with proper food. Milk is one of the best foods for bacteria that exists. Therefore, unless precautions are taken to exclude bacteria from milk, any that may enter it will rapidly multiply to such an extent as to spoil the milk, and render it unfit for human consumption. Bacteria do not spring spontaneously into existence. Each one comes from some previously existing one. If they are found in milk they have come from some bacterium that has entered the milk, either in the cow, or after it has been drawn from her. Not all of these bacteria are dangerous to health. In fact but few out of the thousands that are known cause disease in man. But nearly all of them will cause a milk to spoil if they enter it, and so are a source of loss to the producer.

In previous papers before this Association I have dwelt at considerable length on the kinds of bacteria that enter milk at various stages in its passage from the cow to the consumer, and have dwelt mainly on the economic aspects of the problem, merely stating that there are certain diseases that can be transmitted through the agency of this food. Tonight I shall simply enumerate the causes of economic loss to the producer, and mainly call your attention to the possibilities of disease among the users of a dirty milk, with illustrations of cases on record.

While bacterial dirt is invisible, and so escapes our notice, it is just as much dirt in a milk as is the manure, hay, hair, and earthy matters, which are so common. It is the most important kind of dirt in a milk, both from an economic point, and from a health point of view.

While physical dirt is never present in the milk as it comes from the cow, some bacterial dirt is always present in the first milk drawn from a cow, even if she is in the best of health; and it is always present in the milk from a diseased cow; especially from one with a diseased udder; in which case the bacteria, which are causing the disease of the udder, are drawn from the udder with the milk in countless numbers.

We thus have to consider two sources of bacteria in milk, i. e., those which are in the milk as it comes from the cow, and those that enter it after leaving the cow.

The bacteria in the first drawn milk from a healthy cow are those that have worked up through the milk ducts from the outside of the teats, and are derived from dust and any matters that have touched the moist ends of the milk ducts. They are almost always harmless in so far as affecting health is concerned; but they may be the cause of economic loss to the farmer through rapid souring of the milk, unless precautions are taken to inhibit their growth after they leave the cow. Aside from the economic loss resulting from their presence, unless the milk be at once cooled, we need not consider them.

The milk from a diseased udder, whether the seat of the disease be located within or on the outside of the udder, will always contain the bacteria that cause the particular disease. Most of these disease bacteria are able to set up either mild or severe disease symptoms among the human users of the milk, as well as among the calves. Thus *tuberculosis* of the udder will result in the presence of the germs of this disease in the milk, which may later cause the same disease among the human or animal users of the milk. Ulcerative processes, which pass so commonly under the name of "garget" deliver their causative agent to the milk, and these streptococci, as they are called, can set up varying degrees of sickness in the bodies of the users of the milk. Many an epidemic of septic sore throat, some with a long list of fatalities, have been traced to such a source. In such milk as it comes from the animal there is no physical dirt. It is entirely bacterial and invisible.

There is now no question but that milk from a tubercular udder will contain the bacteria of this disease, and can be the cause of the disease among the users of the milk. There is also now quite general agreement in the view that general tuberculosis of the animal, not affecting the udder itself, will result in the presence of the bacteria in the milk. There are cases where the germs of tuberculosis have appeared in the milk after being injected into the shoulder of the animal, and so far removed from the udder. There is also now general agreement in the view that the bovine strain of the tubercle bacillus can result in human tuberculosis not only in children but in adults, and not only in the intestines but also in the lungs. As a result, milk drawn from a tubercular cow, even though the degree of infection of the cow be so small as to be detected only by the tuberculin test, should not be considered safe to use in a raw state. If absolutely necessary it can be used after pasteurization, which kills the germ.

The cow is never affected by the disease we know as diphtheria, yet there have been cases where ulcers on the outside of the udder have become infected by the diphtheria bacillus, and have dropped from thence into the milk during milking. Out of 27 milk borne outbreaks of this disease, studied by the U. S. Public Health & Marine Hospital Service, 2 were reported to have been thus caused.

There are also two cases, recorded by the same Service, of outbreaks of scarlet fever, caused by eruptive disease of the udders of cows.

Seven outbreaks of septic sore throat, resembling pseud-diphtheria, have also been recorded. In the case of septic sore throat and scarlet fever the ulcerative process may be within the udder as well as outside of it, and so the milk as it comes from the cow may be infected. When from the outside, the bacilli drop in with physical dirt. Enough has thus been said to show the necessity of excluding a cow, diseased in any way, from a milk herd. It should be an axiom that milk should be taken only from healthy cows. If there is the slightest degree of suspicion as to the health of the cow the milk from her should be pasteurized if it is to be used for consumption in any way.

Aside from the danger from tuberculosis, the greatest danger of milk causing disease in the human subject lies in the bacteria that enter it after it comes from the cow's udder. Aside from tuberculosis and garget, there is no danger from inside the udder; no physical dirt comes from inside the udder. After the milk has left the cow, bacterial dirt can enter it either attached to the physical dirt from the cow, her surroundings, or the different milk utensils and the places where they are kept; or from the person of those who handle the milk, whether in milking, preparing the milk for the market, or in the marketing. Some of these cause disease in the users of the milk; some cause rapid souring of the milk, but no disease in the human subject; and some cause odors, tastes, colors and changes in the physical appearance of the milk, as in the case of ropy milk, without causing disease among the users of it, although, in these latter cases, the physical condition of the milk unfits it for use, and would cause its rejection by farmer and consumer alike. The dangerous, disease causing germs give no hint, however, of their appearance until the person is taken sick.

The most common forms of bacteria that gain access to a milk are the lactic acid group, which cause souring. These are present everywhere about farms and dairies, and, as they are everywhere in the air attached to dust particles, it is impossible to entirely keep them out of the milk; although proper precautions in cleaning the cow, keeping the stable and milk rooms scrupulously clean, and protecting the milk pails from the entrance of dust by proper strainers, will practically eliminate them; and will make it possible to thoroughly control the growth of the few that do enter the milk. These bacteria do not cause disease among the users of the milk. They are harmless to the human family, but a source of very great economic loss to the producer through the lessened keeping power of his product. In addition to the lactic acid group there are very many other bacteria that cause souring of milk; many of which are of intestinal origin, and produce harmful results in the human subject. These being derived from the intestines of the cow both can be, and should be, excluded from the milk.

The various bacteria that change the physical condition of the milk through making it ropy, or giving it color, odor or taste, also enter it in the dirt and dust about the stables and milk rooms. They do not naturally belong there, as do the lactic acid group, and so can be removed by suitable cleansing of these places. They may also enter the milk through the water, used to clean the utensils. This of necessity implies a polluted water supply, and so the way to eliminate this source of trouble is both plain and easy.

Aside from the above two classes of bacteria, which are of economic significance only, disease bacteria can enter the milk in the stable or milking room attached to the manure flakes that may fall into the milk. This may be in the form of dust. kicked up in the stable, or in the form of the larger particles of this substance that fall from the dirty flanks and udder of the cow during the manipulations of milking. A strainer in the mouth of the milk pail will remove the solid dirt, but it will not remove the greater part of the bacteria, which are so small as to pass through cloth. With absorbent cotton the greater part of them can be removed, but we cannot depend on any method of mechanical straining to remove all of them. A clean and dustless tieup, together with a clean cow, whose udder has been wiped off with a moist cloth, and a covered pail, will reduce their number to a minimum.

The intestinal bacteria that thus enter a milk are of considerable significance from a health standpoint. A cow with *tuberculosis,* whether of the lungs or intestines, eliminates the bacilli mainly in the feces, so that the dried manure flakes from such a cow will carry the germs of this disease. and transmit it to the milk into which it falls, to later cause trouble for the consumer, especially if he be young or in poor health.

In addition the streptococci and bacteria of the colon group, which are always present in feces, will not only cause souring of the milk if they enter it, but they are also able to set up intestinal disturbances among the users of the milk. Much of our terrible infant mortality is due to the diarrheas caused by these organisms among the children using the raw milk. This is well shown by the great difference in the mortality of children fed on pasteurized milk or mother's milk as compared with those fed on raw milk. So well is this recognized that many cities now maintain milk depots where pasteurized milk is dispensed for infant consumption. One notable historic proof of this condition was afforded at the siege of Paris in 1879. During the starvation period of the siege, although the adult death rate was greatly increased, yet the infant death rate fell off over a half, owing to the mothers having to nurse their children, there being no cow's milk available. These infantile intestinal infections of children, with their enormous mortality, are due mainly to these intestinal bacteria from the cow, which will always be present in a milk unless the above methods of cleanliness be practised during milking. The substitution of a pasteurized milk supply for infants in New York City has resulted in a drop of a half in the summer infant mortality. The importance of this subject is well seen when it is considered that the infant death rate is over 10 times the adult death rate, and that at only one time of life,—at an age of over 90 years, is the possibility of death as great as for the child of under one year.

In addition to the bacteria that enter milk during the act of milking, from sources other than the milker, there is opportunity for bacterial contamination after the milk enters the milk room. Here the lactic acid bacteria can enter it from the dust and air, unless the room be scrupulously clean; or they may enter it from the dishes used in handling the milk, especially if they have seams from which it is hard to entirely dislodge the bacteria during the act of washing. The only way in which we can be sure of the absence of bacteria on the dishes is by sterilizing them with steam. This is too expensive for the small dairy. The use of pressed metal pails and pans will largely obviate this trouble.

In the milk room also enters the same possibility of the milk being contaminated with the bacteria which cause odors, tastes, colors, and changes in the physical condition of the milk. These have often been the cause of great trouble in the milk room. If the shelves and tanks be kept scrupulously clean by the liberal use of hot water and soap these bacteria can be kept out, as they are foreign invaders, and not natural inhabitants about all dairies.

The use of polluted water in washing the milk utensils has also been the cause of trouble in many cases. Not only can a polluted water cause odors, tastes, colors, etc., in a milk; but, if it be polluted by typhoid discharges, it can become the means of introducing these germs into the milk, which is later put in these dishes. In the milk they will multiply rapidly, and cause disease among the users of the milk. There are a number of such cases on record. The use of a pure water supply will do away with all trouble from this source.

In the distributing depot there also enters the possibility of infection of a milk supply by the use of an infected bottle, which has been returned from a house where there is a case of infectious disease, and which has not been sterilized before being used again. Here also the receipt of a single can of infected milk from a single small producer can produce infection of the entire supply with which it is mixed. It should be an axiom that all bottles sent out from a milk depot should be sterilized with live steam before being filled. This would not be an expensive matter for the large distributor, any more than it would be for the Creamery.

Up to this time we have considered the possibilities of baeterial contamination of the milk by agencies other than man, and we have seen that tubercle bacilli may be transmitted from the cow to the milk, both in the udder, and by manure flakes falling into the milk. We have also seen that eruptive diseases of the udder may be caused by the organisms causing diphtheria, scarlet fever, summer complaint, and others; and that these bacteria may fall into the milk to later make trouble for the users. We have also seen that the souring bacteria enter the milk with this same dirt. Tubercular infection of milk is due almost entirely either to infection within the udder or to infection by the bacteria in fecal discharges from the tubercular cow. Those who handle milk play but little part in the infection of the milk with this disease. The same is also true of the organisms causing summer complaint. There are records of outbreaks of diphtheria, scarlet fever, and typhoid fever in which the cow infected the milk, but they are few as compared with the many cases where the milk received its infection from the human being who either did the milking, or handled the milk at some point between the cow and the consumer.

To understand how milk is infected by the human factor we need to understand a few facts about how these germ-caused diseases are transmitted. They are mainly infectious, although also contagious. The organisms enter mainly through the nose and mouth. The diphtheria organism and probably also the scarlet fever organism are eliminated mainly in the discharges from these organs. The typhoid and cholera organisms are eliminated mainly in the feces.

Now when the germs of these diseases enter the human system there elapses a space of from 3 to 4 days in the case of diphtheria, to about 2 weeks in the case of typhoid fever, before the symptoms of the disease appear. When the disease appears we can take care to disinfect the discharges and keep the sick person away from milk so as to free them from danger; but during this preliminary incubation period we are unaware of any danger from the infected person, and so he goes about his business, although eliminating the bacteria of disease unknown to himself and all others. If the infected person, during this incubation period, handles milk either in milking or at any point in its marketing he will introduce into it the bacteria of the disease in question, which will be transmitted to the users, and so be the cause of an epidemic. It is almost impossible to do anything with these incubation cases, as we do not know that anything is the matter with them until they become sick.

Then there is the person who may have any one of these diseases in such mild form as to simply feel mean and run down; but is not sick enough to call a doctor or take to his bed. Such persons are represented by the so-called "walking typhoid case" and the "latent diphtheria case." These persons are eliminating the germs of the disease just as well and fast as would one who is so sick as to be confined to his bed. If these persons handle milk in any way they will infect it, with very serious results in the form of an epidemic. This element of danger we can control by never allowing any person to be employed in any way in the production of milk who is not in the best of health. Any person feeling in any way indisposed should be excluded from all contact with milk.

Then there is the person who has clinically recovered from these germ diseases, but who, although physically well, is still eliminating the germs of the disease. He is free from the disease, but not from the cause of it, and so can infect any milk or other food with which he may come in contact. This class of persons is known as the "Bacillus Carrier." Some carry the bacilli for but a short time, while others have been known to carry them for years,—in one case for 18 years. This class of persons we can control if we insist on only considering a person well and safe to release from quarantine when the germ of the disease has been found to be absent by bacteriological examination. This we do in the case of diphtheria and once in a while in the case of typhoid fever. This factor is one that can be eliminated in the case of diseases whose causative agent is known to be a bacterium.

Not only can the person carrying the germs of disease infect milk himself, but the attendants on the sick person will get the germs of the disease on their hands and clothing, and, unless they are very careful to sterilize their hands and clothes, they may carry the infection to the milk, if they afterwards handle it. Any person or thing that has touched, or been touched by the sick person or his discharges can carry the germs of the disease to whatever it may later touch. Experience has shown this to be a very fruitful means of spreading disease. It can be avoided by allowing no person who has been in contact with the sick patient, or in contact with any of his possessions to have anything to do in handling milk.

We have thus examined the human agency in transmitting disease through milk, and have seen that the possibility of infection from this source enters at all stages of the handling of the milk from the time it is drawn from the cow to the time it is consumed. Some of the danger from this source, and in fact the greatest part of it, can be eliminated by having only healthy individuals handle the milk, and by allowing no one to come in contact with it who has been in contact with a case of infectious disease. The lesser part of the danger is due to the incubation and carrier cases of the disease. The incubation case cannot be eliminated with our present knowledge, but typhoid carriers and diphtheria carriers can be eliminated by refusing to release the sick person from quarantine until bacteriological examination has shown them free from the germs of these diseases. This is a procedure that should always be done in the case of diphtheria. It is too expensive to do in all typhoid cases, but it should be right to demand it in the case of any person who is to handle a food of as wide distribution as is milk.

Just a word now in regard to the class of persons who make the greatest use of milk. There is probably no single food, out-

side of water, which is so much used as is milk.   The great
users of milk are children and sick persons, for both of whom
its easy digestibility makes it an ideal food, provided it be pure
and clean.   But this very class of persons, who through deli-
cate health have to use milk as a food are the very ones who
are least prepared to resist the onslaught of the diseases that
are borne in milk.   Thus we find diphtheria, measles, scarlet
fever, and summer complaint to be especially children's diseases, and to reap their greatest mortality from this class, while
typhoid fever requires a weakened system to permit the germ to
gain a foot-hold.   Thus the contamination of the ideal food
for these two classes of persons will result in the greatest
amount of danger to them.   The same statement holds good in
regard to any adulteration of milk, although not to be noticed
as quickly or in as marked a degree as in the case of bacterial
contamination of the milk.

Now in this discussion I am not arguing that all milk ought
to be of the very highest quality that it is possible to produce it
from a bacterial standpoint.   I am not arguing for the production of all milk as of a "certified" grade.   If a person wants
this grade of milk and is willing to pay the cost of it, he has
the right to get it.   But the expense of production puts this
class of milk out of the question for the ordinary consumer.

I do, however, go on the assumption that nothing is fit for a
food, or ought legally to be sold for a food, that will cause disease among its users.   This is the assumption that all of our
pure food laws go on.   There is, of course, no question but that
we have the right, and that we will exercise it, of throwing out
any milk that contains the germs of infectious disease, such as
typhoid and scarlet fever, diphtheria, measles and cholera.   But
the greatest trouble from milk comes in the case of infants,
and the common diarrheal diseases in their case.   These complaints are caused, in the main, by bacteria which enter the milk
through carelessness, and enter it on the solid physical dirt
which enters the milk during the process of milking, and which
contains intestinal bacteria from the cow's intestines.   Such
dirt, both physical and bacterial, is preventable, and is but a
mark of carelessness.

To get an acceptable milk, that is physically clean, and of
such low bacterial content as to be free from danger, both when

drawn and when delivered, is possible; and it is the right of every consumer to demand it of his milkman. If we observe the following precautions such a milk can be obtained and delivered to the consumers.

First of all the milk must come from a cow that is free from all signs of disease, which can be detected by either physical signs or by chemical reactions. This will exclude *tuberculosis*. This point should be an axiom in all milk production.

Second, milk should be handled only by persons who are in the best of physical health. This should exclude from the milk most of the cases of infectious disease, such as typhoid and scarlet fevers, diphtheria, measles, smallpox and cholera; and leave only the small number of cases due to the physically well carriers and incubation cases. This second point should also be axiomatic.

Third, the healthy cow should also be clean, so that no filth can drop from her into the milk. This can be done by housing her in a clean stable, so that the minimum amount of filth will accumulate on her; and she should be brushed down before milking, and the udder should be wiped off with a damp cloth. This will eliminate the major part of the solid filth, and the major part of the bacterial contamination of the milk due to intestinal bacteria. This will cut off the most of the infantile troubles which now follow the use of dirty milk. Covered pails also aid in excluding dirt from the milk.

Fourth, the milker, and all who later handle the milk should not only be healthy, but they should also be clean. If we should compel the milker and those who later handle the milk to be as clean about this work as they would be when they sat down to the table, the chance of dirt and bacterial filth falling from their persons and garments into the milk would be eliminated, and still more of the infant mortality would be cut off. This is not an expensive proposition, and is one that the consumer has a right to insist on.

Fifth, the milk, when it has been drawn from a clean and healthy cow by clean and healthy individuals, in clean dishes, and handled in a clean and healthy way, should be at once cooled to a temperature at which the bacteria do not multiply. This will reduce the chance of souring through the retardation of the growth of the lactic acid group of bacteria, and will, at the same time, keep any chance intestinal bacteria from multiplying to a harmful extent, for the number of bacteria that a person ingests has an important bearing on the likelihood of disease following.

Sixth, the farm should have a pure water supply, both to prevent the entrance of economically harmful bacteria, and water-borne disease bacteria, into the milk. This is not a source of added expense to the producer. The State will tell him free of charge if his water supply is pure or contaminated.

If the producer will observe these 6 points he will be able to produce a clean, and at the same time a healthy milk; and at practically no added cost. The consumer has a right to this degree of protection, and the sooner he demands it of the producer the better it will be for both parties. If the producer will not go to this extent in giving his trade a healthful article of food, then the law should compel him to pasteurize his milk before sale, and to mark it plainly as being so treated. Pasteurization is but a makeshift at the best. It does not imply that any kind of milk, from any kind of an animal, and handled in any kind of way ought to be used, but that, if some persons will produce, and some persons will buy such milk, then they should know what they are buying. Pasteurization is no apology for carelessness.

The question naturally arises in such a body as this, "Does such a condition as this exist?" The answer, so far as it affects this State, is plain. During the last two years 49.7 per cent of all milk samples, and 5 per cent of all cream samples collected by the inspector of the State Commissioner of Agriculture have contained such quantities of dirt as to be visible to the naked eye, when looking at the bottom of the milk bottle. These samples have not been collected with an eye to dirty samples, but were taken in the routine course of collection of samples for examination for adulteration. This is a serious condition, and is the warrant for such a paper as this at a meeting of the dairy interests of the State.

THE GIPSY MOTH SITUATION IN MAINE.

Portion of Illustrated Lecture by A. O. Pike, Field Agent
Gipsy Moth Work.

During the first year of Gipsy moth work in Maine in 1906,
eight towns were found infested with this pest. By the end
of 1909 the number had increased to twenty-two and comprised
practically all of York county. During 1910, thirty-one more
towns were found to be infested, in 1911 fifteen more were
added to the list, and during the present year twelve more new
towns have been discovered to date. In all there are now
eighty towns which are known to contain the Gipsy moth. This
infested area includes Fryeburg on the north, stretches beyond
Lewiston, Gardiner and Bath on the east and includes all the
territory between those points and the Atlantic ocean and New
Hampshire line.

This rapid increase of infested area is serious in itself but
even more serious is the enormous increase in the number of egg
clusters of the moth found in the badly infested towns of York
county. The comparative record for 1911 and 1912 in the
towns named is as follows:—

Town.	Egg Clusters Destroyed.	
	1911.	1912.
York	10,327	77,484
Wells	4,829	33,651
Berwick	4,031	24,249
Kennebunk	1,428	3,383
Acton	315	8,899
Totals	20,930	147,666

From these figures, it may be seen that in these towns more
than seven times as many egg clusters were found and destroyed
in 1912 as in 1911. The same ratio of increase will un-

doubtedly hold true in all other parts of York county. Moreover no less than three thousand egg clusters were destroyed
in Cornish this year where last year less than fifty were reported. Again, a serious woodland infestation was found in
Brunswick this fall and over four thousand egg clusters were
destroyed. Last year the number found there was less than one
hundred. A serious situation confronts the State of Maine
when infestations of such size are found so far towards the interior of the State.

But the real menace of the Gipsy moth is in the fact that the
caterpillars eat foliage and thereby destroy trees. Ever since
the start of the work in Maine, this Department has been warn-
ing the public that unless sufficient money was provided for
this work, the woodlands of the State would be in danger of
destruction. Until last summer there has not, to my knowledge,
been any extensive Gipsy moth defoliation in Maine. Last
summer, however, about twenty acres of oak growth in the
town of York were nearly stripped of foliage. There was one
pine tree sufficiently defoliated to cause its death and it is, I believe, the first pine lost through work of the Gipsy moth in this
State. This defoliation occurred in the vicinity of Mount Agamenticus in York. Next year in the same section probably forty
acres will be devastated and a good part of the growth will be
killed. Smaller defoliations occurred in Wells, So. Berwick,
Eliot and Kittery. With the increased number of caterpillars
sure to hatch next year, more and more defoliation will take
place throughout this entire county.

This is the Gipsy moth situation in Maine today. The reason
for its seriousness is that we have been unable to place in the
field a sufficient force of men to check the increase of the pest.
From the start, the appropriations for this work have been
inadequate and particularly so for the past four years. The
result is that the Gipsy moth is at present destroying woodlands in York county and will soon be doing likewise in other
parts of the State, if indeed it is not already doing so. After all
that has been written and spoken on this subject during the
past six years, the present Gipsy moth situation in the State of
Maine should be a surprise to no citizen.

ANNUAL MEETING MAINE SEED IMPROVEMENT ASSOCIATION.

Held in connection with meeting of Maine Dairymen's Association at City Hall, Portland, December 3, 4, 5, 6, 1912.

TUESDAY EVENING, 7.30 O'CLOCK.

In the absence of Mayor Curtis the welcome in behalf of the City was given by Representative-elect John B. Kehoe, who spoke in an appreciative way of the progress which the farmer has made and is making, emphasizing especially the thought that the day of slipshod methods on the farm has passed, these being followed by scientific methods in the dairy and other branches of farm life.

Silas B. Adams, vice president of the Portland Board of Trade, extended a cordial welcome in behalf of that organization, speaking of the spirit of co-operation which existed between the board and the two organizations which are holding their annual sessions here this week. He spoke of the Board of Trade as appreciating the fact that agriculture is the basic industry of the State and the measure of its prosperity, the members being anxious to see it prosper.

Col. Fred N. Dow brought the greetings of the Portland Farmers' Club of which he is president, and in his remarks urged greater loyalty to the State and devotion to its welfare. Speaking of business men buying farms and conducting them as a side issue, Col. Dow stated that seldom did the business man profit greatly if any from such a project, yet he contributed to the general advancement of agricultural interests by improvements in methods, by which the community profited.

RESPONSE TO ADDRESSES OF WELCOME.

By Dr. L. S. Merrill, Orono.

Your words of welcome are warmly appreciated, because knowing you and the splendid citizenship you represent, we know that you are indeed glad to have the Maine Dairymen's and the Maine Seed Improvement Associations meet in your city. In turn, we are equally glad that circumstances have so directed the affairs of our Associations that their annual meetings can be held in the city of Portland.

We are glad because Portland is a beautiful city, because it is the chief city of this great commonwealth, because its citizens are public spirited, because of its strong and aggressive business organizations, because these organizations have shown an active interest in the development of agriculture, and because many of the members of the Portland Board of Trade and the Portland Farmers' Club are active members of the Associations which are tonight and will be for a few days your guests.

These Associations represent organized agriculture along two fundamental lines of the industry,—plant, and dairy husbandry. It is from these two lines that Maine agriculture derives its principal income, amounting to quite fifty million dollars annually.

The Maine Dairymen's Association was organized to fill a definite need in the dairy industry. It has helped to educate and unify its membership; to improve the quality of dairy products; to place the industry on a firmer business basis. It has labored under difficulties and its efforts have been practically limited to holding an annual meeting and exhibition, simply because no direct appropriations have been made by the State for its support.

Its plans for the future must include liberal support from the State and an aggressive promotion program. As business men we must recognize the fact that it costs money to do things worth while.

The dairy farmer produces a product which constitutes not only one of the greatest necessities but also one of the greatest luxuries among human foods. As a people we are growing more fastidious in relation to our food. While the dairy industry of the State has had a slow but steady growth, the farmer has for some time been feeling the pressure of the growing fastidiousness among the people. He has also been feeling pressure from higher priced cattle feeds; from scarcity and inefficiency of farm help.

Shall the products of the dairy continue to fill an important place in the living of the people? If so, then dairy farming must be encouraged. The quality of dairy products, it is true, must be improved but at the same time the consuming public must be educated both to care for such products in the home and to have a proper appreciation of their value as articles of food. It is our part to improve the quality; it is your part to educate the people who are consumers. Let us work together.

The Maine Seed Improvement Association centers its activities around a big idea, "increased seed efficiency." Efficiency is a crying need in all industries, whether we deal in terms of men, machines, plants, or animals. Efficiency in seeds makes success in plant husbandry surer. It adds its contribution to harder working acres, to increased food supply, to profitable agriculture. It helps to erect standards and then aids to surpass them.

In its efforts the Association represents high ideals and deserves the support of the State it is trying to serve. The membership of our Associations includes leading farmers of the State. These men are interested in Maine and the development of her agricultural resources. We are here to counsel together for the advancement of Maine's greatest industry. Successful agriculture means happy and prosperous farm homes; it means the maintenance of high ideals among American farmers; it means stability in business—in your business; it means national welfare and progress.

In conclusion we thank you most heartily for your cordial welcome; we are happy to be with you and enjoy your hospitality.

INDUSTRIAL EDUCATION.

By Hon. Payson Smith, State Superintendent of Schools.

The main address of the evening was by State Superintendent of Schools, Payson Smith, whose subject was Industrial Education. He spoke in substance as follows:

What then should be the attitude of the Maine school system towards those practical phases of education that are included in what we call industrial education?

COMMON SCHOOLS FURNISH FOUNDATION.

It goes without saying that the primary purpose of the common schools is not to fit children for specific vocations. The elementary schools, dealing with children up to the fourteenth or fifteenth year should place their strongest emphasis on the teaching of those fundamental subjects that form a basis of other education. The historic subjects of the common schools should continue to be the vital elements around which the instruction of these schools should center.

SCHOOL SUBJECTS VITALIZED.

These subjects need, however, to be taught in a more direct connection with the affairs of the real world in which the child daily lives. The instruction given in school should not be detached from the realities, but should deal with them. Arithmetical problems should be of the kind that the boy will have occasion to use outside of school. Geography should deal more with facts nearer the child and less with those remote from him. History should be more than a recital of events. · It should become, so far as good teaching can make it, a guide to good citizenship. All subjects taught in the common schools are not parts of that which we generally term industrial education, but all of them may be so taught as to lead the child into a better realization of his own powers, into a clearer vision of the demands the world will make of him and to that extent they make for a more effective contact of the individual with society. Hence they do have a bearing in increasing the efficiency of each social unit.

MORE HAND WORK.

There is place, however, in the lower schools for a vast increase of the attention paid to those forms of education that involve hand training. It has been demonstrated again and again that the process of education is often more effectively conducted by means of an appeal to the motor activities than in other ways. We learn by doing as well as by thinking. The schools ought to be given very much greater opportunity than they now have to apply in action the education that is so largely limited to a study of theory. Hand work in the form of manual training for boys and domestic subjects for girls ought to extend very rapidly into all elementary schools and very much more time should be given to them.

THEORY SHOULD BE APPLIED.

I have no doubt that pupils would be more efficiently educated if half the day were to be devoted to an application in practice to the theories studied. Some communities will soon have the courage to place the work of their elementary schools on some such basis. Indeed at Gary, Indiana, the school course is already organized somewhat on that plan with great economy in money cost and with an apparently considerable educational gain. Maine has a most liberal law for the encouragement of manual work in elementary schools. There remains only the necessity of an aroused public opinion in the several towns in favor of adequate attention to courses of this kind.

WHAT SECONDARY SCHOOLS CAN DO.

A peculiar opportunity is open to Maine high schools and academies in the direction of a more vital connection between school and life. The youth who attend these schools are, many of them, just about to pass into some active contact with industry. Such schools will and should pay very large attention to these courses that make for culture— for the ability to enjoy the finer things their lives will present to them. They will render a very sorry service, however, if they leave their graduates with only the taste to enjoy and without a liking and desire for work. It is a dangerous thing to educate a person in such a way that he wants fine things unless it leads him to see those things in their true values and right relations, and unless he becomes able to get honestly the things his taste leads him to desire or to need.

SHOULD HELP STUDENT TO FACE LIFE.

Maine secondary schools in both country and city should pay increasing attention to the problems that are so soon to press upon their young students. The individual and society will suffer unless these young men and women are led through their education to realize that its goal is service and unless to some extent they get a realization of the ways in which they are best adapted to serve.

AGRICULTURE IN RURAL HIGH SCHOOLS.

Rural high schools should pay greater attention to agriculture in all its forms. This attention may come in many cases through subjects now offered. Chemistry for example is being removed from the field of the abstract and is being made specifically to apply to soil study, food values and other specific ends. Chemistry is not less valuable, but it is more valuable when given this concrete application. The comparison may be made of many of the already accepted subjects of the secondary schools. There are schools that should go beyond this, however. Some that have proper equipment and adequate public sentiment as a support should frankly enter the ranks of special vocational schools, making the agricultural course a central and controlling purpose of the institution. A few schools such as Parsonsfield Seminary are already doing this and from being schools of somewhat uncertain mission are becoming strong and virile with the new purpose. Maine ought to have at least twenty schools that should frankly and avowedly undertake seriously agricultural courses. With the large number of secondary schools in Maine it would appear to be unnecessary and unfortunate to increase the number of institutions. Some of these we already have are admirably situated for the purpose.

CITY HIGH SCHOOLS.

In the cities the 'opportunities for a closer contact of school and industry are not less evident. The so-called Fitchburg plan which has passed out of the experimental stage has shown conclusively that schools and shops may coöperate in giving the boy an education that preserves for him the education of the schools while it adds the practical value of shop application. Outward traditions must yield to successful evidence of the kind produced at Fitchburg. The high schools of all our large towns and cities will, I believe, in the near future, pay greatly increased attention to a study of local industries and the opportunities offered by them. Through extended manual courses in some cases related to the trades, and through coöperative courses they will open new avenues of approach by which young men may enter employment with right ideals of labor's significance and with such practical equipment as will lead them to more satisfactory returns for their labor. At the same time the young women will be better prepared for all the fields that may appeal to them, not forgetting the chief of them all, that of home making.

DOES NOT IGNORE COLLEGE PREPARATION.

These changes in our secondary schools are not inimical to such higher education as the colleges now offer. They merely indicate that the boy who will not go to college has his rights which the school must recognize, on at least an equality of plane with those for whom the secondary school course is college preparatory. The public school is indeed for all the children of all the people and upon any other basis it loses its claim to the support of all the people.

CONTINUATION SCHOOLS.

In addition to the things that should render our ordinary schools more effective there is vast opportunity for increasing the industrial capacity of the people through courses that will enable those already engaged in the industries to increase their capacity in them, or to change from one to another.

To discover how general is the desire for such opportunities it is not necessary to turn to the enormously successful public continuation schools of Europe. We find evidence in the hundreds of thousands in our country who at personal expense undertake the so-called correspondence courses. For the present the continuation courses in Maine are likely to be largely in connection with evening schools.

SHORT COURSES RECOMMENDED.

The short evening school course making a direct appeal to some specific need of the student is capable of immediate development. For example, an evening course of a few weeks in the reading of blue prints would be valuable in any community where there are a number of machine shops, a short course in the principles of salesmanship would be distinctly valuable in at least a dozen of our cities, the domestic science equipment ought not to be idle when by means of short evening courses it could be employed for the advantage of those whose interest is in the betterment of household and domestic service. The manual training equipment could similarly go to assist young men just entering certain occupations. Short courses in bookkeeping and stenography would increase the interest and earning capacity of those already engaged in such work. These are but examples of the ways in which short courses may be made valuable. You have only to visit an evening school where such courses are offered to realize how direct an appeal is made as soon as the student can connect his evening study with the next day's task.

CONTINUATION DAY SCHOOLS WILL COME LATER.

Doubtless the continuation day school will soon be possible in Maine. Its coming will depend in part upon the coöperation of employers of labor. In some European countries the employe is entitled by law to attend a continuation school for a certain specified time. Thus the nation aims to protect its industrial efficiency. A few continuation day schools in America are already successful in large communities where employers realize the advantage of such means of increasing the capacity of their workmen.

THE VOCATIONAL SCHOOL.

There remains the independent vocational school of which we have thus far none in Maine, although our state law provides for its liberal aid by the State when any community is prepared to establish one. The distinct grade school usually takes boys and girls at the end of the elementary school course at the age of fourteen or fifteen and gives them training in the elements of a chosen trade. Only the largest cities would be likely at present to provide a patronage large enough to warrant the establishment of such a school. It is to be hoped, however, that at least one or two such schools may soon be started to provide for some of the youth who now pass directly from the common school into industry to their own ultimate loss and to the depreciation of the service of the industry they enter.

INVOLVES EXPERIMENT.

We do not see our way to the end of our industrial education plans. It is not necessary to do so in order to undertake these things that now appear right and just. Experiments are involved and some mistakes are likely to be made. I am not disturbed, however, either by the charge of experimentation in the schools, or by the possibility of mistakes. All of our educational progress, as well as other progress, is the result chiefly of experiment. Without it we should be at the beginning of time. The unchartered course may be less easy to follow, but it leads to the undiscovered continent of new achievement. And if we are to hold still our plans for educational betterment until the danger of mistakes has passed, then there is little hope for that growth of which we have believed public education to be the best guarantee.

Maine faces a future of brightest industrial prospect. No other State surpasses ours in the possibilities of the economic improvement of her people. But let us remember that Maine's future is in her children. As they are being educated with respect to personal rectitude, to civic responsibility and to useful service so will the Maine of the future realize the potential prosperity we believe is hers. It is our present obligation in our school system as in all our other institutions to point our youth to all possible ways of self realization and social service, at the same time swinging as wide as we can the doors of their opportunities.

WEDNESDAY, December 4.

A business meeting of the Association was held at 9.30 A. M. The meeting was called to order by the president, W. G. Hunton of Cherryfield. The annual address of the president followed, in which he outlined the work of the Association.

The annual report of the secretary was given, as follows:

REPORT OF SECRETARY MAINE SEED IMPROVEMENT ASSOCIATION.

It is with pleasure that the secretary submits his report at the annual meeting of the Maine Seed Improvement Association. It is a pleasure because the work that the Association is doing is to raise the standard of crop production by the use of better seed. The necessary change in secretaries this year has no doubt impeded the work of the Association, owing, perhaps, in a measure, to your present secretary's lack of facilities for handling such a large volume of work.

The executive committee have met once since the change was made, at Lewiston, September 4th, where the program was arranged for the annual meeting. The members present were Guy C. Porter, Houlton; Dr. G. M. Twitchell, Auburn; Frank Lowell, Gardiner, and L. C. Holston, Cornish. The subject of a corn score card was discussed and Dr. Twitchell requested that the subject be taken up at the annual meeting. The members have been very prompt in the payment of dues. $32.50 . has been received since the last annual meeting.

There is very little different information available, regarding the detailed work of the Association this year, probably due to the fact that no field agent was appointed to fill the vacancy caused by the resignation of Mr. Barber. The secretary is in hopes to get an account of the work that has been done as soon as the present field agent, Mr. Jones, has had opportunity to get it together.

Owing to the bad year for corn the Association was unable to send as large an exhibit to the New England Corn Exposition as in previous years, but a few members sent a very excellent exhibit of sweet, flint and pop corn. The same is on exhibition at this meeting. With a few suggestions the secretary will conclude his report.

First. That the executive committee be authorized to draw up plans for next year; and that immediate steps be taken for procuring the best varieties of grains and possibly corn, to be put into the hands of members of the Association who can and will guarantee to take care of the crop produced therefrom.

Second. Limit the distribution of seed to only one or two members in each county in the State. Have the field agent visit and inspect the farms of each of these members. Also have him on the ground to see that the ground is properly prepared, the seed properly planted, and the crop cared for and harvested. By limiting the scope of our work to only a few, and making the work as thorough as possible with the aim of getting quality and at the same time an increased remuneration to the seed grower, we can soon build an association that will be as solid as the one in Canada.

As a seed association we have got to have something to sell. For, say as much as you will, the success of this organization depends fundamentally on the profitableness to the seed grower.

If we adhere to the plan of membership which states that a Class A member shall be a breeder of seed, the work will not progress as rapidly as it should, because the average farmer cannot afford the time or the money to develop strains of economic plants. Such work requires the painstaking care of the scientist. Why not begin a campaign immediately by signing up one or two members in each county as outlined above, to plant next spring so many acres of oats or other grains, potatoes or corn, as the executive committee might deem advisable, and in the furtherance of this work we will begin with the highest type of the variety of plants it is possible to procure. In this way the Association will have some crops next fall in a limited way, for seed.

In all of this work there should be a rigid inspection of the farm and all of the methods by the field agent.

Very respectfully,

R. P. MITCHELL,

Secretary.

———

The treasurer, Mr. C. M. White of Bowdoinham, was unable to be present, and his report was read and approved.

———

REPORT OF THE TREASURER.

———

BOWDOINHAM, MAINE, Nov. 27, 1912.

C. M. White in account with Maine Seed Improvement Association.

DR.

To cash on hand at last report		$123 85

CR.

By amount paid W. G. Hunton, for expenses at Augusta during legislature of 1910 and 1911	$14 75	
By amount paid Leon S. Merrill for postage, etc., 1911	21 50	
By amount paid Maine Farmer Publishing Co., for 100 badges	3 65	39 90
Cash on hand		$83 95

The following committee on resolutions was appointed by the Chair: Dr. Raymond Pearl, Orono. Guy C. Porter, Houlton, and E. C. Carll, Augusta.

It was voted to have the committee on resolutions also act as a nominating committee.

The report of the Field Agent, Mr. Austin W. Jones of Bangor, was read as follows, and approved.

THE WORK OF THE ASSOCIATION DURING THE YEAR OF 1912.

A. W. Jones, Augusta.

To the Members of the Maine Seed Improvement Association:

The work of the Association has not prospered as well this year as it would have if there had been a field agent during the whole year instead of only half of it.

I began my duties as field agent on the seventeenth day of June. In some respects this was an unfavorable time, as all of the crops were planted or if not planted the time did not permit any selection of seed. There was one advantage, however. I had the best opportunity to see what the different members were doing and to find out the ones that were most interested in the work.

Since June seventeenth, I have called on 160 farmers at their farms, and of these I have called on 36 a second time. During the month of September I attended 8 fairs. I also had the pleasure of attending the New England fruit show at Portland and the New England corn show at Boston.

During this time I have made but few attempts to offer advice or suggestions. This line of work was a little different from any I ever did before, so I thought I would study the condition of things as I found them, and then I could offer suggestions where they were needed.

In the course of my work I have tried to help the farmers in solving the immediate problems and hope I have been of some assistance in that way.

During my conversation with various farmers and by observing their methods and the general appearance of their farms, I have found the following points to be true in nearly every case, to a greater or less extent. Please bear in mind that what I am about to say is only the impression I received; I leave it with you to decide whether my impressions were correct or not.

First and foremost, I find a great lack of system and business principles among the average farmers. These two things alone almost double the cost of production in many cases; especially is that true where the farms are cut up into several small fields instead of being in one big field. The markets are not watched closely enough to enable the farmer to sell with intelligence and to the best advantage. The farm is nothing but a factory and the cost of production must be kept down.

The second point that became apparent to me was a lack of interest, in quite a large number of cases. I believe this fact is due as much to me as to anyone. I have not been with you the whole year. I have not had an opportunity to talk to many of you for any length of time. I have not been able to show you examples of men who are doing good work along these lines.

The third point that I noticed was the inconsistency of some of the members. Changes of any importance do not come in this work in a short time, but it takes several years. If you start to improve one crop and do not get satisfactory results the first year, keep at it until you are not only doing well, but you are doing the best of any man in the State.

With regard to the crop conditions as they appeared to me from my conversation with farmers over the State, I would say that as a whole the crops are a little below the average this year. Aroostook suffered most decidedly from an over supply of rain. As a result the hay crop was ruined in many places. The grain was injured to some extent and the potatoes turned out about 20 per cent lighter than last year.

Through the central and southern parts of the State the crops were somewhat better, but the cold weather, combined with the rain, made a very light corn crop, both sweet and field corn. The potatoes on the average did very well in this section and there was a good crop of hay. The grain was rather light, due to the hot week in July and the damp, cold weather that followed. Of apples there was a good crop through all parts of the State.

I am going to devote most of my time to plans for the coming year. There are two reasons for this: First, I have not much to say about the year just past, and second, it seems to me more desirable to lay before you my ideas for the coming year, and to receive here and now your approval or disapproval, than to spend my time in telling you what we have already done, a thing that most of you know.

Some of the following points I have worked out in part and others are still unsolved.

First,—By use of the post cards which most of you have received, I plan to make as complete a list as possible of all of the seed for sale by the different members. I will send one of these lists to each Grange; it will then be up to you if you sell your seed or not.

Second,—I am planning to run germination tests on as much seed as is sent to me for that purpose. The germination test will tell you if it is worth while or not to plant that seed the coming spring. The germination percentage is a very good point to mention in advertising your seed. With a high germination percentage you can ask a higher price. The result of this work depends on you. If you send the seed in, I will test it. If you don't send it in I can not test it. I will do this testing in January and February.

Third,—I hope to send out to as large a number of farmers as advisable, plans for seed improvement. Whether these plans will be of any value or not depends on two things; first, on my ability to make the plans hit each individual, and second, on the following out of those plans by you.

Fourth,—I hope to be able to obtain a small amount of money so that I can buy good seed from reliable houses. I plan now to buy only the small grains, as oats, barley, etc. Then to any man that seems worthy (I will judge his worth by the work he has already done and the interest he has taken), I will send as much seed of any one (but only one) kind as he wants for his own use next spring. In return I shall demand that he sign a regular contract to return to the field agent or department next fall the same amount of seed as I gave him in the spring and one-half as much more. The seed that he returns must be cleaned in a fanning mill and free from all weed seeds. To illustrate,—if I give John Smith ten bushels of oats this spring, I shall expect him to return to the field agent next fall fifteen bushels of clean seed.

Fifth,—I expect to be about with the farmers next spring at planting time and aid them in the selection of seed. I hope also to keep in close touch with them through the whole season until after the crops are harvested.

Sixth,—I think that you will agree with me that 160 people scattered through the whole State is a rather large number for one man to keep in close touch with. Therefore, if it is possible in any way to obtain the aid of the teachers of agriculture in the secondary schools, I shall try to do it. That is, I will talk with them and put before them the plans I have made for the farmers in their section. They will then for a slight compensation, act as my deputies and will watch and advise the farmers as I direct them. This will allow me more time in places where no other assistance can be secured.

Seventh,—I am going to try to send out a monthly card to all of you in an endeavor to bring to your minds some of the necessary and advisable things that should be done at that time. I hope also to get out other printed matter, perhaps more in the nature of advertising.

Eighth,—I would like to see an exchange or store established where you could sell your seed at wholesale and yet get a fair price for it. I have not yet talked with Mr. Embree, but I hope he will be able to solve this question for me, if the Farmers' Union has not done so already. It does not seem to me to be good business, to sell little amounts of seed to this farmer or that farmer. I know if I had 500 bushels of oats to sell I would much prefer to sell all of them at once at a slightly lower price than to job them out at a higher price. To my mind the wholesale trade is business and the other is a Jew trade.

The last plan I have and perhaps the biggest is to assist the farmer in every way possible and along every line of farming. Seed Improvement is my business, but I know that that is not the only way to make money on a farm. I don't know it all, but I am, or can become, acquainted with those who do know it all. I can get the information for you. Don't be afraid to ask me; I will not tell you if you do not ask.

Just a few words now to sum up how things stand.

I have used my time since June seventeenth to get acquainted with the situation and the people. I have tried to help you when I could at the same time.

There seems to be a lack of system and business principles in the average farmer, and a slight lack of interest and a little inconsistency in the Seed Improvement Work. I can remedy these three things to a great extent, with your coöperation. *But I Must Have Your Coöperation.*

The crops this year are perhaps a little below average, but I am glad to say that I have yet to see a farmer who was ruined by the hard year.

I hope in the following year to:—

1. Send out lists of the seed for sale by the different members.

2. Run a large number of germination tests and thus aid you to get a larger crop next year.

3. Furnish Seed Improvement plans that will be of value if you follow them.

4. Send out to a small number of you good seed free of charge.

5. Coöperate with you and assist you at all times along all lines of farming.

6. Secure the aid of the secondary schools in this work.

7. Send out a large amount of printed matter that will be of service if you read it and think it over.

8. Find some means of selling the seed at wholesale to good advantage.

There is enough there to keep me busy for one year at least, but I want to say right here, I can do nothing unless every one of you helps me all he can. I am merely planning the work, showing you how, why and when to do these different things. It is you who have got to do the work. It is you who will make a success or failure of your own work as well as mine. It is you who will get the greater benefits and the larger profits, and it is you who will get the credit. I am only your silent partner, "The man behind the gun."

THURSDAY, December 5.

GROWING POTATOES FOR SEED.

By Guy C. Porter, Houlton.

In introducing this subject, I wish to state that I am not a potato expert, but simply a practical potato grower, also that my experience in growing potatoes has been confined to Aroostook County. In addressing this meeting, I shall consider that I am speaking to practical farmers.

I heard of an incident the other day, which will illustrate what a practical mind the average farmer has. A certain Chemical Company was erecting a building near the highway under the direction of a chemist. When a farmer drove up and inquired what he was building, the chemist replied that it was a chemical laboratory. Want to know, said the farmer, what you are going to do in there. Why, we are in hopes to discover a universal solvent, that is, a liquid that will dissolve any solid. Fine! fine! said the farmer. Say, what are you going to keep it in?

This topic, growing potatoes for seed, is a very practical one and has a large commercial significance. Three-fourths of all the potatoes grown in Maine could be sold for seed at a good price every year, if we would but exercise proper care in growing and shipping our seed stock. We have the best soil and climate for growing potatoes of any State in the Union, and recent tests have proved that Maine grown seed is superior to that of any other section when planted in the South.

The potato seed business is at present in a very crude state. Varieties are not standardized. We often find one variety posing under three or four different names in different parts of our State. I am in hopes that something may be done by the Maine Seed Improvement Society towards standardizing the varieties of seed potatoes.

There are several ways of obtaining better seed, the simplest of which is to buy from some other grower, who has been selecting his seed, provided that man can be found and is willing to sell some of his selected stock. Then again, we may improve our own seed, either by mass selection, seed breeding or hill selection. I have tried all three, but think hill selection the most practicable for the average farmer. Mass selection is better than no selection, but we must remember, when we pick out an ideal potato from a pile, that it may have been the only nice potato in that hill, in which case the progeny of that potato is more likely to resemble the average of the hill, than this parent, for the potato seed is not properly a seed but a cutting or a scion of the potato plant. Seed breeding is rather a long process and requires more time and attention than the average farmer can afford. The best way to make hill selections is to dig a hill at a time with a hand digger, throwing two rows together, keeping the rank and file of the potatoes on one row, and whenever a hill is found containing five or six smooth, even sized potatoes, with no small or rough ones, throwing this on the other row, so that they may be picked up separately. It is not a very hard matter in this way to select enough good hills to plant a plot of sufficient size to grow seed enough for the entire crop for the following year. If the selections are made carefully, I believe that in a few years a decided improvement, both in yield and quality, may be obtained. Having secured as good seed as possible to plant, it is necessary to exercise special care in cutting, planting, cultivating, spraying, harvesting, storing and shipping the seed crop.

Clover seed is the ideal ground upon which to plant. In Aroostook the more successful growers practice either a three or four years' system of crop rotation. Following potatoes with oats and seeding down to clover, growing clover either one or two years, plowing in the fall ready for potatoes the next spring, after a thorough harrowing with both the disk and smoothing harrow, we are ready to plant.

I have treated my seed with the formaldehyde solution for the past two years and believe it pays. Not that the black-leg disease has ever done much damage in Aroostook, but seed showing a very small per cent of disease here may develop as much as fifty per cent when planted in the South, and it is for our interest to do everything possible to protect the Southern grower.

Care must be taken in cutting seed, to discard all potatoes which show disease, and we should disinfect the knife which has cut the diseased tuber. It is desirable to cut the potatoes so as to make as square and blocky pieces as possible, avoiding thin edges.

In Aroostook, we think we get better results by planting close together, about ten inches, and using a liberal amount of high grade fertilizer. We use the high ridge method of cultivation, doing practically all of the work with the wheel cultivator and horse hoe. A new two-row wheel horse hoe has been put on the market this year, which will save the work of one man. We go through the crop about every week during the summer, keeping the ground entirely free from weeds and keeping a fine dust mulch on the rows at all times. I am afraid many of us are not careful enough in preparing our Bordeaux Mixture for spraying. It is very important that only diluted solutions be mixed together and it is a very easy and inexpensive job to erect a platform from which the diluted solutions can be run directly into the sprayer. I believe in using a power sprayer, giving a good pressure, using fine nozzles and spraying rather than sprinkling the vines. We are spraying from three to seven times, depending on weather conditions. A few years ago, we waited for fine weather to spray, but we have learned that the time it is most needed is in wet weather, and we spray any time when the tops are dry. I have noticed that potato vines will dry off very quickly, fully an hour before the grass is dry.

We should go through the fields two or three times during the summer and remove all plants showing any signs of disease, also any plants whose blossoms prove them to be of another variety. I have found, however, that the best time to remove any late varieties, which have become mixed with Cobblers or other early varieties, is to wait until the early potatoes have died down and then go through the field and remove all potatoes which are attached to green stalks.

We need to improve our method of digging potatoes. I suppose until someone invents a good potato digger, we will have to use the ones we have at present, but the way our potatoes are cut and bruised is really a shame. I did not realize how bad this was until I tried to pick out a bushel of nice potatoes for exhibition purposes. It then seemed that, whenever I found a potato that came up to my ideal in size and shape, in almost every case I would find it bruised or cut. We must have a radical change in our diggers. I do not know just how and if I did, I would not tell you, at least until after I had secured a patent.

Special care should be taken in handling our seed stock from the field to the storehouse. Many are careless, even using barrels in which the nails are not properly clinched, and some drop their potatoes from the floors of storehouses to the bottoms of the bins and this bruises them badly. We should remember not only that each bruised place may cause the tuber to decay, but also that it furnises a hiding place for the black-leg, or other disease germs, which will remain ready to appear the next year.

The question of selling and shipping our seed, is one in which I am especially interested just at present, but Mr. Embree is here to speak to you on this subject. He is much better qualified to speak on this than I, therefore I will leave it entirely to him.

There are many ways in which seed stock may get mixed and some Maine growers and shippers have not been any too careful in the past, so that it behooves us as farmers of the State to work together to produce and ship pure seed stock, so that Maine may take the place she deserves, as the leading seed potato state of the Union.

A judging contest for men, on corn and potatoes, was held in the afternoon, and also one for boys.

In the evening a very interesting address was given by Dr. Raymond Pearl on *"What Plant Breeding can do for Maine."*

Dr. Pearl pointed out that the State of Maine in 1911 in its seven leading crops, corn, wheat, oats, barley, buckwheat, potatoes and hay, had a valuation of $42,736,000, and that one per cent of this amount would endow a seed producing and distributing farm with a yield of $25,000 annually. To give such a farm $25,000 annually would cost but six one-hundredths of one per cent of the total value of these seven crops, or six-tenths of a mill for every dollar of value.

Experiments in plant breeding at Highmoor Farm, Monmouth, were interestingly described, and in spite of the more or less scientific terms which alone express adequately the work and results in many instances it was made very interesting and comprehensive to the people present who are not familiar with the scientific work. He spoke of the great increase in the yield per annum of plants with which experiments had been made, and this, the speaker stated, proved what a great advantage a seed-producing and distributing farm would be to the farmers of the State. Under the present plan it is possible to serve but a small proportion of the farms of the State. It could be placed within the reach of all with the improved facilities.

Dr. Pearl devoted considerable time to the description of the method of breeding oats. He stated that a necessary preliminary to plant breeding is to discover which varieties are best adapted to a locality. Of the varieties planted three were selected, the first yielding 149 bushels to the acre, the second 141 bushels, and the third 139 bushels. He pointed out that the average yield in Maine is 38 1-2 bushels per acre. This he stated shows that the quality of the oats had been improved in breeding.

Like experiments with corn had been made, the most successful being one in hybrid breeding, a variety of yellow corn and one of sweet corn being crossed. The first yield the corn was entirely yellow, while in the second there were four varieties—starchy white corn, starchy yellow corn, sweet white corn and sweet yellow corn. The sweet white corn was selected for propagation and when bred was found to be double in size that of the original plant, to have a larger ear and a much finer kernel. These were pointed out as three marked evidences of the success of the experiment.

During the evening three new varieties of oats, all bred by Dr. Pearl in the series of experiments conducted by him, were christened, each of these being capable of producing even under adverse conditions double the present yield in this State. They have been named by Dr. Pearl, Maine 281, Maine 247 and Maine 250, he having named them after the State in which they were bred.

Oat Field of J. C. Peterson, Gardiner.

FRIDAY, December 6.

GROWING SMALL GRAINS.

By R. L. Copeland, Holden.

Some years ago our attention was first called to the importance of pure or good seed by the remark of a friend, who said "I hear you have a large crop of oats. Have you got any good seed for sale?"

We had to reply that we had not, as the oat we grew at that time had been on the farm many years, was light in weight and somewhat infected with foul seed.

We at once asked ourselves why it was that we were growing an inferior grain when with but small expense and a little care we might grow the best, and resolved to grow only the best in the future.

With this aim in view we sought the best or the ideal oat according to our mind, i. e. one strong in stalk, with large, branching head, kernel well filled, and hull comparatively thin. The result has been highly satisfactory.

According to the best of our recollection the yield from the old oat was from 40 to 50 bushels to the acre, whereas at the present time we consider a yield of 60 bushels rather light. This amount was our average yield this season. Last year it was 86 bushels per acre, and we have grown 110 bushels on a measured acre in one season.

We do not wish to be understood as claiming that all one has to do is to procure some improved or high cost seed in order to reap a harvest of nearly 100 bushels of oats to the acre. The experienced farmer knows that there are other conditions which enter in, in order to make a successful harvest.

This fact was forcibly illustrated the past season by a neighbor who had more money than experience. He paid $3.00 per bushel for oats enough to sow one acre. The oats were remarkably heavy, and had a thick, flinty hull, which seemed to make up a large per cent of the weight. He sowed them when the ground was wet and cold, in a poorly prepared seed bed. The yield was 23 bushels from the acre.

To grow a good oat crop there are four prime essentials:

    1st.   Pure seed of known germinating power.
    2nd.   A fertile soil, but not over rich in nitrogen.
    3rd.   A good seed bed.
    4th.   A favorable season.

A fertile soil sown with poor seed will give only a fair crop in the most favorable season. Sown to the best varieties of seed, the soil yields the greatest returns. In recent years a vast amount of attention has been given to the preparation and treatment of the soil and but very little attention given to the purity and productiveness of the seed.

If one has any doubt in regard to the great loss sustained by the farmers of Maine through the use of poor seed he has only to drive in the country during the first week of August to be convinced. He will note acre after acre so infested with charlock, commonly called mustard or kale, as to render them not worth the harvesting.

Those who have not had experience little realize the damage to the farm and the difficulty in eradicating these foul weeds when they have once got established.

Dr. Woods says, "Spray with iron sulphate when the plants have attained a growth of three or four leaves." This method may be effectual for the present crop but it is characteristic of these seeds to germinate at all times of the season and some lie dormant in the soil for several years even when the ground is cultivated. Frances Willard is credited with saying, "The proper time to begin to bring up a child is one hundred years before it is born." The same principle holds true in regard to exterminating weeds. Begin before the seed is planted.

From experiments covering a series of years at the Ontario Experiment Farm the pure and selected seed gave an increased yield over the ordinary seed of approximately 20 per cent.

This gain agrees with our own experience and observation.

Some will say: We cannot all grow seed oats and sell them at a fancy price. Possibly not. But the best in kind and quality can never become too abundant.

We have sold oats for feed purposes at ten cents a bushel above the market quotation to a party who believes it economy to buy a clean, bright, heavy oat even at an advanced price.

At the present time it is difficult to obtain a market price or quotation for a Maine grown feed oat on account of its poor quality.

The manner of harvesting and curing has much to do with the value of the crop. We cut our oats with a reaper which leaves the grain in bunches of any desired size. The second day turn two or three rows together leaving them evenly spread, and the third or fourth day turn again. At this time if the weather is good, the crop will be evenly dried and ready for the barn.

We do not use the horse rake in the oat field as it gathers up more or less stubble, sticks and roots which are not desired as the separator in threshing breaks them up and they pass into the grain.

Oats we sell for seed are run through a fanning mill and those for home planting are treated with formaldehyde also.

THE SILO—CHARACTERISTICS, LOCATION, COST AND CONSTRUCTION.

By Professor R. W. Redman.

In any factory the supply of raw material largely determines the possibilities of the business. If the raw material is limited in quantity or quality, or the cost is excessive, the profit is necessarily curtailed. In the dairy business the storage of large quantities of palatable, nutritious, yet low cost feed, is fundamental for success. At the present time there is no method for storing dairy fodders equal to siloing them. A part of the ration will profitably be the dried fodders and another part the concentrates or grains; yet the silage is the greatest factor in making an economical and palatable ration.

By use of a silo, large quantities of green food may be economically stored for winter use. True it is that this same fodder could be dried, yet the drying process is expensive for many of the leaves are lost, and in the case of corn, small animals and birds frequently eat an appreciable amount, especially if the ears are at all matured. Also the labor of handling the dry fodder is nearly, if not quite, as great and many times as much storage room is required.

The building of a silo by the dairyman usually marks a great advance in the net returns from his business. The chief time for feeding silage is during the winter, when otherwise only dry feeds would be available. A secondary time for feeding silage is during those summer months when the pasture grass is short and dried. Silage will help the dairyman over this trying time, usually at a smaller expense than by the use of soiling crops.

The popularity of the silo in Maine is shown by its presence on so many farms. Its value is attested by every dairyman who keeps an account with his cows, and the majority of cow owners who keep no records believe that the silo is a necessity. Yet, notwithstanding this constant demonstration of the silo as an important part of the business equipment, there are many cattle owners who have not yet investigated silo construction. For this reason I present to you some of the phases of silo location, cost, and construction. I do not attempt to prescribe a cure-all for your feeding troubles. Neither can I tell you what it will cost to build a silo on your own farm, since conditions differ widely. The ideas and figures which I bring to you are not new. Some of them have been obtained through concerns manufacturing silo material, others from experiment station investigations, and still others from my own observation and experience in eight states of this country and two of the Canadian provinces.

SILAGE CROPS.

The principal crop for the silo is corn, though numerous other green crops have been used successfully—such as clover, oats and peas, various grasses, Japanese and German millets, soy beans, and beet tops, besides other crops which grow farther south.

DEVELOPMENT OF THE SILO.

The first silos to be constructed were merely pits dug in the earth, in which fresh vegetables and fodders were tramped. These pits were covered with earth and not infrequently weighted with stones. It is said that the first silos on the western hemisphere were used by some tribes of South American Indians to preserve fish for winter use.

The next step in the development was a rectangular room of varying proportions, but usually with the height not exceeding one of the floor dimensions. This type of silo did not prove particularly satisfactory on account of the lack of depth and hence lack of pressure, as well as because of the relatively great surface exposed to the air.

The next general class of silos was those having a greater depth than any one floor dimension. These were first rectangular or square, and the farmer often built them in a band or joint in the barn. He soon found, however, that there was a great tendency for the silage to spoil in the corners of the silo, and also for the walls to separate at the corners. He attempted to remedy this by cutting off the corners, making the octagonal silo. The round silo followed quickly, and is today, for obvious reasons, the most satisfactory type to build. It is true that today there are in Maine many square silos giving good satisfaction and possibly there are places in which it would be advisable to build them, but this does not apply to average conditions.

Advantages of a round silo over a square or rectangular one:

1. The round silo requires less lumber.

2. The round silo is easier to reinforce.

3. There is less difficulty in filling, as no corners have to be cared for.

4. The silage settles more evenly and compactly.

The materials used for building silos are:

1. Wood—(a) single thickness, stave; (b) two or more thicknesses, with air space, as King, Gurler, or Wisconsin type.

2. Stone—usually single wall.

3. Brick—either single or double wall.

4. Hollow tile.

5. Concrete—(a) monolithic or one-piece; (b) blocks.

Of these materials, stone and brick may be disregarded under most Maine conditions, for on account of the extra cost to build them another type is chosen. The cost of double wall wooden silos is nearly as much as that required to erect a concrete silo. Further, they are not as permanent, and require much more care while they do last.

A hollow tile silo can be built without the use of the forms necessary for concrete. From what few figures I have been able to gather, the expense is slightly greater than for concrete, but the silo could be built where gravel is not readily obtained. Hollow tile are worthy of further investigation.

Thus discarding these materials for the reasons named, we have staves, concrete, and concrete blocks for silo construction. Time forbids the extended discussion of all three of these, and as detailed information can be obtained from the cement companies concerning the last two we will devote the major portion of the paper to stave silos.

Before building, a man should know how large a silo he needs. Further, a consideration of the desired essentials of a silo will help him determine the material.

THE SIZE TO BUILD.

The capacity and proportions of a silo are governed by these five factors:

1. Number of cows to be fed.
2. Number of days fed.
3. Number of pounds silage fed per animal per day.
4. Depth necessary to feed each day to prevent spoiling.
5. Effect of additional depth on capacity.

The first factor needs no comment. Many of the Maine dairymen plan to feed silage from their winter silo for eight months; that is, from the middle of September to the middle of May, or 240 days. To each cow thirty or forty pounds of silage are fed each day. To prevent spoiling, about two inches should be fed off the top each day.

A deep silo holds a proportionally greater amount than one of less depth. For example, a silo 20 feet high, 14 feet in diameter, holds 51 tons, while a 30-foot silo of the same diameter holds 91 tons. This is a gain of 40 for the additional 10 feet, while the first depth averaged only 25 1-2 tons per 10 feet.

To answer the question of size, I refer you to the following table taken from publications on silage:

TABLE I.*

RELATION OF SIZE OF SILO TO SIZE OF HERD, FED 240 DAYS.

No. Cows.	Silage Consumed.	Size of Silo.
10	48 tons	10x31
12	57 tons	10x35
15	72 tons	11x36
20	96 tons	12x39
25 ·	120 tons	13x40
30	144 tons	15x37
35	168 tons	16x38
40	192 tons	17x39
45	216 tons	18x39
50	240 tons	19x39

CAPACITY OF SILOS OF VARYING SIZES IN FEET.

INSIDE DIAMETER OF SILO IN FEET.

Depth of Silo in Ft.	10 Tons Silage.	12 Tons Silage.	14 Tons Silage.	16 Tons Silage.	18 Tons Silage.
25	36	52	68	96	122
28	40	61	81	108	137
30	44	68	90	115	150
32	50	72	95	126	162
34	53	77	108	142	171
36	57	82	114	158	194

ESSENTIALS OF A GOOD SILO.

Under this heading I can do no better than to give you the substance of a report of the agricultural engineers of Iowa State College. These essentials are:

Imperviousness of the Walls.—The fundamental principle involved in preservation of silage is the retention of moisture within the silage and the exclusion of air. For this reason the silo wall must be nonporous. Moisture must be prevented from passing in.

*Mo. A. E. S.—Bul. 103.

Rigidity, Strength and Smoothness of Walls.—An ideal silo must have rigid walls. It must be strong enough to resist the bursting pressure of·the silage. This acts outward in all directions as the silage settles. The friction of the silage against the wall and the weight of the wall produce a crushing action which is great near the bottom of the silo. A silo when empty should be heavy enough to stand against heavy winds. The inside of a silo wall should be reasonably smooth to permit the silage to settle freely. If the wall is not smooth, or if there are shoulders or offsets on the inside surface, air pockets will be formed and a considerable loss of silage will result.

Durability.—After due consideration to all other points of merit to be found in silos, the most desirable silo is the one that is the most durable and will give the longest term ·of service. The durability of a silo depends first upon its strength, and, second, on the durability of the material used in its construction. To be durable, any material must resist the action of the weather, the constant wetting and drying, freezing and thawing in the winter season, and any disintegrating action which may be due to the silage itself. Some material will disintegrate with age, and other materials suffer from rapid decay when subject to the warm, moist conditions which exist in the silo.

Care and Repair.—It is desirable that a silo require the minimum expenditure in the way of labor and material for its upkeep. A silo which must be adjusted for shrinkage and expansion is of less value than one which does not need such attention. Often this work is neglected, and loss results. Some silos must be frequently repainted in order to present a pleasing appearance. This means added expense. All parts should be equally durable and lasting. The replacement of parts which are short-lived, the substitution of new pieces for those which have become decayed or faulty for any other reason, adds materially in many cases to the cost of maintaining the silo.

Convenience.—A silo should be convenient for filling, and so arranged that the silage may be easily removed from day to day during the feeding season. The doors should be so constructed that they can be put in place and removed with the least effort. They should permit easy access to the silo and allow the removal of the silage with the least possible amount of labor.

Portability.—There are instances where tenants and others desire a silo which may be used in one place for a time and then moved to a new location. Under such circumstances, this feature should be given due consideration.

Fire Proof Construction.—It adds materially to the value of any building to be made of fire-proof material. The importance of this feature is realized when the large annual loss from fire is taken into consideration.

Appearance.—All farm buildings should be of good appearance. This feature adds both to the attractiveness and the value of the farm. A permanent silo of neat appearance is the most desirable silo to construct, other things being equal.

Simplicity of Construction.—It is an advantage to select a silo which can either be constructed without special skilled labor, forms or tools, or can be purchased ready for erection without the aid of skilled labor.

Cost.—One of the most important features to be considered in the selection of a silo is its first cost. The silo which will furnish storage for silage at the least cost per ton is the silo to build, other points being equal.

Frost Resistance.—In Maine the winters are so severe that it is difficult to construct a frost-proof silo. The silo wall which will prevent freezing to the greatest degree is the most desirable. A roof probably does as much as the walls to prevent freezing.

Some silos are made with double walls, with an air space between, as the King silo; others have double walls of brick or concrete; wood offers considerable resistance to the escape of heat. Single wall stave silos have given good satisfaction in this State. It may be necessary to keep the outside of the silage slightly lower than the middle when feeding during cold weather, or to cover the top of the silage with blankets, or with the doors of the silo which have been taken out—usually a little thoughtful attention prevents any serious trouble from freezing. Freezing does not hurt the silage but more labor is required to take it out of the silo, and it is harder on the animals to warm the food if it is frozen.

FAILURES OF SILOS.

If the essentials of a good silo are observed in its construction, there will be but few failures. However, some silos have failed, and these have been object lessons to us. With a stave silo, sometimes the staves shrink, the hoops loosen, and unless tightened before filling, the cracks may be large enough so that air gets into the silage and allows it to spoil.

Unanchored silos are likely to blow over when empty if the hoops are not well tightened. Occasionally a silo bursts. This may be due to an excessive swelling of staves, to lack of reinforcement, or an accumulation of juice from immature silage. If crops containing a large amount of juice—as refuse from a pea cannery—are to be used for silage, a drain should be provided in the bottom of the silo to remove excessive moisture.

To prevent bursting, extra reinforcement should be provided in building a concrete silo, or in case of the stave silo, hoops should be larger or put nearer together. A silo may be anchored by setting pins in the concrete when the foundation is made. These may be straight and have the staves set upon them, or have rings in the upper end and the staves bolted to them.

Guys may be attached from the top of the silo to the ground. Concrete silos have vertical reinforcement set in the foundation.

Some double-walled wooden silos have lasted but a short time because insufficient ventilation was provided between the walls to allow them to dry out during the summer.

LOCATION.

Advantages of Inside Silo.—Silos are sometimes put inside of barns on account of the following advantages:

1. Some men desire to build a square silo and find that they can do so by the use of the timbers of a joint or band in the barn to support the walls.

2. A silo inside the barn should freeze less than one outside.

3. A cheaply-made silo may last longer if it is inside and not exposed to the weather.

4. When the silo is placed in the center of the barn there is less distance to move the feed.

Reasons for Outside Location.—At the present time the majority of silos are being built outside of the barn for:

1. The inside location is not an economical use of barn room. The man who is working his plant to its full capacity will need that space for storing materials which will not go into the silo.

2. The average silo usually does not need the protection of an inside location.

3. Often the inside silo is unhandy to fill, while a silo on the outside may be reached easily.

4. The location keeps the odors from the barn. Nearly every outside silo has a door between it and the barn, and if this is closed, one of the chief objections to the use of silage is removed.

The outside silo should not be over four feet from the barn, and should be located so that the chute or communicating passageway leads into the feeding alley. The silo should be so placed in respect to other buildings that there is room to run the ensilage cutter and for teams to reach the cutter with their loads.

COST.

Stave Silos.—The figures on the cost of stave silos are very unsatisfactory for comparison with the other estimates, for the reason that the labor of erecting and the cost of foundations are not figured. Further, while I have written nearly all of the companies who are selling many stave silos, only one concern has given me prices in such shape that they can be used here.

These silos are made with splines between the staves, and metal splines are used if staves are pieced. These prices do not include roof, foundation, nor labor for erecting.

SIZES AND PRICES OF ROUND SILOS.

2-in. White Pine.	Approximate Weight.	Diameter Feet.	Height Feet.	Listed Capacity Tons.
$69 86	2,000	8	20	18
73 40	2,300	9	20	23
129 71	3,800	10	30	42
142 39	4,200	11	30	51
155 40	4,600	12	30	60
167 09	5,000	13	30	72
179 73	5,300	14	30	86
218 81	6,400	14	36	103
234 00	7,100	15	36	116
276 44	8,100	16	40	147
310 97	9,100	18	40	186
351 19	10,100	20	40	233
440 09	12,600	20	50	300

2-in. spruce, 5 per cent. less than white pine.

PRICE OF CONICAL SILO COVERS.

Diameter Feet.	Weight.	Price.
8	195	$16 95
9	225	19 91
10	425	22 55
11	500	25 81
12	575	28 88
13	650	32 65
14	750	36 34
15	875	39 77
16	1000	44 32
18	1125	54 08
20	1450	65 56

Estimates for foundations as given by agricultural engineers vary from $15 to $135, and for labor from $16 to $125.

As previously stated, the amount of material required for the foundation and floor varies with soil conditions. The following estimate has been given for cement, for substantial work, where the whole foundation is concrete: Silo 8 feet in diameter, 2 1-2 barrels cement; 16 feet, 6 1-2 barrels; 20 feet, 9 barrels.

STONE SILOS.

The cost for stone silos varies with the distance which the material has to be hauled, the size of the stone, also the size of the silo. A silo large enough to accommodate 15 cows will probably cost about $400. This according to the Wisconsin Agricultural Experiment Station is greater than the cost for the same size silo of any other make excepting iron silos.

The figures for brick silos were furnished by the Iowa Experiment Station (Bulletin 100), and are based upon the following cost: Brick, $8 per M ; mason, $4 per day; helpers, $2 per day.

Single Wall Silo: 14 feet in diameter, $9 per foot of height; 16 feet in diameter, $10 per foot of height; 18 feet in diameter, $11.50 per foot of height.

Double Wall Silo: 14 feet in diameter, $13 per foot of height; 16 feet in diameter, $14 per foot in height; 18 feet in diameter, $16 per foot in height.

HOLLOW TILE.

These are used to some extent for silo building and probably will be used more in the future. I have been unable to obtain figures as to cost applicable to New England.

CONCRETE SILOS.

Actual cost of any number of concrete silos is as difficult to obtain as for stave silos for much of the labor of erection is done by the men on the farm and no account of time kept. Estimates from several states indicate a total cost of $2.50 to $3.00 per ton capacity for silos holding 90 to 120 tons. These figures are not exact. Concrete block silos seem to cost slightly more in total expense but more of the labor can be done by the ordinary farm help.

This means that monolithic (or solid wall) concrete silo of 100 tons capacity should cost $250 to $300.

The cost of any silos for any specific location can only be determined by the dairyman by securing estimates for his particular conditions and for the silo he desires. All silo companies and many cement dealers will cheerfully assist in determining cost.

CONSTRUCTION.

It is necessary to establish a foundation below the frost line. Usually it is not advisable to go over 6 feet below the surface of the ground on account of the extra labor required to throw the silage out. Also the cost of construction at a greater depth is often more than that for the additional height. If the ground is hard and firm, a footing 2 feet wide by 1 foot deep will be sufficient to support the weight of the walls; but if the soil is soft or loose, it may be necessary to make a footing 3 or 4 feet wide. If a chute is to be used, a footing should be provided for it when the foundation for the walls is being put in.

Unless good drainage is natural to the location, tile should be laid to conduct the water away from the foundation of the silo. It may be necessary to put cinders, 3 in. to 6 in. deep, under the floor, in order that the water which seeps under the silo may reach the tile laid around the outside of the foundation.

FORMS.

If a heavy clay soil, a form will not be required for a foundation, but if the soil is somewhat light, it may be necessary to use heavy building paper or tarred paper to line the trenches; if the soil is still lighter and has a tendency to cave in, boards will need to be bent around some stakes to serve as forms. A satisfactory mixture for foundation is one sack of cement to three cubic feet of coarse, sharp sand, to five cubic feet of screened gravel.

FLOORS.

The floor may be made of the same mixture as the foundation. If the silo is likely to be filled with immature crops or crops containing a large amount of water, as refuse from a pea cannery, it would be necessary to provide for a drain, which should be laid at this time. This drain should have a trap in it so that air will not come up through it to allow decomposition of the silage. It should be provided on top with a screen so that the silage will not go down through.

A floor is not really a necessity, provided the soil is well drained and rats do not burrow through to get into the silage. A floor cleans easier than the earth, and will care for the two above-mentioned troubles. A floor 5 in. thick, with a pitch of 1-4 in. to 1 in., gives good satisfaction. The floor supports the great weight of the silage, but this weight is evenly distributed, so that a heavier floor is not required.

FOUNDATION WALL.

If the silo is to be made of concrete, the foundation wall may be the same thickness as the walls of the silo; that is, 6 in. to 8 in. If not a concrete superstructure, 6 in. to 12 in. will be sufficient for the walls. If this wall comes above the surface of the ground (it usually does), reinforcement must be provided. This reinforcement may be of wire or iron rods, depending upon the size of the silo. These data may be obtained from the cement companies or dealers when purchasing cement for the foundation. If a concrete or stone silo is to be built, vertical reinforcement rods should be placed in the foundation; if a stave silo is being built, eye bolts should be placed in the concrete so that the silo may be anchored.

The foundation may be made of other material than concrete, such as stone, brick, hollow tile filled with concrete, or concrete blocks. These are used according to conditions.

STAVE SILO.

Any substantial weather-resisting lumber can be made into a good silo. The following woods are used for staves: Cypress, white pine, cedar, redwood, tamarack, long leaf southern pine, spruce, and sometimes even hemlock. The Bureau of Forrestry, U. S. Department of Agriculture, makes the following statement regarding the average number of years wood will remain without decay (Mo. A. E. S. B. 103):

TABLE VI.

Species	Ave. No. Yrs. Life Untreated
Cypress	14
Redwood	14
Douglas fir	10
Yellow pine	8
White pine	8

Dipping in or painting with a preservative is recommended and many silo companies furnish such preservatives or treat the lumber by dipping before it is shipped. Coal tar preservatives can usually be purchased from dealers in any of the larger towns.

Directions for the erection of patented stave silos are usually sent with these silos. Each piece of lumber is usually numbered so that the farmer should have no great difficulty in putting the silo together.

In conclusion, I am going to tell you about building a home-made silo—a silo for the small dairyman who is trying to get on his feet. It is true that this silo may cost more in the end than a permanent structure of concrete might cost. It may represent as many dollars invested as would a patented stave silo, but it does not call for the actual cash outlay.

My attention was called to this home-made stave silo several years ago by a dairyman in Penobscot county. While the silo may not be very long lived, especially if placed outdoors, it has given sufficient satisfaction so others have been built in the same neighborhood.

A silo 12 feet in diameter and 20 feet high needs 10 hoops of 5-8-inch round iron. This means 10 holes in each side of the door frame and 20 holes in the post at the back. The hoops are made in two sections each, threaded for 6 inches on each end. The door frame and middle post are stood in place on the foundation and held by braces. Two or three hoops are put in place, the staves stood up inside, and fastened by cleats of laths or barrel staves. The other hoops are put in and all tightened.

For lumber, this 12 x 20 ft. silo requires 105 staves 4 inches wide and 20 feet high, three 6 x 6 in. x 20 ft. posts, two 6 x 6 in. x 22 ft., and about 75 feet of 1-in. boards. The door is made of pieces of 1-in. board, which are 4 inches longer than the width of the doorway, this latter being usually 18 inches. Two thicknesses of 1-in. board are used with a layer of building paper between, taking care these pieces of board break joints.

The objection to this type of silo is lack of permanence and the amount of care it requires. As the staves are square, they touch only on the inner corners. This leaves cracks outside where decay starts. The silo dries during the summer, and the hoops must be tightened to keep it from falling down. In spite of these two objections, this type of silo will serve to help the struggling dairyman to put up ensilage for his cows. He may be able to get on his feet by using such a silo, even though it costs him more in the long run than a more durable one would, had he been able to build it in the first place.

CONCLUSION.

The silo is a business necessity for Maine dairymen. Its purpose is to preserve large quantities of succulent feed at a low cost. It should be convenient to fill and to empty. The cost varies greatly, but some kind of a practical silo is within reach of every farmer who expects his cows to return a profit.

Business meeting, called to order by the president. The report of the committee on resolutions was received and approved. The following resolutions were adopted:

Resolved: That one of the most pressing needs of the live stock interests of Maine today is a more adequate knowledge than now exists in regard to the laws of breeding domestic animals for particular economic purposes. The Maine Seed Improvement Association is of the opinion that in order to meet this need the Maine Agricultural Experiment Station should undertake at the earliest possible moment thorough and systematic investigations in the field of animal industry, with special reference to the laws of breeding cattle for productive qualities, and desires hereby to extend its hearty support to the proposed plan to secure an annual appropriation of at least $5000, to be continued until the investigation is completed.

Resolved: That this Association recognizes the great need for new barns at the University of Maine and endorses the movement to secure an appropriation from the next Legislature for this purpose.

Resolved: That this Association give its hearty support to the effort to secure aid from the Federal Government for the support of the extension work in each state, under the direction of the College of Agriculture, and that we therefore urge the passage by the Congress of the United States of the so-called Smith-Lever Bill, Agricultural Extension Bill H. R. 22871, hereby reaffirming the position which this Association has constantly maintained in the past.

Resolved: That the agricultural interests of the State would be better served by a Commissioner of Agriculture appointed by the Governor, with the advice and consent of the Council, and answerable to them for the conduct of his office, than by one selected under the present law. This resolution is offered without any reflections expressed or implied, regarding the present incumbent of the office of Commissioner of Agriculture, but as an expression of the opinion of the Association as to the future policy which will be most conducive to the welfare of Maine agriculture.

Resolved: That we believe that this joint meeting of the Maine Seed Improvement Association and the Maine Dairymen's Association has been a great success; that we favor the continuance of these gatherings and that we believe it would be for the best interests of the agricultural organizations of the State if as many as possible of them should unite in such joint winter meetings.

Resolved: That as an Association we deeply appreciate the splendid hospitality which has been afforded us by the City of Portland, the Portland Board of Trade, and the Portland Farmers' Club. We desire to express our hearty thanks for the manner in which this convention has been entertained. To these bodies is due in large measure the success and pleasure of our meeting. We appreciate the courtesies extended by the press, the railroads, and the people of the city of Portland.

Signed GUY C. PORTER,

R. O. JONES,

RAYMOND PEARL.

The committee on nominations reported as follows:

President, W. G. Hunton, Cherryfield.

Vice President, A. P. Howes, Palmyra.

Treasurer, C. M. White, Bowdoinham.

Secretary, Prof. W. L. Slate, Orono.

Executive Committee: Guy C. Porter, Houlton; R. T. Paten, Skowhegan; R. L. Copeland, Holden, and Frank Carvell, Gardiner. Member of Experiment Station Council, W. G. Hunton. Visiting member to College of Agriculture, L. C. Holston, Cornish.

The above were duly elected. The bills were read and approved and ordered paid.

An invitation to hold the next annual meeting in Lewiston and Auburn was presented by L. C. Bateman of the Lewiston Journal.

Announcement of prizes awarded was made as follows:

Best peck of Late Potatoes—1st, W. L. Hannah, Freeport; 2nd, Dexter Burnell, Cumberland Center; 3rd, Guy C. Porter, Houlton.

Best peck Early Potatoes—1st, Guy C. Porter, Houlton; 2nd, Dexter Burnell, Cumberland Center; 3rd, F. W. Bonney, Monmouth.

Best display, one peck each, of three different varieties— 1st, Dexter Burnell, Cumberland Center; 2nd, F. W. Bonney, Monmouth; 3rd, Frank Lowell, Gardiner.

Sweet Corn, early, best ten ears—1st, Dexter Burnell, Cumberland Center; 2nd, Eugene Lowell, Gray; 3rd, George C. Merrill, Gray.

Dent Corn, best ten ears—1st, Uriah Duncan, Houlton; 2nd, Hiram Cornforth, Waterville.

Ensilage Corn, best five stalks—1st, H. G. Beyer, Jr., Portland; 2nd, H. G. Beyer, Jr., Portland.

Sweepstakes in any Corn—Dexter Burnell, Cumberland Center.

Beans, yellow eyes, best peck—Dexter Burnell, Cumberland Center.

Kidney Beans, best peck—Dexter Burnell, Cumberland Center.

Potatoes, best peck any variety, showing least waste in preparation for cooking—1st, Dexter Burnell, Cumberland Center; 2nd, F. W. Bonney, Monmouth; 3rd, Frank Lowell, Gardiner.

Corn, northern zone, best ten ears—Roscoe Bigelow.

Corn, southern zone—1st, H. M. Moulton, Cumberland Center; 2nd, H. M. Moulton; 3rd, W. B. Williams.

Sweet Corn, late—1st, Eugene Lowe, Gray; 2nd, Dexter Burnell, Cumberland Center; 3rd, George E. Merrill, Gray.

Pea Beans, best peck—Dexter Burnell, Cumberland Center.

Oats, best peck—1st, R. L. Copeland, Houlton; 2nd, Guy C. Porter, Houlton; 3rd, H. B. Whipple, Bingham.

Barley, best peck—H. B. Whipple, Bingham.

STATISTICS OF AGRICULTURAL SOCIETIES.

OFFICERS OF AGRICULTURAL SOCIETIES.

Name of Society.	President.	P. O. Address.	Secretary.	P. O. Address.	Treasurer.	P. O. Address.
Me State Agricultural ion.	B. J. Hly	d	I. L. Lowell	Auburn	T. F. dn	Lewiston.
Eastern Me Fair	F. O. Beal	Bangor	S. P. Emery	Bangor	A. S. Field	Bangor.
l Me Fair Co.	L. G. dr	Waterville	R. M. re	rle	L. G. Whipple	Mrville.
Maine State Pomological Aion.	H. L. Keyser	Greene	E. L. White	Bowdoinham	E. L. Lincoln	We.
Me State Poultry	H. L. h	Oakland	A. L. Merrill	Auburn	W. E. Scott	ll.
Androscoggin County Gn Fair As-	Fred A. Pike	East Livermore	Os. D. Dyke	Livermore Falls	H. F. Jones	e Corner.
Androscoggin, Greene in.	L. C. Mendall	Greene	W. L. Mer	Greene	B. P. Rackley	ne.
Aroostook, Northern Maine Fair As- n	A. E. Irving	Presque Isle	Ernest T.	Sn Presque Isle	Jhn E. Bishop	Presque Isle.
roostoo, Houlton	Nathaniel Tompkins	Houlton	G. T. Holyoke	Houlton	Roland E. Clark	Houlton.
Cumberland ity i i	Cl ss. W. i i	Sebago Lake	C. H. lh	Cumberland Mills	Harry C. Palmer	Gun, R. D. 1.
d Farmers' Club	A. W. Stanley	Cumberland Ct	Fred E. t ll	R. F. D. 2.	Willard Mhn	Cumberland Ctr. R. F. D. 2.
ll, New Gr a n d						Cr.
Danville	F. H. Grav	New Gester	J. P. Witham	New Gr	A. S. Gli lch	New Freeport.
li, Freeport Poultry Ass'n	L. E. Curtis	Freeport	Geo. P. Coffin	Freeport	A. P. Winslow	Mo's Mls.
Cumberland, tle Rigby Park	Sumner O. Hancock	Casco	Ernest U. hald	West Poland	dil H. Poore	Farmington.
Franklin t ly	Chas. W. ods	Farmington, R. F.	Geo. D. Glk	Farmington	Geo. M. Currier	
		D.				
i i, rh	E. Dill	Plps	J. I Harnden	lh	A. W. lleaport	Plps.
Hancock ity	F. P. Merrill	ll	C. S. Gman	dl	M. R. lley	ull.
Hancock, North	Forrest O. Silsby	Amherst	tcn. aHl M. Kis-	nt	J. G. Dunham	nt.
Hancock, Eden	A. S. Bunker	West Eden	F. A. Wool	Salisbury Cove	Chas. F. King	Eden.
Kennebec ity	E. E. Peacock	Readfield	P. G. i	dd	El A. Mr	Readfield, R. F.D. 27.
Kennebec, South	Leslie B. Hisler	Windsorville, R.F. D. 54.	Edwin t Glk	Mrville, R.F. D. 54.	J. S. Gray	Windsorville, R.F. D. 54.
Knox, North	E. E. Thurston	Union, R. D. 3	H. L. Grinnell	Union	Go. C. Hawes	Union.
Lin ity	Leslie Boynton	Jefferson	A. L. Shaw	Damariscotta	Harvey E. Mw	Damariscotta.
Lin Bristol	Emery P. Richards	Round Pond	J. Wilbur Hunter	Damariscotta	C. B. Woodward	Damariscotta.
Oxford t lg	W. L. Mr	So. Paris	W. O. Frothingham	So. Paris	W. O. Frothingham	So. Paris.
Oxford, Mt	Alt R. Hll	East Brownfield	B. Walker Mh	Fryeburg	A. D. Merrill	Fryeburg.
Mord, Androscoggin Valley	W. W. Rose	th	O. M. Richardson	th	W. S. Marble	Dixfield.
Oxford, rh	Charles T. Poor	Andover	nh F. Talbot	Andover	R. A. Grover	Andover.

Society					
Oxford, Western Maine Poultry Association	A. E. Shurtleff	So. Paris	E. P. Crockett	So. Paris	D. H. Bean	So. Paris
Penobscot, West	E. M. Atkins	Dexter, Route 3	E. E. Colbath	Dexter, Route 3	F. C. Barker	Exeter
Penobscot, North	H. B. Lewis	Springfield	I. R. Averill	Prentiss	O. A. McKenney	Springfield
Penobscot, Orrington	Chas. H. Chapman	So. Brewer, R. F. D. 1	F. Elmer King	So. Brewer, R. F. D. 1	F. Elmer King	So. Brewer, R. F. D. 1
Penobscot, Bangor Poultry and Pet Stock Association	F. H. Tupper	Bangor, Hammond St.	F. G. Bishop	Bangor, R. F. D. 8	F. G. Bishop	Bangor, R. F. D. 8
Sagadahoc County	C. W. Hayes	Foxcroft	E. C. McKechnie	Foxcroft	A. J.	Foxcroft
Sagadahoc, Richmond Farmers' and Mechanics'	E. C. Patten	Topsham	John R. Stanwood	Brunswick	Lyman E. Smith	Brunswick
Somerset	H. F. Smith	Richmond	N. H. Skelton	Richmond	W. R. Fairclough	R
Somerset, East	B. Frank Burns	Madison	Orlando Walker	Anson	J. F.	M sin
Somerset, Central	A. W. Miller	Hartland	E. A. Webber	Hartland	A. K.	Hartland
Somerset, Embden	Clyde H. Smith	Skowhegan	S. H. Bradbury	Skowhegan	W. Fogler	Skowhegan
	G. G. Palmer	No. Anson	Chester K. Williams	No. Anson	D. S.	No.
Waldo	Ralph Hayford	Belfast	W. G. Preston			
Waldo and Penobscot	Frank A. Littlefield	Monroe	Allen D. Colcord	D. 2.	M Mre	Mort, R. F. D. 2.
Waldo, Unity Park Association	Wm. H. Kimball	Burnham	Edwin T. Reynolds		Edwin T. Reynolds	Unity
Washington County	Dr. T. W. Pomeroy	Pembroke	J. M. Morgan	West	A. E.	Dennysville
Washington, West	A. H. Chandler	Columbia Falls	Wm. N. Dyer	Harrington	E. V. Coffin	Harrington
Washington, Machias Fair Ass'n	E. I. White	Machias	W. H. Phinney	Mas.	W. H. Phinney	Machias
Washington, Calais Fair Association	Wilfred L. Eaton	Calais	Thos. J. Doyle		E. C.	
Washington, Passamaquoddy Poultry Association	Jabez M. Pike	Lubec	Walter A. Harriman	Lubec	William L. Porter	Lubec
York, Shapleigh and Acton	John W. Fernald	Shapleigh	Fred K. Bodwell	Acton	Geo. T. Crediford	Shapleigh
York, Cornish Agricultural Ass'n	O. W. Adams	Cornish	Wm. R. Copp	Cornish	Samuel G. Sawyer	

ANALYSIS OF EXHIBITION.

Name of Society.	Number of horses and colts.	Number of thoroughbred bulls and bull calves.	Number of thoroughbred cows, heifers and heifer calves.	Number of grade cows, heifers and heifer calves.	Number of oxen and steers.	Number of animals for beef.	Number of cattle shown in herds.	Total number of neat stock.	Number of sheep.	Number of swine.	Number of poultry (coops).
Maine State	140	70	246	44	256	56	60	496	286	68	760
Eastern Maine Fair Association	74	38	108	14	150	44	146	306	27	14	275
Central Maine Fair Co	226	156	468	20			90	794	247	101	1,487
Maine State Pomological											
Maine State Poultry Association											1,000
Androscoggin County	14	3	8	14	20	4	42	49	4	10	30
Androscoggin, the Town Fair	17	3	6	15	6		95	42	4		2
Aroostook, Northern Maine Fair Association	172	57	132	25	4	8	80	218	34	15	667
Aroostook, Houlton	67	60	125	15	4	10	72	279		11	404
Cumberland	109	45	67	30	187	6	15	411	32	21	131
Cumberland Farmers'	26	7	20	7	32		42	87	8		180
Cumberland, New Gloucester and Danville	24	4	25	11	18			70	9	5	49
Cumberland, Freeport Poultry Association											800
Cumberland, Little Rigby Park	12	49	177	20	22	26	113	42	148		16
Franklin	81	8	25	100	300	16	34	765	95	26	104
Franklin, North	62	10		60	90	8		233	25	5	18
Hancock	25	1	9	25	35			78	4	15	15
Hancock, North	11			7	6			23	8		2
Hancock, Eden	5	21	43			31	49		24	4	15
Kennebec County	60	4	2	25	63	9		232	4		448
Kennebec, South	22	7	14	19	138	9	18	172	4	27	3
Knox, North	30	5	14	28	172	14	10	248			34
Lincoln	33		1	10	60			113	5	6	25
Lincoln, Bristol	22			10	38	42	36	49		1	24
Oxford	104	34	88	87	124		120	381	52	21	194
Oxford, West	118	24	40	87	224	28		364	32	4	45

											Total
Oxford, Androscoggin Valley	72	24	64	33	76	8	50	255	4	—	43
Oxford, North	22	5	15	32	30	12	6	100	28	30	10
Oxford, Western Maine Poultry Association	—	—	—	—	—	—	—	—	—	—	457
Penobscot, West	67	22	56	74	30	4	54	240	90	20	40
Penobscot, North	20	4	44	—	4	—	32	52	—	—	—
Penobscot, Orrington	7	1	5	—	—	—	4	10	—	10	6
Penobscot, Bangor Poultry and Pet Stock Ass'n	—	—	—	—	—	—	—	—	—	—	—
Piscataquis County	50	8	24	20	10	4	30	92	36	17	22
Sagadahoc County	21	44	138	60	56	4	189	491	46	29	80
Sagadahoc, Richmond Farmers' and Mechanics' Club	34	3	8	12	12	2	6	43	—	—	9
Somerset County	43	3	10	53	56	26	6	154	67	2	60
Somerset, East	53	3	5	27	2	3	25	65	—	—	23
Somerset, Central	23	10	22	15	56	16	—	119	52	—	150
Somerset, Embden	17	5	10	13	6	4	23	34	—	—	—
Waldo County	14	14	31	21	12	15	20	113	106	7	80
Waldo and Penobscot	75	17	47	30	54	14	32	194	20	10	91
Waldo, Unity Park Association	77	11	45	40	16	11	32	155	13	20	31
Washington County	17	7	17	37	14	—	25	92	83	13	38
Washington, West	29	15	19	28	48	—	6	116	7	—	41
Washington, Machias Fair Association	19	2	2	6	2	—	—	12	8	29	41
Washington, Calais Fair Association	19	11	13	11	—	10	15	60	—	—	297
Washington, Passamaquoddy Poultry Ass'n	—	—	—	—	—	—	—	—	—	—	16
York, Shapleigh and Acton	4	—	—	—	65	6	—	71	4	10	73
York, Cornish Agricultural Association	27	9	18	19	100	10	—	160	—	—	—
	2,164	824	2,211	1,204	2,598	426	1,521	8,080	1,616	552	9,036

ANALYSIS OF AWARDS.

Name of Society.	Amount of premiums awarded trotting bred stallions.	Amount of premiums awarded trotting bred brood mares.	Amount of premiums awarded draft stock stallions.	Amount of premiums awarded draft stock brood mares.	Amount of premiums awarded family horses.	Amount of premiums awarded gentlemen's drivers.	Amount of premiums awarded matched carriage horses.	Amount of premiums awarded colts.	Amount of premiums awarded horses for draft.
Maine State ...	$108 00	$30 00	$120 00	$26 00	—	$5 000	$10 00	$4 000	$97 75
...rn Me Fair ...son	71 00	15 00	30 00	16 00	$17 00	18 00	—	25 00	88 00
...al Me Fair Co.	35 00	27 00	28 00	32 50	—	50 00	—	37 00	102 60
Me State Pomological	—	—	—	—	—	—	—	—	—
Me State Poultry	—	—	—	—	—	—	—	—	—
Androscoggin County	4 00	4 00	1 50	4 00	—	15 00	—	12 00	12 00
...n, ...rn Fair Association.	—	—	120 00	—	—	—	—	2 50	118 00
..., Northern Maine Fair Association.	51 00	25 00	78 00	92 00	17 00	8 00	15 00	259 00	—
Aroostook, Houlton	50 00	25 00	15 00	46 00	—	6 00	—	130 00	85 00
... ...y	50 00	30 00	2 00	9 00	—	—	—	25 00	16 00
... ... Kib	3 00	2 00	4 00	2 00	—	—	—	17 50	13 00
..., New ...r and Danville.	6 00	—	—	—	—	3 00	—	18 00	—
..., ...t Poultry ...ation.	—	—	3 00	—	—	—	16 00	—	16 00
..., Little Rigby ...rk	9 00	9 00	21 00	9 00	8 00	20 00	7 00	3 00	52 00
Franklin County	15 00	3 00	—	4 50	2 00	6 00	2 00	42 00	13 00
Franklin, North	3 50	10 00	8 00	8 00	—	3 00	—	17 60	4 00
Hancock ...ty	5 00	—	—	—	—	3 00	—	18 00	11 25
Hancock, North	—	—	—	—	—	—	—	—	—
Hancock, Eden	15 00	7 00	11 00	5 00	—	30 00	—	13 00	24 00
Kennebec ...ty	3 75	3 75	2 50	2 00	3 00	3 50	2 50	22 50	38 00
Kennebec, South	2 00	2 00	10 50	3 00	3 00	3 50	—	7 00	42 50
Knox, ...	13 00	5 00	3 00	2 00	—	10 00	—	21 50	18 00
...in County	—	—	—	—	—	—	—	11 00	8 00
Lincoln, ...tol	—	—	—	—	—	—	—	3 00	—

Society									
Oxford, ...	45 00	27 00	—	—	—	25 00	—	83 00	208 00
Oxford, ...	25 00	21 00	8 40	12 00	—	—	10 00	23 60	64 00
Oxford, ...	17 00	10 00	8 00	10 00	—	10 00	10 00	19 00	89 00
Oxford, North ...	2 00	3 00	3 00	—	—	—	5 00	2 00	64 00
Oxford, ... Me ...ry Association	—	—	—	—	—	—	—	—	—
Penobscot, North	10 00	7 00	13 00	6 00	—	6 00	5 00	36 50	104 00
Penobscot, Orrington	1 50	—	—	2 50	—	—	—	7 25	7 00
...or Poultry ... Pet Stock Ass'n	—	—	—	2 50	—	3 00	—	5 00	—
Piscataquis County	8 00	5 00	8 00	—	—	—	3 00	—	66 00
Sagadahoc County	29 00	5 00	3 00	6 00	8 00	7 00	—	16 50	90 00
Sagadahoc, ... Farmers ... Ms' Club	—	—	—	10 00	—	—	—	39 00	11 75
Somerset	2 00	4 50	1 00	1 00	6 00	6 00	—	5 60	8 00
Somerset ...	12 00	8 00	3 50	4 50	—	5 25	—	16 00	102 00
Somerset, Central	8 50	3 00	4 50	4 50	—	20 00	18 00	15 25	84 00
Somerset, ...	6 50	—	3 00	5 00	—	—	—	9 00	18 00
... City	—	6 00	3 00	—	—	5 00	—	10 00	85 00
... City Park	15 00	9 00	15 00	6 00	12 00	—	8 00	52 00	41 00
Washington ... ion	17 50	6 00	20 00	5 00	6 00	8 00	7 00	19 50	29 00
Washington, West ... Ms Fair	—	4 00	11 00	5 00	—	—	—	18 00	8 00
... as Fair	8 00	—	3 00	9 00	2 00	144 00	2 00	18 00	94 00
... ly Poultry Ass'n	14 00	—	—	—	—	—	—	14 00	—
...	—	—	10 00	11 00	—	8 00	—	27 00	—
...	—	—	8 00	—	3 00	—	—	—	—
York, ... Agricultural ...iation	4 00	4 00	—	—	—	3 00	4 00	38 00	50 00
	$665 25	$320 75	$582 90	$361 00	$87 00	$483 25	$124 50	$1,208 80	$2,081 85

ANALYSIS OF AWARDS—Continued.

Name of Society.	Amount of premiums awarded thoroughbred bulls and bull calves.	Amount of premiums awarded thoroughbred cows, heifers and heifer calves.	Amount of premiums awarded grade cows, heifers and heifer calves.	Amount of premiums awarded herds.	Amount of premiums awarded working oxen and steers.	Amount of premiums awarded matched oxen and steers.	Amount of premiums awarded trained steers.	Amount of premiums awarded beef cattle.	Amount of premiums awarded town teams.	Amount of premiums awarded oxen and steers for draft.
Maine State Agricultural	$334 00	$514 50	$280 00	$420 00	$32 00	$66 00	$32 00	$73 00	$146 00	$343 00
Eastern Maine Fair	115 00	278 00	42 00	96 00	—	—	—	133 00	60 00	206 00
Central Maine Fair Co.	281 25	338 50	48 00	240 00	103 00	38 00	—	—	—	—
Maine State	—	—	—	—	—	—	—	—	—	—
Dairy Association	7 00	15 00	30 00	4 00	—	8 00	4 00	7 00	12 00	37 00
Town Fair Association	—	—	—	2 50	1 50	—	—	—	—	—
Northern Maine Fair Association	392 00	850 00	40 00	162 00	6 00	—	8 00	—	—	—
	376 00	764 00	46 00	194 00	—	15 00	—	36 00	16 00	124 00
	110 00	130 00	48 00	30 00	35 00	30 00	8 00	22 00	27 00	49 00
New Danville	19 00	42 00	13 00	15 00	9 00	13 00	10 00	9 00	5 00	—
Poultry, Danville	8 00	41 50	12 50	10 00	5 50	2 00	2 00	—	—	—
Rigby Park	—	—	—	—	—	—	—	—	—	10 00
Franklin County	99 50	174 00	17 00	117 00	12 00	111 00	9 00	27 50	145 00	99 00
Franklin, North	10 50	13 40	90 00	24 00	20 50	8 90	1 50	6 50	36 94	28 00
Hancock County	19 00	—	17 10	5 00	3 00	7 50	—	7 50	—	28 00
Hancock, North	1 00	6 50	25 00	—	5 00	—	50	—	—	—
Hancock	—	—	4 50	—	1 50	—	—	—	—	—
County	33 00	59 00	19 00	24 00	24 00	10 00	10 50	21 50	50 00	18 00
South	15 50	2 50	23 50	—	22 50	33 50	17 50	10 50	59 00	71 00
Knox, North	21 00	19 75	29 50	17 00	27 25	18 00	1 00	5 00	35 00	31 50
Lincoln	10 75	17 00	10 75	8 00	7 00	15 00	—	9 50	—	88 00
Bristol	—	1 25	3 25	—	6 15	2 75	—	—	—	21 50
Oxford County	152 00	196 00	178 00	60 00	147 00	65 00	10 00	32 00	95 00	232 00

Society										
..., West... ... in Valley	16 40	120 00	96 50	60 00	42 00	30 20	—	28 00	150 00	65 00
Oxford, ...	32 00	80 00	40 00	24 00	30 00	44 00	5 00	9 00	50 00	39 00
Oxford, ... Western Maine Poultry Association	15 00	40 00	35 00	15 00	42 00	20 00	13 00	25 00	7 00	13 50
Penobscot, West	53 00	128 00	88 00	60 00	32 00	10 00	5 00	4 50	—	—
Penobscot, ...	4 25	—	—	38 00	3 00	—	—	—	—	—
... Poultry and Pet Stock Ass'n	3 00	—	8 50	4 00	—	—	—	14 00	50 00	227 00
Piscataquis ...	16 50	32 50	20 25	27 00	4 50	4 50	10 00	—	—	—
Sagadahoc ...	295 00	591 75	125 75	147 00	80 00	47 00	—	15 00	—	—
Sag... ... and Farmers' and Mechanics' Club...	1 65	5 45	2 30	1 00	2 20	1 85	60	4 50	28 00	35 00
Somerset County...	3 00	9 75	35 25	3 00	11 50	13 75	—	22 00	—	—
Somerset, East...	8 50	10 50	36 50	13 50	2 00	—	—	15 00	—	—
Somerset, Central...	19 00	37 50	22 00	—	17 50	18 00	—	4 50	30 00	84 00
Somerset, ...	3 00	3 00	2 00	11 00	—	5 00	10 00	22 00	—	—
... County... ...	45 00	58 00	10 00	5 00	23 00	24 00	9 00	9 00	30 00	123 00
Wo... at ... ...tion	79 00	155 00	79 00	16 00	18 00	37 00	3 00	26 00	10 00	18 00
Wo, ... ty Park ...	24 75	61 50	24 50	47 00	5 00	14 00	—	22 50	—	—
Washin... ...	13 50	20 00	24 00	26 50	17 00	—	—	—	—	40 00
..., West... ...s Fair	103 00	106 00	84 00	12 00	66 00	—	—	100 00	—	—
..., ...s Fair	5 00	5 00	9 00	—	5 00	—	—	—	—	—
..., Passamaquoddy	41 00	50 00	11 00	20 00	—	—	—	—	—	11 00
York, ... al Acton...	—	—	—	—	6 00	29 75	—	6 00	45 00	—
York, ... As...ation	39 00	100 00	58 00	8 00	136 00	71 00	4 00	20 00	60 00	95 00
	$2,823 05	$5,076 85	$1,789 15	$1,966 00	$1,010 60	$813 70	$173 60	$705 50	$1,166 94	$2,136 50

ANALYSIS OF AWARDS—Concluded.

Name of Society.	Amount of premiums awarded sheep.	Amount of premiums awarded swine.	Amount of premiums awarded poultry.	Amount of premiums awarded grain and root crops.	Amount of premiums awarded fruit and flowers.	Amount of premiums awarded bread and dairy products.	Amount of premiums awarded honey, sugar and syrups.	Amount of premiums awarded agricultural implements.	Amount of premiums awarded household manufactures and needle-work.	Amount of premiums awarded objects not named above.	Total amount of premiums and gratuities awarded.
Maine S...	$640 00	197 00	$335 75	$77 50	$206 00	$432 50	$38 50	—	$315 14	$150 00	$5,124 64
Eastern Maine ... Association	60 00	30 00	131 25	163 15	275 75	11 00	19 00	—	238 25	163 25	2,012 65
... Maine Fair Co.	522 00	213 00	775 25	87 00	219 80	241 75	51 75	—	234 16	1,363 65	5,468 21
Maine State ... Association	—	—	—	—	1,178 30	—	—	—	—	—	1,478 50
...	—	—	2,322 65	—	—	—	—	—	—	—	2,322 65
... Town Fair	4 00	4 00	12 75	7 00	5 00	3 00	3 50	—	13 55	53 00	269 50
... Maine Fair As-	—	—	—	4 00	4 00	—	—	—	—	17 85	45 85
... in	130 00	42 00	529 25	108 65	44 65	62 25	30 75	—	252 80	406 55	3,854 90
...	—	45 00	375 30	75 50	56 90	18 00	—	—	218 30	69 00	2,624 30
... Farmers Club	21 00	12 00	163 75	22 50	30 50	35 00	—	—	42 00	20 00	1,128 75
...d, W... ter and	7 00	—	84 25	19 75	25 85	12 50	50	—	40 00	19 50	457 85
Danville...	4 50	10 00	15 75	30 00	10 00	10 00	8 00	—	14 00	—	232 75
..., Freeport Poultry As-	—	—	511 18	—	—	—	—	—	—	10 50	521 68
..., the Rigby Park	—	15 00	3 00	—	—	15 00	—	—	—	50 60	138 00
Franklin ...	135 50	8 50	50 25	24 90	65 60	5 20	14 75	—	90 65	95 60	1,585 80
...	32 25	2 00	5 25	7 90	12 70	12 00	75	—	31 10	38 00	341 59
Hancock ...	20 00	—	15 00	75 00	40 00	1 00	8 00	—	54 50	10 00	389 50
Hancock, North...	2 60	75	1 00	17 00	16 75	—	35	—	14 55	—	82 25
...	6 00	—	9 75	109 80	33 70	2 00	—	—	14 45	13 00	201 70
Kennebec ...	21 50	13 00	125 25	89 50	81 50	27 50	5 00	—	58 50	59 00	814 25

Society											Total
Kennebec, South	8 00	—	3 00	9 00	17 50	6 25	70	—	42 00	39 00	432 45
Knox, North	11 50	11 50	24 50	37 50	36 05	4 50	5 50	—	28 30	14 19	493 04
…u…	—	2 00	21 50	31 75	41 40	17 50	3 25	—	43 15	6 00	432 55
…l, Bristol	3 00	1 50	13 25	17 20	13 45	3 75	1 00	—	29 25	18 45	146 75
…t…	57 00	66 00	142 00	78 75	446 25	39 05	21 00	36 00	117 35	240 00	2,798 40
…d, …th Valley	32 50	7 20	26 30	25 40	14 40	10 80	13 40	3 00	30 80	116 60	1,049 00
…n Valley	—	—	30 50	13 25	21 80	16 85	6 30	—	25 05	74 40	718 65
…d, …th Valley	23 40	19 50	7 50	10 35	16 00	12 00	5 27	—	25 00	12 00	435 52
Oxford, North…Wn Maine Poultry Association	—	—	496 96	—	—	—	—	—	—	—	496 96
…d, association	48 00	35 00	97 50	47 05	46 75	12 85	6 75	—	65 85	81 40	1,009 15
Penobscot, West	—	—	—	44 00	43 00	4 25	—	—	40 85	—	195 60
Penobscot, North	—	5 00	3 75	8 75	20 05	2 25	1 50	—	62 15	7 00	136 45
Penobscot, …r Poultry …l …t	—	—	496 65	—	—	—	—	—	—	—	496 65
…Stock Association	9 50	8 00	8 25	6 00	14 50	7 50	—	—	14 50	26 50	309 25
Piscataquis	58 00	95 75	185 80	126 25	150 50	78 50	36 75	—	101 75	315 16	2,926 96
Sagadahoc	—	—	1 80	9 10	13 45	1 65	—	—	11 80	2 60	77 60
Sagadahoc, …l Farmers' …s' Club	—	80	23 75	8 00	4 90	2 25	50	—	35 05	4 00	322 45
…d	29 25	—	18 50	1 50	7 25	3 50	50	—	16 00	30 75	302 00
Somerset	—	—	190 00	16 00	22 00	24 75	1 00	—	34 00	3 00	771 25
Somerset, East	82 00	—	—	4 00	—	—	—	—	—	—	59 00
Somerset, Central	—	—	76 00	61 30	73 25	6 00	6 00	—	61 25	3 00	610 50
Somerset, …h	24 00	20 00	34 00	32 50	58 20	33 50	1 00	—	109 00	49 00	1,280 50
…o …l Penobscot	87 00	43 50	60 50	4 75	13 50	10 50	18 00	5 00	59 25	42 25	591 75
…o, …k Association	7 50	60 50	23 25	75 00	3 25	22 75	—	—	45 25	36 75	298 50
…o, …n	10 00	10 00	45 50	75 00	67 75	35 00	1 75	—	208 40	—	1,216 40
Washington, West	98 00	18 00	54 00	24 00	41 00	19 40	1 00	—	56 35	—	273 25
…n, …s Fair …'L	9 00	—	61 50	45 75	68 50	19 50	—	—	100 25	—	608 50
…n, …s …r Ass'L	8 00	25 00	—	—	—	—	—	—	—	—	—
…n, …ly Poultry Association	—	—	98 50	58 75	48 75	8 75	—	—	13 50	134 75	98 50
York, …n and …n	3 25	—	13 75	15 00	23 75	5 50	—	—	51 90	—	385 25
York, …n Agricul…al Ass'n	—	16 00	98 00	—	—	—	12 00	—	—	—	913 15
Total	**$2,216 25**	**$980 00**	**$7,823 69**	**$1,730 35**	**$4,031 85**	**$1,395 80**	**$326 52**	**$44 00**	**$3,059 95**	**$3,795 70**	**$48,981 30**

FINANCES.

Name of Society.	Amount received from State.	Receipts for membership.	Receipts from loans.	Receipts from entry fees for trotting purses.	Receipts from all other sources.	Total receipts.
Me State Agricultural	$2,500 00	$100 00	$1,500 00	$2,555 00	$19,103 80	$25,758 80
Eastern Me Fair	2,500 00	—	2,000 00	2,555 00	16,933 38	23,988 38
All aine Fair Co...........	1,000 00	182 00	—	—	1,456 70	2,68 70
Me State Ial dation...........	1,148 91	61 00	—	—	1,791 48	3,001 39
Maine State W dation...........	467 08	32 84	15 85	—	728 61	1,28 53
An, Greene Fn Fair Association...	—	16 00	—	—	36 46	68 31
Wak, Northern Me Fair Association...	1,699 25	38 00	7,000 00	1,056 00	11,303 71	21,06 96
A, h...........	—	—	—	—	—	—
nd W...........	525 08	20 00	—	370 00	5,427 34	6,82 42
nd Farmers', Gb...........	180 09	79 00	—	427 50	1,683 60	2,70 19
nd, New Gr and Danville...	107 49	5 00	—	135 00	694 49	91 98
Cumberland, Freeport W Avion..	163 49	15 00	200 00	311 50	297 11	87 10
Wd, Lsle dy Pak...........	704 65	716 00	—	162 50	1,41 32	1,63 82
Franklin W...........	139 52	271 00	700 00	993 50	3,722 12	6,86 27
I rfn, oth...........	178 97	—	300 00	211 25	683 54	1,65 31
k, Gty...........	44 50	—	—	83 00	1,797 36	2,69 33
k, North...........	89 66	5 00	—	—	470 26	34 76
k, Eden...........	320 92	—	—	129 00	1,180 57	1,99 23
Che W...........	158 88	—	950 00	105 00	973 08	1,404 00
Cho, South...........	203 85	3 00	200 00	113 75	1,063 15	2,285 78
Kk, North...........	41 16	28 30	570 24	56 25	1,961 13	2,424 23
Ln, Bol...........	54 84	25	—	92 25	1,391 02	2,22 97
Oxford W...........	1,233 12	24 00	500 00	765 00	6,261 05	8,83 17

Oxford, ...	574 90	35 00	500 00	145 50	3,317 60	4,53 00
...d, Androscoggin Valley	304 88	1 00	—	314 00	1,731 05	2,50 93
Oxford, ...th, ...	165 16	—	—	—	574 77	39 33
Oxford, ...ern Maine Poultry Association	188 69	48 00	—	—	604 77	81 46
Penobscot, ...	432 97	69 00	200 00	320 00	2,406 00	47 97
...t, North	133 94	1 00	—	275 00	1,510 80	3,90 74
..., Bangor Poultry and ...t Stock	49 54	50 00	—	60 50	698 25	1,88 29
...s	143 06	45 00	—	—	335 25	83 31
	158 64	—	—	—	648 53	87 17
Sagad... ...	1,244 86	490 00	—	1,200 00	7,301 72	10,36 58
Sagadahoc, ...	33 89	—	—	—	100 00	33 89
Somerset, ...al Farmers' and M... ...rs' Club	123 22	10 00	157 00	180 00	763 05	1,33 27
Somerset, East	163 61	94 00	333 48	—	1,352 37	1,93 46
Somerset, Central	412 61	60 00	—	1,175 00	3,154 66	4,82 27
Somerset, ...	22 54	—	5 00	—	45 25	72 79
...o ...	289 22	30 00	800 00	105 00	2,095 90	1,24 22
...o ...d Penobscot	640 74	—	1,300 00	294 75	959 25	4,31 39
...o, ...ty ...k Association	262 15	1 00	—	120 00	1,146 90	1,82 40
...	156 45	1 00	539 00	89 00	3,553 49	5,93 35
...	574 06	2 00	—	360 00	1,669 48	2,68 93
..., ...es Fair	199 45	—	—	780 00	4,943 12	5,9 18 82
..., ...ty ...ly Association	255 70	—	62 17	720 00	159 13	31 30
York, Shapleigh ...d ...	178 08	10 00	60 00	—	39 00	68 08
..k, ...h ...gul ...tal ...cia ...on	458 84	191 00	—	550 00	2,735 90	3,74 74
	$20,728 66	$2,734 39	$17,892 74	$16,810 25	$122,329 69	$180,495 73

FINANCES—Concluded.

Name of Society.	Amount expended in improvements.	Amount expended in trotting purses.	Expenses during the fair.	Amount expended for all other purposes.	Total amount paid out, including premiums and gratuities.	Value of property belonging to the society.	Amount of liabilities.
Me State Agricultural	$3,438 65	$4,925 00	$5,433 24	$5,698 27	$24,619 80	$63,000 00	$14,500 00
Eastern Me Ar Association	75 50	4,494 96	10,770 40	1,106 67	21,415 74		3,552 80
[...]l Maine hr Co			1,160 20		2,638 70	1,750 00	
Me State	100 00	300 00	1,146 80	634 99	4,104 44	2,000 00	600 00
[...]e State	10,400 00		21 70	221 55	1,162 75	40,000 00	11,200 00
[...]ge Town Fair Association				9 90	55 75		
[...]n, Me hr Association	1,137 51	3,600 00	2, 90 87	542 06	20,817 83	40,000 00	1,600 00
[...]		1,002 50	2,475 73		5,744 49	8,000 00	
[...]		900 00	360 09	350 46	2,068 40	3,000 00	
[...]d, New Enville	18 75	450 00	119 50	109 00	911 25	2,500 00	00 00
[...]al ati a.	200 00		367 85		908 28	300 00	1, 30 21
[...]d, Freeport y Park	924 14	700 00	257 82	2,023 15	1,295 82	1,700 00	2,459 00
Franklin	70 00	990 00	959 89	420 00	6,482 98	12,500 00	
[...]	50 00	500 00	298 05	100 18	1,629 64	2,500 00	
[...]a, North	5 00	613 65	940 00	33 70	2,093 33	5,000 00	
[...]			389 86	127 55	510 81	200 00	
Kennebec County	50 00	319 00	182 20	304 20	830 45	2,400 00	1,095 00
Kennebec, South	127 60	530 00	117 38	165 25	1,815 83	3,000 00	2,400 00
[...]x, North	300 00	625 00	224 75	517 96	1,575 05	1,000 00	950 00
[...]		617 50	678 00	900 42	2,606 50	1,000 00	400 00
[...]n Bitol	72 60	390 00	500 00	5 00	2,222 97	2,000 00	550 00
Oxford	1,341 00	1,915 00	116 02	768 24	340 37	11,000 00	500 00
[...]			2,361 09		9,183 73	12,000 00	

Oxford,		250 00	940 00	680 00	175 00	3,094 00	10,000 00	1,300 00
(di) Androscoggin Valley		141 47	800 00	847 26	137 65	2,507 38	6,000 00	2,605 00
Oxford, North		15 00	12 50	20 00	97 81	620 67	2,500 00	250 00
(di) Western Maine Poultry Association		39 16	–	118 88	597 77	752 81	300 00	–
at,		366 39	800 00	349 40	50 00	3,122 71	6,500 00	5,150 00
(di) North		200 00	650 00	300 00	271 84	1,395 60	3,000 00	–
(di) Bangor (di) Poultry and Pet Stock Association		45 00	245 00	160 00	–	858 29	1,800 00	1,200 00
		200 00	–	102 50	–	799 15	300 00	–
Piscataquis County		650 00	700 00	3,309 77	–	1,659 25	3,000 00	–
Sagadahoc (di)		1,700 00	2,700 00	45 75	–	10,636 73	–	–
Sagadahoc, nal Farmers' and Mechanics' Club		–	–	223 96	127 00	123 35	1,500 00	585 00
Somerset, City		93 74	450 00	60 00	1,034 46	1,217 15	2,000 00	1,170 00
Somerset, East		45 00	502 00	903 39	683 25	1,943 46	5,000 00	2,862 75
Somerset, Central		150 00	3,225 00	4 50	–	5,732 89	–	5 00
Somerset,		–	–	–	–	63 50	–	–
do		–	–	834 00	1,635 63	4,726 13	10,000 00	1,884 00
W do and Penobscot		200 00	976 00	230 00	481 45	1,596 75	–	254 35
do, ity Park Association		70 30	575 00	102 10	–	1,393 35	1,936 00	125 00
Washington, West		309 71	441 00	2,210 51	292 09	4,636 62	–	2,039 00
Wash di, M ds Fair on		–	900 00	909 05	–	3,014 39	12,000 00	31 75
An, ds Fair		1,199 06	1,540 00	3,603 96	52 05	7,061 52	–	86 07
An, dly Association		–	1,650 00	80 75	19 50	231 30	2,000 00	–
York,		–	–	26 25	147 00	431 00	4,500 00	–
York, nal Association		428 44	1,160 00	828 33	–	3,476 92	–	–
		$24,514 02	$41,139 11	$46,901 80	$19,841 05	$176,129 83	$238,686 00	$65,974 93

SPECIAL REPORT

OF THE

Maine Agricultural Experiment Station

FOR THE

COMMISSIONER OF AGRICULTURE

For the Year 1912

17

MAINE
AGRICULTURAL EXPERIMENT STATION
ORONO, MAINE.

THE WORK OF THE MAINE AGRICULTURAL EXPERIMENT STATION IN 1912.

DIRECTOR CHAS. D. WOODS.

Introductory to this brief outline of the work of the Maine Agricultural Experiment Station for the year 1912 a few paragraphs covering the purpose for which the Station was established, the limits of the field of its operations and a brief history of its more than a quarter of a century of work seem essential.

HISTORICAL SKETCH.

The Legislature of 1885 enacted a law establishing the Maine Fertilizer Control and Agricultural Experiment Station. The purpose of the Station as defined in Section 1 of the act was as follows: "That for the purpose of protection from frauds in commercial fertilizers, and from adulterations in foods, feeds and seeds, and for the purpose of promoting agriculture by scientific investigation and experiment, The Maine Fertilizer Control and Agricultural Experiment Station is hereby established in connection with the State College of Agriculture and Mechanic Arts." The act was approved by the Governor March 3, 1885, and early in April the Station was organized with a director, who was also chemist, an assistant chemist, and an assistant in field and feeding experiments.

It depended for its quarters upon the hospitality of the Maine State College. A chemical laboratory for the Station was partitioned off from the College laboratory and supplied with apparatus. Part of the dairy room of the College was fitted up with apparatus for use in experiments involving the handling of milk. A part of the new barn just erected by the College was turned over to the Experiment Station for feeding experiments and was fitted up with stalls, scales, etc. Field experiments were started by laying off about three acres of land into blocks, and box experiments for growing plants were also begun.

While the principal object of the establishment of this Station was the maintenance of a fertilizer control, in the first months of existence lines of investigation were entered upon, many of which have been continuously followed by this Station.

The Maine Fertilizer Control and Agricultural Experiment Station existed about two and a half years and issued twenty-six bulletins and three reports, the former being published only in the leading papers of the State and the latter as a part of the report of the Maine Board of Agriculture. Upon the passage by Congress of what is known as the Hatch Act, establishing agricultural experiment stations in every state, the Legislature of 1887 repealed the law of March 3, 1885, by an act which took effect October 1, 1887. It was expected at the time this act was passed, that by October 1 a station would be in operation under the provisions of the national law. This did not prove to be the case owing to the failure of Congress to appropriate money, and had not the College assumed the risk of advancing the funds to pay the expenses of the Station, work would have ceased on the date in which the old Station law stood repealed. As it was, the work was continued until January, 1888, when the Station force disbanded to await the action of Congress. It was not until after the passage of the deficiency bill early in February, 1888, that the funds became available for the payment of the expenses of the year 1887-1888. Prior to this, the Maine Legislature of 1887 had accepted the provisions of the Hatch Act on the part of the State, and at the meeting of the College Trustees in June, 1887, the present Station was organized as a department of the College by the election of a director and two other members of the staff of officers.

At a meeting of the Trustees, held February 16, 1888, a general plan for carrying out the provisions of the Hatch Act involving the expenditure of $15,000 per annum, was presented to the Board of Trustees and was accepted by them, and the development and management of the Station under this plan was placed in charge of a Station Council, made up of the President of the College, the Director of the Station, the heads of the various departments of the Station, three members of the Trustees and a representative from each of the state agricultural organizations.

The Station Council meets once a year. At this meeting, the Director and other members of the Station staff outline the work which has been undertaken in the past year and make recommendations for the following year. Such of these as commend themselves to the Station Council as well as suggestions from that body are approved and the Director is instructed to carry them out in detail. The appointment of members of the staff is made by the Trustees, and the recommendations of the Council are subject to their approval.

The Director is the executive officer of the Station and passes upon all matters of business. The members of the staff have charge of the lines of work which naturally come under their departments.

INCOME OF THE STATION.

For the year which ended June 30, 1912, the income of the Station in round figures was:—Hatch Fund, $15,000; Adams Fund, $15,000; U. S. Department of Agriculture for poultry investigations, $1,000; State printing, $5,000; Inspections, $1,700; Sales, $8,800. All of the receipts and expenditures are audited by the State Auditor and those from the Federal Government by the Office of Experiment Stations of the U. S. Department of Agriculture.

RELATION OF THE STATION TO THE UNIVERSITY OF MAINE.

The Station is by act of legislature a department of the University of Maine and in the organization of the University is co-ordinate with the different colleges. The function of the colleges is to teach. It is by the Act of Congress establishing the Station, "The object and duty of said experiment stations to conduct original researches or verify experiments .... bearing directly on the agricultural industry of the United States as may in each case be deemed advisable, having due regard to the varying conditions and needs of the respective States or Territories." None of the funds received by the Station can lawfully be used for teaching, for demonstration, for exhibition purposes or for any purpose whatever outside of research into agricultural problems, and carrying out the provisions of the laws regulating commerce of which the Director is the executor.

ORGANIZATION OF THE STATION.

While the work for which the Experiment Station was primarily established is that of investigation it has been found much more convenient for the State, because of the Station laboratory facilities, to make the Director of the Station the executive officer of the laws regulating the sale of agricultural seeds, commercial feeding stuffs, commercial fertilizers, drugs, foods, fungicides and insecticides, as well as calibrating the creamery glassware used in the State. It is necessary to have the work of investigation and that of inspection distinctly organized in order that the funds for these two distinct purposes may be lawfully expended. From necessity the Director and the office force must divide their time between these. two divisions of Station work. But outside of this there is no overlapping of the duties of the staff. Those who are engaged upon the work of investigation devote their whole time to the carrying out of the various scientific projects that bear upon the solving of the problems that confront Maine Agriculture. The remainder of the staff devote their whole time to the work of inspection.

DISSEMINATION OF INFORMATION.

It is not the function of the Station to disseminate general agriculture or other information. That is for the College through its extension department. It is, however, the distinct duty of the Station to publish the results of its investigations. Although the correspondence that bears upon general agriculture is referred so far as practicable to the correspondence department of the University the Station receives and answers many thousand letters each year.

The Station publishes: (a) Bulletins which contain the results of investigation; (b) Official Inspections which give the results of the work of inspection; (c) Miscellaneous publications; and (d) a series of publicity letters that are issued Fridays of each week and sent to a limited number of papers to be released for publication on the following Wednesday. The bulletins, the official inspection and the chief miscellaneous publications are bound together at the close of the year and make up the Annual Report of the Station. During 1912 there were issued 11 bulletins containing about 475 pages; 10 Official Inspections containing about 200 pages; 20 miscellaneous publications and 52 Publicity Letters.

The following are the principal publications although there were numerous circulars not here listed as well as more pretentious papers that were printed in scientific periodicals, both American and foreign.

List of Principal Publications in 1912.

Work of Investigation (Bulletins)

198 Orchard Spraying Experiments
199 Orchard Notes
200 Fungus Gnats Part IV
201 Sweet Spirit of Nitrous Ether
202 Aphid Pests of Maine, Psyllid Notes
203 Elm Leaf Curl and Woolly Apple Aphid
204 Triplet Calves
205 Inheritance of Fecundity in Poultry
206 Histology of Oviduct of Hen
207 Insect Notes for 1912
208 Meteorology, Finances and Index

Work of Inspection (Official Inspections)

36 Seed Inspection
37 Carbonated Beverages. Ice Cream
38 Feeding Stuff Inspection
39 Miscellaneous Foods
40 Sundry Drugs
41 Jams, Sausage, Vanilla
42 Fertilizer Inspection
43 Clams, Oysters, Scallops
44 Creameries
45 Soda Water, Ice Cream, and Cream

All publications are distributed free to residents of Maine. The demand for the Station bulletins outside of the State has made such inroads upon the printing fund that a price is put upon them to non-residents with the exception of exchanges, scientific investigators and libraries.

EQUIPMENT OF THE STATION.

The Station is well equipped in laboratories and apparatus, particularly in the lines of chemistry, entomology, horticulture, pomology, plant pathology and poultry investigations. Its poultry plant is probably the most complete for the purposes of investigation of that of any Experiment Station in the country. While the Station carries on some coöperative work such as orcharding, and field experiments with farmers in different parts of the State, most of the work is conducted in its own laboratories and poultry plant at Orono, and upon Highmoor Farm, situated in the town of Monmouth.

Its offices and laboratories are chiefly located in Holmes Hall (named in honor of Dr. Ezekiel Holmes, the first Secretary of the Board of Agriculture) on the University of Maine campus, Orono. It is a two story brick building, 81 x 48 feet. On the ground floor are five large chemical laboratories used for the analysis of foods, feeding stuffs, drugs, fertilizers, fungicides and insecticides; the laboratories of the plant pathologists; and two of the biological laboratories. The general office and mailing room, the Director's office, the laboratory for seed testing and photography, the entomological laboratories and the library, are on the second floor. In the basement there is a chemical laboratory; rooms for the grinding and preparation of samples; culture and preparation rooms used by the plant pathologists and rooms for the storage of chemicals and glassware. The large attic is also used for the storage of samples and supplies. The building is connected with the steam heating plant of the University; is supplied with gas and electricity; and is thoroughly equipped with apparatus for the work of agricultural investigation. The library consists of about 3000 volumes, chiefly agricultural and biological journals and publications of the various experiment stations. Holmes Hall is situated near the University Library and card catalogues of books in the University Library that are likely to be used by the Station workers are also in the Station Library.

The poultry plant is also situated on the University of Maine campus and includes two long houses built on the curtain front plan. It is possible in these houses to carry over the winter from 800 to 1000 laying hens. One of these long poultry houses is used for pedigree breeding work during the breeding season in the spring. In this house it is possible to carry from 200 to 300 breeding hens in such condition that the exact pedigrees of their offspring may be recorded. The entire portion of the poultry plant devoted to laying hens is equipped with an improved form of trap nest which makes it possible to obtain exact records of the egg production of each individual bird. Besides these two laying houses the poultry plant has a house 35 x 16 feet which is divided into three compartments used for hospital purposes in connection with the experimental work of the department and for special physiological investigations with poultry. The incubator house and brooder houses include ample facilities for the annual hatching and rearing of about 4000 pedigreed chickens during the breeding season from April 1 to June 1. There is also a well equipped laboratory on the poultry range that is chiefly used and especially equipped for physiological work. It includes three rooms arranged in a linear series. The outer one of these rooms is devoted to general laboratory purposes and the conducting of post-mortem examinations on poultry. The two inner rooms are devoted to experimental physiological work. The first of these rooms is the sterilizing room and is equipped with the usual instruments and facilities for the sterilization of instruments, etc., including steam and hot air sterilizers. The last room in the series in this laboratory is the experimenting room. The rooms are so constructed as to be practically dust proof, and the walls and ceilings are entirely covered with white enamel which makes it possible to thoroughly sterilize the rooms.

HIGHMOOR FARM.

The State Legislature of 1909 purchased a farm upon which the Maine Experiment Station "shall conduct scientific investigations in orcharding, corn and other farm crops." The farm is situated in the counties of Kennebec and Androscoggin and largely in the town of Monmouth. It is on the Farmington Branch of the Maine Central Railroad two miles from Leeds Junction. A flag station called Highmoor is on the farm.

The farm consists of 225 acres, about 200 of which are in orchards, fields and pastures. There are in the neighborhood of

3000 apple trees upon the place which have been set from 15 to 25 years. The fields that are not in orchards are well adapted to experiments with corn, potatoes, and similar general farm crops. The house is two story with a large wing, and contains about 15 rooms, well arranged for the Experiment Station offices and for the home of the farm superintendent. The barn is large, affording storage for hay and grain. The basements of the building afford a moderate amount of storage for apples, potatoes and roots.

Although the farm is used as a laboratory by the different departments of the Station and some of the work in progress upon the farm is described in other parts of this report it may be of interest to briefly note the more important investigations that were carried on upon the farm during the growing season for 1912.

FIELD EXPERIMENTS HIGHMOOR FARM.

ROTATION EXPERIMENT.

The object of this experiment is to ascertain the differences in yields and in the exhaustive effects of corn and potatoes in relation to land treated with chemical fertilizers and with organic manure. The whole field was planted to potatoes on chemical fertilizer in 1911. It is to be seeded to grass with oats in 1913.

Plot 5 A. One acre Irish Cobbler potatoes (planted 3½ inches deep), with 1700 pounds of 4-8-7 chemical fertilizer.

Plot 5 B. One acre sweet corn (planted 18 inches in the row), with 1700 pounds 4-8-7 chemical fertilizer.

Plot 5 C. One acre sweet corn (planted 18 inches in the row), with 600 pounds 4-8-6 chemical fertilizer plus 8 cords manure.

Plot 5 D. One acre Irish Cobbler potatoes (planted 3½ inches deep), with 600 pounds of 4-8-7 chemical fertilizer plus 8 cords manure.

CYANAMIDE FERTILIZER EXPERIMENT.

This is in continuation of an experiment started in 1911 to test the efficiency of a chemically prepared nitrogen supplying fertilizer, known as cyanamide, with the other forms of nitrogen fertilizers now in common use.

Three plots of one acre each, planted to Irish Cobbler potatoes, 3½ inches deep, treated uniformly in respect to phosphoric acid and potash. Nitrogen fertilizers as follows:—

Plot 15 A. 190 pounds nitrate of soda plus 425 pounds dried blood per acre.

Plot 15 B.   385 pounds cyanamide plus 190 pounds nitrate of soda per acre.

Plot 15 C.   580 pounds cyanamide per acre.

POTATO CULTURAL EXPERIMENT.

This is a continuation of the experiment started in 1910, comparing the results of planting at different depths with different cultural methods. Three plots of land are planted to Irish Cobbler potatoes, treated with 1700 pounds of 4-8-7 chemical fertilizer (1000 pounds in the hill, 700 pounds worked in) per acre.

Plot 19 A.   Planted 2 inches deep.   To be highly ridged.

Plot 19 B.   Planted 5 inches deep.   To receive level culture.

Plot 19 C.   Planted 3½ inches deep.   To have a low ridge.

"MINERAL FERTILIZER" EXPERIMENT.

A comparative test of the New Mineral Fertilizer with barnyard manure and with complete chemical fertilizer, on corn and potatoes was made in 1911. It was planned to repeat it in 1912. The results of 1911 seem to be conclusive that this material is of no value on this land. The experiment is cancelled.

TOP DRESSING ON GRASS.

The third year of an experiment comparing acid phosphate and Thomas slag as a source of phosphoric acid. Plots 16 A and 16 C each receive 112 pounds of muriate of potash and 100 pounds of nitrate of soda. Plot 16 A has in addition 600 pounds of high grade soluble acid phosphate. Plot 16 C has 600 pounds of Thomas phosphate powder. Plot 16 B received no top dressing of any kind.

EXPERIMENTS WITH THE APPLE.

EXPERIMENTAL NURSERY.

About an acre has been reserved for growing of young apple trees to be used later in experimental plots. There are two thousand one-year-old French Crab seedlings for budding or grafting, and about one thousand grafts of Tolman Sweet cions, root grafted on French Crab, for experimental work.

FERTILIZER EXPERIMENT ON APPLE TREES.

Thirty-two Baldwin trees have been divided into three sections. Ten at each end have been treated with 4-8-7 chemical fertilizer at the rate of 1000 pounds per acre plus nitrate of soda at the rate of 100 pounds per acre. The 12 trees in the middle of the row have received the 4-8-7 chemical fertilizer at the rate of 1000 pounds per acre.

The Baldwin orchard has also been divided into two parts for a fertilizer test. Rows 1 to 26 inclusive (beginning at the north end of the orchard) have received the 4-8-7 fertilizer at the rate of 1000 pounds per acre plus nitrate of soda at the rate of 100 pounds per acre. The remainder of the orchard has received the 4-8-7 formula at the rate of 1000 pounds per acre.

An experiment to compare the effect of fertilizer over a series of years is begun this year. The orchard has been cultivated and fertilized for three years and has been brought into good condition. All the lots will be cultivated and everything (other than apples) that grows upon the land will be plowed in each spring.

9 A. Rows 1 to 4 will receive no fertilizer.

9 B. Rows 5 to 8 will receive annually 500 pounds per acre of a 5-8-7 commercial fertilizer.

9 C. Rows 9 to 12 will receive annually 1000 pounds per acre of a 5-8-7 commercial fertilizer.

It is planned to begin in 1913 a similar experiment with more mature trees which will also be carried through a series of years.

For the past three years this plot has been used for testing swine and sheep in orchard management. A few missing trees have been replaced. This year the plot is treated with 1000 pounds commercial fertilizer (4-8-7 goods) and is kept in clean cultivation in order that the trees may be in good vigor when the fertilizer experiment is begun.

PLANT BREEDING EXPERIMENTS.

SWEET CORN.

Experiments with sweet corn were begun at Farmington in 1907. An experiment is being started this year to test the effect on yield and quantity of crossing two highly bred, closely related strains of white sweet corn, in each of which earliness is a fixed characteristic.

YELLOW FIELD (DENT) CORN.

Preliminary experiments with dent corn were conducted at Farmington 3 years ago. This work has since been continued at Highmoor. Plots No. 17, 18 and 18a are planted with a variety of corn originally obtained from Mr. Hiram Cornforth of Waterville. During the past three years the corn has been selected on the ear-to-row system, until finally some highly desirable types have been bred. These are being tested this year in the plots here noted (17, 18, 18a) on a larger scale. A further ear-to-row test is also being carried on on these plots.

ORCHARD SPRAYING EXPERIMENT.

This is a continuation of last year's work, and is a test of the home made concentrated lime-sulphur spray as a fungicide used at different strengths, with arsenate of lead as the insecticide. Tests of arsenate of lead as a fungicide are also included. One plot of trees is treated with bordeaux mixture for comparison. No trees have this year been left unsprayed for insects, as the desirability of spraying has been fully established.

There are 25 rows in the experiment. The first six trees in each row are treated as follows:

Rows 1 to 3, inclusive, arsenate of lead at the rate of 4 pounds to 50 gallons of water.

Rows 4 to 9, inclusive, home made concentrated lime-sulphur solution, used one-fifth stronger than the strength recommended by the latest dilution tables, with 2 pounds arsenate of lead to 50 gallons of water.

Rows 10 to 15, inclusive, the same lime-sulphur solution used at the dilution recommended, according to its density, plus 2 pounds arsenate of lead to 50 gallons of water.

Rows 16 to 21, inclusive, the same lime-sulphur solution used at a dilution of one-fourth weaker than the strength recommended by the latest dilution tables, plus 2 pounds arsenate of lead to 50 gallons of water.

Rows 22 and 23, arsenate of lead, at the rate of 2 pounds to 50 gallons of water.

Rows 24 and 25, bordeaux mixture of the 3-3-50 formula, plus 2 pounds aresnate of lead to 50 gallons of water.

Orchard Management Experiments.

In 1910 and 1911 two plots were pastured with hogs and sheep in a comparison with the cultivated plots. The results showed so decisively that cultivation is essential on the soil of Highmoor Farm for growing the apple that they are discontinued.

12. Rows 19 to 25, inclusive, beginning with the seventh tree in each row, have been left in grass, to compare with the cultivated and pastured plots.

13 A. Rows 26 to 30, inclusive, throughout their entire length, have been dressed with barnyard manure at the rate of 6 cords per acre, to compare this means of fertilizing with the three preceding plots and with 13 B.

13 B. Rows 31 to 35, inclusive, have been treated with the complete 4-8-7 chemical fertilizer at the rate of 1000 pounds per acre.

All of the plots included have been pruned and sprayed; all excepting 12 are cultivated, and all excepting 13 A have been fertilized with 4-8-7 chemical fertilizer at the rate of 1000 pounds per acre.

These orchard management experiments are to be continued in order to obtain data covering long periods of time.

OAT SELECTION EXPERIMENTS.

This year the seed from the individual oat plants, selected from last year's plots because of their excellence in one or more qualities, is planted on the head-row system. 25 grains from each of 225 selected lines are planted in short rows in the oat-breeding garden No. 1. The visitor should note the many different types to be found among these pedigree oat rows. Next year the best of these rows will be used for further propagation. The effect of individual plant selection within a pedigree line is being tested in this oat-garden.

BEANS.

This plot contains the continuation of an experiment in breeding yellow-eyed beans, of both the old-fashioned and improved varieties. One bean was planted to a hill. Strains embodying desirable characters are being propagated on a larger scale. Variety tests of unselected seed of standard varieties are also being conducted in connection with the pedigree work.

VARIETY TEST OF OATS.

The object of this variety test is two-fold. First, to demonstrate the great differences in the yield and other characters of the different varieties. Second, to serve as a check and basis of comparison in a series of breeding experiments with oats. The variety tests this year are a continuation of those of last year.

There are 22 varieties under test this year. Of these 8 are new (i. e., have never before been tested at Highmoor) and 14 have been in these tests in previous years. Each plot is 1-10 acre in size, and there are 44 of them. Each of the 22 varieties has two-tenth acre plots assigned to it. One of these duplicates is on 4A, and the other is on 4B. The plants are seeded (with a grain drill) at the rate of two bushels to the acre.

The following table shows the names of the varieties and the sources of seed used:

Plot Nos.	Variety Name.	Source of Seed.
167, 168.....	American Clydesdale......	1911 Plot 43
169, 170.....	Danish Island............	1911 " 44
171, 172.....	Kherson................	1911 " 45
173, 174.....	Irish Victor.............	1911 " 46
175, 176.....	Early Champion.........	1911 " 47
177, 178.....	Prosperity.............	1911 " 48
179, 180.....	Silver Mine.............	1911 " 49
181, 182.....	Lincoln................	1911 " 50
183, 184.....	Swedish Select..........	1911 " 51
185, 186.....	President...............	1911 " 52
187, 188.....	Senator................	1911 " 53
189, 190	Victor................	1911 " 54
191, 192.....	Imported Scotch........	1911 " 55
193, 194.....	Banner.................	1911 " 56
195, 196.....	White Plume..........	L. L. Olds Seed Company, Madison, Wis.
197, 198.....	Rebred 60 Day.........	L. L. Olds Seed Company, Madison, Wis.
199, 200....	Early Pearl............	R. L. Copeland, Brewer, Maine.
201, 202.....	Daubeney..............	C. R. Gies, St. Jacobs, Ont.
203, 204.....	Gold Rain.............	Experimental Farm, Charlottetown, P. E. I.
205, 206.....	Siberian...............	Wm. Lewis, Dunsford, Ont.
207, 208.....	Minnesota, No. 26.......	Garton-Cooper Co., Chicago, Ill.
209, 210.....	Abundance............	James Ferguson, Dalmeny, Ont.

PURE LINE OR PEDIGREE OATS.

In 1910 about 500 of the best single oat plants to be found in the plots of that year were selected. In 1911 the 200 best individuals out of these 500 were planted in rows in the oat garden. This year there have been selected for further propagation the 83 best rows of last year's planting. The seed from each of these rows will be separately planted in two plots, each of which will be just 1-2000 of an acre in area. These "two-thousandth" acre plots will be found in 4B. Each plot represents a "pure line," all the plants on it being descended from a *single head* grown in 1910. Some of these pure lines give great promise of being exceptionally fine oats.

WORK OF INSPECTION.

The inspections entrusted to the Maine Agricultural Experiment Station include agricultural seeds, apple packing, commercial feeding stuffs, commercial fertilizers, creamery glass ware, drugs, foods, fungicides, and insecticides. In the course of the year this work leads the deputies to visit practically every town of importance in the State at least once and many of them several times.

The work of inspection comprises much more than the actual collection of the samples. The deputy has constantly to be on the watch for goods which are not registered in the case of fertilizers, feeding stuffs, fungicides and insecticides; labels and tags have to be constantly examined in order to see that the statements thereon are apparently in accord with truth. Weighings are often made in order to see that the net weight actually contained in the package does not fall below the guaranteed weight; and there must be constant watch for old, shop-worn and damaged goods.

The fertilizer inspection must of necessity be carried on almost entirely during the early spring months just before that commodity is used by the farmers. While a large amount of fertilizer comes into the State during the fall and winter and is stored in large warehouses, more and more is being shipped into the State by rail and directly to the points of consumption so that the collection of samples of the various brands becomes more and more difficult and involves a larger expenditure of time and money each year.

The feeding stuffs inspection comes naturally during the fall and winter months when commercial feeding stuffs are most in use. This work also increases year by year as the consumption of commercial cattle feeds increases. The importance of this inspection becomes more and more apparent as the number of compounded feeding stuffs on sale increases. The tendency to use waste and inferior materials, screenings, chaff, oat clippings, hulls, cob meal, and other low grade materials, is ever increasing and the importance of having such compounds marked plainly so that the consumer may know exactly what he is getting is, of course, apparent.

The inspection of agricultural seeds also comes during the spring months just before the seed is placed in the ground. A comparatively few samples of seeds are actually analyzed because the seed analyst himself does the actual work of inspection and no samples are taken unless the appearance of the goods indicates that the guarantees accompanying it may be too high, or for some other reason there is cause for suspicion.

The insecticides and fungicides inspected include all classes of materials which are used to destroy, repel, or mitigate in any way insect and fungus pests. The requirements of the insecticide and fungicide law are more recent than the other inspection laws of the State, but the importance of the work is already evident.

The inspection of foods and drugs goes on constantly throughout the year, and the number of samples collected does not represent in the least either the importance of the work or the scope of the ground covered by the deputies.

The importance of manufacturing, storing and dispensing food materials under sanitary conditions is just being realized by the public. Just how much disease is spread because flies carry with them and deposit upon exposed foods the germs of dangerous diseases, or the dust of the streets containing dangerous disease germs is scattered upon food materials, or the spray from human mouths contaminate food products, can never be ascertained. That diseases are spread by these means, however, is indisputable. In like manner it can never be ascertained of just what value various inspection laws are to the commonwealth, but by comparing the reports of many other states with our own we can feel certain that at the present time the old statement that Maine is the dumping ground for inferior materials can no longer hold true. The character of the various materials offered for sale in the State, which come under the requirements of the various inspection laws, is constantly improving.

The actual work of inspection in the field is accomplished by means of several deputies. The collection of samples of fertilizers, feeding stuffs and seeds is done, as noted above, at certain short definite periods of the year and is usually done by special deputies who search for these particular materials only. The remainder of the inspection work is at the present time done principally by local inspectors appointed to look after some limited locality in which they reside.

By this means the larger towns and cities are at present being constantly inspected and the sanitary conditions of food displays are being constantly improved.

The prosecution feature of the enforcement of these laws is a disagreeable duty. For the most part Maine dealers are and desire to be law abiding. As it is the object of the law to protect the public in the future rather than to impose penalties for the past, cases are only prosecuted as a last resort. It has been found necessary to bring about 125 prosecutions during the year.

CHEMISTRY.

The work of this department, as for the past four years, has been confined almost entirely to inspections and is briefly considered under the following heads: Fertilizer Inspection, Feeding Stuffs Inspection, Food and Drug Inspection, Fungicide and Insecticide Inspection, Paint and Oil Inspection.

FERTILIZER INSPECTION.

About 450 samples of fertilizers and chemicals were analyzed in connection with the fertilizer inspection work. Considerably more work was done this year than usual in determining the quality of the nitrogen in mixed goods by the method adopted by the New England State Stations and New York and New Jersey Stations. This additional work on nitrogen increases the time required to analyze a fertilizer about one-third, but in view of the importance and desirability of having this information the directors of the several stations felt warranted in incurrng this additional expense.

FEEDING STUFFS INSPECTION.

In connection with the feeding stuffs inspection work about 1300 samples of feeds have been examined the past year. The larger part of them were only tested for protein, but owing to a change in the law requiring a guaranty of fiber as well as protein and fat, one complete analysis of each brand of feed sold in the State was made. A large number of the samples examined for nitrogen were sent in by dealers who wished to know if the goods were up to standard before offering them for sale. The official samples, or those taken by the regular Station inspector, were the ones on which complete analyses were made. Complete analyses also were made on 55 samples of oats for the Department of Biology in connection with oat breeding experiments.

FOOD AND DRUG INSPECTION.

In connection with this inspection about 800 samples of foods and drugs have been examined. The work in this line covers a very great variety of materials and varies to some extent with the season. During the summer considerable time is given to examinations of ice creams on the market. During the early fall when preservatives are most likely to be used, oysters and clams were collected in the open markets and tested. It is pleasing to note that not a single instance of a preservative being used was found and only a few instances in the case of oysters was an undue amount of water found to be present—a very great improvement over the condition in which these goods were found a few years ago. A notable improvement has also been noticed in the vinegars and molasses. Canned goods and drugs are examined at any and all times of the year when-ever occasion calls for such examination.

FUNGICIDES AND INSECTICIDES.

Owing to the passage of a fungicide and insecticide law the Maine Agricultural Experiment Station collected and turned into the laboratory for analysis 75 different insecticides and fungicides. These have nearly all been examined and the results will soon be reported in a bulletin.

PAINTS AND OILS.

With a view of learning something about the character of the paint and oil materials on the market, about 60 different kinds of materials were bought and examined. These comprise some dry pigments, pigments ground in oil, and several kinds of mixed paints. Also several oils and driers were tested. The results of this work will soon be published and will be of con-siderable interest to people who use paint.

BIOLOGY.

The Department of Biology is chiefly engaged in the study of plant and animal breeding. The final goal of this work is to find out how the common farm crops and live stock may be improved in quality and productivity by breeding. On the animal side the experimental work is largely with poultry, while on the plant side corn, oats and beans have been the crops chiefly studied.

During nearly the whole existence of the Maine Agricultural Experiment Station it has carried on work with poultry along one line or another. Two phases of the poultry work of this Station have attracted wide attention, namely its experiments in breeding for increased egg production, on the one hand, and in poultry management on the other hand. In recent years an increasing amount of attention has been paid to the former line of work. This is warranted by the great practical importance to agriculture of the subject of breeding for performance in general. Not only will a working out of the fundamental principles upon which successful breeding for egg production depends be useful and valuable to the poultryman, but also to the breeder of any kind of live stock who is seeking to improve utility qualities. Poultry probably furnishes more favorable material for working out the laws of inheritance and breeding than any other of the domestic animals.

Breeding for Egg Production.

The work in breeding for increased egg production is now drawing to a close. During the past year the essential features of the mechanism by which egg production is inherited have been finally worked out. These final results have been published during the present year in Bulletin 205, thus completing an investigation which has engaged the attention of the Station for over 14 years.

The essential facts which have been brought out in this study are the following:

1. The record of egg production of a hen, taken by and of itself alone, gives no definite, reliable indication from which the probable egg production of her daughters may be predicted. Furthermore mass selection on the basis of the fecundity records of females alone, even though long continued and stringent in character, failed completely to produce any steady change in type in the direction of selection.

2. Egg production must be inherited, however, since (a) there are widely distinct and permanent (under ordinary breeding) differences in respect of degree of fecundity between different standard breeds of fowls commonly kept by poultrymen,

and (b) a study of pedigree records of poultry at once discovers pedigree lines (in some measure inbred of course) in each of which a definite, particular degree of fecundity constantly reappears generation after generation, the 'line' thus 'breeding true' in this particular.

3. A careful experimental analysis of the inheritance of fecundity in both pure bred and cross-bred fowls has demonstrated the following unexpected and practically important facts, viz.:

High egg productiveness may be inherited by daughters from their sire, independent of the dam. This is proved by the numerous cases presented in the detailed evidence where the same proportion of daughters of high fecundity are produced by the same sire, whether he is mated with dams of low or of high fecundity.

High productiveness is not inherited by daughters from their dam. This is proved by a number of distinct and independent lines of evidence, of which the most important are: (a) continned selection of highly fecund dams does not alter in any way the mean egg production of the daughters; (b) the proportion of highly fecund daughters is the same whether the dam is of high or of low fecundity, provided both are mated to the same male; (c) the daughters of a fecund dam may show either high fecundity or low fecundity, depending upon their sire; (d) the proportion of daughters of *low* fecundity is the same whether the dam is of high or of low fecundity provided both are mated to the same male.

A low degree of fecundity may be inherited by the daughters from either sire or dam or both.

These results receive their best interpretation through the application of Mendel's law of inheritance. A detailed discussion of the matter will be found in Bulletin 205. They make possible a definite system of breeding for high production, in which success is assured if the guiding principles are carefully followed. The most notable practical feature of the work is to demonstrate the very great importance of the male bird in breeding for increased production. The goal of the practical breeder must be to get a strain of birds in which the males carry the hereditary factor for high productiveness in pure form.

How Many Eggs Can a Hen Lay?

In connection with the studies on breeding for egg production an anatomical study has been made of the potentialities of hens in regard to production. The eggs which a hen can by any possibility lay are limited by the number she carries in·her body in the ovary or egg cluster. How many of these primitive eggs does an ordinary hen have? The following table shows the results of some counts which have been made in this department of the primitive egg *visible to the naked eye,* in various individuals.

Bird No.	BREED.	Total Number of Eggs Laid in Life.	Actual Winter Production.	Total Visible Primitive Eggs on the Ovary.
8021...	Barred Ply. Rock.....	10	3	1,228
8017...	Barred Ply. Rock.....	10	0	1,666
8030...	Barred Ply. Rock....	7	0	914
8005...	Barred Ply. Rock. . .	17	5	1,174
1367...	Barred Ply. Rock....	34	3	2,306
8018...	Barred Ply. Rock....	16	0	1,194
8009...	Barred Ply. Rock....	15	0	2,101
8010...	Barred Ply. Rock... .	19	5	1,576
425...	Barred Ply. Rock.....	23	0	1,521
3546...	White Leghorn.......	198	54	2,452
2067...	White Leghorn.......	197	32	3,605
3453...	White Leghorn.......	10	0	1,701
3833...	White Leghorn.......	2	0	2,145
52...	Cornish Ind. Game...	52	13	1,550
71...	F1 Cross.............	124	106	2,000
	Guinea hen..........	–	–	765
	Guinea hen..........	–	–	586

It is evident that the potentialities in respect to production far outrun the actually realized laying. Laying is a physiological matter rather than an anatomical. All hens, whether good or poor layers, have a vast lot more eggs available for laying than they ever actually lay.

The Function of the Comb and Wattles of Poultry.

Curiosity is often expressed by the poultry man as to the practical utility to the bird, or to himself as a poultryman, of the comb and wattles of fowls. The following brief discussion of the subject was prepared for the purpose of answering such inquiries.

The comb and wattles of poultry are what are known to the biologist as secondary sexual characters. According to Darwin's theory of sexual selection the original purpose and function of these structures was to make the male conspicuous and attractive to the female. It is supposed on this theory that those males which had the largest comb and wattles would be most attractive to the females and would, therefore, stand a better chance of mating and perpetuating themselves in the offspring. Like many other secondary sexual characters the comb and wattles while present in both sexes are very much better developed in one sex than in the other. It is doubtful whether the sexual selection theory really accounts for the presence of large comb and wattles in the male. It is more in line with modern biological opinion to suppose that these organs are merely one representative of the surplus of growth energy and physiological vigor which characterizes the male as compared with the female. It is doubtful, in other words, whether they have any selective value.

It is quite certain that neither the combs nor wattles serve any useful physiological function. That is to say, a bird from which these structures has been removed is quite as healthy and lives as long and is fully as able to perform all its vital functions as a bird which possesses them. They are in some degree, however, and in a manner which is not yet fully understood, connected or correlated with the primary sexual organs (that is, the testes in the male and ovary in the female). Further proof of this has recently been furnished by the work of an English biologist who shows that throughout the life of a hen every period of laying is preceded by an enlargement of the comb. This enlargement is due to an actual growth of tissue in the comb substance. The enlargement in many cases is not marked and can only be detected by very accurate measurements.

The fact that the comb and wattles diminish in size and become pale in color during periods of physiological depression such as molt or in various diseases finds its physiological explanation in the considerations which have been advanced above. These organs being in the nature of non-essential excrescences or ornaments, with a very considerable blood supply when the bird is in health and vigor, it stands to reason that when that vigor is diminished for one reason or another, the supply of blood and nutriment to the tissues of these organs will be diminished in order that it may be diverted to other more vital parts. The reduction of the comb in size and color during periods of depression is physiologically comparable with the fact that a person when ill is usually pale. This means that the supply of blood to the skin is smaller than in condition of full health and vigor.

A large comb does not necessarily indicate strong constitution. In the first place it must be recognized that comb size in part depends upon the breed. The most vigorous specimens of some breeds have by nature and inheritance relatively small combs as compared with other birds. While it is practically always true that a bird with a comb relatively small in proportion to the size normal for its breed is a weak and worthless bird, the converse is not always true. That is to say, some weak, poor specimens will have large combs. The size and condition of the comb should be taken as only one indication along with a whole series of others in judging the constitutional vigor of a bird. Simply selecting large-combed birds regardless of everything else would not result in a strong vigorous strain.

Poultry Management.

At all times efforts are being made to improve the methods of management of poultry on the Station plant. During the past year a new concrete shed for the storage and proper conservation of poultry manure has been built on the plant. A full description of this with directions for the care and use of this valuable fertilizing material will be issued as a bulletin during the coming year.

Green Food for Poultry.

During recent years an increasing amount of attention has been paid by poultrymen everywhere to the furnishing of green food to their fowls during the winter months, when it is imposible in northern parts of the country, at least, for the birds to get fresh succulent pasturage out of doors. It has been the universal experience that an addition of green succulent food to the ration of laying hens tends to keep them in better physical condition and helps towards a better egg production, with consequently increased profits to the poultryman. On the poultry plant of the Maine Agricultural Experiment Station considerable attention has been given to this matter of supplying green and succulent food to poultry, and as a result of experience extending now over a number of years a very satisfactory scheme of supplying this necessary part of the ration has been worked out.

It is, of course, obvious that if it is to be satisfactory not only must the green food given to poultry be of the proper kind to give good results in egg production, but also it must be something which can be produced and handled at small cost. Furthermore a factor which is frequently lost sight of here is that fowls need something besides succulence in their so-called "green food." There is a distinction between a succulent fodder and a "green food" in the strict sense. One can supply succulence in the form of root crops like mangolds or other similar crops. A careful examination of the situaton, however, indicates that probably the fundamental need of the fowls is not for succulence as such, but rather for the tonic effect which is produced by green plants. The green color of plants is due to the presence of cholorophyll, a chemical compound which is very rich in iron. In feeding fowls for high egg production it is necessary that they be given a ration rich in protein. Only birds of very strong constitution and with thoroughly sound digestive systems can continuously handle for a long period the heavy laying rations carrying meat scrap and oil meal, which are now so widely used by poultrymen, with successful results for egg production. On these heavy rations there is always a tendency for the bird's liver first to become impaired in function and ultimately to become enlarged and diseased. As the matter has been studied at the Maine Agricultural Experiment Station it would appear that one of the chief, if not indeed the most important functions of green food in the ration is to counteract this tendency of the digestive system, and especially the liver, to break down under the strain of assimilating heavy laying rations over a long period of time. It would appear that the green food given to poultry acts primarily as a mild tonic rather than as a food in the proper sense. There is very little of this tonic effect produced from succulent non-green foods like mangolds. For this dependence must be placed primarily upon cholorophyll bearing plants.

The practical problem then becomes to find a satisfactory and economical system whereby a supply of green food may be kept at hand for the birds at all seasons of the year when wanted. The following system of rotation in the green stuff supply has been in use for several years on the poultry plant of the Maine Agricultural Experiment Station with entirely satisfactory results. It should be said that, owng to the small area of ground available for the poultry work at the Station in relation to the number of birds it is necessary to carry, green food must be added to the ration practically throughout the year, not only for the adult fowls in the laying houses, but also for the chicks growing on the range. The number of birds reared is so great in proportion to the area which can be devoted to them that the natural pasturage is very quickly exhausted.

Beginning with the time in the fall of the year when the pullets are put into the laying house they are given green corn fodder chopped fine in a feed cutter. This is fed stalks, leaves and ears (if there are any) all together. The pieces are cut from a quarter to a half inch in length by the feed cutter used. This green corn fodder is one of the most satisfactory sources of green food for poultry which the Maine Agricultural Experiment Station has ever been able to discover. The birds eat it ravenously and in large quantities. It may be safely fed in larger amounts than any other green food yet tried. After the corn has been killed by frost so as no longer to be available the birds are given cabbage and mangolds fed with the tops on. These plants serve until well into the winter (December or January). Then the oat sprouter is started and green sprouted oats serve as the chief source of green food until well on into the spring (April or May). The green oats are supplemented with mangolds or with clover hay cut in short lengths with the feed cutter and steamed. In case clover hay is not available cut alfalfa is sometimes substituted for this. As soon as possible in the spring fresh green clover is cut from the range and fed to the birds in the houses. To the young chicks in the brooders, however, the best source of green food which has yet been found is green sprouted oats. To these little chicks only the tops are fed and these are cut fine. In the regular crop rotation system carried out on the range green corn, Dwarf Essex rape, mangolds and cabbages are planted each spring.

The green corn, Dwarf Essex rape and the thinnings from the mangolds are used during the summer to feed both the adult birds in the houses and the growing chickens on the range after the natural pasturage has become exhausted. Dwarf Essex rape is an excellent source of green food for poultry but it must be, fed with great caution to birds which are laying, because if eaten in any considerable amounts it may color the yolks of the eggs green with disastrous results in the market.

Following such a system as is outlined above it is possible to have throughout the year a continuance of green fodder well calculated to keep the birds in the best of physical condition and at the maximum of productivity.

Natural Enemies of Poultry.

One of the difficulties that the poultryman has to contend with is the continued loss of chicks, and sometimes even of nearly or quite full grown birds, as a consequence of the depredations of natural enemies. It is safe to say that the magnitude of the loss from these sources is not anything like fully realized by anyone who has not kept an accurate account of all his birds. In the experimental breeding work with poultry at the Maine Agricultural Experiment Station it is necessary to keep account of every single bird on the plant. It has, therefore, on this account been possible to check up and form an adequate estimate of the losses due to the creatures that prey upon poultry. A good deal of attention has been devoted to the problem of how these losses may be cut down and the results of this experience may be of benefit to other poultry keepers in this State.

In the experience of the Maine Agricultural Experiment Station the most destructive natural enemy of poultry, in the long run, has been found to be the crow. The depredations of hawks are more spectacular perhaps but on the whole far less destructive. A hawk will only visit a poultry yard occasionally, and especially if he is shot at once or twice will be very wary about approaching it again. On the contrary the crow is a steady and persistent robber. He will continue his depredations just as long as it is physically possible for him to do so. While there may be some doubt as to whether crows are beneficial or harmful as regards other phases of agriculture, there can be no question that, so far as the poultryman is concerned, the only good crow is a dead one. For a number of years the crows killed and either carried away, or left behind partly eaten, a large number of chicks on the Maine Agricultural Experiment Station poultry plant. The losses were not by any means confined to the small chicks, but half grown birds, nearly if not quite equal in weight to the crow itself, were killed and partly eaten and left behind on the range. In a single year the crows destroyed something over 500 chicks. One after another all the devices which had been suggested by others or could be devised by those in charge of the poultry work, were tried in order to stop these ravages. Various sorts of scarecrows were put up but with no effect whatever. Dead crows were hung up on stakes about the yard as solemn warnings to their fellows, but instead of operating as warnings they appeared rather to serve as "invitations to the dance." Decoying the birds in various ways, so that they might be shot, was tried but with very slight success, and no substantial effect on the steady losses. Poisoning, which is reported to have been used with success in other places, has never been tried on the Maine Agricultural Experiment Station plant and it is very doubtful whether it is ever justifiable, save under very exceptionable circumstances. The point is that it is difficult to manage a poisoning campaign in such way as to insure that the crows and only the crows will get the poison. There are so many useful and valuable animals about the farm, which might very easily get the poison before the crows did, with resulting losses greater than those caused by the crows, that it would seem wise to resort to poisoning only when it can be done under well controlled conditions.

The plan which has finally been adopted on the Maine Agricultural Experiment Station poultry plant for dealing with crows is one which is perfectly safe and sure in its operation. It consists simply in running strands of binder twine about two feet apart over the whole of the poultry range occupied by the young birds. These strings are left in place until the chicks attain such size that they are able to take care of themselves. These strings are run over the tops of the brooder houses and on supports made by running cross strands 20 to 30 feet apart of either wire or of five or six strands of binder twine twisted together. These cross strands are held up where necessary by posts. The whole network of strings thus formed is put at such height that the attendants in working about the yard will not hit them when standing upright. The area covered in with strings in this way on the Station poultry plant is usually about 3 acres per year. The expense of covering this area is from $15 to $20 for twine. The labor of putting it up is comparatively small. It forms a perfect and complete protection against both crows and hawks.

Next in importance to the predaceous birds as poultry enemies stand the rats and the foxes. In times past foxes have destroyed many chickens from the Station's poultry plant. Of late years, however, none has been lost. The protection is afforded by a fox proof fence surrounding the whole plant. Rats may become a very pest. They live under the brooder houses and take the young chicks. Various methods have been tried at the Station, but no wholly satisfactory way of dealing with rats has yet been found. Trial has been made of one of the most widely advertised of the bacterial rat destroyers, which when fed to rats is supposed to induce a disease which kills them all. No effect whatever was observed to follow the use of this preparation. The rats ate freely of grain which had been moistened with it and if any disease developed as a consequence it has not yet manifested itself, and the trial was made some three years ago. Digging the rats out of their holes and shooting them is on the whole about as effectual a method of dealing with them as the Station has yet found. Several good cats on the place also aid materially in fighting this pest. If someone will discover an effective, non-poisonous rat repellant or destroyer he will confer a great boon on all mankind, and especially on the poultryman.

WORK WITH DAIRY CATTLE.

Proposed Plan for a Comprehensive Investigation of the Inheritance of Milk Production in Dairy Cattle, with Special Reference to Breeding for Improved Production.

There has never been carried through anywhere in the world any systematic or comprehensive scientific investigation of the

laws of the inheritance of the function of milk production in
dairy cattle. Whatever progress has been made up to this time
in breeding for this quality has been built largely on an empiri-
cal basis. There is no body of well-grounded scientific principles to guide a person at the present time in building up a high
producing dairy herd or improving what he already has in such
a way that the improvement shall be definite and permanent.
The need for investigation which shall lead to the accumulation of knowledge of the principles referred to has been keenly
felt for sometime past by the dairymen in the State. The dairy
industry in Maine is just now in a critical condition. The increased prices of feed without anything like a corresponding
increase in the price of milk and other dairy products has
materially reduced the profits of the business. For several
years past the Maine Dairymen's Association has had a Committee empowered to discover ways and means if possible
whereby the Maine Agricultural Experiment Station might
undertake a comprehensive investigation along the lines indicated. Furthermore, this matter has been taken up by the
Experiment Station Council and efforts have been made by
that body to secure funds for this purpose. It is felt that the
experience which the Station has gained in its long continued
experiments on breeding for increased egg production in poultry would be of very material advantage in undertaking work
on the problem of breeding for dairy production. The amount
of work, however, under way at the Station uses up all the funds
which it has available and it is therefore not possible to embark
on any new project of this kind until additional funds are provided from some source.

A plan of coöperation between the Agricultural College and
the Experiment Station has been worked out, whereby the barns
and herd of the College will be available for this investigation.
It is hoped that during the year the necessary funds will be
provided and the Station can then undertake this important line
of work.

TRIPLET CALVES.

A tendency towards increased fecundity in any domestic
animal, provided it is not associated with loss of other valuable

qualities, is a thing much to be desired. During the past year a bulletin (No. 204) has been published, dealing with the subject of multiple gestation in cattle in general, and describing a case of triplet calves in detail.

The triplets were the progeny of a grade Guernsey cow that produced 14 calves in her first eight pregnancies, bearing triplets twice, twins twice, and single young four times. This cow undoubtedly inherited and transmitted a tendency to high fecundity.

The triplets described consisted of two females and one male. The latter was sexually normal in every particular, and was used in service, getting normal offspring. The females never came in heat and probably were freemartins.

In color and pattern inheritance the triplets exhibited the following peculiarities: The male was typically a Guernsey, resembling closely his dam. The females were of quite different color and pattern, resembling more closely their sire, a grade Hereford. A possible Mendelian interpretation of these facts is discussed in the bulletin.

WORK WITH PLANTS.

Beans.

During the year the experiments looking towards the improvement of the old-fashioned yellow-eye bean were continued. Owing to the unfavorable season, however, but little progress was made. A committee of the Station Council and Maine Seed Improvement Association have been actively engaged in the question of bean grading and standardization. Considerable progress has been made, and it is possible now to go forward with the breeding work with a definite standard as to types and quality in yellow eye beans, which will be in accord with the demands of the market.

Variety Tests of Oats.

In 1912 the oat variety tests were continued at Highmoor. It was a very unfavorable season but the yields considerably exceeded those of the year before.

The yields in 1912 are shown in the following table.

Oat Variety Test

1912.

NAME OF VARIETY.	Yield in Bushels Per Acre.
Reg. Swed. Select............................	–
Reg. Swed. Select......	56.5
Silver Mine..	52.9
Banner................................	62.6
Irish Victor.........	61.6
Lincoln....	68.3
Kherson.........	52.6
President......	56.5
Early Champion........................	50.4
Prosperity............................	67.4
Imported Scotch	62.2
Victor................................	56.9
Senator.......	53.5
Danish Island.	57.7
Clydesdale.	54.5
Early Pearl.......	64.2
White Plume....	44.1
Rebred 60-Day....................	47.5
Gold Rain....	53.8
Abundance............................	47.9
Minnesota, No. 26.......................	52.7
Siberian.............................	50.0
Daubeney............................	· 43.3

These tests have been running for three years now. The ten best yielding varieties with their average yields for the three years, in bushels per acre, are given in the following table. These tables should be of value to the Maine farmer in deciding what variety of oats to grow.

The Best Yielding Varieties of Oats on the Basis of Average of Three Successive Years Test.

NAME OF VARIETY.	Average Yield for Three Years in Bushels per Acre.
Irish Victor..................	62.6
Lincoln......................	62.0
Prosperity...................	61.9
Imported Scotch..............	61.5
Banner......................	59.7
Silver Mine..................	59.3
President....................	58.0
Victor (a black oat)...........	57.0
Kherson (an early oat).........	56.6
Regenerated Swedish Select.....	56.5

The breeding work with oats has consisted of the study of individual pedigree strains to find what are most promising. Several strains which appear to be very valuable will be propagated on an extensive scale in 1913. Some of these new sorts have yielded in trials on small plots at rates of 100 bushels or more to the acre. Seed from some of the best of these will probably be available for distribution in 1914.

Corn.

Work with sweet corn and with field corn (yellow dent) is being continued. The field corn of the Cornforth strain has been now bred up to the point where it appears to be a highly desirable sort for the Maine farmer.

An experiment was tried this year to determine the exact stage of development at which sweet corn should be picked for seed, in order to give the best results.

This year a more extended test was given a new sort of white sweet corn, with fine kernels and large amount of stover, which has been bred by the Station. It promises to be superior to any corn now grown in the State for canned purposes.

ENTOMOLOGY.

The year of 1912 has been in some ways of unusual entomological interest. The ravages of the spruce bud moth, the

19

abundance of a new spruce leaf miner and the occurrence of other spruce insects have turned much of the attention toward the conifers, both native and those introduced for ornamental purposes. The increase of the Gypsy moth area and the continued spread of the brown-tail moth have given the emphasis of one more year's experience with these two pests of paramount importance. The season has been so favorable to the development of scale insects that even those species ordinarily little noticed have been conspicuous in many parts of the State. Fortunately correlated with the abundance of injurious species the insects of 1912 have included beneficial species in great numbers. The syrphus maggots and other predaceous insects, for instance, have practically exterminated many species of plant-lice over large areas, and parasites have been actively engaged in their natural warfare against injurious caterpillars and other insects.

Dr. O. A. Johannsen has completed this year a study begun ten or fifteen years ago of the Fungus Gnats of North America and this Station has published this work in four parts, the last of which contains those gnats of most economic importance, dealing with a group which attacks apples and corn as well as potatoes and other root crops.

As a basis for studies of New England Psyllids, or "Jumping plant-lice," a series of systematic studies was undertaken and the results of this preliminary work have been published this summer. The "Jumping plant-lice" are sucking insects which injure plants in much the same way as the aphids. This family of insects has heretofore received such meager attention in this country that it has not been possible to recognize some of the commonest species in the United States from the published accounts and many have been known merely as manuscript species. It is proposed to continue this work until we are much better acquainted with the Maine Psyllidae than at present.

APHID INVESTIGATIONS.

It is a fact familiar to students of this family of insects that certain aphids live for a few generations (usually wingless) upon one food plant and then produce a winged generation that migrates to an entirely different species of plant for the summer, where it establishes a series of summer generations and by fall produces a second migrant generation that flies back to the original food plant. It is here the true sexes occur and that the winter egg is deposited,—stages absolutely essential to the continuation of the species.

Such a dual personality of certain aphid species is a condition which, before it is detected, betrays the economic entomologist into many futile combative attempts; but on the other hand the same duality may reveal, when once discovered, the most vulnerable point of attack. It is not necessary to go out of our own State for illustrations. The discovery that *Chermes abieticolens,* Thomas 1879, which makes cone-like galls on black and red spruce is the same species as *Chermes pinifoliae* Fitch 1858,* which lays eggs on new growth white pine for progeny that render the pine shoots weakened and unthrifty, gives the landscape gardener his clue. If he treasures the beauty of a group of white pines he would do well to exclude red and black spruces from the vicinity, or conversely if he wishes to grow black spruces with normal branches it is an indiscretion to place them near white pines. Again, when once it was ascertained that the common Alder Blight, *Pemphigus tessellatus* Fitch 1851, was masquerading on the maple *(Acer saccharium* L.—*dasycarpum* Ehrh. and cultivated varieties) as *Pemphigus acerifolii* Riley 1879† the owner of ornamental cut leaved maples had a theretofore unsuspected means of protecting their foliage by the control of the pest on its alternate food plant, the alder, which in many circumstances is an easy point of control.

It is with no slight interest that we have ascertained that the woolly aphid of the apple is such a migratory species with two distinct types of food plants;—the elm, or "original food plant," on which the true sexes occur in the fall and deposit the over-wintering egg, and on which it lives in the curled leaves in the spring; and the apple to which it migrates from the elm-leaf-curl and where it establishes itself as a bark feeder during the summer. This species, in addition, produces in the fall a generation that passes the winter at the roots of the apple, a

---

* Bulletin 173 Maine Agricultural Experiment Station.
† Entomological News, 1908, p. 484; Journal of Economic Entomology 1909, Vol. II, p. 35; Bulletin No. 195 Me. Agr. Exp. Sta., Feb. 13. 1912.

circumstance which has led to the assumption that the apple alone was concerned in the life cycle of this pest, and the elm-leaf curl which shelters the wolf in sheep's clothing has been previously unsuspected of other danger than that which threatened the elm itself, which except in the case of young trees is not usually great. But the discovery of the annual migration of a fresh infestation from the elm to the apple and the knowledge that the elm generations are an essential portion of the life cycle of the woolly aphid of the apple put a new significance upon the economic status of the elm curl.

There is probably no more interesting line of insect investigation than working out the full life cycle of the migratory aphids and such projects find sufficient economic justification in the fact that there are possibilities of control of certain species of plant lice or aphids by such methods as rotation of crops or the destruction of weeds which serve to maintain a species of aphids dangerous to neighboring crops; or the selection by the landscape gardener of ornamental shrubs and trees which are not susceptible to attacks of aphids common on native vegetation. In some cases circumventing the aphid by means of a knowledge of its food habits and migrations would be simpler and more effective than the direct methods of spraying which need to be repeated each year of attack.

PLANT PATHOLOGY.

As was pointed out in the 1911 report the department of plant pathology of this Station is equipped for making and does make studies of diseases of the various economic plants of the State. In the past, however, the work has been largely confined to the diseases of the potato and the apple on account of the importance of these crops and on account of the fact that, as a rule, success or failure in potato and apple growing is to a great extent dependent upon proper and efficent disease control.

With regards efficiency in disease control, the commonest methods of spraying potatoes illustrates a case in point. Spraying potatoes for late blight is probably more widely practiced and better done in Maine, as a rule, than in any other part of the United States, but there is still much chance for improvement. Much of the spraying is far from being efficient. Field studies made in comparison with the results obtained from the Station's experimental work in potato spraying have shown that the bordeaux mixture used on many farms was improperly made and not applied at the proper time. Almost without exception potato spraying as practiced by the average potato grower lacked in thoroughness. Usually only one spray nozzle is used for each row of potatoes, applying but 50 gallons of spray per acre. With the rows 32 inches apart and the plants 12 inches apart in the row this means that one pint of liquid must cover 41 plants, or over 100 square feet of surface when the plants cover the ground.

There is much need for demonstration work in various parts of the State to show the farmers what has been done and what can be done in the way of efficient disease control, when the proper methods are used and properly applied. In fact there is probably as much immediate need for this sort of practical work as there is for research upon plant disease problems, although the latter should be of greater permanent value. However, no matter how great the need for demonstration work along the lines mentioned, the Station is not allowed to use the funds available for plant disease studies to carry on work of this nature, except to test under field conditions the conclusions drawn from laboratory studies. The funds available are from the National Government and it is expressly stipulated that they shall be used for original research and experimentation.

IDENTIFICATION OF PLANT DISEASES.

One of the important lines of pathological work now being carried on at the Station is the study of the prevalence and distribution of the different diseases of economic plants within the State. This work is being done in coöperation with the Bureau of Plant Industry of the United States Department of Agriculture, and the Station pathologist is supplied with printed shipping tags which will carry packages of diseased plants without prepayment of postage, and which can be furnished to those who will send specimens. This is an important line of work and its success depends upon the coöperation of the farmers of the State. An increasing number are sending in such specimens each year and it will greatly increase the efficiency of the work if a still greater number will avail themselves of the opportunity. In return for the specimens the Station will endeavor to determine the nature of the disease and advise methods of control if such are known. Such specimens often suggest needed lines of investigation and as the practice of sending them in for identification becomes increasingly common it will become increasingly difficult for a new and dangerous plant disease to establsh itself within the borders of the State.

PREVALENCE OF PLANT DISEASES IN 1912 WITH SUGGESTIONS FOR THEIR CONTROL.

Diseases of orchard trees and fruits. Apple scab, while always of the greatest economic importance in Maine, was particularly severe the past season. This was due to the very favorable climatic conditions during the early part of the growing season, namely an abundance of rainy, cloudy weather. Not only was the fruit crop badly damaged by this disease but the foliage suffered severely in many instances with certain varieties, and in one case specimens were received from a young orchard where the twigs were killed back by the fungus. Wherever spraying was properly done and at the right time the disease was largely controlled. In some cases pink rot of the fruit was very destructive in storage on apples affected by scab.

Black rot is probably next to apple scab in importance as the same fungus causes the leaf spot and canker, as well as the decay of the fruit. About the same amount of damage was recorded from this fungus in 1912 as usual, although a few cases were recorded where the owners reported that the canker was quite destructive and increasing. For the treatment of this and other apple diseases the reader is referred to Bulletin 185 of this Station or pages 380 to 440 of the Report of the Commissioner of Agrculture for 1910.

Crown gall appears to be becoming increasingly common upon the nursery stock shipped into the State, judging from the specimens received. Trees so affected should not be set and nursery men supplying them should be refused patronage. Numerous specimens of various other diseases of the apple were received but those mentioned are of the greatest importance.

Three very common diseases of the stone fruits as usual did much damage within the State last season, and many specimens of them were received. These are the brown rot, black knot and plum pockets.

More specimens of brown rot of the plum were received last season than for several years. The disease also attacks the cherry and the apple in this State, and is one of the most destructive diseases of the peach farther South. Last season it was reported from Bar Harbor as doing considerable damage where the English custom of growing peaches under glass is carried on commercially. In 1911 a very severe outbreak of brown rot was reported from a cherry orchard where not only were the young fruits destroyed but young branches and twigs were killed back by the fungus. Plum fruits are attacked by brown rot about the beginning of the ripening period. The diseased portions turn brownish, forming soft spots which rapidly grow in size till the whole fruit is infested. The fungus then breaks through the surface in the form of small grayish tufts or nodules which are masses of summer spores which scatter and infect healthy fruits. The decayed fruits dry up and form mummies which hang on the trees, or fall to the ground. In either case these mummies are the most important means of carrying the disease over winter and serve as the source of the new infections of the following seasons, when the young twigs, flowers and young fruit may be attacked.

The mummied fruits should be destroyed in the fall, and the trees sprayed with a 5-5-50 bordeaux mixture early in the spring before the leaves appear. After the leaves appear the trees should be sprayed with lime-sulphur the same as is used on apple trees. See Bulletin 185 mentioned above.

Black knot is too common to need description. It is especially common in Maine on wild cherries, particularly the chokecherry, which is one of the sources of the spread of the disease to cultivated plums and cherries and these plants should be rooted out and destroyed wherever found. The knots on the cultivated cherries and plums should be pruned out and burned as fast as they appear. The trees should be sprayed in the same way as described for brown rot.

Plum pockets, judging from observation and from the number of specimens sent in, appears to be a widely distributed and destructive disease of the plum in Maine. In some years, as in 1912, it does much more damage than in others. Cherries are also affected with a similar malady. In this disease the fruit early in the season becomes enlarged to several times the natural size. No stone is formed and the entire fruit is converted into a large, thin-walled, bladder-like structure, at first yellowish but later becoming gray as a coat of spores forms on the surface. The disease does not seem to spread with great ease but the fungus may live over winter in the twigs so that a tree once infected may continue to produce a crop of plum pockets each year instead of normal fruit.

The treatment consists of pruning back severely all affected twigs as fast as the diseased fruits appear on them and spraying the trees heavily with a 5-5-50 bordeaux mixture just before the leaf buds open in the spring.

DISEASES OF FIELD AND GARDEN CROPS.

While many plant disease specimens of this nature have been received and examined during the past season, bean anthracnose, onion mildew and the various potato diseases are by far of the greatest importance.

Bean anthracnose or "pod spot," more commonly known as "rust" by Maine farmers was very destructive last season, some fields being entirely ruined by its attacks. The term "rust" as applied to this disease is a misnomer. Moreover there exists in Maine a true rust of beans, but this produces small brown or black pustules on the leaves, particularly on some varieties of pole beans. These are most conspicuous in late summer. The bean anthracnose is much more destructive, and attacks both the leaf petioles and the pods. On the former it produces brown streaks, finally girdling the leaf stems and causing defoliation. On the latter the appearance is well known to every bean grower. The attacked pods are covered with what are first small brownish or discolored areas, which later enlarge forming rusty-colored pits or ulcers. The fungus frequently grows through the pods into the seed beans beneath, and beans so infected carry the fungus over winter.

To avoid bean anthracnose, rotation of crops is advised, and perfectly clean seed obtained from fields where the disease has not appeared, if possible, should be used. Some varieties are more resistant to the disease than others. Varying results have been obtained from spraying with bordeaux mixture but this is advised as a precautionary measure.

Onion mildew is an important and destructive disease of onions. It is mentioned here particularly because a case reported from Hallowell in the summer of 1912 was the first record of its occurrence in Maine since the department of plant pathology was established at the Station. It appears in late June or July. The fungus which causes it belongs to the same general class as that to which the fungus causing the late blight of the potato belongs. The disease is characterized by a sudden wilting and death of the foliage and rapid spread of the malady where large fields of onions are being grown. In the early stages the attacked portions of the leaves have a furry appearance with a slight violet tinge. Later these become mouldy, pale, streaked or blotched, collapsed and broken.

For treatment, spraying with bordeaux mixture, particularly a modified form having an addition of a sticky substance composed of fish oil, resin and potash, has been found to be very effective.

With regards potato diseases, particularly late blight, the season of 1912 gave very unexpected results. From past experience any prolonged period of rainy weather after the plants have reached the blossoming stage is, in this State, practically certain to result in widespread and destructive epidemics of late blight on all but the most thoroughly sprayed potato fields. The summer of 1912 was probably the first exception to this rule that New England has experienced in many years. While the potato growing season was abnormally wet and late blight of the foliage and the associated decay of the tubers appeared, no real severe cases of this disease were reported to the Station or observed by the pathologists.

There is one possible explanation for this failure of the disease to appear in epidemic form. The fungus is carried over winter in the seed tubers and spreads from these to the young plants in the spring. At this time of the year it is propagated very slowly, does no apparent damage, and consequently is never seen by the average observer. In this region it never breaks out in epidemic form till after the plants attain considerable size and the weather conditions are favorable. The fungus causing the disease is very sensitive to high temperature. Exposure for any considerable period of time to a temperature of 90% to 95% F. or over kills it while continuous and prolonged exposure to a temperature above 86% or 87% F. will accomplish the same results.

The month of July in both 1911 and 1912 was characterized by a period of about 10 days, at the beginning, of the most severe and continuous hot weather recorded in Maine in many years. Not only were high temperatures recorded but the days were very bright and sunny and the nights abnormally warm. During this period young apples on the exposed portions of the trees were partially cooked on one side as a result of the extreme brightness and heat of the sunlight. It seems quite possible that the air and soil temperature were so high that the late blight fungus was in many instances practically killed out during this period. Moreover it came at a time when the fungus was probably no longer alive in the seed tubers but existed in a vegetative stage in the young stems and leaves above or at least very close to the surface of the soil, if below the ground at all.

The hot period of July 1911 was followed by a fairly dry season and there resulted the most healthy crop of potatoes, so far as late blight was concerned, that Maine has produced in years. Consequently the seed tubers used in 1912 contained very little of this disease. The only dry period of the growing season of 1912 was the month of June. This was followed by the hot period of July, already referred to, and apparently furnished the final causes which nearly eliminated late blight from the State this year.

Early blight normally does little damage in wet seasons, but some cases were observed this season where, associated with flea beetles it caused considerable damage. Blackleg and scab caused about the usual amount of losses. The wet weather was quite favorable to the development of the former. Very favorable reports were received from those who used the formaldehyde seed-treatment for these diseases.

DISEASES OF CEREALS AND FORAGE CROPS.

The Station pathologists have made some quite extensive field observations upon the distribution of oat diseases in the State during the past summer. An apparently new leaf blight disease of oats has been found which seems to be very generally distributed throughout Maine. Not enough is known about it as yet to suggest methods of treatment or prevention. It is apparent, however, that it does considerable damage and that a large number of varieties are quite susceptible to it, although some are probably more resistant than others.

Oat smut was found to be much more common and destructive in the State than was at first supposed. In some cases 10% to 25% of the crop was destroyed in this way. This is, perhaps, the most conspicuous illustration of the need for demonstration work in plant pathology. A perfectly successful, cheap and effective method of seed disinfection is known, and it can be carried out by any man of average intelligence. To do this the oats to be treated are spread out on a canvas or clean barn floor and are sprinkled with a solution of one pint of formaldehyde to 40 or 50 gallons of water at the rate of a gallon per bushel, and then shoveled over to insure thorough wetting of each seed. Cover with a blanket or canvas for at least four hours, but not longer, and then spread out to dry.

One of the serious obstacles to growing alfalfa in Maine appears to be the alfalfa leaf-spot. Many specimens of this are received and practically all fields examined show bad attacks of the disease. No practical method of controlling it has been developed, but frequent cutting is said to help. Even though alfalfa is a valuable forage crop it may be wiser to turn attention to the more hardy red clover, which reaches its highest perfection of development in Maine. However a new disease of red clover was found in Maine last season. This is an anthracnose and is apparently similar to one described in Tennessee for the first time a few years ago. How wide-spread and destructive it is has not been determined but some sections of the State were found to be free from it.

DISEASES OF SHADE TREES.

Each year a considerable number of specimens of diseased sugar maple leaves are received the last of June and on through July. Almost invariably these are the result of late frosts, or result from the effects of strong drying winds, associated with bright sunlight, following a period of moist, cloudy weather when the young leaves have been growing rapidly and consequently are very tender

Much complaint is received from a leaf-spot of the horse-chestnut. The disease is so common and destructive that it is strongly advised that other species not susceptible to disease be used when planting shade trees.

Another quite destructive disease of shade trees in Maine is the elm leaf-spot, caused by *Gnomonia Ulmea* (Sacc.) Thum. Shade trees are frequently badly defoliated by attacks of this fungus and many complaints were received regarding such instances during the past summer. Doubtless spraying would be beneficial in the case of this disease as well as the horse-chestnut leaf-spot. However it would doubtless be impractical except where the matter of expense would be no consideration or in those municipalities where special equipment has been purchased to fight gipsy and brown-tail moths or other insect pests.

ORCHARD SPRAYING EXPERIMENTS IN 1912.

When Highmoor Farm came under the management of the Maine Agricultural Experiment Station the pathologist planned a series of experiments, particularly designed to test the effect of lime-sulphur and other sprays in controlling apple scab upon those varieties of apples like the Ben Davis and Baldwin which are quite susceptible to bordeaux injury. Bordeaux mixture is a most effective agent in controlling apple scab but on the varieties mentioned, and certain others, it frequently produces, especially in wet seasons, much damage to both foliage and fruit. So long as a horticulturist was stationed at the farm during the summer months he could best conduct these experiments, therefore they were transferred to his department. This work has again come under the control of the pathological department.

The apple spraying experiments of the past season were the third of the series. A brief résumé of the results of the two preceding years was included in this report for 1911. Weather conditions for 1911 were such that very little scab developed, therefore the experiments for that year were duplicated for 1912 with much more satisfactory results. On account of the more severe outbreak of scab these results regarding certain features of the experiments were quite clear cut and conclusive.

The most important lesson to be drawn from the work of the present year is with regard to the value of the application of the spray made first at the time the flower buds are showing pink. It is not recommended to omit the later sprayings, but where they were made last season and the first spraying omitted the work was probably done at a loss. Where all three applications were made almost perfect results were obtained. In other words last season *the application of the spray made just as the blossoms were showing pink was several times more effective than the other two taken together.*

Lime-sulphur applied at the proper time effectually controlled scab and was very free from leaf injury and produced only a small amount of russeted fruit. Bordeaux mixture, under like conditions controlled scab better than did lime-sulphur but upon the very susceptible Ben Davis produced so much russeting of the fruit that this more than off-set the beneficial effects.

Four pounds of arsenate of lead to fifty gallons of water plainly was of considerable fungicidal value. In fact the results were fully as good as on adjoining plots where two pounds of lead arsenate to fifty gallons of lime-sulphur were used. The heavy application of lead arsenate did result in considerable leaf injury, however. Arsenate of zinc and dry arsenate of lead were used with entire success with regards effect on foliage and fruit, and controlled insect pests, including codling moth, as effectually as did the ordinary lead arsenate paste.

POTATO SCAB.

The work on potato scab is being continued. Recently specimens of a new form of scab called "powdery scab" have been received from an adjoining County of Canada. This like the blackleg and potato canker or wart disease were probably

imported to Canada from Europe. Specimens of scabby potatoes are being secured from as many localities in Maine as
possible and these are being studied to learn if there is more
than one form of the disease in this State. This is only a part
of the very extended study that is being made of this disease
and the organism causing it.

Some very interesting results have been obtained from feeding scabby potato tubers to the horse and the cow. It was found
that the germs of the scab organism could pass through the
digestive tract of both these animals and still be able to cause
the disease if their manure is used for fertilizing a potato field.
However it was concluded that as a rule there is little danger
from feeding cows an ordinary amount of scabby potatoes
provided none of the uneaten tubers were allowed to get into
the manure. Uncooked potato peelings or potato refuse should
not be thrown on the manure pile.

STUDIES UPON THE POTATO BLACKLEG ORGANISMS.

Last year's report stated that a practical method of the control of blackleg had been worked out and found to be quite
successful. Since that time the more technical studies of the
organisms associated with the disease have been completed and
will soon be published as one of the research papers from this
laboratory. It is sufficient to say in the present instance that
only one type of organism was found associated with the disease in this State so that the remedial measures which succeeded
in one case should be effective in all.

FUSARIUM DISEASES OF PLANTS.

There are a rather large number of plant diseases caused by
species of the genus Fusarium. More than 300 species have
been described for this genus and many of the descriptions
have been very incomplete so that in many cases it has been
impossible to determine from the written descriptions whether
a form which was being studied had been described or not. As
a result of this, it has happened in some cases that the same
species has been described under two or more different names.
This has led to much confusion. This is especially true in the

case of forms which cause disease in plants. In some cases the occurrence of a form on a certain host plant has led to its being described as a new species, whereas the same form had already been described on another host under a different name. In such cases where one species can cause disease in two or more hosts it is of great importance to know that it is the same fungus which causes the diseases because that knowledge determines largely whether one of the plants can be used to follow the other in a rotation or whether two or more such host plants can be grown near together. It will be seen that a knowledge of the effect of such a species on its hosts may become of great practical value.

On account of the lack of knowledge in regard to diseases of plants which are caused by species of this genus in Maine, studies have been made of Fusarium forms which have been found in connection with diseased conditions in a number of plants which are of economic importance. This work was begun in 1908 when 3 species of Fusarium were isolated from decaying apples and it was found by inoculation experiments that each of these was capable of causing decay of apple fruit. Since no species of Fusarium had been reported as a cause of apple decay in America it was decided to study these forms carefully for comparison with a species which had been described in Europe as a cause of apple decay. One of the Maine forms has been found to agree closely with this fungus. Fusarium forms have been isolated from apples a number of times since but in each case the characters of the fungus have agreed with those of one or the other of the forms isolated in 1908.

In connection with the study of one of the forms from apple it was found that a very similar fungus has been described in other places as the cause of a bud-rot of carnation. The apple fungus was tested by making inoculations of carnation buds and was found to cause the rot. Since that time a fungus similar to, if not identical with, the carnation bud-rot fungus has been isolated from diseased parts of the following plants: Potato, sunflower, sweet corn, and the culms of five grasses which had been injured by the grass thrips. All of these fungi have been grown under the same conditions as the apple fungus for comparison and all have been tested by means of inoculations on carnation buds. As a result of this work it has been found that the same fungus may cause disease in a number of plants which are not closely related. The practical bearing of such work is seen when the chance of infection of one host by the spores produced on another is considered. For example the effect of the growth of this fungus on the grasses is probably not of much importance because the primary injury is caused by the grass thrips but the presence of the fungus on the grass may become of importance if the sod.is used for potting soil in a greenhouse where carnations are being grown. If grass in an · orchard is, affected by this fungus, the spores may be carried to apples and thus bring about their decay.

One of the other species from apple has also been isolated from diseased wheat and from potatoes. The fungus from wheat was tested on apple fruit and found to cause as much decay as the fungus isolated from apple. This species also caused the rot of carnation buds when it was used in making inoculations which shows that this fungus also may cause disease in more than one host.

On account of the difficulty in distinguishing one species of Fusarium from others which closely resemble it, it is necessary to grow the forms from different sources under the same conditions for comparison. In order to determine the extent to which each may cause disease it is necessary to carry on inoculations. In this work species of Fusarium have been isolated from the following hosts in addition to those already mentioned: potato, 3 species; corn, 2 species; cucumber, 3 species; squash, 3 species; garden pea, one species; China Aster, one species; tomato, one species. It has been found that two of the species from potato are very similar to two of those from cucumber and that one species from corn agrees quite closely with one from squash. Inoculations have been made in potato, cucumber, tomato and pea.

When the great·number of species of Fusarium is considered in connection with the fact that a given species may cause disease in more than one host plant, it becomes apparent that studies in which inoculations and cross inoculations are made, using material from pure cultures of the fungi, not only have value from the scientific standpoint but are also of great practical importance.

Exhibit of C. E. Hardy & Son, Hollis, N. H., at Annual Meeting State Pomological Society, Portland, November 12-14, 1912

APPENDIX.

––––––––

Annual Report of the State Pomological Society.

1912~13

OFFICERS FOR 1912.

President.

HOWARD L. KEYSER, Greene.

Vice Presidents.

W. H. CONANT, Buckfield.

A. K. GARDNER, Augusta.

Secretary.

E. L. WHITE, Bowdoinham.

Treasurer.

E. L. LINCOLN, Wayne.

Executive Committee.

WILL E. LELAND, Sangerville.

E. F. HITCHINGS, Orono.

F. H. MORSE, Waterford.

Member Experiment Station Council.

ROBERT H. GARDINER, Gardiner.

Vice President N. E. Fruit Show.

HOMER N. CHASE, Auburn.

Trustees.

Androscoggin County—Silas A. Shaw, Auburn.
Aroostook County—Edward Tarr, Mapleton.
Cumberland County—John W. True, New Gloucester.
Franklin County—E. E. Hardy, Farmington, R. F. D.
Hancock County—William H. Miller, Bar Harbor.
Kennebec County—E. A. Lapham, Pittston.
Knox County—Alonzo Butler, Union.
Lincoln County—H. J. A. Simmons, Waldoboro.
Oxford County—W. H. Allen, Buckfield.
Penobscot County—A. A. Eastman, Dexter.
Piscataquis County—C. C. Dunham, Foxcroft.
Sagadahoc County—J. H. King, Bowdoinham.
Somerset County—Frank E. Nowell, Fairfield.
Waldo County—Vacant.
York County—J. Merrill Lord, Kezar Falls.

CONTENTS.

MEMBERS OF THE SOCIETY.

LIFE MEMBERS

Allen, Wm. H................Buckfield
Andrews, Charles E.............Auburn
Atherton, Wm. P.............Hallowell
Atkins, Charles G......... ....Bucksport
Averill, David C.................Temple
Bailey, W. G..................Freeport
Bennoch, John E.................Orono
Bickford, Lewis I.......Dixmont Center
Bisbee, George E................Auburn
Bisbee, Stanley............Rumford Falls
Blanchard, Mrs. E. M...........Lewiston
Blossom, O. E.............Turner Center
Boardman, Samuel L.............Bangor
Briggs, John..................Turner
Burleigh, Miss Clara M........Vassalboro
Burr, John....................Freeport
Butler, Charles M..............Wiscasset
Butler, Alonzo..................Union
Butnam, J. W.................Readfield
Chadbourne, C. L.......North Bridgton
Chandler, Mrs. Lucy A . ...Freeport
Chase, Henry M., 103 Federal St. .Portland
Chase, Homer N.................Auburn
Clement & Taylor..............Winthrop
Conant, Geo. I..................Hebron
Conant, W. H.................Buckfield
Conant, W. G...................Hebron
Corbett, Herman............Farmington
Crowell, Mrs. Ella H..........Skowhegan
Crowell, John H.............Farmington
Cushman, Chas. L..............Auburn
Dana, Woodbury S.............Portland
Dawes, S. H..................Harrison
DeCoster, Virgil P.............Buckfield
Denison, Mrs. Cora M..........Harrison
DeRocher, Peter........Bradentown, Fla.
Dirwanger, Joseph A............Portland
Douglass, C. S..............Douglass Hill
Dunham, W. W..............North Paris
Dyer, Milton.............Cape Elizabeth
Emerson, Charles L...... ..South Turner
Farnsworth, B. B..............Portland
Felch, Chas. E................Limerick
Flint, John M................E. Baldwin
Frost, Oscar F.... ....Monmouth
Gardiner, Robert H.............Gardiner
George, C. H. ....Hebron
Goddard, Lewis C............Woodfords
Grover, Franklin D................Bean
Gulley, Alfred G...........Storrs, Conn.
Hackett, E. C...........West Gloucester
Hall, Mrs. H. A.................Brewer
Hanscom, John....................Saco
Hardy, E. E................Farmington
Harris, William M...............Auburn
Hayes, William................Gardiner
Heald, U. H.....................Paris
Herrick, A. A..................Norway
Hitchings, E. F..................Orono
Hoyt, Mrs. Francis............Winthrop
Jackson, F. A.................Winthrop
Keene, Charles S................Turner
Keyser, Howard L...............Greene
Knowlton, D. H............Farmington
Lang, Ivan E..................Augusta
Lapham, E. A.................Pittston
Leavitt, L. C................Kezar Falls
Leland, Will E.........East Sangerville
Lincoln, E. L....................Wayne
Litchfield, J. H................Auburn
Litchfield, Mrs. L. K............Lewiston
Littlefield, Harry W.............Brooks
Lombard, Thurston M...........Auburn
Lord, J. Merrill..............Kezar Falls
Luce, Willis A............Columbia Falls
Macaulay, T. B............Montreal, Can.
McAllister, Zaccheus.........West Lovell
McCabe, George L..........North Bangor
McLaughlin, Henry..............Portland
McManus, John................Brunswick
Merrill, Oliver F...............Gardiner
Merrill, Rupert B...............Gardiner
Mitchell, Frederick H.............Turner
Mitchell & Co................Waterville
Moody, Charles H...............Auburn
Moore, William G.............Monmouth
Moor, F. A..................Waterville
Morse, F. H.................Waterford
Morse, W. J....................Orono
Moulton, Dr. John F..........Limington
Newell, G. E....................Turner
Page, F. W...................Augusta
Palmer, George L.............Kents Hill
Parsons, Howard G.......Turner Center

LIFE MEMBERS—Concluded.

Patten, Mrs. E. C...............Topsham
Prince, Edward M......West Farmington
Pope, Charles S..............Manchester
Pulsifer, D. W..................Poland
Purington, E. F..............Farmington
Richards, John T...............Gardiner
Ricker, A. S.....................Turner
Ricker, Fred P..................Turner
Roak, George M................Auburn
Sanborn, Miss G. P..............Augusta
Sawyer, Andrew S........Cape Elizabeth
Saunders, Ernest...............Lewiston
Seavey, Mrs. G. M...............Auburn
Simmons, H. J. A.............Waldoboro
Skillings, C. W.............North Auburn
Smith, Frederick O.........New Vineyard
Smith, Henry S...............Monmouth
Snow, Mary S..................Bangor
Stanley, H. O................Winthrop
Staples, Geo. W., 904 Main St.,
                        Hartford, Conn.
Starrett, L. F...................Warren
Stetson, Henry.................Auburn
Stilphen, Asbury C.............Gardiner
Supt. Maine Sanatorium Farm.....Hebron

Taylor, Miss L. L. (Lakeside)....Belgrade
Thomas, William W............Portland
Thomas, D. S..............North Auburn
Thurston, Edwin......West Farmington
Tilton, William S..........Boston, Mass.
Townsend, Mrs. B. T...........Freeport
True, Davis P..............Leeds Center
True, John W............New Gloucester
Twitchell, Geo. M...............Auburn
Vickery, James.................Portland
Vickery, John...................Auburn
Wade, Patrick.................Portland
Walker, Charles S.................Peru
Walker, Elmer V................Oxford
Waterman, Willard H.......East Auburn
Waugh, F. A.............Amherst, Mass.
Weston, Joseph...............Gardiner
Wheeler, Charles E..........Chesterville
White, Charles M...........Bowdoinham
White, Mrs. Annie..........Bowdoinham
White, Edward L...........Bowdoinham
Woods, Chas. D...................Orono
Wright, Frederick.................Bath
Yeaton, Samuel F......West Farmington

6

AGRICULTURE OF MAINE.

ANNUAL MEMBERS FOR 1912.

Bass, Lizzie E................... Wilton
Bass, Mary A.................... Wilton
Bryant, J. B................... Buckfield
Bumps, Leon A................. Wilton
Campbell, D. W...........Cherryfield
Cardmus, H. C.........Auburn, Route 1
Carll, E. C..................... Augusta
Chadbourne, J. A..............Bridgton
Conant, E. E.................Buckfield
Conant, H. L................... Hebron
Corliss, Geo. H..............Cherryfield
Cardwell, Roy................. Hebron
Cornforth, W. H................Auburn
Davis, W. H.................. Augusta
Dearborn, Hall C...Hampden Highlands
Dearborn, Mrs. Annie S.......Limington
DeCoster, Miss Helen...........Buckfield
Dickey, Miss E. A.............. Greene
Dolloff, E. W................. Standish
Dunn, Charles, Jr...........So. Portland
French, E. O.................. Norway
Gardner, A. K................. Augusta
Granville, Harvey D..........Kezar Falls
Guptill, Edward G.............. Cornish
Haines, William T............ Waterville
Hardy, Walter M................ Brewer
Harris, M. H.................... Greene
Harrison, J. C. & Sons.........Berlin, Md.
Hawkes, Allie E.............So. Windham
Heath, Gardner K.............. Augusta
Hennessy, W. A................. Bangor
Hitchings, E. F.................. Orono
Ingraham, William M..........Portland
Jewett, P. E.........Whitefield, Route 1
Johannsen, O. A.................Orono
Jones, George T................Fairfield
Jones, O. R................... Sabattus
Knowlton, G. H.............. Vassalboro
Leavitt, Frank................. Newburg
Lee, Fred W.................. Augusta
Libby, E. H................. Auburn
Littlefield, J. R................. Brooks
Lincoln, Mrs. E. L............. Wayne
Lang, R. D.............. No. Raymond
Maloon, W. L................. Sabattus
Maxwell, J. H................ Sabattus

Mendall, L. C.................... Greene
Merrill, Harvey T............. So. Poland
Millett, Charles R........... West Minot
Milliken, E. C.....Portland, 87 Market St.
Milliken, A. H...............Parsonsfield
Millspaugh, Lewis H..Winthrop, Route 21
Moody, J. F..................... Hebron
Mosher, Claire................... Wilton
Newell, Mrs. Geo. E.............. Turner
Nichols, Dr. Estes............... Hebron
Nichols, W. A.................. Hebron
Noyes, Reno P.................. Wilton
Nowell, Frank E.............. Fairfield
Page, E. E................. East Corinth
Patch, Edith M.................. Orono
Perley, C. A................... Winthrop
Pierce, Arthur W............. Woodfords
Pierce, Franklin......... Hebron Station
Philbrook, E. E...Portland, 233 Spring St.
Philbrook, H. H................. Greene
Pike, W. W..................... Cornish
Pratt, B. G..New York City, 50 Church St.
Record, G. B.................. Buckfield
Reed, R. C.................... Temple
Reynolds, W. E.............. Monmouth
Rines, J. Henry................ Portland
Robertson, B. E................ Hebron
Robinson, W. E.............. No. Anson
Sawyer, C. F.................. Hebron
Sawyer, L. W.................. Greene
Savage, Will N............... Waterville
Sinclair, W................... Monmouth
Small, Edgar A.................. Cornish
Smith, V. M.................. Buckfield
Smith, Geo. S................. Monmouth
Stack, Garrett M........Still River, Conn.
Stetson, C. S.................... Greene
Sweetser, H. P........ .Cumberland Ctr.
Townsend, J. G..........Shelbyville, Del.
Tucker, Benj.................. Norway
Twomey, M. Joseph.Portland,14 Wilson St.
Usher, E. E.............. West Baldwin
Washburn, C. C...........Mechanic Falls
Wentworth, Howard..........Kezar Falls
Wilson, Geo. T..Portland, 519 Congress St.
Wing, Fred A............... Waterville

ANNUAL MEETING
OF
MAINE STATE POMOLOGICAL SOCIETY,

TUESDAY P. M., AT 2.00 O'CLOCK.

ADDRESS OF WELCOME.
HON. OAKLEY C. CURTIS. Mayor of Portland.

Mr. Chairman, Ladies and Gentlemen:

It is always a pleasure to welcome societies, conventions and gatherings of all kinds to the City of Portland, and it gives me special pleasure to extend to the Maine Pomological Society a most hearty greeting and a sincere and cordial welcome.

Portland aims to be a convention center and that was one of the main ideas which inspired the building of this auditorium and spurred on the builders to construct suitable quarters to enable the city to care for all gatherings regardless of size. This season does not mark the beginning of this idea, for Portland has been favored by visits of many organizations in the past, but we now hope to take a wider range for the future.

Portland is unquestionably destined to be a much larger and more important city than it is today. Its geographical and natural position viewed from all points is secure. It was but a few years ago (practically the span of a life) when Portland was nothing more than a seaport town. In Blunt's "American Coast Pilot" of the issue of 1833, the following reference is made on sailing instructions entering our harbor:

"In steering the above courses you will see a round bushy tree to the north of the town, and a house with a red roof and one chimney; bring the tree to west of the house, which course will carry you up the channel in six or seven fathoms of water;

but when you come abreast of the fort which stands on a hill haul away W. S. W. as there is a shoal bank on your starboard hand that has not more than ten to twelve feet on it at high water, which you are to avoid."

This was only 79 years ago and simply illustrates the crude methods of navigation, and in contrast we see the development of the present day. I refer to this more particularly as a point on which to form a basis of the steady increase in growth of the largest city in the State.

The rise of the tide in Portland is 8 to 9 feet. If you will go to Fort Allen Park where the remains of the old fort referred to now exist, and look over the hill you will see the spot in the harbor where, 79 years previous there was only two to three feet of water at low tide, and today you will see anchored on the spot the largest vessels which exist in the maritime trade and there is thirty feet of water at low tide.

Foreign steamers are continually coming to Portland and the increase in the size of them is remarkable in comparison to those of but a few years ago; and to accommodate them large expenditure has been made and as time goes on a large amount must be appropriated to keep pace with the greater development.

The growth of cities depends largely on the push and activity of their inhabitants, but the large commercial activity is caused to a great extent by the "stranger within our gates" or what might be termed the transient visitors. Boston and New York and all the other large cities are dependent more or less on the transient guests for it is this class who give life to the city, society, amusement and trade.

And so today we are particularly pleased that this active and important society comes to us and is grafting into our system renewed incentive to still greater efforts for development as a center of exhibition and display of the products and industries of our State.

We have a great and beautiful State with wonderful resources of almost every description, and all that is required is to make them known in order to attract the attention they so well deserve and be the means of promoting wider expansion and greater activity; and for these reasons it appears to me that a city like Portland is a most favorable place to hold such gatherings, as naturally the larger the city the more people to view the exhibits and thus the more probability of creating still further interest in our industries and resources.

We people of the State of Maine, to a certain degree, know what we have, but the principal idea is to have others know it so they may become interested with their capital and energy.

The City of Portland is particularly favored with railroad and water connections. but the increasing traffic is pushing them to still wider expansion.

This State is destined to more advancement and to my mind the railroads have made but a mere scratch on the surface on what is to become a vast commercial area.

Our harbor also demands further attention as ocean commerce is taking enormous strides and tonnage is becoming greater and greater. While we have had ocean liners running from Portland to European ports for many years, the steamers are gradually becoming larger, and today some of the very largest are coming to Portland and loading with our apples and products, together with grain, cattle and in fact all farm produce from the far West.

It may be said that we are just commencing to grow, and this probably is due to the fact that Boston and New York and the large Atlantic ports are fast becoming congested and the expansion of trade is seeking new ports to facilitate shipments.

In conclusion, it is not for me to enter into the science of fruit culture, store housing and the care of your products as I notice there are other speakers to follow me who are far more capable of enlightening you on such affairs, but will say that Portland is in a position to offer you all the facilities necessary for your expansion process and for the widening of your field of advertising. We are always open to suggestion for it is our desire to have this and similar organizations come here as often as possible and we wish to extend to you every courtesy within our power and trust this visit will be so agreeable and profitable that you will decide to again hold your meeting here in the immediate future.

I wish you all success at this and all future meetings wherever they may be and hope that they will inure to the benefit of the State and profit to its people and your society.

ADDRESS OF WELCOME.

Mr. Charles F. Flagg, President Portland Board of Trade.

Mr. President and Members of the Maine Pomological Society:

As we gather around these harvest tables like a great Thanksgiving family, I want to tell you a secret. It was my privilege to be present when the Mayor dictated your invitation from the city a year ago, and in addition to testifying to the interest and promptness of his action, I want to tell you of the undying admiration with which I heard him successfully charge upon that word "Pomological," a word before which so many other good men have gone down to humiliation and defeat. I want also to say a word to you members about your president, Mr. Howard L. Keyser of Greene. He is the smartest man I ever met. Last summer in the midst of a prolonged drought, Mr. Rines and I telephoned him about some details of this coming fruit show, and in the course of the conversation we asked him jokingly if he had seen any rain up there at Greene. To our surprise, he said, "Oh, yes; it has been raining two or three hours." Mr. Rines asked him to send some down to Portland, and he said he would. And he did. In half an hour it came: thunder, lightning, hail and rain; and the wind blew such a gale that nothing but the fear of electricity prevented our telephoning again to have him shut it off. Perhaps you have plenty of men as smart as that up the State but they are rare down here.

You come in distinguished company, you members of the Pomological Society, and we welcome with you these rosy cheeked dwellers of the orchards of Maine and New England. Like you they are products of the modern scientific world. Indeed I understand that they consider themselves such quality that they have a sovereign among them, and that Mr. Tompkins has put a crown upon his head and calls himself king. And, Mr. Chairman, with your permission, I want to say, through you, a word to King Tompkins and his subjects.

Undoubtedly, King Tompkins, you have the most brilliant company which has ever assembled in the new City Hall; but you have a great deal to answer for in the history of the world. You turned us out of the garden of Eden, you upset the kingdom of Troy with your golden apple of discord, you gave William Tell a bad half hour when you perched on the top of little Tellie's head, and you are responsible for much apple jack and more hard cider. But for all these things we forgive you because of the men and women you have brought to Portland today.

Members of the Pomological Society, on behalf of the Port-- land Board of Trade with its eight hundred and twenty-five members I welcome you, and may your coming draw closer the bonds between your home and our home, so that more and more we may realize that we are neighbors. I congratulate you upon your harvest exhibition. You are steadily raising the standard of the fruit of Maine, and I can assure you that we stand ready to assist you in every way possible. I can understand why laws upon fruit marking have been imperfect in this State in the past. Rigid laws would have been like some of those whist rules, very good if one held the cards. But every year you are now producing an increasing crop of the highest quality, which cannot afford to be dragged down by short sighted and even blind legislation. You all remember the barrel of Maine "Number 1" Baldwins purchased last year in the open Boston market and brought down to Augusta and opened there. Hardly a "Number 1" Baldwin in the barrel. You may also know of the Maine man in Liverpool who said to a consignee half jokingly, "I should think you would be ashamed to beat down the price of our good Maine apples so." "Do you want to see some?" said the consignee. "Pick out any barrel you want with the Maine label on it and turn it out." And the man did, and he told me afterward that he was the one who felt ashamed.

And therefore, knowing how the name of the State under present law is liable to be abused we feel the more grateful to you members of the Maine Pomological Society who are doing so much to honor it. We feel that the time must come when the name "Maine apple" shall be such a sacred term that every marking upon the package shall be made to tell the truth, and that no man shall be permitted to inflict an injury upon his neighbor by pulling down the reputation of his State. It all comes out in the market price. I say, therefore, that we want to assist you in whatever you may deem wise and prudent.

And in this present exhibition over a hundred citizens of this city have contributed actively toward your reception and enter_ tainment. I wish I could mention all their names, and I am going to mention Mr. J. Henry Rines and his Agricultural Committee of the Board of Trade. But in closing I desire to say for them all and for the Board of Trade that we welcome you because we know you, because we honor you, and because we believe that you are today one of the shining hopes of Maine.

·

RESPONSE.

DR. G. M. TWITCHELL, Auburn.

Mr. President, His Honor the Mayor, Mr. President of the Board of Trade, Ladies and Gentlemen:

It is a pleasant duty assigned to me this afternoon to express our thanks, the thanks of the officers and members of the Maine State Pomological Society for the very cordial words of welcome extended to us by your Honor the Mayor, and the President of the Board of Trade. But, gentlemen, it was not necessary that you should speak these words for us to know that we were welcome to the City of Portland, or that you were coöperating with us in doing all that was possible for the suc· cess of this exhibition. The magnificent list of special prizes, unknown by any other State Society, in all the East, has been speaking to us all these months, telling us of your desire and of your kindly interest, testifying to your appreciation of the work of this Society, to your faith in the fruit industry, to your purpose to help promote its best interests.

But, gentlemen, this is not our exhibition. Yours it is, as much as ours. We are not here to compete for prizes only. That is but a secondary matter. We are here to help build up the great fruit interests of the State, and therefore it becomes your exhibition as much as ours, and its chief purpose will fail unless every man and woman in Greater Portland visits this hall during the next two days and inspects what is spread upon the tables and in the boxes and barrels.

We have proven that we can grow apple trees as rapidly as they can in the far West. We have proven that these trees will come to maturity as early as in the far West. We have proven that we can grow fruit of a quality which the West can never hope to equal. What more do you want us to do as workers for the good of the State? This fruit spread upon the tables came from the hills of York, Cumberland and Oxford, from Franklin, Androscoggin, and Kennebec, from Sagadahoc, Somerset, and Piscataquis,—yes, from Knox and Lincoln as well; from the same hills where some of you men grew to manhood. And we want you to come back to this hall frequently and get a sniff of the old farm and of this fruit, for I venture that some of it came from the trees where as boys you used to steal apples. We want you to come back and get a fresh inspiration by this close contact with mother earth, to touch elbows with the workers, and be better men because of that contact with the giant forces of God manifested in this work before us, in the fruit on the tables. We need your coöperation for the work of the Society. We need above all—you need rather—such a show as this to prove the interdependence which must exist between all classes. The sucking power of the towns is today a serious menace to our civilization. Life, energy, growth can be maintained only as rich, fresh blood runs free upon the hillsides. The city, left to itself, dies with the third generation. It is only the incoming of the boys and girls from the hill farms all over our eastern country,—it is only in this way that new life and energy can be vouchsafed to us and that the city can make that progress which you hope to see in coming years.

The agricultural possibilities of this State insure a tremendous asset to you, gentlemen of the City of Portland. The fruit in this State is worth in round numbers about three and one-half million dollars yearly. In 1910 there were set 100,000 trees, in 1911, 120,000, and in 1912, 150,000. Properly cared for, by men who are studying the question as carefully as you are studying any of the questions which confront you in your business, do you not see that in the immediate future there must be a large increase in the revenue of the farms, and whatever adds to the value of the farm adds to the value of the city; whatever increases the output of the farm increases the revenue of the men engaged in the many enterprises here.

So friends, we are all workers together. You can increase this work, you can help this work, by uniting with the men upon the farms in solving some of the great problems confronting them. There is the great question of unjust discrimination in distribution of our products. You can aid materially through coöperating with growers in the disposal of those products, by bringing about a more harmonious relation. Surely we can never hope for that increase in farm life and farm work in the good old State of Maine, which we desire, until there comes the incentive that can come only when the producer is receiving a fair share of the consumer's dollar. There comes to my mind just now an illustration in point. In the City of Portland during the past two months one of your grocers, paying, as he said. all that he could possibly pay, because of what he could realize, purchased apples of one of our growers, paying $1.50 per barrel. Those apples were sold by the grocer for fifty cents per peck, or $5.50 a barrel, and when some of the purchasers complained, the grocer said, "What can we do? We are at the mercy of the farmer." There is the condition which exists more or less everywhere, and so long as it exists you cannot expect that there will be the incentive necessary for the proper growth of this industry. Remember this, friends,—the farmer can live without you, but you cannot live without the farmer. That fact alone, it seems to me, should quicken us to a better appreciation of the need of hearty and more complete coöperation. Your industries, great as they are, your mills, your factories, your great manufacturing interests, produce nothing. You simply change the form and add to the value of the raw product. Agriculture, and agriculture alone, is the productive industry, and therefore it has claims upon you over and beyond all others. You must have fresh blood from the country if your city is to live. Uncle Solon Chase was right when he said that "the grass would grow in the city streets if it were not for the tramp of the cowhide boots in the barnyard." Remember that our dependence one upon the other must be mutual. We recognize' our dependence upon you. We ask you to coöperate with us. as you never have in the past, in helping to bring about those relations which will swell the volume of farm products, which will bring fair returns to the producer, which will lift some of the burdens from the man upon the farm, which will make aggressive and positive our agricultural interest, which will surely build up the vast resources of Maine. By thus working together, believing in Maine and laboring for its advancement, we shall find in the years, that, on the hillsides and up and down the valleys of the Pine Tree State, God has showered his richest blessings and made possible the largest, fullest, truest life vouchsafed to any people. This is indeed a goodly heritage and it is for us to enrich in every way possible. If we believe in Maine let us prove faith by honest service.

ADDRESS.

Hon. Wm. T. Haines, Waterville, Maine.

Ladies and Gentlemen:

I see by your program that I am down for an address upon this occasion. I feel that there is nothing that I could say that would be as eloquent in the cause of pomology in Maine as the splendid fruit display which you have on exhibition in this hall.

I am, as you know, always interested in the Maine farm, and I am particularly interested at the present time in the Maine orchard. I wish all those who live upon the Maine farms and have orchards could be here to witness the splendid exhibit which is the result of modern methods and the splendid care, in the line of orcharding, which some of our Maine farmers have been giving of late to this subject. There is nothing like the object lesson to teach the people, and especially the lesson in agriculture and horticulture. You are here for the benefit of this object lesson. Those who are absent do not benefit by it except as they hear of it through others, but I feel that its influences must of a necessity be very large throughout the State, and that the work which you are doing as a society will constantly exert an influence for the better understanding of the best methods of fruit growing in our State.

I want to call your attention, briefly, to a few facts about
the Maine farm, and make some suggestions which may affect
the subject of orcharding. It is well enough to know a few
statistics on any subject.

The last census report in 1910 shows 60,016 farms in Maine,
comprising 6,296,859 acres, with an average of 105 acres to the
farm. This is an increase of 717 farms in the last ten years
and a decrease of about 1 1-4 acres in the average size of the
farms. The value of farm property, including farm buildings,
machinery and stock thereon is placed at about $200,000,000,
an increase in ten years of nearly $77,000,000, or about 62
per cent. The average value of these farms is placed at
$3,320, an increase of about 60 per cent since 1900. The in-
crease in these values would seem very encouraging, but there
are some things about the farm statistics gathered in 1910 that
are not so encouraging, namely: The improved land is only
2,360,657 acres and slightly less than it was ten years ago, and
comprises only about one-eighth the entire area of the State,
and is not as much as it was in 1880 by 124,000 acres. The
population of Maine seems to be divided very nearly equally
between the rural and the urban. New Hampshire has lost
10,000 and Vermont 8,000 and Massachusetts has gained only
5,000 in the rural population during the last ten years, while
Maine leads all New England and has actually added 6,026 to
her rural population. These figures look very small in comparison with the great relative gain in the country in the farming population in the same period, which averages over 11 per
cent, but it is quite a favorable comparison with the other New
England states.

I give you these figures to impress upon your minds our
position in the matter of agriculture. There is being so much
said of late about the high cost of living, the relative opportunities in the country and the city, and the advantages of
rural and city life, that it is well enough for all of us to understand how we in Maine compare with the other states. Certainly there is a chance for further development and improvement in our agricultural resources, as clearly shown by these
figures.

But it was not my purpose to speak of Maine farms, but to
speak particularly of orcharding, which I know you are all

Portion of Exhibit from Highmoor Farm, at Annual Meeting State Pomological Society, Portland, November 12-14, 1912

much interested in. The same census report for 1910 gives us some very interesting data on this subject. It reports 42,976 farms as having in bearing 3,476,716 apple trees. It also reports 17,362 farms as having, *not* in bearing, 1,047,128 trees (whether on the same farms or not I don't know), making a total of 4,522,373 apple trees in Maine, and it gives the value of the apple crop gathered in 1909 at $2,123,816, being 3,636,181 bushels, and a gain over 1899 of 1,421,773 bushels.

I remember of reading somewhere in an old publication, I think issued about 1700, in regard to the State of Maine, that it was then not determined whether apple trees could be raised in Maine or not. The report said that there were a few old trees found living, along the coast, that it was assumed had been planted by the early French settlers, but the drift of the article was to the effect that apple trees could not be raised profitably in this climate.

There are many other very interesting figures that might be given in regard to our orchard products, but these are enough to show something of the business within our borders. The past few years have demonstrated the practicability of spending more time and money on the orchards. We have found that an apple tree does not differ much from a hill of corn. It needs plowing and harrowing, weeding, and to have the suckers removed, and plenty of fertilizer to produce good ears or good apples. The scientists have come to our aid and shown us that both fungous growth and insects which prey upon the trees and upon the fruit can be avoided by the simple and inexpensive process of spraying with chemicals and poisons. We have also passed the period when we believe that an orchard can be expected to bear only once in two years,—if properly fertilized and care is taken that both years' crops are not picked at one time. So, at least, I may say that we have arrived at a stage in the understanding of the science of orcharding where we know that trees can live and thrive in the State of Maine, and this exhibition demonstrates the fact that we can produce as fine fruit as is produced anywhere in the world. More than this, if you will go to the agricultural department at Washington, you will find charts showing where different agricultural products in the United States grow naturally, and as strange as it may seem, you will find certain sections of Maine marked upon that map as the place where apple trees grow wild.

The State of Maine has the advantage of the natural re source. The country has all been explored and settled and the period of large emigration from one section to another is passed, and it stands every locality in hand to develop to its fullest extent what it can do best. Pennsylvania has been doing this with both coal and iron; Maine has done it for years with her lumber; and the great prairies of the West and Middle West are furnishing the cereals for feeding not only our ninety millions of people but many in foreign lands. It is said that the Riverside district of California produces three-fourths of all the oranges, lemons and grape-fruit produced in the United States, and some sections of Washington and Oregon have undertaken to furnish all the apples eaten in America, and no one will doubt their ability to produce them in great quantities. But there is no state in the Union that can produce the good apples, that is, apples with the fine flavor and keeping qualities, as the State of Maine, and there is no land for sale in any other state at as low prices, that is better adapted for apple raising than is much land found in Maine.

But as we go about the State and notice these apple trees on the different farms and by the roadsides, we are all shocked at the lack of care and cultivation which these trees are getting. An occasional farm shows that its owner appreciates the value of his orchard, but the most of the trees are unpruned, the ground lacks cultivation, the leaves of the trees indicate the lack of fertilizer, and too often insects of different kinds are plainly visible within their branches. The object lesson as taught by the State Farm in Leeds, commonly known as Highmoor Farm, during the past two or three years has been seen by many and its value has been far reaching, although not yet known by any very large majority of our rural population. The State is too large for any such lesson as is being taught there in this short time to be brought home to a great extent to the farmers of the State. Its influence must spread like infection, by affecting a farmer here and there in different parts of the State, who in turn shall make a similar object lesson for his neighbors to see. Thus in time by such teaching may modern methods of orcharding be understood throughout the State.

The bulletins which are issued from our Experiment Station as the result of work at Highmoor Farm, also those bulletins which are to be had on application from the Agricultural Department at Washington by any farmer in the State, showing experiments made in orcharding in different states of the Union, are a source of help to all our farmers who have these bulletins and who read them. But comparatively few applications are made and there are thousands of farmers within our borders who have never seen or read them and whose orchards of apple trees are but a by-product in the economy of the farm. If a few apples are raised, they are so much ahead, without any labor or trouble, except the picking of them, and what are not suitable for the market are fed to the pigs or made into cider. With many it would seem that the orchard is not looked to as one of the substantial farm crops. Now, this is the condition under which we are living in regard to the orchard. A few are alive and awake to its value and importance in our State, but the great mass are asleep to its possibilities. I have no doubt that those who are awake will continue to awaken others, and that the State in the near future is to largely increase its orchard product. The 1,047,128 trees, which are young trees, are soon to come into bearing, and the gain made in the last ten years, as shown by the last census report, is small in comparison with what we may expect for a gain within the next ten years. This means that Maine during the next ten years is likely to become a great producer of apples, apples not only for its own people, but apples which may be shipped into every State in the Union, and into foreign countries.

Now, the thing that I want to speak about, and the one point that I want to make in this address—and all that I have said has simply led up to it—is the question of marketing and handling this crop after it is gathered. The question is, to whom are we to sell it, and when are we to sell it and what are we to get for it? Now, this depends upon several things: First, the quality of the apple, but that is all settled in the method of growing. The next is the manner of picking, and that is being understood to-day. The next and most important is the handling of the product at the time and soon after it is harvested. The old method of the farmers in Maine was to take the apples into the cool, damp cellars, which were found under a great many of the homes on the farms,—put them into the bins where they were kept till such time as the farmer had the opportunity to take them to market, a few at a time, as the entire crop of most farms could be put into bins in small cellars. But this period is passed, as the most of the farmers who have any orcharding worthy of special consideration have more fruit than can be kept housed and cared for in such a way. More than this, the most of these cellars that were once damp and cool, now have furnaces placed in them for the heating of the house, so that they become dry and this is not a fit place to keep fruit in. Consequently, to my mind, one of the most important questions before the orchardist of Maine is the place in which to keep his apples until the market calls for them. There are plenty of apples throughout the middle states for the fall and early winter consumption, but after January these apples have mostly disappeared, and the Maine apple is in competition with the Oregon and Washington apple in all the markets of the East. The western apple grower has provided for the care of his apple through methods of cold storage in the large cities which provide for the keeping of them until such time as the market demands them.

The Maine apple has no provision whatever made for it, except through the buyers who come into the State in the fall, make their own bid for the apples, and carry them off, as the farmers are obliged to sell for almost anything they can get, for the reason that they have no place in which to care for them. These buyers use cold storage plants in the large cities, or ship them abroad. The Maine farmer or apple grower in most cases has no choice in the matter of the disposition of his apples. He can let them rot on the ground or sell them to some speculator for just what he will give him for them. Hence, the next step toward advancing the interests of the apple growers in the State is some manner and place for handling this crop. The Aroostook farmers have made large potato houses on their own farms, which give them a certain independence in regard to their potato crops. When they first commenced to raise potatoes, they were absolutely at the mercy of the buyer. With a place in which to keep them, they can now hold them and dispose of them at their own satisfaction. The apple grower in this State has not even the opportunities that the potato grower has. This is the situation, and you will ask what is my solution of it. A very simple one and one not very hard to put into operation, and it is for the farmers themselves who produce apples to any great extent and who have orchards coming into bearing, to arrange for lots of land on side tracks, or where side tracks can be built near the railroad stations, along the apple growing sections of the State, upon which they can build storage houses for their apples; cold storage or such storage as will keep the apples till the time when the market calls for them. Every product has a time during the year when it is needed for consumption, and those who want it will find it wherever located. To illustrate, if there were 50,000 barrels of apples stored in different storehouses along the line of the M. C. R. R. from Waterville to Lewiston, which is all an apple growing country, the selling houses and jobbers of Boston and New York would know just how many apples were there in those houses, the minute they were filled, and the minute the market called for those apples, they would have them. In other words, they would come to the farmers for this product, and the time to sell anything is the time when somebody wants it, and when one wants to buy a product, he will pay a fair price for it. Under these circumstances the farmer would be master of the situation. The only question is, How are we to tackle the problem of building the store house? An investment of money is required, and the cost of building and expense of maintenance and care must be borne by the apple grower. What better way to get the net result to the Maine farmer than for the Maine farmer to do it himself, or for the community in which the apples are grown. And our Maine farmers have plenty of money, in many instances deposited in our Maine Savings Banks, which could be used toward this enterprise, and it is simply a matter of investing more capital in their own business. The question simply is,—Have these men confidence enough to invest their own money in this their own business?

While the Maine apple has the flavor which no other apple raised in the Union has, it can also be kept till the apples of the other states are practically all out of the market, if provision is made for properly keeping them, and the situation is entirely in the hands of the apple grower. All he needs is the courage to tackle the problem and thereby make money on his own crop by being in a position to dispose of it when the market demands it. To my idea, it can be done through the coöperation of storage houses of a proper kind, which I believe should be built near to the railroad stations, so that the apples can be handled with a great saving of labor, taking them direct from the orchard to the storage house, and then at the proper time shipping them from there to the market.

I have listened a good many times in the past to speeches upon what ought to be done in Maine to make apple growing profitable but I have failed to hear many men discuss this question of the selling of them, the methods of handling to a good advantage the apples grown in Maine. For that reason I thought the first opportunity I had I would offer these suggestions. To my mind it is the most important question to-day in connection with the business. I have not undertaken to tell you what kind of storage houses should be made, whether cold storage or storage to keep out frost because I don't know, but it is the kind of storage houses such as are used in other places where they are cared for to the best advantage, that our Maine farmers need.

I understand that the suggestion is to be made that the State provide a cold storage plant for the apples raised on Highmoor Farm, at the railroad station near the farm. I believe this will be a very profitable experiment along this line. If done, it will be done at the expense of the State. If mistakes are made, they can be remedied and the lesson learned, and the people can all have the advantage of it. I sincerely hope it will be undertaken in the near future, because I thoroughly believe that unless we provide for the better handling of the apples grown in Maine by the farmers having orchards of five hundred, a thousand and two thousand trees, as many have, and which trees will soon come into bearing, the prices will be so poor for the crops, that it will lead to discouragement in this industry and hinder its further development.

CO-OPERATIVE AGRICULTURAL CREDIT ASSOCIA-
TIONS.

Address by PROF. G. W. STEVENS of the University of Maine.

Ladies and Gentlemen: It will be noted on the regular program that President Aley of the University was to have ad-
dressed the gathering at this time. To those of you who may
have been in some degree induced to come this afternoon in
the expectation of hearing President Aley, I offer my sympathy. I shall upon my return to Orono extend my sympathy
also to President Aley for his failure to have opportunity to
witness the magnificent display here before us, but I am re-
minded in this connection that there is apt to be no loss without
some gain and I most heartily congratulate myself upon being
here to have some humble relation to the program this afternoon
and above all to have opportunity to observe this magnificent
display of apple products.

The subject to which I am to address myself for a few moments this afternoon is perhaps not entirely adapted to such
an occasion as this. It is one which in the nature of the case,
to be presented with any fullness calls for a mass of detail that
the limits of time will not permit to be presented this afternoon; and it is, of course, as the chairman of the meeting an-
nounced, one of a general character. It has no special relation
to any specialized set of people in agriculture. But I am very
sure that this movement, which is already finding a beginning
in this country, if it advances to successful fulfillment will require as a condition of that advance the effort of just such
progressive organizations as this, and therefore it is not unfit-
ting, I am sure, to briefly consider some of the elements contained in this movement.

Agriculture as an industry has made very material advance in
this country in the last several decades. The farmer has aban-
doned the more or less indifferent, slipshod methods in his
industry. He has been acquiring information as to the methods and processes of his industry. He has been acquiring
knowledge of the nature of his materials and his product. In

other words, he has been applying what we call the method of scientific agriculture to his industry. The agencies by which he has been able to do this may be summarized under the word *education,* and the specific agencies in that direction have been primarily the Federal Department of Agriculture, and under it in more or less close relation the Experiment Stations, the Agricultural Colleges, and by no means least such organizations as that here represented.

But agriculture as an industry has made less advance, so far as those features of it that we might call of economic efficiency are concerned, than any other basic industry today. In comparison with transportation, in comparison with commerce, in comparison with manufacture, in comparison with mining, agriculture has in general failed to take advantage of the economies and the efficiencies that lie before it, and we have in the experience of a foreign people methods and policies in operation in connection with this matter of efficiency that we may very well give attention to.

Not the least point in which the American farmer has failed to take advantage of the economies that are possible to him is in that of credit—the capital whereby he may accomplish more, whereby he may obtain a larger product to get a larger result from his farm, from his occupation, than he has been able to do thus far. Now the economies that we associate with the other basic industries, such as transportation, such as manufacture, are those in general that we may classify under associated effort, combined effort, the economies of large scale production, the economy of large scale buying, of large scale selling, the economy that promotes an avoidance of the leaks and wastes that have in former times been associated with all industries and have in this way been largely removed by reason of combination. Coöperation is the great form of business organization that predominates in all these other fields. It is not my purpose to enter into a discussion as to the reasons why there seems to be little probability that we can ever expect successful coöperation so far as the direct operation of farms is concerned, but we may very safely say that there are possibilities in the nature of combined effort on the part of farmers, not the least of which is in the matter of combined effort to obtain better credit facilities. That will give to the farmer very great return indeed.

Now the principle that underlies this matter of combined credit is simply the point that a number of people by guaranteeing their combined capital, by guaranteeing their combined warranty, are able to obtain capital when they want it at a smaller cost than any of them are able to do individually. That is the underlying principle of the matter of combined credit. This may not seem to be at first thought a particularly important matter. It may not occur to us that it matters a great deal whether the ordinary farmer is obliged, as he is, to pay on an average over eight per cent interest, taking into account the cost of commission and renewal, on his ordinary loans, instead of as low a rate as three and one-half or four per cent, as the ordinary German farmer, the ordinary French farmer, the ordinary Belgian farmer, the ordinary Italian farmer, is able to do. And yet when we realize that the farmers of the United States are today operating on a borrowed capital of over eight billion dollars on which they pay an annual interest charge of over eight per cent, we perhaps get a better conception of the significance of this.

The possibilities that lie in this matter of cheaper credit, as a consequence enabling the farmer to utilize in a better way his land, are significant not only to the farmer, enabling him to get a larger net profit out of his activity, but they are of course of great significance to those of us who are not actively engaged in farming,—the consuming class. The outcome of this finally cannot fail to be, as a consequence of the larger production from the more economic processes that will be made possible, a cheaper food supply, cheaper articles of consumption in the case of commodities of an agricultural character than we have had thus far.

Now I want to briefly describe one or two of the general methods of coöperative agricultural credit that have been in highly successful operation for a long while in a number of foreign countries. There are, I may say, a variety of these organized credit associations which differ among themselves in some rather important respects, but chiefly in detail. Substantially these credit associations are all alike, and on account of the limits of time I shall not undertake today more than rather briefly to describe two that in the judgment of those who have been making careful inquiry into the operation of these credit systems abroad are best adapted to American conditions. The first of these is the so-called Raiffeisen system, so called because of the name of the founder, a man in Germany who in about the year 1849 observed the handicap that rested on the German farmer in the matter of obtaining credit to handle his activities and organized among local groups of German farmers these so-called Raiffeisen associations. They were based upon certain, rather few, fundamental principles. One of these was the unlimited liability of each member of the association for the obligations of the association. Another feature of this system was the confining of the borrowing privilege to members of the association only. The credit of those who belonged to this association was of a personal character only. That is, there was no mortgage upon any real estate individually. It was simply the matter of combining the personal credit of those who wished to join the association and who contemplated becoming borrowers themselves to a greater or less degree. Again, the cost of maintaining these associations was made very low. There was only one officer—and that, I may say, is still the feature of this system—who received any compensation, the treasurer. And when I say that today the expense of maintaining these local agricultural credit associations averages only about $150 or $175 a year, we appreciate the great economy that is associated with their conduct.. A further feature of these associations is a committee, a supervisory committee, that passes upon the application of any would-be borrower, who, it is to be remembered, must himself belong to the association, and inquires into the purpose for which he wants his loan. The loan must be applied to a so-called productive purpose, it would not be permitted to be applied to a consumptive purpose; a man would have to demonstrate to the satisfaction of this committee that the purpose for which he wanted this small loan was one that was reasonably likely to succeed. If in the judgment of the committee the purpose was not apt to be a successful one he would be refused a loan. The man as a borrower would also be required to have two sureties on the note he would give representing the loan, the names of two people, also themselves members of this association, acceptable to the members of the committee. Now possibly that is enough, on account of the limits of time, as a general description of this so-called Raiffeisen system. I may say that these associations average about ninety-five people in number. They are purely local. They accept deposits from members and also from non members. The average loan, as possibly I have stated a few minutes ago, is about $150. The average borrower makes a loan of about.$150. The average deposit is about $300. And when I say that all the funds at the disposal of these local credit associations run up into the billions of marks in terms of German money, and that by far the greatest part of these funds is furnished by members themselves who are not at a given time in need of money and who may happen to have a little surplus of their own, it gives a better idea of the economic and valuable character of these associations.

The local associations are combined into federated groups. At the head of each group is a bank, itself coöperative in character, made up not necessarily of the members of the local Raiffeisen associations, though usually so made up. Now these banks are sort of equalizing agencies that in times when the local associations may have surplus funds on hand, loan these funds in the great commercial centers of the country, or at least distribute them there to other rural credit associations; and, on the other hand, when a given local association may have need of more funds to lend than it has at its disposal these federated banks furnish such association with the funds needed. Still above these federated banks is a great central bank which carries on substantially, except on a larger scale, the same activities that the federated banks carry on.

Over all this combined activity is exercised the very careful supervision of the German government. I mention in connection with these Raiffeisen associations which exist to the number of several thousand throughout Germany, that in the entire history of them in the sixty or seventy years they have been in operation, not a single man, not a single member who is legally responsible to an unlimited extent for any failure of a local association, has ever been obliged to contribute a penny to make up a deficit as a consequence of failure. They have been conducted with the highest degree of success.

The general purpose of these so-called Raiffeisen associations is to enable the man who may not need a large amount of funds, who is not in a position perhaps to mortgage his real estate, but who could use to very good advantage more and better utensils and could enlarge his activity in some such way as that,—to enable him to branch out in that small way as he may desire and thereby carry on his activity with a larger efficiency than he had theretofore been able to carry it on. So much for the present for the Raiffeisan associations.

Another form that has met the strong approval of those who have investigated it from this country is the so-called Landschaften association which in perhaps all substantial respects is similar to the Raiffeisen association, and yet in a number of important ways differs from it. It is an association of a corporate character and is based upon land mortgage, the members of which are supposed to be people who themselves want to mortgage their farms for the purpose either of acquiring more land or for the purpose of making some large improvement. Now ouly people who are borrowers of considerable amounts of money belong to the Landschaften association. There is not in this, as there is in the Raiffeisen association, any expectation of dividends simply from the holding of stock. There would be no special motive for anybody's joining a Landschaften association unless he expected to borrow a considerable amount of money and unless he was willing to mortgage his real estate for the purpose of so borrowing. Now in that connection I desire to call attention briefly to a contrast which we may all readily observe between the character of the credit furnished by such an organization in this country as a railroad and that furnished by the ordinary farmer. In the case of a railroad, or an industrial plant, or a mine, you have a highly negotiable instrument in the form of a bond that anybody as an investor of experience may readily recognize the character of and which has, as we say, a very high degree of negotiability. It is a very fluid instrument. It is a liquid instrument. The man who may be uncertain as to how long he will care to keep a given bond has no hesitation whatever in putting his surplus cash into that, realizing, as he does, that he can dispose of it very readily at any time he sees fit. Consider then, if you please, the difference between that and the case of the farmer who like the railroad wants to borrow money, because of course a bond of a railroad represents nothing but a loan of substantially the same character as the loan made by the farmer secured by mortgage. In the latter case we have complicated laws governing the mortgage. They are essentially local in character. A mortgage held by a person a long distance away from the site of the mortgage is rare indeed. As a consequence of that, and primarily I maintain owing to the fluidity of the loan instrument the railroad is able to borrow at a rate of 4 or 4 1-2 or 5 per cent while the farmer with security often better than that of the railroad is obliged to pay 6, 7, and as I said earlier in the discussion on an average throughout the United States of 8 1-2 per cent. Now let it be plainly understood that the reason for this difference is not difference in the character of the loan but it is a difference in the nature of the instrument representing the loan. The theory or principle underlying the Landschaften association is to form an association whereby farmers banding themselves together and wanting to borrow money can mortgage their farms and have as the representation of that mortgage debenture bonds substantially similar in nature to the railroad bond or debenture bond in this country. These bonds are highly negotiable. In Germany they are generally as acceptable as the bonds issued by any industrial plant of any kind whatsoever. Now it is more commonly the case than not that a rural loan association bond can be circulated at a lower rate of interest than the average industrial bond.

Now another feature about this Landschaften association is a scheme whereby the farmer who as a borrower mortgages his farm, pays back his principal gradually, let us say in a period of twenty years. Suppose a German farmer wants to borrow $10,000. Now the average rate on farm mortgage loans in Germany is 4.3 per cent. The association would require him to pay each year in addition to that 4.3 per cent, 3.2 per cent to create a sinking fund gradually throughout a period of let us say twenty years. This man would pay therefore, $750 a year as a total upon that loan of $10,000 that he had made, let us say to purchase an addition to his farm. He would pay at the end of twenty years $15,000 as a total and he would have acquired in that time the piece of land that he had purchased in addition to paying interest on his loan during the time.

Contrast that with a typical case of the American farmer. I am not so sure about the conditions here as I am in the Central West with which I have been associated until very recently, but I know that on the average out there the farmer would carry the loan for twenty years, have paid over $15,000 and have in addition not a cent toward the purchase of his land. We have maintained seemingly a very haphazard system in connection with our real estate mortgage business. The theory seemingly has been that a mortgage ought to be drawn up merely for a period of three or four or five years, whereas the statistics show that the average life of a mortgage is vastly longer than that in this country, causing very decided inconvenience at times and embarrassment to the borrower as well as the lender. Now a distinct feature of this Landschaften system is the sinking fund feature whereby in addition to the low rate of interest that is charged as interest the borrower is obliged to pay a slight additional rate of interest that gradually accumulates as a sinking fund, so that at the expiration of the given period, twenty, twenty-five or thirty years, he has paid for the real estate that he has purchased.

Possibly this is sufficient in general explanation of the character of the two forms of local agricultural credit associations that have been operated with such great success in foreign countries. There seems to be no doubt whatever that they are, in substance at least, adaptable to American conditions. There is no question whatever of the possibility of applying the general principles of some of these local credit associations to American rural life. It will certainly be necessary, as one condition to this adaptation, that we have strict government supervision of these associations; that we proceed gradually. The process ought to be one of building up locally. The American farmer has been a distinctive individualist heretofore. He is now in contrast with the European farmer. And undoubtedly the movement of such organizations as this will be slow because the American farmer hesitates to enroll himself in coöperative efforts with others. The preceding speaker spoke in brief upon the fact that the American farmer has lagged behind in the adoption of up-to-date and improved methods and in contrast with his industrial brother in other fields of activity in this country he has remained altogether too distinctively individualistic. Now that individualism will have to be stopped. There is no possible question about the need of American farmers everywhere for more working capital, and if by reason of putting into operation associations of this general character they are able to obtain their loans at a rate not more than half of the average rate at the present time, and do it under circumstances that if we may judge by foreign experiences do not jeopardize the financial security of the individual farmer, that will not occasion loss if governmentally supervised, there is no reason whatever why they may not succeed. It may be of interest to know that several associations in general similar to that holding session here today have after rather careful consideration of organization of this kind, endorsed it. The American Bankers' Association has endorsed it, the Southern Commercial Congress has endorsed it, a number of industrial organizations have endorsed it. And as most of us know, the Commission appointed by Congress recently made its preliminary report only a few weeks ago, and in that report gave what may be called an unqualified endorsement of the principle of these local credit associations and their adaptability to American conditions. And I would say in conclusion that an organization such as this is eminently suited by reason of its progressive character, by reason of its organization, to at least investigate and study, and if convinced that there is merit in principles such as these, to lend aid in furthering the idea. Certainly benefit will come to you as individuals and to our country as a whole.

TUESDAY EVENING.

———

ORCHARDING IN DIFFERENT REGIONS OF THE UNITED STATES (ILLUSTRATED).*

By H. P. GOULD, U. S. Department of Agriculture, Washington, D. C.

"Mr. President; Members of the Maine State Pomological Society; Ladies and Gentlemen:

A man would indeed be devoid of all sentiment if he could be in the circumstances in which I find myself tonight and not have a great many fond recollections come to his mind. Though I have not been a resident of the State of Maine for quite a good many years, a good deal more than half of my life has been spent in this State, and I have been coming back once a year for all this time that I have been absent to see just a little of my people who still live in the State. It makes it doubly pleasant when I can be greeted by some of my old teachers as I was just a few moments ago.

The course which I will try to take you over tonight will be presented in views showing some typical orchards and some typical orchard methods in various representative fruit-growing regions of the United States. The views are not in all cases quite as representative as I would like to have them, but still perhaps they may not be without some interest. A few views will be suggestive, I hope, with reference to practical orchard management.

The matter of atmospheric drainage has been a good deal emphasized in much of the horticultural literature during the past few years. It has not been over-emphasized, however, because atmospheric drainage is one of the most important

* Condensed and revised by Mr. Gould for publication from stenographer's notes.

considerations in selecting orchard sites in their relation to successful orcharding. To a great many it is a more or less unintelligible thing, this matter of atmospheric drainage. Two or three slides will perhaps show the effect of atmospheric drainage in such a way that even if you cannot see it you can get a very vivid idea of its results. (A view of an orange tree in Florida was here thrown on the screen.) This shows a condition which the tree displayed following a severe freeze which occurred in Florida a few years ago. You know after a very severe frost occurs while plants are in active growth the leaves will be killed and will dry right up on the tree without falling off. That is a common observation. If slightly injured, enough just barely to kill them, they will drop in a little time. These conditions were apparent in the case of this orange tree. The lower leaves were killed so entirely that they dried up on the tree without falling off. In the middle portion of the tree, the leaves were injured just enough to kill them, so that they dropped. The top of the tree was uninjured, thus showing three gradations in temperature—three climatic conditions, if you please—within the height of the tree.

The next view shows atmospheric drainage in another manner, in a large mountain peach orchard in West Virginia. The picture was taken in the morning, with a fire burning on the side of the mountain. The smoke is seen drifting down the hill showing simply that the current is downward; in other words, a visible illustration of atmospheric drainage.

Atmospheric drainage is further illustrated by two views of an apple orchard in West Virginia. There was an interval of one week between the dates on which the photographs were taken. The views show a depression between the point where the photographs were taken and the remote portion of the orchard, that portion being elevated 50 feet or such a matter above the lowest point of the depression. The earlier view shows the trees in the distance in full bloom, while those in the depression had not yet come into bloom. The second view displays the same orchard a week later, showing the trees in the distance on the elevated portion of the orchard going out of bloom, while those in the depression were in full bloom. A comparison of these two views makes it apparent that there were really two climates within the short distance indicated in the illustration. The cold air had settled into the depression to such an extent as to retard the blossoming of the trees nearly a week in comparison with the blossoming of the trees in the elevated portion of the orchard.

Another thing of great importance in selecting sites for orchards is the soil and especially the subsoil. I am coming to lay more and more importance upon the character of the subsoil. It should be deep and porous, at least relatively so; porous enough to admit of a fairly rapid percolation of the water through it.

The next view shows a section of soil in the Ozark Region in which apple trees and other fruit trees make a rapid growth during the early years of the orchard. This rapid growth is not due to the extreme fertility of the soil as much as it is due to the great moisture reservoir that is furnished by the deep, porous subsoil.

In contrast to the last view, the one now on the screen shows a solid ledge formation within three or four feet of the surface. There is nothing on the surface of the soil to indicate that the solid rock is near the surface without an examination of the subsoil. One could very readily have purchased an area of land in the section in which this view was taken thinking that he was securing soil that was suitable for any purpose and being totally unconscious of the fact that its usefulness was greatly restricted by the character of the subsoil. Fruit trees have done fairly well during seasons of normal rainfall on soil having such characteristics as those in the section of country in which this view was taken. But the season of 1911 was one of excessive drouth following two other years that were very dry. As a result of this drouth, coupled with the fact that the moisture reservoir—that is, the subsoil—was very limited, thousands of apple trees died.

A thin stratum of rock two or three feet from the surface underlaid by good soil conditions would be equally as undesirable as a solid rock formation because of the fact that the rock stratum would effectually cut off all communication between the soil above the rock and that below."

Following these views, several were thrown on the screen showing typical orchards or orchard conditions in various sections of the country. These included a view illustrating the sod-mulching method as practiced by Mr. Grant G. Hitchings of Onondaga County, New York; a Maiden Blush apple orchard about 30 years old in New Jersey, the symmetry of the trees and the heavy crop of fruit which they were bearing being the points of chief interest; one showing a Gravenstein orchard in New Jersey which was planted before the matter of low heads had been as much agitated as has been the case during the past few years, the present orchard showing very high heads; two views showing early apples loaded at the orchard for further disposition, one going to the Philadelphia market, the other loaded with 7-8 bushel baskets ready to be taken to the shipping station.

In the same manner typical views were shown in important orchard districts in West Virginia, Illinois, Kansas, the Ozark Region, Iowa, Colorado, Washington, Oregon and California. In the Rocky Mountain and Pacific Coast States where fruit growing is confined quite definitely to particular districts and river valleys, the views shown were representative of the various districts and valleys in which important fruit interests have been developed. Several packing scenes were shown indicating packing houses, packing tables, the packing of apples in boxes, etc.

The two citrus packing houses in California were shown and commented on because of the fact that one of them was an old style packing house in which a great deal of overhead machinery was used. In this type of packing house, the fruit was elevated to a relatively high point and then allowed to drop by gravity through various spouts, runs, etc., as it passed through graders, sizing machines and other apparatus in its transit to the bins from which it was packed. The other citrus packing house was a modern one showing the changes which had been made in recent years following the work of the Office of Field Investigations in Pomology in connection with the serious losses which the shippers sustained, due to the decay of the fruit in transit from California to eastern markets. This work showed very clearly that the decay of the oranges was very largely traceable to injuries which the fruit received either in the orange groves before it was taken to the packing houses or while it was being handled after it reached the packing house.

The bruising of the fruit and other injuries which resulted from its passing by gravity through the overhead machinery shown in the old style packing house contributed a great deal to the decay of the fruit. The taking out of the overhead apparatus and the substitution of that which would eliminate all dropping of the fruit was considered essential in order that the fruit might be handled with the least possible injury. When all injuries were eliminated and the fruit was handled with the greatest possible care from the time it was picked until it was packed, the decay of the fruit was almost entirely prevented.

Similar investigations carried on in connection with the handling of other fruits have further emphasized the fact that much of the loss and other difficulties which fruit growers and fruit dealers have experienced is due to the rough handling of the fruit. Where all bruises and other injuries are eliminated, the keeping qualities of the fruit, other things being equal, are very greatly enhanced. A great many of the injuries which result in trouble in storage or subsequent to storage after the fruit is removed for marketing are due to bruises and other injuries which are almost imperceptible.

Attention was called to the heating of orchards to prevent injury by frosts in two or three views showing smudge pots, storage tanks for oil, etc. In contrast with this operation which has become a prominent one in some sections of the country in the management of the orchards, attention was directed to the fact that in Maine injury by unseasonable spring frosts was practically unknown and that the growers in this State were particularly fortunate in this respect as they had no occasion to consider the matter of orchard heating so far as the management of their own orchards was concerned.

In order to give some idea of the character and the extent of the root system of apple trees, several views were thrown on the screen showing the roots, their ramifications through the soil and some of the influences in their development. As a matter of general interest, the portable refrigerating plant which was built by the Office of Field Investigations in Pomology was shown. This refrigerating plant is used for experimental work in the fruit transportation and storage investigations conducted by that Office, the principal object of this plant being to precool the fruit either for immediate transportation or for storage.

In connection with the view of a monument which has been erected to indicate the spot on which the original Baldwin apple tree stood, the speaker called attention to the fact that a number of monuments and tablets had been erected to mark the spot where the orignal tree or plant stood of some fruit which has become famous and which has contributed largely to American pomology.

Concluding his address, the speaker said:

"I have talked quite a good many times with fruit-growers in the East who have made extensive trips through the western fruit-growing regions. They have come back home feeling more satisfied than ever with their surroundings; feeling that they are able to meet successfully in competition with what their brother fruit-growers in the famous regious of the West are able to force upon them; and so if any of these views make the fruit-growers here in Maine feel that their conditions are just as good as they are anywhere else, possibly it may give you a happy feeling—happiness leads to contentment and contentment is great gain."

ADDRESS ON EUROPEAN HORTICULTURE.

By PROF. FRANK A. WAUGH, of Amherst, Mass.

Mr. President, members of the Maine State Pomological Society and Friends:

After Brother Gould has taken you all over North America it only remains for me to show you about over the rest of the world. Now the time has gone by when a man who comes home from a trip to Europe is thereby made a curiosity. Anybody can go to Europe who can grow a barrel of apples, and pretty nearly for the price of a good barrel of apples nowadays. It is as easy to go to Europe as it is to go to Boston or New York, and a good deal easier than it is to go to some of the back towns of Maine. I suppose that there are a good many people here tonight who have been to Europe, some of them more times than I have, and some of them have stayed longer, have seen a good deal more than I have and know a good deal more about it, but I shall do the best I can in spite of that. All I can say for myself is that I have been there a time or two, that I had some little acquaintance with the country principally because my mother was born in Germany, that after going there twice and getting acquainted with the country I could find my way about pretty well because I could speak some of the language, and that I was able to stop there for five or six months on the last trip and become settled and acquainted, and so to see and understand a good. many of the things which the ordinary tourist does not see and which perhaps he cannot understand.

I was located for a time at a little horticultural school near Berlin, and the first picture I show you is taken from the garden there. You will see it is a very nice, well-kept garden, that the trees are planted close together, and that, in fact, they are all of the forms which we call dwarf trees. The standard tree, as we call it, in our orchards, is almost unknown. These are dwarf pear trees which we see along the border of the walk, and these which we see here (picture 2) are dwarf peach trees growing in pots which are kept along here at the fruiting age and are used for replanting in the orchard whenever there is a vacancy.

Here is a peach tree trained out against the wall, and beside it you see blankets on rollers so that if there is danger of frost the blankets can be rolled over the peach tree and it can be guarded and kept from frost. The peach tree is very carefully trained there, very carefully taken care of.

Here in a closed garden carefully walled in on all sides are numbers of pear trees spread on trellises and very carefully trained as to form. You may imagine that these bear large quantities of fruit, as indeed they do, and that the fruit is of a very high quality, as indeed it must be to pay for all that care.

Now here is an example of apple trees trained against a work building on the grounds of the school. These apple trees are 5 years old, and have borne four crops. Each apple tree there will bear eight or ten apples of the very finest quality. Those which we see are fronting to the south. They get the best and brightest light of the day, the warmth of the sun, and the brick wall against which they grow takes up large quantities of heat which it gives out to the fruit all through the night so that they just grow day and night. They work them there twenty-four hours a day.

We have in this picture the explanation of why they can take so much care of their fruit trees. The work is largely done by women. The major portion of their hard work is done by the women. It is a country where they have genuine women's rights. These girls, about twenty-two years old, work ten hours a day and receive forty-eight cents a day throughout the summer. From the enormous savings which they amass during the nine months of the growing season they go home and live with their parents and support the family for the rest of the year. Every house has a few fruit trees—not an orchard scattered out behind the barn as we have it in New England, but usually a few fruit trees trained up against the side of the house.

This is more of a business orchard which you see here. This is composed of cordon apple trees, each one trained obliquely to a stake and the stakes tied to a trellis. This is a business proposition and the man who runs that makes money out of it. He gets good prices for his fruit. and he puts lots of work into it so he has to get good prices.

Here we have a little inclosed garden such as we find in all private estates. This is on a large private estate, where a number of gardeners are kept. For comparison we have here the little peasant's cottage in the little town where my mother was born, and very near her old home-—a pear tree growing against the end of the house and a grape vine growing under the eaves. The amount of land these people have is extremely limited. Between the house and the front fence is about two and a half feet, but they manage that land to pretty good advantage and get something from it.

Here in the middle of a little village in Silesia we have a garden running along between the sidewalk and the grocery store; growing against the side of the house an apricot tree which bears abundant crops of fruit.

This is an orchard of fruit trees on a private place in one of the suburbs of Berlin. It was photographed early in the spring. The trees have been whitewashed which gives them that striking appearance. It is rather advantageous from the photographic point of view because it gives us a chance to see just how the tree looks. These trees are old and neglected, by the way, and do not show the nice symmetrical, clean-cut, well-kept forms which you will find on carefully trained trees.

This is another portion of the same place, showing horizontally cordon apple trees. These apple trees will be a foot and a half or two feet from the ground. Now there are great advantages in that. They have the advantage which I spoke of in respect to the trees growing against the side of the brick wall, that they receive the reflected heat from the soil and that they receive during the night a considerable amount of heat taken up by the soil during the day and given back to the fruit during the night. It is much easier to take care of trees eighteen or twenty-four inches high.

This is a little apple tree growing in a little private garden down in Kent in southern England. You will see they vary a great deal, some of the trees being very symmetrical, very fine, and others poor and untidy. Of course a tree in these various forms requires constant care—not merely one pruning once in five years as some of our trees get in Massachusetts, but five prunings every year—looking after all the while.

These trees are peaches, of course under glass, for in England peaches are grown practically only upon walls and under glass. One must have a good deal of faith in horticulture when he can afford to glass over his orchard. As a matter of fact some of these glass houses grow fruit for the market, not so much in England as in Belgium and northern France; but still there are hundreds of acres of them altogether—I don't think I could say thousands, but hundreds of acres in fruit trees in the old country which are grown as a commercial enterprise in glasshouses.

This is a typical tree for use in a glass house. Some of them are bush-formed trees in pots, and some of them are spread out on trellises as you saw them in a former picture. This happens to be a nectarine which is grown in England largely in preference to the peach, and I am unable to understand why it is not more widely grown in America. As one finds them in the old country they are fully as good as peaches and in many ways superior.

This little fig tree reminds us of our forefathers because that is what they started housekeeping with. This one is grown in the greenhouses with the other fruit. In order to show that the small fruit proposition, the small fruit tree, is not necessarily confined to England, I am putting in two or three pictures from a garden which I used to have in Massachusetts. The one in the foreground is still growing but the apple trees have been dug up. They were very attractive and interesting and very satisfactory during their day. I may say they were dug up simply because the ground had to be used for the erection of a new building. These are cordon apple trees, upright, trained against a wire fence. The trees are planted eighteen inches apart and have ample space, and you will see are bearing good crops. Bro. Gould has stated tonight that many of us are making mistakes in planting our apple trees too near together. He thinks they ought not to be closer than thirty-five feet. I don't recommend everybody to put them in at eighteen inches apart, but this picture will show that it can be done, and done successfully.

Here we have another picture from my own garden of a dwarf pear tree. A six-year-old boy beside it will indicate pretty clearly what is the size of the tree, and the crop speaks for itself. This small apple tree bearing four or five first rate good-sized apples had an entire height, we will say, of twenty inches. Now that is a small tree. I believe in heading them low and keeping them under careful attention. However, that is a garden proposition and not an orchard proposition. And while I am speaking about that I might as well say that while I have a good deal of enthusiasm for dwarf fruit trees, and have said something about them, and written about them from time to time, I have never recommended them as a commercial proposition and do not do so at the present time. They are splendidly adapted to the needs of the ordinary city and suburban dweller, the man who finds it a great deal more comfortable to move once in three years than to pay his rent. Now the man in that condition cannot possibly go into fruit growing unless he can have some small trees which he can put in the back yard and bring into bearing in one or two years. He can do that with a dwarf fruit tree and get a lot of fun out of it, and under many circumstances when he has got to move to another neighborhood he can pull those trees up after dark and take them with him. I know because I have done it and they will go on growing almost as readily as the chickens which you move along at the same time. Here we have currant bushes in the same style of garden, simply to show that when one starts out in that suburban back yard gardening he can do almost anything he pleases.

Now we are back in Europe and find ourselves in the Covent Garden Market which I think is far and away the most interesting fruit market in the world. In some ways it is the largest fruit market in the world—I don't know but it is really the largest in the volume of fruit that it handles; it certainly is the most interesting one in the extent of country from which it draws, for one finds there fruit literally from all parts of the world. He finds the best from all parts of the world because it is a discriminating market, a market which selects well. There are some of the keenest and brightest fruit handlers in the world, men who have correspondents everywhere, in every country, and they know what the fruit markets of the world are, what fruits of every kind are, where they come from. One gets all kinds of information and all kinds of courtesies from these men, and it is extremely interesting. Of course we self-satisfied Yankees see a great many things to criticise. For instance, those baskets piled up in the background, willow baskets, they use for every sort of thing, and they ship everything in them, including strawberries. Strawberries are mostly shipped in quarter bushel baskets made out of willow in that fashion. And moreover, they are returnable baskets, shipped up from Kent to London, berries sold and poured out into the old woman's apron, and then the crate is shipped back to Kent, thrown in the red mud in the early morning, and is packed full of fruit again and shipped back to Covent Garden, and the next day it comes back to Kent again, and so after making about twenty trips and resting in the red mud twenty different mornings, and having the strawberry juice run through twenty different times, you can imagine the sort of package in which the strawberries are distributed in the market in London.

Here is another corner of the market, with the usual things. This place here in Liverpool shows many of the same features of the ordinary fruit market. It is quite late in the day—it usually is when I get round to anything of that sort—and the market is being cleaned up, but here on the curb throughout the early morning thousands of bushels of fruit are sold and carted off to the local markets of which this picture shows a type. It looks like an ordinary corner grocery, and it is. You see the half-sieves sitting there on the corner from which all kinds of fruit and vegetables are distributed to all kinds of customers—you have them there as you do here.

Now going on to the continent of Europe we find ourselves in the city of Mainz, in a typical continental market of one of the most strikingly beautiful and interesting cities in all Europe. There is nothing more picturesque and from every point of view more interesting than these city markets. Here you see the marketing going on, mostly conducted by women who bring the produce of their own farms into market and sell it there direct to the customers. Now you and I know that the greatest problem we have to face is that of marketing, and the thing we are trying to arouse people to do is to bring the producer up to the consumer, to get the two together, and that is done better in the local markets of Central Europe than anywhere else in the world, and I haven't the slightest doubt in my mind that some of the improvements in the next few years will come in this direction. I am pretty sure that some of the cities in America could support these public markets with very good advantage. I am especially sure of that. not because I have seen it in Germany and France and Switzerland and Austria and Italy, but because I have seen it in America. Lots of things you see over there will not apply in this country. But the open curb market supported by the municipality can be made successful in this country, perhaps not so easily and universally, but certainly it can be made successful. This particular market is the one with which I am best acquainted for I lived six months in this little village and used to go almost every market day, that is two days in the week, Tuesdays and Fridays, to this place and used to buy the things which I needed for supper. I did it because I wanted something for supper and because I wanted to know how this business was handled. It was very interesting. I could spend all this evening telling stories of the way in which things are sold there. I used to buy a quarter of a pound of butter, or cheese—which was quite enough of some kinds—or a quarter of a pound of sausage and other commodities in like quantities. It is a retail market in the most literal sense of the word.

The flower market here in front of the great city hall in Brussels is simply another example of a retail market. It is beautiful and picturesque.

I thought perhaps this picture would be interesting although it is not one of my own. This shows one of the typical city markets at Sofia in one of the public squares, and this one here shows a market at Cairo, Egypt. These open air markets in public places are almost universal outside of the United States of America. I was going to make an exception of Canada, but in French Canada particularly the open air markets are maintained in a great many places.

Now I am going to leave behind the fruit-growing business and the fruit marketing business for the present because I am personally more interested in other branches of horticulture. I am personally particularly interested in the ornamental phases of agriculture known as landscape gardening, and the old and beautiful gardens of England have been a special delight to me. Here you have an example of one of them. They are characterized by the enormous quantities of flowering plants and of very, very great luxuriance. There is no other country where such quantities of flowers can be grown in such a magnificent and luxuriant manner and no place in the world where such beautiful lawns can be developed. Uufortunately it is not convenient to show the beauty and the luxuriance of a lawn in a photograph, and so in these pictures which we run over we don't have the opportunity to see the lawns as we ought to see them. This picture of the old fashioned bee hives is interesting perhaps, and I ought to say that the bee hives are kept there for ornamental purposes rather than for the growing of bees. In this country we have heard of the rose as the queen of flowers, and many of us suppose that it is so although we have very small demonstration of it in our own gardens. It is not possible to grow roses, in the Eastern States, at any rate, at all as they are grown in England. After one has seen roses in England he is pretty nearly ready to give them up in this country and devote his land to cabbages.

This is a typical garden at the height of summer, with its multitudes of larkspurs, hollyhocks, phlox and other things. You may think there is some hocus-pocus about that because you find a lot of plants there in blossom which here in Maine do not blossom simultaneously, and yet they are pictured here together. But although I did not take that photograph, I think the picture is genuine. We find in England, in the long slow spring and the long slow summer many plants coming on together which here are total strangers. This is a pleasant little valley in rural England,—shows the fine, pleasant, rural seenery. The picture here is particularly interesting to me because it shows an old orchard and a deer park combined right near London. This is about ten miles from London. Now we have tried in Amherst, Massachusetts, to run an apple orchard and a deer pasture combined for a number of years; we do not supply the deer, however, and we do not own them. The State of Massachusetts claim that they own the cattle and we have to support them. We do not like the business and have been trying very hard to keep the deer business and the apple business apart. As a matter of fact, they do not conduct the two together in Europe, but when they have a flock of deer over there they make use of them. They keep them and they are all tagged and numbered like so many Jersey cows and as soon as they mature they go to market. And if the State of Massachusetts would conduct its deer business in that fashion I should think very much more of it than I do at the present time.

This little sketch along one of the pleasant rural paths in England gives a nice idea of the country, one of the pleasantest and most attractive countries in the world for the tourist, and I think also for the one who lives there. These pleasant paths lead about all over the fields and are really public paths so that one may wander about almost where he chooses in the country and not feel he is trespassing anywhere, and come upon all such pleasant, rural bucolic scenes as this where we have the hay stack in the barnyard and all the farm work going on. It is very interesting for a man who has been brought up on a farm and who loves farm life and who likes to stop and talk with the men and women at work in the fields.

This is a pleasant country house in England, a house which has stood for a little over two thousand years, and which as

far as I can see will stand for two thousand years more. It
gives one some little idea of the permanence of that country.

And just to show that everything in that country is not as
bright and beautiful as some of the photographs, I have also a
few pictures of the back yards, some of which look just as
they do in this country and make one feel as though he was
entirely at home.

A pleasant rural church of this kind is a common scene in
England and reminds me that our country churches in New
England are, some of them, beautiful, but very few of them
are as permanent as this, and some of them, in fact, are very
squalid and unsatisfactory. It happens that this particular
church is like a good many of our New England country
churches, it is entirely deserted except by these good old friends
in the foreground who can't get away. A village farmhouse in
the same neighborhood is shown here, showing something of the
type of rural architecture which is quite familiar, especially on
the hills of Gloucester. This is a substantial school building in
a little village in Gloucester, showing two or three little items
of interest, the closeness and narrowness of the streets, the
sharp corners that are turned, the way in which all the little
corners of land are used for buildings, and the fine and clean
and substantial character of the public buildings themselves.
. Those people have been there, as I say, for two thousand years
and they expect to stay two thousand more, and so they are
willing to have things fixed up as they ought to be.

Here we are again back on the continent, for with the collection of these slides around various paragraphic topics, I
have looked to the topics rather than to the particular localities
in arranging the slides, and am therefore keeping you jumping
about from one place to another; but I hope that will not con-
fuse you or cause you any seasickness or discomfort. We can
cross the channel in this way without any seasickness, though
some people find it difficult to get across in fact without some
trouble. We are now in southern Germany, in a very pleasant.
beautiful, private garden in the early spring with the magnolias
in blossom. The same girls stand for us here in this photograph, showing the same magnolia tree, and a very attractive
view down the main street of the garden. You see the pretty

Japanese plum trees, very attractive and beautiful, strong bushes, which will not grow in this country.

Here we are in Dresden at the lilac blooming time. It is one of the fête days of Dresden, for there are thousands of people that go to Dresden every spring simply to have a smell of the spring and see the lilacs in blossom. Here are also the wistarias growing against the side of the house, and we have a typical arrangement of a dwelling-house of the better kind—there are a good many things which I have not time to explain. Here we see the lilac bush at the private house leaning over against the wall, and the pear tree growing against the gable end of the house—there isn't much room, as you will see; wherever there is a foot of land it is made use of, either in fruit trees or useful plants or something which is attractive to the family. This is rather a better house here, with its nice fence and its splendid lilac bush growing against the wall. These arrangements are perfectly practicable in any of our American communities. In American cities we have what we call slums. We are ashamed of them and we try to get rid of them, and we are doing something very slowly and very unsatisfactorily to rid our cities of the slums. I think that on the whole the better cities of Germany and Austria have made more progress than any other cities in the world. The picture which is taken here is in one of the poorer districts of Vienna and shows a little courtyard around which six or eight families live, all opening out into this little square, and yet you see it is a fine, pleasant, attractive place. It has a home-like look and it is greatly enhanced by the fruit trees and vines which are growing there. In every one of these little courtyards you will find some sort of gardening going on.

You and I, however, who like to be in the country, are more interested to walk along the country roads and to view scenes like this. When the fruit trees are in blossom there we find something really more attractive than the set and cultured gardens such as some of those I have been showing you. These wayside views are always attractive. This is one of the suburban gardens of the poor working classes in the neighborhood of Berlin. All about the European cities you will see small gardens of a quarter or an eighth of an acre set apart and rented on long terms of years to workmen of the poorer classes in the

city, and they go out there and work all day Sunday and work
in the evening after hours, and very often take their families
out there too, put up a shed or two dry goods boxes and live
there all summer, in that way getting a touch of rural life, at
any rate of out-door life, doing some gardening and fruit-
growing. And nothing is more attractive, nothing is more interesting anywhere in the old country than to go and spend a day
in one of these little settlements where perhaps four or five
hundred families are located. This is something which the
ordinary tourist misses altogether, partly because it isn't down
in the guidebook and partly because one doesn't get into these
places easily. They do not like to be looked over. If one goes
there sociably and talks and visits with the people and spends
some time in getting acquainted, he finds them very amusing
and interesting and the stories one could get would be well
worth the entire trip.

Here we are on a large estate in Silesia showing one of the
fine old castles with its splendid grounds. It is the estate of
Prince Pückler of Moscow who wrote a famous book on landscape gardening. This is his own estate built a little over a
hundred years ago on one of the most magnificent stretches of
land I ever saw, on which today are developed thousands
of beautiful trees planted over a hundred years ago, because he
preserved many which were old trees when he went on there,
and the trees which he himself planted about a hundred years
ago are now full grown beeches and oaks such as we cannot
have in our gardens and our yards in this country because we
haven't lived long enough yet to accomplish so much.

The beech trees in this picture are a part of the Kaiser's
hunting property. The land belongs to him personally. A
tract of 640 acres right in the center of this big capital city
(Berlin). You will notice the fine rural character. You
would think that you were out in the woods there. It is only
ten minutes walk from the main streets of the city, and there
you are in this splendid woodland. It gives every one the opportunity to get a breath of the fresh out-door air and look
at the trees, a chance to remember that there is something else
besides streets and buildings.

But speaking of buildings there are some of these in the old
country which are very interesting and which teach us really

valuable lessons. The two buildings which we see here are known as the old and new town hall in a little town of southern Germany. The new one, on this side, was built two or three hundred years ago, and the old one long before that. They are both pretty good buildings, and when we remember that the poor people who built these buildings five or six hundred years ago were working for wages of ten cents a day or less, and that out of these meagre incomes they were able to save the money to build such magnificent town halls, it rather puts us to shame that we with our greater wealth and our greater opportunities, and the greater productiveness of our land and labor are not able to do better things in this country. I mention this somewhat freely here in Portland where you have done something splendid, something magnificent in the way of a town hall. There are not many places that have done as well as Portland, and there are very few indeed in this country which can compare with anything in the old country in the way of a town hall.

This is one in a little country town. It shows an old town hall, built many years ago, and still fine and well kept. The one in Hamburg is in a large, modern, prosperous city, but it is a fine building with a nice plaza in front of it which opens out onto a fine water front. The city hall in Dresden is the latest one to be built. It was finished within the last few years and is regarded as the very last word in city halls, a splendid modern building in every respect.

And here is one of the school buildings. We think a great deal of our schools in this country and suppose that they are the greatest in the world, and yet the men who study the school problems tell me without any reserve that the German schools are better than ours, and I can say with great emphasis, having visited a good many of them, that the school buildings are certainly better than ours. This is a typical example of a building I knew very well. This is an example of a girls' school in one of the German cities, and shows the fine type of architecture which one sees over there in the public school buildings. Here is a public building which has always interested me a great deal. It might be an art gallery, but as a matter of fact it is a department store, a splendid department store in the center of Berlin. It might be out in the country, from the looks of the picture, a pleasant, roomy, attractive place, and yet it is in the busiest part of the city of Berlin, and in front of the building there pass two hundred thousand people a day. Now that is a good deal of traffic to pass along one street. There is some business going on there. It shows, however, from our point of view that a little open space in a city with a tree or two and a strip of grass are well worth while.

Another public building which is somewhat unique is a public theatre. I believe there are two in the United States. One of them is in the neighboring town of Northampton which owns its own theatre and controls it and manages it in the interest of the public. These public theatres are common in Germany. Performances are given frequently. This is one of the least of them in a country town—a very attractive public building. And this is a post office. Of all the public buildings the one which comes nearest to the average man is the post office. This is one of the thirty-six post offices in Berlin. This is one in one of the small suburbs, where I used to live and used to go frequently to mail packages. It is interesting to me on a great many accounts. That looks like a good deal of a building— we see only one end of it here—and to imagine that there are thirty-six of them in Berlin would indicate that they put a good deal of money into public buildings. But their post office department does some business. It handles all the telephone business—not very well; it handles all the telegraphic business, most admirably, and it handles all the stuff which in this country we call the express business but which over there is the parcels post,—a real, genuine, honest parcels post. It used to be interesting to me to go over and see all those packages of every sort of thing, butter, sausage, live geese and one thing and another, coming in there to be mailed. Why, if a man has a yellow dog he wants to get rid of, what he does is to take it down there. write an address on a tag, tie it on the dog's tail, address it to some one, put a stamp on the dog's back and send it along. I had some experiences with this parcels post which interested me. I collected some apples to send to my friend Professor Sears, in Amherst, and I had them packed in a box weighing four or five pounds which I knew could not have got into the mails in the United States unless it was inserted from the outside. It was not mailable here, but it had

to be intruded from across the water. I put the stamps on it
and mailed it to Professor Sears and he got it and ate the
apples. I counted up what it had cost me and the postage on
that box of apples, entirely unmailable in this country, from
Berlin to Massachusetts was just a trifle less than half it would
cost to send it from Portland to Old Orchard, supposing
I could have mailed it in this country. Now that was
a lesson to me along with a good many others, and I made up
my mind that I would not vote for anybody in this country
who would not vote for parcels post. I could tell stories all
night about the parcels post. It is an interesting theme.

In the old country they have taken up very seriously the
questions of beautifying their streets, and one problem which
they have solved is that of taking care of their water fronts. I
am told that there is a problem in Portland of taking care of
the water front, and while I have not looked the situation over
I am not afraid to make a guess that there are not many miles
of the Portland water front that look as well as this little strip
of Hamburg I showed you a moment ago. The city hall is at
the left corner here fronting out upon this beautiful square of
water. We see it here in its narrowest dimension where this
magnificent plaza sets out into it. Here is a fine boulevard.
The great department stores are located at the left. On this side
are the big hotels of the city. Here are the finest and biggest
offices in the city. This used to be simply an old tide flat. Here
we have a flowing stream, a little narrow stream running
through a country town in Central Germany. You know how
they look up here in Maine with saw-mills and slab dumps and
things of that sort along the sides. In this case the banks have
all been cleaned up, used for the best buildings, and they have
been ornamented with double rows of trees, made into fine
promenades. Let us take a nearer look. Here is a nice public
music hall in the center, a nice friendly beer garden at the right,
with trees growing along both sides, pleasant, clean, sanitary,
attractive, ornamental, making all the property fronting on this
river ten times more valuable than it could be if that river was
treated in the manner we treat our streams as they run through
our American villages and cities. Even here in the country
there is no such treatment of the trees as we are liable to see.
This is a pleasant little German country village with its one

winding street and a pleasant stream back of it; altogether a
fine, clean, wholesome neighborhood to live in. And this view
is taken from the old factory of Nuremberg. There is the
bridge. This canal which runs here turns the wheels of industry, as we say. You may think that factories necessarily mean
a lot of waste and rubbish and squalor and dirt, but they don't
in any country which is cleaned up and cleaned up to stay.
This is a water front view also, where a little stream runs
through a pleasant English village. It also used to be a sewer,
but it has been cleaned up and is now as nice and attractive as
any place you could imagine.

This view shows some of the fruit growing and farming interests in Central Germany, near Berlin. This is a cherry
orchard at blossoming time. This shows the terraced banks on
the hills upon which the vineyards grow, terraced up with stone
walls to hold in a little patch of land and then the vines are
grown there. The fields of Germany and Central Europe are
always picturesque and interesting. I have referred before to
the wide recognition of woman's rights in the old country, for
one finds them there always in the harvest fields, early and late,
working with the men, even doing more work than the men,
perhaps, because they are more industrious.

Here we have the fields of northern Germany on the flat low
land at the harvest time, and I would like to have you notice
what a splendid heavy growth of grain there is. I have one or
two other pictures which show that growth of grain. Look, for
instance, at this on the line next to Denmark. There is a crop
of rye that a man might be proud of. Notice how the land
is farmed up to the very eaves of the building. There is a place
where people have been farming for five hundred years and
the land growing richer all the time. That is agriculture on a
permanent basis, and agriculture which is sure of itself and
understands what it is doing. And here we see agriculture
crowding up not merely to the eaves of the houses but crowding up to the foot of the mountains. Here are the snows in the
upper mountains, and below them are the fields, some of them
in grain and further back in forests, but all of them busy, all
of them doing something, all of them bringing in a revenue.
Notice here as we get near to the mountain we have those fine
forest lands running up there. That is all public forest, all
carefully managed, all bringing in a good solid revenue. They

cannot afford to let any piece of land loaf over there, or any-body loaf over there. These public forests are extremely in-teresting to everybody. You have heard, of course, always about these public forests, but one of the things that has im-pressed me is not so much the technical management of the forest as the political aspect of the thing. The forests are owned by the towns in which they exist. The little town in which my mother was born and which I have visited has several hundred acres of public forest. It is managed by a professional forester, and the crop is cut whenever it is matured, and what we call the waste here, the rubbish or brush is taken out, wrapped up into bundles and is distributed pro rata through the town, and the lumber is sold and the proceeds are returned to the town, and there is money enough brought in from the public forest owned by the town to pay all the town's bills, every cent of running expenses, the care of their roads, the care of their schools, and even the salary of their preacher who gets a good salary from the town, the best salary in the town. There are not any town taxes at all. Here in this country we say a man can escape anything but death and taxes; in that country he can escape taxes, and he only dies once. There are towns in that country, they tell me, where from the thrifty man-agement of their own property they not only pay all their run-ning expenses, but they have money left over and on the first day of January they distribute $10 apiece to every man, woman and child in the place, making him a present for living there. I don't know any place in this country where they are liable to do that. We do not manage towns and cities that way. It looks like good business. I know there are a good many thou-sands of acres of land in Maine, as there are in Massachusetts, which could be put to work if we had the brains to do it and if we had the political integrity and the political efficiency to manage those things as public enterprises in the way they are managed in the old country.

Now friends, I have covered the trip as far as I expected to go. I have taken these various ideas from various parts of the country, not in a very connected manner, but I hope some of them have interested you and I hope some of them seem to have some bearing or other upon our problems here in Maine and in New England.

I thank you for your kind attention.

WEDNESDAY FORENOON.

WEDNESDAY FORENOON.

PRESIDENT'S ADDRESS.

MR. HOWARD L. KEYSER, Greene, Maine.

On behalf of the officers and members of this society I wish to express our thanks to the citizens of Portland, who, by their efforts and generosity have made this meeting of the Maine State Pomological Society the largest in its history and thereby stimulated increased interest in the pomological work in the State.

We are pleased and proud to have with us as our guests at this meeting, the officers of the New England Fruit Show as well as many leading orchardists of New England and glad they are exhibiting fruit in competition with our own—made possible by the hearty coöperation of the Portland Board of Trade.

On every hand is the evidence of the awakening of hundreds of fruit growers to the questions of the hour,—the best and most practical methods for the improvement of general conditions.

Where a few years ago the orchardist who sprayed was not considered quite sane, he is now sought by his neighbors for information, and the small amount of knowledge possessed by many growers notwithstanding all the publications, bulletins and various educational meetings, illustrates the fact that a very large per cent remain in the primary class and a great work still remains for such societies as ours.

Since our last meeting the season of 1911 has passed into history and we have again harvested a bountiful crop of fruit, the culture of which I am going to leave for discussion to the many able authorities we have with us, and, in a brief way, speak of some of the ills we have with us on the business side.

The fruit crop of the state of Oregon was placed at 1,100,000 boxes for 1911 for which was received $1,094,000, not quite one dollar net per box. I am not quite visionary enough to grasp the figures of the speaker who figures that Washington, Oregon, Idaho, and Montana have 19,500,000 boxes planted and growing and by 1915 will produce 97,500 cars of fruit, equal to 3900 trains of twenty-five cars each, or the dispatching of seventy-eight trains a day for fifty days. But I do say to our fellow fruit growers of the East, it is time for Rip Van Winkle to arouse. They do things on a large scale in the West and if we remain dormant, they can and will take our markets. If we awake to the new ways and methods, we have all in our favor,—cheaper lands, nearby markets, less cost of production. They are averaging three dollars a barrel for their best fruit, with no market for seconds. The same prices to us, owing to our advantages, would mean five to six dollars per barrel and markets for cheaper grades. What is the reason for this vast discrepancy? Coöperation. Does it need any more convincing argument? How much longer shall we talk and argue, while the other produces and sells?

No doubt there are many present who recall the time New England produced her own corn, wheat, etc., but now she purchases in the West. Are you going to permit history to repeat the story and purchase your fruit? I am not an alarmist, but you must not overlook the fact that in another year the Panama canal will be open to traffic. At the same time our European apple market will open to our western competitors and unless all signs fail they will land fruit at foreign parts at thirty-five cents per box. Under our present methods of production and packing how long can we hope to control these markets? To dominate them we must use the progressive culture, grading, packing, and marketing methods of our competitors,—the Pacific coast orchardists.

During the past year, I have received numerous complaints through our new foreign consuls of our careless pack, and I regret to say most of them mention New England States in particular. It is time to "stop, look and listen," the locomotive and cars are coming.

I was very much impressed at our last meeting with the address of a former secretary of this society on the want of proper storage facilities. This, at present, is one of the greatest crying needs of the fruit growers of this State. Thousands of barrels of apples pass annually into the hands of speculators simply because of lack of facilities for storing. To my mind, cold storage and coöperation go hand in hand. When we solve the former, the latter will follow, enabling us to avoid the fall rush of fruit to glutted markets and make a more equal distribution at all seasons, and insuring a larger profit to the grower without adding any hardships to the consumer.

I was approached a short time back, as to the feasibility of the erection of a cold storage warehouse in the fruit belt. It did not, however, in this particular case, appeal strongly to me, as the capital would come from out of the State entirely, while I firmly believe it should and could be raised here among our citizens, who have the welfare of their own State more at heart. This proposition, however, illustrates the fact that if we do not take the initiative, the opportunity will be lost and I recommend the appointment of a committee of this society with power to act if sufficient capital can be procured. To accomplish anything a beginning must be made.

Four years ago at the earnest solicitation of this society, the legislature passed the Maine apple law, without any appropriation to secure its enforcement. We are all too familiar with the present conditions, which seem nearly a calamity to those who are doing their utmost to make our apples known not as the "big red apple" but the "best red apple." There are a number of sections of the law which are open to criticism and for the purpose of discussion and that the sense of this meeting may be laid before our next legislature, I recommend the following changes:—Omit after Sections 2, 3, 4, "Any package, barrel or box of apples containing more than ten per cent of apples below this standard shall not be marked, etc."

The success of our western competitors is in their honest package, not superior quality.

This is the age of progress; we must keep in the procession or be spectators. This will work no hardships except on such parties as pack 106 barrels of fruit in six hours with a crew of five men, as was done in the town of Monmouth last winter. Let us be honest and pack our goods true to label, leaving the tolerance to the court or proper authorities.

If our present law was enforced we could not secure a conviction under a tolerance of fifteen or sixteen per cent. Surely five or six per cent is sufficient. This, I am informed, has been the usual custom in all pure food decisions, relating to protein.

When the apple buyers of the world understand that the word Maine means just what the label reads, the results will surprise the opposition to this change. Try and be convinced.

Your presiding officer has made his stencil bring a premium price, and surely what a few can do many can accomplish with much better and quicker results. The world's greatest trust, the Standard Oil, has been accused of watered stock, but we never heard that they watered their oil.

Let us also recommend a change in size of our apple box to 18x11 1-2x10 1-2 owing to the simplicity with which it can be packed in comparison with our present standard, and also for the sum of two thousand dollars for the enforcement of chapter 247 of the public laws of 1909. In this connection I have heard the argument advanced, that more can be accomplished by education, than by statute; that you cannot prevent a dishonest pack by law. Possibly not entirely, but we can control it. You cannot prevent murder by statute, but how many of this audience would repeal the laws relative to murder for this reason?

At the same time I believe in education along packing lines and our State Department of Agriculture has offered to give box packing demonstrations in the orchards, upon request.

I do not know how many have availed themselves of this offer, but coming at the busy season, I fear but few. Such demonstrations given in the granges during the winter months, would no doubt be well attended and do much to improve general conditions. Of one thing we can rest assured, the apple box for fancy fruit has come to stay.

A story is in circulation so absurd that it may seem foolish to refer to it here and I would not except for the fact that it is so persistent in its circulation and it has come to me from so many sources. I want it distinctly understood (and I am quite sure I voice the sentiments of every grower present) that there never has been and never will be on the part of this society any effort to prevent the sale of *any* grade of apples grown in this State. All we are fighting for is that they should be so graded and marked as to truly represent the stencil. The farmers who listen to the doleful tale of some apple buyers, that they will not be able to sell their number two apples, if this law is enforced, can rest easy that there is a market for their fruit, but if they persist in growing number two grade it must be sold as number two and not as fancy. At Augusta last year we had a good sample of a fancy pack of one of our prominent buyers. The man who circulates such a story among a class of growers who do not understand that the apple law is intended as an uplift to the industry, certainly is no credit to that industry, his state, or nation, in trying to create the prejudice that he may still continue his dishonest methods.

Our society has made such rapid growth in the past few years that it is impossible with our present funds, to keep up the past high standard of our meetings and perform all the various committee work without assistance from the cities we visit, and while it has been freely given in the past, it places your officers in an unenviable position and bars us from visiting some places where the fruit industry would be much benefited. I therefore suggest requesting the legislature to increase our stipend to two thousand dollars. I am firmly convinced in making this suggestion that standing committees of this society can in time rectify many existing evils. As an illustration look at the tremendous increase in ocean freights on apples in the last few years, an increase worse than injustice.

Look at the arbitrary rates of the M. C. R. R. on the so-called "freezer" cars, a special rate of three dollars per car to Portland and five dollars to Boston on apples, while cream and other commodities are carried at regular tariff rates. We surely are not making an unreasonable request and in a State where the fruit industry is so important, the State should give freely to assist such work in every legitimate channel.

Your officers had hoped at this meeting to be able to set a standard of sizes to assist the judges in awarding prizes, and while we have procured much valuable data, we did not feel that we had sufficient to add to our rules and rather than commit an exhibitor to an injustice, preferred deferring same for further consideration.

A very large per cent of the fruit raised at Highmoor Farm is Ben Davis and it certainly, as a rule, is not a good business proposition to dispose of them early in the season. Here the storage question is again a serious matter and our member of the Station Council has requested me to call your attention to it, with the request that we endorse their action in asking for an appropriation of five thousand dollars from the State for the erection of a cold storage plant to be used also for experimental work.

This society has accomplished a great work in the past for the fruit growers of this State, and it has always seemed strange to me that its membership has not increased in proportion. I am inclined to believe that we have not been active enough in extending invitations to our fellow fruit growers to join us. At our field meeting at Highmoor Farm, an appeal I made was met with a ready response and believing there will be a great many visitors with us here, who would be glad to join our ranks, if given a personal invitation, I would like to see a special committee appointed at this meeting to solicit members.

· Since we met together last, God, in His infinite wisdom, has seen fit to remove from our midst one of those noble characters which are only too rare, one who not only crowned his own personal work with success, but gave freely of his time to his fellow farmers, to this society and to his State. We have lost a member of sterling worth of character and mind. Such a man was our ex-president of this society, the Hon. Z. A. Gilbert of Greene.

ADDRESS: LIFE, HABITS AND DEVELOPMENT OF THE HONEY BEE.

By Dr. James P. Porter, Worcester, Mass.

Mr. President, ladies and gentlemen and fellow scholars:

I have here on the screen the representation of a cucumber. Every year in the State of Massachusetts the cucumber growers use one thousand colonies of bees. They use them in order to make sure that their cucumber vines produce cucumbers. As many of you know, the cucumber is peculiar, the male flower being on one plant and the female flower on another plant. Now in order that the cucumber vine produce cucumbers the grower, before he made use of the bee, would take a little brush and go from one plant to another and carry the dust or the pollen that is grown on one plant and put it on another. Unless that is done the cucumbers which grow in the greenhouses will not produce, so the cucumber grower has found that each season he must bring to his greenhouse a colony of bees and allow those bees to fly inside. They go from one blossom to another and fertilize those cucumbers, and thus he is enabled to produce a crop. We see then that there is direct use for the honey bee in the fertilization of the cucumber plant. Now I want to show you something of the life and the habits of the honey bee, and above all to show you the relation of the bee to the work of the apple grower.

This slide represents the different parts of the blossoms of plants. One part of the plant produces the pollen or the yellow dust which you find on the apple blossom and on the blossoms of many other plants. Another part when a grain of pollen falls on it is fertilized. The grain of pollen passes down through a tube, and therefore this plant will produce seed. Darwin, working nearly a hundred years ago, found that a great many of our plants will not produce seeds unless they are properly fertilized and properly pollenized. That means that the pollen from one plant must be carried to another, or, in other words, we must have cross fertilization. If we do not have cross fertilization very soon we shall have too close inbreeding and the plants will deteriorate, and the apples grown on apple trees of course will become poorer and poorer.

You can see that as the bee flies from one blossom to another blossom he has some dust on his body and as he alights he fertilizes the plants. Therefore the bee is most useful in this process of cross-fertilization. Darwin is responsible for the statement that nature abhors self-fertilization; that is, that we must have some method of cross fertilization.

This picture shows the worker bee, the bee in the hive which does all the work or most of it. Here we have the queen bee. The queen bee can best be described by this phrase,—that she is an egg-laying machine, and more of that I will show you later. Here we have the drone which exists for the purpose of fertilizing the female and for no other purpose. In this cell you see the egg as laid by the queen bee. Now that egg is carefully cared for and it is fed by the worker bee inside the hive. We may never understand the honey bee until we know from whence it has come. Flying around among our flowers and fertilizing them are a great many other bees in addition to the honey bee, and these are the bees from which the honey bee has developed. I show you here a little bee which digs a hole in the ground. That hole is lined, pollen and nectar are put in the bottom of the hole, the egg is laid which you can see on top of the nectar and pollen, the hole is closed up, and the little bee goes away and allows that egg to hatch and feed on the food stored there, and after a little while the little bee flies out and gathers nectar and pollen just as the mother bee has done. You see that the bee has dug the hole in the ground, but now runs it horizontally after it has entered the ground a little ways. It lines this hole with leaves cut from the rose. After a while this little bee hatches and grows into a bee and digs its way out and goes the way of the mother bee. This slide will show you the bee flying over toward the entrance of that hole in the ground. Here we have several nests, all with a common entrance, and that suggests the beginning of social life in bees. Here we find by digging down into the ground several females, in there together, and there again we have the first example of bees living together.

This shows you a little bee which searches out a snail shell and uses that as a nest. It does not go to the trouble of digging a hole in the ground. It lays its eggs in the different turns of the snail shell, and then covers the shell with pine needles and bits of straw to protect it from other insects.

Here we have a very interesting condition of things because we have several cells instead of one. This mother bee lives until she sees the young hatch and grow, and this is said to be the first example in bee development of real contact of mother and child, and it forms an important step in the development of the honey bee.

Here is a very interesting thing. The nest which I have just shown you, with several cells, belongs here. That is placed in the ground, being reached by a tunnel down below. That tunnel does not end with this nest. It goes on below. We have been set to thinking, trying to reason out why that hole went on below. Some say it is for the purpose of allowing the bee, when danger threatens, to run below. Not so, I believe. That hole below the nest proper is for the purpose of draining the nest of water and keeping it dry, and so we must with our honey bees at all times keep them free from moisture. In fact, the reason so many of them die during the winter is that they become covered with moisture.

Here we have a bumblebee's nest. You know that at one time the growing of red clover was introduced in Australia but it was found that from the clover grown in Australia seed could not be produced. What was the reason? The reason was this, —that they had no insect to fertilize the clover. Along with the clover they had to import the bumblebee, and after that was done they had no further trouble in growing seed from their clover. That shows you that the bumblebee is a most valuable insect. It ought to be cared for much more than it is. And indeed, we ought in this country to begin to develop a honey bee with a long tongue which could do the same work as the bumblebee now does. I want to tell you a very interesting story about the bumblebee. If you visit the nest of the bumblebee early in the morning you will find that above that nest, which is mound-like above the ground, along about daylight there appears a large bee, as it were on the roof of the house, and he begins to fan his wings rapidly and make a buzzing noise. What is that for? It has been found that if you remove him from the top of the nest another one will take his place. The first explanation was that the reason he appears there is to wake up the rest in the morning. We know, of course, that with us it requires one member of the family, usually, to wake the rest up in the morning. That was thought to be true of the bumblebee, but it is not the case. The real explanation seems to be that those bumblebees coming back at night loaded with food from clover and other plants and lying there in the nest all night make the air impure so that the nest needs ventilation, and the first thing in the morning it is the business of the largest bees to mount to the top of the nest and fan their wings and get air currents so that the nest will be ventilated. The same thing takes place all the time in the honey bee hive. Ventilation is carried on by the bees fanning their wings.

We have here a very interesting bee, not a native of this country, but you see the life is much more complex. This comb is made to hang from a branch of a tree. Above you have the cells made for the storing of honey, below you have the cells made for the workers, in which the workers grow and develop, and finally come out and do the work of the colony; you have the large drone cells, much larger than the others, and at the bottom you have the large queen cells. I can tell you a very interesting thing about the honey bee. Just as soon as the workers find they have no queen in the hive they set about to produce a queen. How do they do that? They build one of these large cells from a small worker's cell, they begin to feed that young bee inside, wormlike now in form, a peculiar kind of food called royal jelly and they soon develop there a queen bee simply by feeding this young a different kind of food. You will notice of course that the queen cell is a good deal thicker and heavier. That is to protect her from the cold. The temperature must be kept constant in this hive.

This shows you the real honey bee hanging as the one shown before. It has been found that bees will live out-of-doors. They do not have to have hives in which to live, and indeed they can pass through the winter, a very cold winter, hanging out of doors with no protection whatever. Formerly of course they lived out of doors. A little later they lived in the trees in the forest, and since we domesticated them they live in the hives which we make for them.

This is a very interesting section from a bee hive. You see here a great brood of worker cells and along here a great row of queen cells. We have found that after we have had a hive of bees two or three years the queen wears out. She gets old, she cannot lay eggs as rapidly as she did once, so we have to take out the old queen and put in a new one. For this reason we have men who make it their chief business to grow queens. They cut out these queen cells, put them up to the top of the hive where the temperature is constant, and move them along gradually, and then these little bees feed them royal jelly. They take them out gradually and sometimes they can produce as many as three hundred queens in one season from a single hive. You will see that the comb cells are larger for the drones than for the workers. Here you have drone cells used for the storage of honey. That recalls to my mind a very interesting story. It is found by bee-keepers that when bees lack room in the hive they store the honey in the drone cells; these being larger hold more honey, and it is said that the bees reason that out and show wisdom thereby. But such is not the case. They use these larger drone cells for the simple reason that you, when you are in a crowd and excited, will do things which you would not do when you are alone or when you are with the members of your family; that is, they fall back on some old way of doing. Here you have the queen cells shown in their characteristic grouping. It has been found that the queen bees need to be cared for every moment by the worker bees. And so you see the queen bee in the center, larger than the worker bees and surrounded by them. They follow every movement she makes. They go wherever she goes. They guard, protect and keep her clean. Of course she is wandering over the cells here, laying eggs in them. How does she know when to lay an egg which will produce a drone and when to lay an egg which will produce a worker? Well, I don't think she knows very much about it. She lays an egg which will produce a drone, which is a fertilized egg, she lays an egg which will produce a worker, when she comes to a cell of a certain size, and I think that is all there is about it. She is an egg-laying machine in the truest sense of the word.

The next slide will show you something about the ant. You know among the trees, in the grass, all through the soil, we have ants everywhere, and sometimes they give us no little trouble. Now the queen ant is very different from the queen bee. After she mates with the male she drops to the ground, searches out some spot which is protected, some hole in the ground—lays the eggs, takes care of them, takes care of the young after they hatch and until they are grown, and then they take care of her. You see a condition of things very different from that of the queen bee who has to be cared for at every step. The queen ant is in no sense a laying machine, or not at all in the same way as the queen bee.

Here you can see very clearly the different stages in the growth of the bee,—the development of the bee from the egg to the adult. Now you know that in the hive when one queen hatches she rules the colony. She goes about over the cells and if there are other queens about to hatch she stings them unless she is prevented from doing it. That means you have a community here which must be ruled over by one queen and one queen only.

Here we have the brain and the nervous system of the bee. Up at the top you see the little bunch of nervous matter which enables the bee to do all the work which it does,—most wonderful little mass of matter in the world.

I wish you would pay particular attention to this picture. Here we have the brain of the drone. I want you to notice how narrow it is and thin. He doesn't do much. He exists only for the purpose of mating with the queen and that does not require much brains. Here is the brain of the queen and you notice how much thicker it is than the brain of the drone. At the top you have the brain of the worker, and you know that the worker bee does nearly all the work in the hive, all but the laying of eggs, and sometimes that, although its eggs produce males. You can find nowhere, so far as I know, a more interesting and more significant set of figures than these. For we find when we examine the brain of man, the brain of adult man, the brain of the feeble-minded man, the same condition as we find here between the worker bee, the queen bee and the drone bee. The feeble-minded child has a brain which is something like this, very small and little developed. Another

24

interesting point. Notice the size of this nerve which runs to
the eye in the male. Notice the size of the nerve which runs
to the eye in the queen, which is smaller, and notice the size
of the nerve which runs to the eye in the worker, which is
still smaller. The nerve in the male is large because the male
has but one use for his eye in his whole lifetime and that is
to follow the queen in her flight and mate with her, so he
must have keen vision. The same thing can be said of the
nerves which run to the feelers or antennae, those parts of the
bee which allow him to find out about the objects which he
meets by feeling of them and smelling of them. The nerve
in the male is large, in the female is large, in the worker small.
That is, the worker in order to do all of its work does not need
to have so keen a sense of smell as the male in order that he
may in connection with his sight follow the female and thus
mate with her. Up here you have the face of the bee shown.
In the middle you see these three small dots. Those are the
three small eyes; on the sides you see those great prominences,
which are the compound eyes. They exist on many birds. The
small eyes of course see objects near by. The large eyes see
objects farther away, but in a blurred sort of way, not clear
as our eyes see. You also see the feelers or the bee's nose.
Now imagine, if you please, if you had a nose as long as your
arm and could move it about, what could you do with it. Well,
you could feel out blossoms, plants that have fragrance, and of
course you could get your food from them, and that is just
precisely what the bee does. It has keen sense of smell because that nose is all covered with fine hollows and it goes
to the plants that are fragrant. I spoke a while ago of the desirability of having bees with a long tongue. European peoples
accuse us in this country of not caring anything about the kind
of bees which we breed. We don't care what breed of bees
we have. We don't spend much time and knowledge in getting
a fine breed of bees or in developing good stock. We take
what we can get. If we could develop a bee with a long tongue,
that bee would be much more useful to us in the pollenization
of our plants. It is said that the honey, bees' wax, etc., produced in the United States are worth annually $20,000,000.
It is also said that the value of the bee to the apple grower

and the florist is certainly five times as much annually, that is, $100,000,000.

Here we have shown a bee hive, the entrance to which leads into a greenhouse where cucumbers are grown. It is much better, of course, to have two entrances to the hive, one leading to the outside and one to the inside, otherwise you will find that you lose your hive of bees too soon. That is, the bees will go to the inside, beat their wings against the glass and so many are killed that you have to replace them with a new hive. Here we have the entrance to one of our hives shown. These are the sentinel bees. Now, as you all know, each bee in the hive has something definite to do. They are the sentinels that guard the entrance. There are those who take care of the ventilation and they are stationed here also, fanning their wings to make currents of air. We see the nurses who take care of the young bees, the worker bees who go out after pollen, the worker bees who go out after nectar, and the bees that take care of the queen; also the bees that clean the hive, keep it perfectly clean. There are the bees that stop up the holes with wax. It is found that these bees remain a certain distance apart. If you remove one the rest will change their position to take care of so much entrance, for often robber bees come to the hive. There are always people that want to get something for nothing and they want to steal it from somebody else. To prevent these robber bees all we have to do is to narrow this entrance down instead of allowing it to reach clear across the hive. We thus can prevent the robber bees from coming in, helping thus the sentinel bees with their work by making this entrance say an inch and a half wide instead of the length of the whole hive.

We have near Worcester, Massachusetts, a man who makes a striking success of growing cantaloupes. He has done this for years. He is an excellent bee-keeper also, and I think one explanation of his success is the fact that he cares so well for his bees and that he keeps enough of them so that they fertilize his melons for him. The melon is like the cucumber, different sexes on different plants, male sex on one plant, female on another and cross fertilization must take place.

This slide shows the kitchen pea. All of you know it. You can be certain that any plant that has a blossom which is very much modified, as this one is, takes especial pains—unconsciously, of course, to attract the bee. The bee flies to this blossom, alights on the wings and another part is lifted up and touches the bee on the breast. The bee in leaving this blossom gets the pollen. Thus we have cross pollenization in the kitchen pea, and without that we should find the seed of the kitchen pea would deteriorate.

Here we have another plant which is most interesting. It is so constructed that, when the bee lights on the flower a portion is made to come down and strike the bee on the back, thus scattering pollen grains all over the back of the bee. Now when that bee visits another flower later in the season it finds the female part developed and what happens is that the dust covered part of the bee comes in contact with the female part of the flower and the flower is cross-fertilized. There you have a flower so developed that the weight of the bee figures in cross-fertilization.

Here we have a still more interesting condition of things, and it was this plant, one of the orchids, which Darwin studied so much. He found that when the bee alighted it touched a spring which let loose the pollen baskets, and they stuck fast to the head of the bee. First they stood upright, then they bent over a little as they hung fast to the head of the bee, later they bent over so that they hung at right angles to the head of the bee. Now the bee visits another flower. What is the first thing to happen? As he visits another flower this bunch of pollen which sticks out touches the female part of the flower and you have cross-fertilization. It seems to me that a thing like that proves beyond question that the plants have evolved or developed or grown along with the insects and that the one cannot do without the other. The bee visits the plant for nectar, for food, for pollen. The plant must have the visit of the bee in order to be cross-fertilized.

Here we have a picture of bee hives as they keep them in New Mexico. We see that they have an orchid also, and it is also a fact that they grow a kind of clover. These three things go hand in hand, one depending on the other. The orchid is cross-fertilized by the bees, and so is the clover. The bees get nectar and pollen from the blossom.

We find that when we start out to test the bee's color vision we have to take very careful pains. We make artificial flowers, bachelors' buttons, for instance, and we find that bees will go to these flowers although they are covered by glass. We find we can get the bees to go to artificial flowers as well as to natural flowers, thus proving beyond question that plants have their beautiful color in order to attract bees, so that cross fertilization may be accomplished. The raspberry is very dependent upon the bee for cross fertilization. We find that when we make an artificial raspberry blossom the bees come to it as often as they do to the natural flower.

This shows a section of the apple blossom. It is proven that if you go out in the orchard and collect say two hundred apples fallen from the tree, you will find that all but eight or ten have fallen because they have not been cross-fertilized. What happens when a bee revisits the same blossom? He fertilizes every part of the apple blossom. Now this apple is a poor one, that is, it is not developed on one side; it remains undeveloped because the bees have done their work imperfectly. They do it imperfectly because there are not enough present. Therefore apple growers should keep bees also. The bees do their work imperfectly because weather conditions will not allow them to come out in the spring. If you have a period of damp cold weather when bees don't fly, you will find that many of your apple trees have apples falling from them when the apples are small. Now the reason for that is that the bees don't fly out in such weather. We should have the bees right near the trees then.

This is my last slide and I want to call your attention especially to this one thing. Apple growers, be very careful when you spray the apple trees. A bee-keeper who is near by has a perfect right to complain in the strongest language if you spray the trees while the trees are in blossom. It is not necessary and many states have laws against it, and we should have. There is no necessity for it. Spraying will do just as much good before or after the blossoming season, and you will not kill your neighbor's bees, or your own. They will do you much more good than any amount of spraying at that time.

WEDNESDAY AFTERNOON.

THE VARIETAL ADAPTABILITY PROBLEM AND ITS BEARING ON COMMERCIAL ORCHARDING.

By H. P. GOULD, Pomologist, U. S. Department of Agriculture.
Members of the Maine State Pomological Society, Ladies and Gentlemen:

I do not presume that it is necessary for me to offer any defense of the subject which is presented for discussion at this time. It may be said in passing, however, that it was suggested, in substance at least, in a letter which I received some weeks ago from the President of your society. This, indeed, furnished me with an adequate topic for it was quite in line with much of my thinking in connection with my work in the Department of Agriculture.

If there is any consistency in the way in which my subject is worded, as it appears on your program, it implies that there is a problem in connection with the adaptability of varieties; it likewise implies that the problem has some bearing on commercial orcharding. We want to find out just what that problem is if we can, and what its solution is. If it bears some relation to success in commercial orcharding, it is important that we know it.

Now, at the outset, the fact ought to be very clearly in mind that a variety is not a definite and fixed thing. A variety as it develops in an orchard in Maine, or in Pennsylvania; in Virginia, or in Georgia; in Missouri, or in Oregon, is the product of the conditions under which it has grown. As the environment varies so the results vary, as manifested in the behavior of different fruits and of different varieties.

But not all varieties respond in the same way or in the same degree to the same or similar influences. For instance, your most extensively grown variety, the Baldwin, decreases in value the farther south it is grown. I have seen it in many orchards in Virginia, where it was planted in an earlier day when it was assumed that because it was good in one place it would of necessity be equally good in all places. While it still retains many of the unmistakable Baldwin characteristics when grown in Virginia and other southern sections, it becomes a very inferior and all but worthless fall apple, except possibly when produced at some of the highest elevations in the mountains. Similarly the Northern Spy at southern points becomes a fall variety—a *fall* variety in more ways than one—because the fruit nearly all falls to the ground before it is ripe, and whether it drops or not the most of it rots before maturity; and further, it lacks the crispness and flavor characteristic of this variety when it is grown under favorable conditions. Again, the Yellow Bellflower, which is familiar to most of you, is usually marketed in August when grown in the Ozark region, as it is in considerable quantities, but little does an Ozark-grown Yellow Bellflower resemble the well grown Yellow Bellflower of the northern orchards. In the Ozarks, it has a pale lemon-yellow color and a sharp, cutting, acid flavor with the peculiar characteristic Yellow Bellflower flavor entirely wanting. And the Winesap, which is to many apple districts in the middle latitudes about what the Baldwin is to the northern districts becomes, when grown in "Baldwin country" what a typical Virginian would call a "very sorry apple," being small, tough in texture and very poorly finished.

A single example will suffice to call attention to the fact that not all varieties respond in the same degree to the influence of conditions. The White Pippin, a variety which I think is not uncommon in Maine, is widely distributed though not extensively grown in any region so far as I know; but I have seen it in the South, in Missouri, in Kansas, and in other widely separated points. The strange thing about it is that it shows so little variation in all these different regions. While there is a difference in its keeping quality, so far as flavor, texture, external markings, etc., are concerned, a White Pippin grown in Maine is not materially different from one grown in the South, in Missouri or elsewhere, so far as my observation goes.

And so we might go on indefinitely multiplying such examples to show how a variety is the product of the conditions under which it develops. In passing, it may not be without

some interest to state that of all the factors of environment
which influence the behavior of varieties, doubtless the climate,
in its complexity, is the most potent of all. I wish we knew
more about it but until we do, it is probably safe to assume
that in the climate factor, heat and moisture constitute, in their
extremes, their distribution and their sum-total, the most important elements which determine the behavior of varieties,
granting, of course, that other conditions do not preclude the
possibility of growing any variety of the species. If for instance the soil of a particular site is so water-logged because
of poor drainage that it is impossible to grow an apple tree of
any variety, all climatic factors obviously cease to operate as
normal limiting or modifying influences.

Now if the Baldwin and the Northern Spy, referring to them
merely as examples, are good in the North and worthless or
nearly so in the South; if the Winesap, a leading variety in
middle latitudes, is entirely impossible as a useful sort in the
North, is it not likely that important differences exist in the behavior of varieties even within the limits of the territory in
which they.are of recognized value and importance? That this
condition actually prevails and more commonly perhaps than
we have noticed is not difficult of demonstration.

In an address before the Maryland Horticultural Society a
year ago, Professor Waugh called attention to the fact that
in the Berkshire Hills it is possible to draw a very well defined
line above which the Baldwin cannot be grown successfully
and below which it develops to a good degree of perfection. I
have made a similar observation with regard to the Winesap
grown at different elevations in Virginia.

In some of the mountain orchards in that state (Virginia),
the Winesap behaves just about as I have seen it do in Maine,
so far as the degree of perfection which it develops is concerned. The Grimes Golden apple grown at a certain elevation in North Carolina will keep a month or more longer than
it will when grown at an elevation perhaps 500 or 600 feet
lower than the first site. In the case referred to, the two
orchards in question are owned by the same party and they are
separated only by a comparatively short distance.

In a West Virginia peach orchard, where there is some 300
feet difference between the elevation of the lower and upper

sides, the same variety usually blossoms two or three days earlier on the lower side than it does on the upper side. There is also a corresponding difference in the ripening of the fruit in some seasons.

If you will note the fact, the differences in the behavior of the varieties just named are very definitely associated with the differences in the elevations at which they are grown. This incidentally emphasizes the importance or at least the influence of elevation in the behavior of varieties. But it should be noted that differences in elevation are primarily differences in climate, especially differences in temperature, so far as they affect fruit growing.

However, not all local differences in the behavior of a variety are directly traceable to marked differences in elevation. The Yellow Newtown apple, or the Albemarle Pippin as it is called in some regions, appears to be unusually susceptible to soil conditions, or what for lack of more definite information is attributed to soil conditions, very marked variations being readily apparent when it is grown on certain soil types; but the relative locations of these soil types with reference to atmospheric drainage, etc., may possibly have as much influence on this variety as have the differences in the types themselves.

You would, perhaps, like to have illustrations which are nearer home. I have no doubt that there is an abundance of them, but I do not happen to know about them. The ones I have mentioned are used merely as types to call attention to the fact that there may be marked local variations within the variety. If there are any principles involved in these variations, as there surely must be, they are operative everywhere and the evidence of their application is only a matter of observation. In Maine, there are plenty of differences based on relative elevation, soil types, latitude, etc., and if these factors are of importance in any region in accordance with fixed laws, they are likewise of importance here. And I venture the suggestion that, with your attention called to the matter, many of you can bring to mind particular orchards, or sections in particular orchards, in which some variety habitually does remarkably well, or it may be it is noticeably poor. No generalization can be made on such a speculative basis as this, yet where there are such noticeable differences in the varieties as have been referred to, the chances are even, at least, that they are due directly to the conditions or to differences in the conditions under which they are grown.

The experience of apple growers in some of the well known apple districts in taking advantage of the special manifestations of varietal adaptability should be suggestive in this connection.

In the Grand Valley of Colorado, they planted pretty nearly everything in the earlier days in the way of apple varieties, as has been the case in many fruit regions during the pioneering period. But, as time has gone on, and the growers in the Grand Valley have become wise, they have gradually eliminated the undesirable sorts until now the orchards consist largely of four varieties which have proved to be of special value under the conditions in that valley. While many trees comprising numerous different sorts still exist, they are gradually being top-worked to one or another of the four leading varieties. In fact, I have never been in a district where so many trees, relatively speaking, have been top-worked as is the case in the Grand Valley.

Another example is the Hood River Valley in Oregon, where two varieties, the Yellow Newtown and the Esopus comprise a very large proportion of all the apple trees in the entire distriet. This is due to no other reason than the high degree of perfection to which these varieties develop and their satisfactory bearing proclivities under the Hood River Valley conditions. It is worth while to note the fact that both of these varieties are very restricted in their distribution and are not to be recommended for planting generally because of the idiosyncrasies with regard to their adaptation to conditions. But these two sorts have made Hood River famous. In fact if it were not for the Esopus and the Yellow Newtown apples, I doubt if anybody in this audience would know there is such a town on the map as Hood River, and I venture to submit that all this was because somebody in an earlier day was keen enough and observing enough, and far-sighted enough to appreciate the value of these varieties in the apple industry of that region and to lead the way in the planting of them.

Again, they claim in the Bitter Root Valley of Montana, that they can "beat the world" in growing the McIntosh. As a result of its merits under the conditions in this valley, the McIntosh is more largely planted in some portions of the valley, than any other sort. Another case of merely finding out a variety that was particularly well adapted to the condition and then being business-like enough to plant it as a leading sort.

Now, as I think of it, what important and widely known variety is distinctively a Maine apple? What variety, when mentioned by name, instantly calls forth the remark, "Yes, that's the apple they grow up in Maine." Or what section in this State has been made famous as the Hood River Valley has been made famous by its specialty—the growing of a variety, or at most a few varieties of apples, because of their superior merit in that particular section? The fault may be mine, if I view these queries in a negative way. Yet I submit the question: Has the variety problem as the apple growers in this State have to face it, been studied very much from the standpoint of the exceptional adaptation of varieties to particular sections of the State?

Of course, it does not necessarily follow that such marked cases of special adaptation of particular varieties as occur in the Hood River Valley and the Bitter Root Valley would be paralleled in Maine. Yet high hills and valleys, upland meadows and river bottoms, seashore and lake influences, and soil types of wide diversity all occur and each with its own little domain of local climatic and other factors of influence; and as the northern part of the State is approached, low winter temperatures become still more a complicating factor. There is no lack in the diversity of conditions prevailing within the borders of the State and under which apples are grown. And it would be strange indeed if there are not well defined cases of varietal adaptability of great practical value within the reach of Maine apple growers.

It may take close observation and require some reshaping of our mode of thought to correctly interpret the things which have been before our eyes so frequently that their significance is unseen. But I'll venture to guess that there are many orchards belonging to you growers here in which the Baldwin,

for instance, habitually excells for its excellence; orchards of
which it is said in the various communities in which they are
located: "It produces the finest Tompkins King of any orchard
in this whole region." Or, it may be that someone says of an
orchard: "It grows good Kings, but I never saw a Yellow
Bellflower come out of it that was fit to eat."

Needless to say, these are hypothetical illustrations used
merely to represent types of cases which are not uncommon,
but the meaning of which is not always rightly interpreted and
the practical bearing of which is sometimes overlooked. The
only object I have in presenting them here is by way of calling your attention to the fact that such cases of marked varietal adaptability are not uncommon and to suggest that where
they become apparent they offer a clue which, other things
being equal, ought to be followed to its logical conclusion. If
the conditions in an orchard give markedly favorable results
with a particular variety, and that variety is a good commercial
sort then plant it and make a specialty of it; if some other
variety established in the orchard seems less desirable when all
its merits have been duly weighed, then top-work it to the better sort. Cut out the star boarder in the orchard as the dairyman cuts out that kind of boarder in his herd of cows. In
other words, take advantage of the information that Nature
thrusts upon you, and use it in a business-like fashion. Study
the behavior of your varieties with a view to ascertaining what
sorts are really best-fitted for filling the place for which you
are growing apples and which ones are not coming up to a
desirable standard either in the excellence of their development
or in the actual cash returns which they bring on the market.

This matter of considering carefully any special advantages
which you may possess for particular varieties, perhaps finds its
most important application in the further development of the
orchard interest of your State. In many regions the fruit tree
agent is a much more potent factor in determining what varieties
are planted than is the grower himself. The grower is more apt
to buy the varieties that the nursery agent suggests than he is
to buy those which, from a critical study of his own conditions
he is convinced are of the greatest usefulness to him. And if
the same community is canvassed by agents of different nurseries that are located in widely separated sections of the

country in which a wide range of varieties are propagated, the multiplicity of sorts that find their way into the orchards of the community is sometimes remarkable. A fine opportunity is thus made for the study of varietal adaptability, but it results rather disastrously so far as commercial interests are concerned.

Now it may be that some one would like to know what sort of a "program of varieties" the speaker would suggest for Maine orchards. I have to admit that I do not know of anything new to suggest nor any variety not already known to you that can be named in this connection which gives promise of a great future under your conditions. Note that I say "any *new* variety." You have the Baldwin, the Rhode Island Greening, Tompkins King, Northern Spy, McIntosh, Hubbardston, Wagener, and various others which are well known standard sorts and which are known to be sufficiently well adapted to a large part of the State to make the planting of them entirely safe as a rule. With these varieties you already have the making of a *great* future. For the northern parts of the State where hardiness of tree is of special importance, there is the Wealthy, the Northwestern, Patten Greening, Eastman, Malinda, Bethel and other hardy sorts from which to select.

Other varieties that are worth consideration for many sections but which are not much grown in this State, so far as I am aware, are Plumb Cider, Milding, Windsor, Mother, Arctic, Akin, and doubtless many others equally worthy of trial.

There are some varieties which, I understand, have been planted here quite extensively that in my judgment are of exceedingly doubtful value. If you want to know it, I suppose I have the Ben Davis especially in mind in making this remark. It is true that the Ben Davis has been the subject of many bitter attacks in recent years. It is a much maligned variety to be sure. But I know it has some staunch friends, even here in Maine—friends who insist that it is an apple of quality; that it is the most profitable variety they grow, etc. Even at the risk of calling down upon my head a "shower of protest;" at the risk of being told that I don't know what I'm talking about, I am going to advise against the planting of the Ben Davis here in Maine and for the reason that I believe you can do better. If the Ben Davis is your most profitable variety, then in my judgment there is something wrong somewhere in what you are getting out of your varieties which possess greater intrinsic merit. The Ben Davis has not sufficient merit to warrant such results. Many apple buyers are now refusing to take this variety or if they take it, it is under protest and only for the sake of getting others in the orchard where it is grown that are desirable.

If this variety could be marketed as a cooking apple and used only for that purpose, it would probably have a better standing. But justly or unjustly, an apple has to "pass muster" largely on the basis of its dessert quality.

I said a moment ago that I believed you could do better than to plant the Ben Davis. If you carefully study the list of possible sorts for planting, I am confident that you can find plenty of varieties which can be produced in Maine in such perfection that they can successfully compete with the best of fruit grown anywhere. The way of your greatest success lies in planting those varieties which are preeminently well adapted to your conditions, regardless of the fact that another variety may be the one which is of paramount importance in a region where conditions differing from your own obtain.

There is another phase of this Ben Davis matter that I want to mention. It is one which I believe is of a good deal of importance, though it has received but little attention. And in this connection I would use the Ben Davis as a type, rather than in its varietal significance, to represent all those varieties that are distinctly poor in dessert quality and which reach the market in considerable quantities. The most of you will admit, I think, that the Ben Davis is a very prominent member of such a group.

I do not know that it stands as a definitely enunciated economic principle, but I believe it is sound doctrine that when a commodity of poor quality repeatedly goes on the market in such large quantities that its presence is constantly conspicuous it is bound to injure the industry of which that commodity is a part. It must be admitted that a very considerable portion of the apples that enter into commerce are relatively poor in dessert quality. If my logic is sound, then the portion of the apple crop that enters the trade which is of poor quality must have .

an undesirable effect on the apple market. If this is really so, it is important, and we ought to realize it. Let us see.

That man who makes two blades of grass grow where only one grew before is said to be a benefactor of the race. Granting this, then the man who makes two apples grow where only one grew before or perhaps even a good apple where formerly a faulty one was produced, ought likewise to be considered a benefactor. Now I submit, from the standpoint of the apple grower who has apples to sell, that he who eats *two* apples where he only ate *one* before must also be something of a benefactor. This matter of dessert quality goes a long way in determining how many consumers eat two apples instead of one. If you will only think of it, you know this is true in your own individual cases as apple growers. It is doubly true in the case of the man who has to part with his hard-earned dollar in order to eat apples at all. If you don't like Ben Davis, and its kind, to eat yourself, why are you so un-reasonable as to expect the man in the city—the consumer—to like it any better than you do? That ultimate consumer is an important factor in your success as an apple grower. It's your job to make him eat as many apples as you can. The better he likes your apples the more of them he will eat. But he doesn't know varieties; he may know the name Ben Davis —it is doubtless the most widely known apple variety name in the world—but to the average consumer, it signifies only a red apple. He buys it. He eats it; and forthwith he says: "I am not very fond of apples anyway." It's a long time before he buys any more. But if he happens by chance to get a variety that really tickles his palate and makes his mouth water, he is going back in a hurry for more if he has a dollar in his pocket, or if his credit is good, lest the supply is exhausted before he can get to its source.

I believe, gentlemen, that my logic is sound, and that what I am trying to tell you about this quality matter is the plain, common, horse sense of the situation.

If what I have been saying is true, then the general effect of much of the fruit that goes into the apple market must be to restrict rather than to increase the demand for apples. I do not know that there is any actual proof of this proposition, but I know, and so do you, that if we care but little for a com-

modity, we get but little of it; the better we like it, the more
of it we buy, as a general proposition. We care but little for
apples of poor dessert quality; fruit of high quality appeals
strongly to everyone. From the argumentative standpoint, at
least, the conclusion is inevitable. I preach the growing of
high quality varieties.

There is yet another phase of the variety problem that I
wish to touch upon very briefly. Reference is made to the
matter of breeding, or if you please to the *making* of varieties
for particular purposes and for growing in definite regions.
Comparatively little has yet been done in the breeding of our
tree fruits. Almost every other field of crop production has
been benefited materially by the result of breeding new varieties
or new strains with definite ends in view. A very little has
been accomplished in the breeding of fruits; but relatively
speaking, the results thus far accomplished are so small as to be
almost negligible, yet enough to give some indication of what
the potential possibilities are. There are perhaps a half-dozen
varieties of apples grown in this State at present which include
the bulk of the fruit that is produced here. A large proportion
of this bulk is doubtless made up of the Baldwin. We may assume that, so far as experience goes, these varieties are the best
there are in existence for general commercial purposes here in
Maine. It does not follow by any means that these leading
varieties represent the limit of perfection attainable. On the
other hand it is entirely possible, even probable, that varieties
could be developed which on every count would excel those
now in existence. It would require a long time to develop a
new set of varieties but the field is a most promising, and to
me, a most alluring one.

With such improved varieties an accomplished fact, they
would of course take the place of old established varieties only
very gradually, but the change would surely come, once the
value of new sorts was recognized. An illustration of this
fact is now in progress. During the past ten or twelve years,
the Stayman Winesap apple has come into much prominence.
It is a variety of great value and it is gradually superceding the
Ben Davis in real Ben Davis districts. Stayman Winesap would
not be likely to be of any value in Maine. This variety is, I
think, doing more to check the planting of Ben Davis in many

regions than any other one thing. The Stayman Winesap apple is of double interest in this connection because it is the result of a definite, systematic effort to produce improved varieties. Its origination was not a chance accident.

That the improving of varieties specially adapted to particular regions is a practical conception and not merely a theoretical possibility is being emphatically demonstrated at the present time in the upper Mississippi Valley. In the early days, some of the people who did pioneer work in fruit growing in northern Iowa, proved to their own satisfaction that the varieties with which they were familiar in the East could not withstand the climatic conditions in their new home. The demonstration of this fact cost them dearly. One or two of these early settlers who had a clearer vision of the future than the others became convinced that apple growing could be made a successful line of industry if varieties could be obtained that would withstand climatic conditions. In northern Iowa, southern Minnesota and other territory in the upper Mississippi Valley, where the climatic conditions are similar the difficulty is not so much a matter of low winter temperatures as it is one of a very dry atmosphere, which, together with low temperatures, makes conditions which call for a tree of remarkable hardiness.

For more than 40 years Mr. Charles G. Patten, of Charles City, Iowa, in a most altruistic spirit, has been devoting a great amount of time and energy to breeding fruit varieties which would be especially adapted to the upper Mississippi Valley. Naturally his earlier efforts were not as well directed and his conceptions of what was needed were not as definitely formulated as has been the case in later years, but the results of his labors have already given several varieties of apples to that section of the country which are of great value. The Patten Greening, the Brilliant and the Eastman are examples; and these resulted from his early efforts. Though now nearly 80 years of age, Mr. Patten is still continuing this work with enthusiasm unabated and with his confidence in the possibilities of effort directed along these lines constantly increasing.

A recent visit to his experimental grounds which include about 20 acres, in which there are under test probably 15,000 to 20,000 seedlings which represent the best selections of the past 10 or 15 years' work, fully convinced me that it was only a question of continued effort when his vision of earlier years will become a great reality. He already has a dozen or fifteen varieties of native plums that have been developed by plant breeding methods which are probably better for his region than most other varieties now elsewhere obtainable. Among his seedlings there are a great number of very promising apples which, in hardiness of tree, mark very distinct advances. In the very nature of the case, much of his apple work is still in a transition period and much still remains to be done. But there is every reason to believe that the ultimate end of this work will give to the upper Mississippi Valley a collection of apple varieties which will be fully adapted to the peculiar conditions of that region. They may be expected also to be of value in other regions where hardiness of tree is a factor.

If Mr. Patten can develop varieties of apples and plums which make fruit growing successful in a region of the country where severe climatic conditions have largely restricted it, it does not require any stretch of the imagination to conclude that great improvement is within the range of possibilities in any region, but it will, of course, require the same sort of devotion to an ideal to develop such varieties as Mr. Patten has displayed in his work in Iowa. One of the greatest difficulties in the way of improving varieties generally is the tendency to let well enough alone, together with the fact that the stress of circumstances is not sufficiently severe to compel action, as was the case in Mr. Patten's region. Moreover, the improving of fruit varieties by breeding is a very long-term proposition. Perhaps this has been the most important reason of all why more attention has not been given to work of this kind. But one of the roads to a higher type of success in fruit growing leads in the direction of breeding varieties which are really fitted to particular conditions and for definite uses—not being satisfied merely with varieties that after a fashion can be made to do.

Now, in order to bring together in succinct form the points which I have tried to lay before you, I present in conclusion the following summary:

1. The fact of wide variability within the variety due to the influence of environment is fully established.

2. Because of the influence of conditions upon the behavior

of varieties, the matter of varietal adaptation becames one of fundamental importance in commercial fruit culture.

3. The influence of even local conditions is sometimes very marked. Because of this, the most critical discrimination in selecting varieties for planting is often necessary or at least contributes largely to success.

4. Every fruit grower who is a real student of his business will take advantage of any local adaptations which he can find and on the basis of them he will specialize with the variety or varieties that he finds are best suited to his conditons.

5. The growing of varieties that are not fully adapted to the conditions under which they are produced results in the grower being less able to successfully meet competition than is the case if he is growing varieties of potential value that reach the highest possible degree of perfection under his conditions.

6. The planting of varieties of poor dessert quality is to be dscouraged by every legitimate means because of the depressing influence of such varieties with reference to the consumption of fruit.

7. As a rule, it is better to plant for commercial purposes a few thoroughly tried and tested sorts known to be adapted to the conditions under which they are to be grown, rather than to take chances with doubtful varieties even though such varieties may be known to be of recognized value under some other conditions.

8. The planting of new and untried varieties for the purpose of determining their value under our own conditions is to be highly recommended if one is situated so that he can devote the necessary attention to such work, but it should be carried on apart from a commercial orchard. That is to say, a variety orchard cannot in the nature of things, be satisfactory as a commercial enterprise.

9. It does not follow that the varieties now shown by experience to be the best obtainable for any particular region necessarily measure the limit of perfection in varieties for the region.

10. The possibility of developing varieties that will be material improvements over present sorts is probably very great. Such development is possible by the application of well known plant breeding methods.

Proper attention to the propagation of present varieties is also doubtless a most efficient means of great improvement, but in due time there will be more definite evidence on this important matter.

With further reference to developing new varieties with a view to securing more valuable types, I want to urge upon this society the importance of this matter. Apparently the Baldwin, your most important commercial variety, is only barely hardy enough to withstand the climatic conditions which are likely to occur almost any winter. In fact, reports appear to indicate that the Baldwin tree has suffered serious injury in some parts of Maine several times during the past 10 years. The developing of a variety or varieties that shall possess all of the good points of the Baldwin and at the same time be better in dessert quality and hardier in tree would doubtless add untold value to the apple interests of Maine. That such an aim is possible of attainment there is no reason to doubt. The road to this end might be a long one. Then all the more reason for haste in beginning the work. The possibilities and the end in view are such as to emphatically justify the giving of early attention to it and when this society supports such a movement with its influence and its demands, it will, in my judgment, be taking a most important step forward in the future welfare of apple growing in Maine.

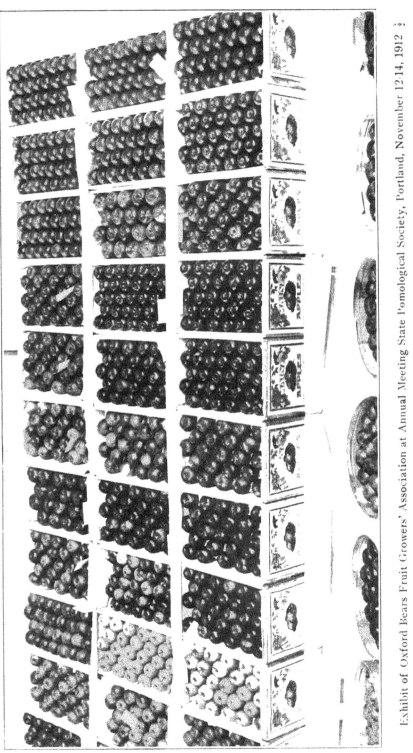

Exhibit of Oxford Bears Fruit Growers' Association at Annual Meeting State Pomological Society, Portland, November 12-14, 1912

WEDNESDAY EVENING.

THE APPLE INDUSTRY,—PAST, PRESENT AND FUTURE.

By MR. J. H. HALE, Glastonbury, Conn.

(Stenographic copy.)

From the earliest settlement of our country apples have been grown. Our first settlers brought seeds with them from the old country, and later scions, and in the march of progress across our great country the apple-pie and cider-mill have kept pace with the church and school-house even to the Pacific coast. Our early settlers planted apples simply for the home supply of food and drink, more largely drink, and it was well into the last century before commercial orcharding became of any considerable importance anywhere, and then only in the few older sections of our country. The few apple trees that were planted under the early conditions were about the home and home grounds, or along the fences of some of the culti- vated fields or mowing fields or pastures, and received practi- cally no attention except what occasionally came from cultivat- ing the fields adjoining them. The question of care as we know it today was never thought of. There was an occasional butchering in the way of a so-called trimming, simply to cut away lower branches that were in the way. That was the only style of trimming, and looking at trees between Boston and Portland this afternoon I saw any quantity of those old time butchered trees.

Our treatment of our trees was not bad method; there was simply no method at all in the old times. In the earlier days I suppose there was not the fungus and the insect troubles that we have today. But long before science came to our aid the fungus troubles of various kinds, and insect pests of every kind, were giving us a very inferior product. With the growth

of cities and towns there was a market for apples such as we
had, and they were marketed in old baskets, in secondhand
barrels, and very largely in bags or any way to get them there,
regardless of results upon the fruit itself; and consequently
we got very little reward for growing the apples and it was
easy enough to say that apple-growing didn't pay. A little later
came the city merchant, the commission merchant we have
heard about, or the wholesale dealer, who found that he could
get the apples in sufficient quantity on the market direct from
the farms and went out into the country and bought and packed
apples and taught us the trick of packing apples, of putting
the best there were in single facing on the head of the barrel,
and then a peck or half a bushel of a little inferior ones, but
the best there were out of the piles on the ground, and filling
up the barrel with anything. And these went upon the market
and apples were sold and handled in that way. Just the way
to destroy a market. Your worthy president of the Pomological Society, and toastmaster, said something about the inferior
packing of apples in Rhode Island, Connecticut and Massachusetts. We have a grange down in Connecticut—which I
hope you have up here in Maine—and it was my good fortune,
and bad fortune for the Pomona Grange of New London County,
to go down to one of their meetings a year or so ago. It was a
fruit meeting and they wanted me to talk. I never want to talk,
but they wanted me to talk on the fruit subject and it occurred to
me that we had better have a text. And to have a text for this
meeting I sent down to the wholesale fruit store and bought a
barrel of apples. It was marked XXX No. 1 Maine Baldwins.
We opened it up there before these Grangers of Connecticut
and we found nine fairly good No. 1 apples on the head—it
was faced up to look pretty well. The balance of the headings
were 2's and 3's. Down the next layer we had a moderate
number of 3's and the balance was low grade cider apples both
in size and appearance—XXX No. 1 Maine Baldwins. You
are just waking up. Within the last twenty-five or thirty years,
or the last quarter of the last century, with the establishment
of the agricultural college and the experiment station, the spread
of the horticultural and pomological societies, the work of the
institutes in the various states, the grange and the farmers'
club and all these organizations working together. there has

come to the aid of the apple tree, the apple grower and the apple consumer, science; the science of horticulture, the science of pomology, the handling of the trees and the plants, and the diseases, insects and fungus troubles, and all have brought about an entire change in the handling of the apple trees and their production. The trouble is, many have heard the story over and over again. We heard the first call of science to the aid of the apple tree, we received those instructions, but paid little or no attention. And so we got left in the great race, the great apple race that is going on today, and our brothers across the Pacific coast went and did what we had been told to do, in the same manner that they were told by some experimenters, by some scientists, by some few successful orchardists who grasped the idea. They have made a success of it; and what has been the result? During the last six, eight or ten years, there has been a wondrous change in the markets of the world, —the fruit stands, the grocery stores, and the tables everywhere, in the show of beautiful apples. Just take the fruit stands and the groceries anywhere as you remember them ten years ago, and then go today and see the bright life that has come into them, say ten months in the year, almost the whole year round, by the glorious beautiful apples that were grown first in the Pacific Northwest, and as shown down here in the hall might just as well have been grown here from the start, but we didn't get the idea soon enough. They have been our teachers. They have been the practical people who have shown us that beauty of appearance, honesty of pack and uniformity of the package were requisite. To be sure, back of all their show of fruit has been the great railroads. The great railroads have financed them by the hundreds of thousands of dollars in their fruit show, in their exhibits all over this country. It has been a land boom in the West. The object has been really to sell land and not apples. It has been a general scheme to get eastern money to go there, and hundreds of thousands of dollars have gone out of Portland, and out of other towns in Maine, have gone out of Boston and all over New England, to help develop these apple orchards in the Northwest, and to buy the lands and to buy interests in the community orchards where by an investment of five times what the land was worth in New England as a first payment and then constantly paying for a

number of years by and by you become the sole owner of a
five acre tract or ten acre tract that would support you to the
end of your days if the apples were to sell at the prices at which
they have sold in the past. But they will not. To any of you
who have an interest in a western community orchard, who
have paid two-thirds of your money, I say, in Heaven's name
quit, and save the few dollars still due on it, because the time
has come when those things will not work out to our great satisfaction. And yet while we may criticise the West in a way, it
has been a teacher and a great teacher. Following the boom in
the West, Virginia and Maryland and West Virginia have
gone to planting apples. In Virginia and Maryland there have
been large plantings of three thousand, five thousand, ten thousand and twenty thousand trees, and the Governor of Maryland
told me last December that there was one set of men in the western part of Maryland planting eight thousand apple trees on
one tract, to be sold out to outsiders if possible and if not to
be carried on to development. The worst of all of the apple
orcharding of the past ten years has been the great number of
inexperienced people who have gone into the business. They
have been made to believe it was a great opportunity, with a
slight investment of capital, with little or no hard work or
care, to plant an apple orchard, and in a few years it would
come into bearing; and look at the markets—apples selling at ten
cents apiece, or $2.50 to $3.50 a bushel box.

There is a craze in New England at the present time on this
apple industry. Now I am not afraid of the countryman who
stays on the land because he loves the land and loves the trees,
who believes in the things that good Mother Nature gives us, and
is going into the apple business. I believe he will succeed. But
there are hundreds and thousands of men, now in the cities and
in the factory villages, and all over this country, that are being
tempted by the beautiful fruit they see on the market and the
high prices of the beautiful fruit, by the wonderful shows like
this one in the hall and the big shows in Boston and elsewhere—
to run into this business believing that it means success every
time. They are willing to take land that they can get anywhere.
They think if they buy a little land and can buy some apple
trees, and can put the two together, that they will have an apple
orchard and success. And they need to stop and think a little.

If the man is all right, if he loves trees. loves the care and culture of them, doesn't mind spraying, doesn't mind all the dirty work on the farm, can get the capital necessary to buy suitable land, suitable trees, and all the necessary spraying machinery and fertilizers and labor, and is willing to watch and wait, and wait and watch, and wait some longer, and put in some more capital, then there is an opportunity. But it takes a long, long time. And it takes a great deal more money and a great deal more energy than it ever did before.

Within a week I was called to visit an orchard property where one successful business man of the city had agreed to pay the capital and a youngish fellow was to furnish the brains, and they planned at the start that for ten years it would take a certain amount of capital. They have reached the fall of the third year and that capital is all gone and they want to know what they are going to do for the other seven years. They can get the money but is it wise to get it? If they figured as best they could and the money for ten years had been absorbed in three years in the care of the orchard, it was a question with the capitalist whether it was advisable for him to put in more money and go to the end of the game or give the orchard to the young man and let him take it and do the best he could. As a business proposition, was it safe or wise to go on investing that amount of money?

I speak of these cases simply to hang out a sign of caution that we are going pretty fast. Some one has said "Why, we can always sell good apples." To be sure we can. But you cannot always sell the kind of apples that you have sold in the past, the low grade apples. Some one says "The poor man wants them." No, the poor man will see these beautiful apples and he will demand as good looking apples for himself as anybody else has. But he must have them at a low price, and the apples of the future have got to be grown, or delivered, at a moderate price. But it is going to cost something to grow them. Prices are low this year. Our friends on the Pacific Northwest, two or three years ago were telling us we should not have to sell an apple below $1.50 a box f. o. b. They were then getting $2.25 to $2.50. This year they can't sell them at all out there. Very few apples are selling on the Pacific coast at any price. Buyers who went there in former years to make money are afraid, and so the western men today are putting their apples in storage or selling them on the market for what they can get. You can go to New York and buy Hood River apples that are not bringing the growers there thirty cents a box. I have seen them within a week, Spitzenburgs, that would not net the growers back in Oregon thirty cents a box in the orchard. The problem that is before us, is to produce the beautiful apples that we are beginning to show now and sell them at a price so that the common people can consume them in the quantities that we are producing them. In the Pacific Northwest only one tree in five is in bearing, and yet they do not know what to do with their product. Multiply it by five and what are they going to do? Why, they say, when the Panama Canal is done we are going to load them on ships and send them to Europe. Europe will soon get filled. It will not give a market at any such high prices as in the past.

At present you have to pay pretty fair wages, you have to spray where you never had to spray before, and you have to cultivate, and then you must have newer and cleaner and better packages costing more money every year; and yet you have got to dispose of the apples that you have already planted trees for, or are planning to plant for, you have got to sell them at the same old price. Can you do it? Are we willing to do all the things that are necessary and then take the moderate reward?

This apple growing proposition is no easy get-rich-quick scheme by any means. We began to think it was. We have seen the fancy prices of apples on the fruit stands and we have got the high price craze. But we are at the top of it. The five and ten cent apiece apples and the $3 a box and the $5 and $8 and $10 a barrel apples have had their day. We have learned to grow good apples. Science has taught us and the West has taught us how. We have learned to pack good apples. We have got more common honesty in the apple barrel than was ever there before. There is a place for some more in the middle of the barrel yet, but we have made a great forward step. The passage of a United States law regulating the packing and grading of apples is a long step forward, and we are making strides along every line, but we must not think that we are going to get a very much greater reward for our labor on the apple than we are on any other line of agriculture or horticulture that we may follow with equal energy, equal skill, equal brains and equal capital. That is the sign of caution that I would like to give you here tonight. With the right sort of soil, elevation and location, the man who loves his business, the man who enjoys caring for the tree for the tree's sake whether it gives dollars or not, the man who wants to grow beautiful apples because they are one of the most beautiful of God's gifts to man, and grows them for their sake alone and for the sake of the production of something better for his fellow men than any one else can produce, who puts love and care and thought into it all the way,—will always get a reward, perhaps not as great as we have anticipated in the past, but there is a great opportunity for him. But there are too many going into it who have not that love of the business, who have not faith in the business, but have simply been led to believe that it is a gold mine. They had better go reasonably slow.

If you are going into it, you must locate your orchard, your commercial orchard, reasonably near to proper lines of transportation. I don't think that the commercial orchard of the future can get much more than two and a half or three miles away from a railroad station with safety. It is a heavy product and has got to be handled at a low price. If you are doing your business upon a large scale, you can go it alone perhaps in the way of packages, in the way of cold storage, in the way of sorting, marketing, grading, and the handling altogether; but in the more modest way that we do things in New England, mostly with small capital and small means, there must be a coöperation, there must be a working together, a general supervision over all the orchards managed in one particular way in such a community, a supervision over the spraying, over the thinning of the fruit, over the harvesting and the grading, a coöperative cold storage house, coöperative marketing, a general working together to cut corners and save expenses. It is the little one cent on a barrel here and the half cent there and the two cents somewhere else that you may save that is going to be a profit that will pay dividends. The dividends come out of the last few cents on top of a barrel of apples or the last few cents saved in the expenses, and that is what we must live up to. We must pull close together. If we don't, we are going to get fail-

ure. It does not matter how much of an acreage we have or
how many trees we have or how much fruit we have in a reasonably small way, we can add to the profits or reduce the expenses of that operation by the most earnest coöperation. The
only possible success that our friends in the Pacific Northwest
have made, and in the Rocky Mountain coast, is largely the profit
in the coöperative handling, in their working together. We of
New England have been a little too independent.

The question of packages for the present and future is a very
serious one. The old, high barrel has been a very easy package
for us to use, and where the groceries break them up in
quarts and pecks and half pecks and half bushels, they have a
reasonably wide distribution. But we must get a wider distribution. We must get the orchard package directly into the home,
into every home in the land where apples are consumed. You
can sell a family a half bushel, or a peck, or a bushel, and once
get them into the family and the children will do the rest to
some extent.

I don't believe in getting around the middleman,—the wholesaler and the grocer are just as necessary as the horse and mule
or old ox on our farm, they are part of the machinery of production and marketing, but at the same time they, as our agents,
want so far as possible to be able to pass the package along from
the grower to the consumer unbroken so as to increase consumption. And whether the box of the Northwest which holds
a bushel is the right size package or not, I am not sure. I am
trying myself in an advertising scheme to reach the consumers direct with that package and we find that it is reasonably
satisfactory. I think it will be better for us to find the largest
possible package we can get into a home and then fill that package full of glorious good apples, top, bottom, middle and all
over—give them more than they expect every time. I believe
that will help us. But we have got to sell at a moderate price,
and that is the thing for us to work out.

I seriously believe, under present conditions of labor, the
necessity for spraying three or four times, the pruning, the feeding, the culture and the new high class package, that you can't
put up a barrel of apples as good as is demanded today for
one cent less than $2. You must reckon two dollars as the
cost of production of a barrel of good apples one year with

Portion of Exhibit of Geo. W. Staples, Temple, at Annual Meeting State Pomological Society, Portland, November 12-14, 1912

another. The West has taught the people to want beautiful apples and we have the quality to give them—and we can't go backward, we have got to produce these beautiful apples.

How can we reduce that cost of $2.00? How can we get a price above $2.50? These are the problems that need to be solved and need to be solved very seriously. And you gentlemen who have only small sums of money saved up, a few hundred or a few thousand dollars, figure out how far that will go in establishing,—not establishing an orchard, but maintaining and caring for an orchard for ten years till it begins to give you some returns. Consider the five-year old Baldwin this year with a bushel of apples on it, but don't expect an orchard to do that. You have got to figure to live for ten years and take expensive care of the trees. It is a business proposition. If the moneyed men here in Portland or in Maine are going to invest money in this enterprise, remember it is a long interest wait. A return will come sometime if the right men are hold of the game as it will with any other solid investment, but don't think it is coming in a pile and going to bring enormous dividends. It will not do it.

Another thing—this is what I am going to say about the future. If there is any one here in this hall who hasn't got an apple orchard and wants one, hold up your hand. Two of you,—only two in this whole company! Have all the rest of you got them? Well, I want to say to you here tonight, those of you who have not orchards and want them, sit down and keep hold of your money and wait five years and you can go out and buy the other fellow's orchard for a quarter what it would cost you to develop it. Yes, I believe that, though it may be heresy, it may be talk that ought not to be given at a Pomological Society meeting. I have been an optimist all my life. I have been a farmer and horticulturist all my life and I have been an optimist from the very start. I believe in looking after the good things in horticulture, and I have faith in the New England people as I have in the people of no other part of America. We are at the head here in quality. We are equal in beauty. We have as strong and as fine soil as anywhere on earth for the production of apples. We have everything here. Within twenty-four hours ride of your Maine farms are thirty million people with more money than any other like number

on the face of the globe, and they desire beautiful fruit, they
want the best and are better able to pay for it than anywhere
else.   And if anybody on earth or in America can make money
in the production of apples, we can here in New England.   It is
a great opportunity.   But, nevertheless, I have hung out the sign
of caution, and I hope it will do some of you some good.

ANNUAL BUSINESS MEETING THURSDAY, NOVEMBER 14, 9 A. M.

Called to order by the President, H. L. Keyser.

The following Committee on Resolutions was appointed by the President: D. H. Knowlton, Farmington, Dr. G. M. Twitchell, Auburn, Charles S. Pope, Manchester.

An invitation from the Bangor Chamber of Commerce, for the Pomological Society to hold their Annual Meeting in 1913 in the city of Bangor, was read.

Voted, to refer the invitation to the executive committee.

The Secretary made his report as follows:—

REPORT OF SECRETARY.

Mr. President, Ladies and Gentlemen:—

A meeting of the Executive Committee was called by the President for January 5, 1912, but owing to a severe snowstorm a quorum was not present.

A meeting of the committee was held at the Augusta House, Augusta, on May 3.

It was voted to hold the annual meeting in Portland and the President was instructed to make the arrangements for the meeting.

It was also voted to invite the New England Fruit Show to meet with us.

The President was instructed to arrange the special premiums. Through his efforts and the hearty coöperation of the Portland Board of Trade, the Pomological Society has the best premium list ever offered for the fruit exhibitors of Maine.

The annual Field Meeting was held at Highmoor Farm, Monmouth, on August 2. A large number of fruit growers from all parts of the State were present and one of the most profitable field meetings was enjoyed by all.

During the year the Society has lost by death one of our most respected and esteemed members, Ex-President Z. A. Gilbert of Greene. It would be very appropriate for those of us assembled here in the annual meeting of 1912 to remember that to him and his associates we owe a debt of gratitude and appreciation for their grand work as pioneers in this department of agriculture and for the safe and sure foundation they laid for a permanent organization solely devoted to the fruit interests of Maine. In all this they manifested great foresight and wisdom in recognizing the splendid advantages to fruit growers arising from the natural adaptability of the soil and climate of *the* State of States.

This present exhibition is a rare and fitting tribute to their much appreciated services.

During the year there has been more interest manifested by the fruit growers of the State to avail themselves of the advantages of membership in the Society.

We have at present 132 life members and 40 annual members, being the largest number of annual members before our annual meeting. Let us use our best efforts to make it 250 life and 250 annual members before the close of this year, making a total of 500.

Our reports for 1911 have just been received and will soon be mailed.

In conclusion let me suggest that as we are about to enter upon a Legislative Session, the fruit growers should remember that no one else will look out for the fruit industry of the State but the growers themselves. Let us then be up and doing, continually.

Respectfully submitted,

E. L. WHITE.

Voted to accept the report.

The report of the treasurer was presented as follows, and approved.

RECEIPTS.

Cash on hand from the year 1911	$132	21
Jan. 2, Received from the First National Bank, Farmington	16	00
interest on bonds	22	50
July 2, from First National Bank, Farmington...	16	00
interest on bonds	22	50
Nov 19, Augusta Trust Co., Winthrop.............	7	49
Dec. 13, for space in hall......................	28	00
20, part of state stipend.....................	413	06
31, life membership fee.....................	90	00
Annual Membership fee	92	00
Feb. 26, balance of state stipend for 1912.........	586	94
Portland Board of Trade	94	88
Total Receipts	$1,521	58

EXPENDITURES.

Nov. 15, Paid E. F. Hitchings	$41	00
E. E. Howard	1	00
Wallace S. Ladd	14	71
Augusta House	3	00
W. E. Leland	3	55
E. F. Hitchings	1	50
Me. Federation Agricultural Associations....	6	00
George W. Staples	35	00
W. F. Dunham	4	25
W. W. Brown	10	62
W. F. Dunham	3	50
Lewiston Journal Co......................	3	25
W. F. Dunham	4	75
Waterville Sentinel Co.	20	91
Me. State Bookbinding Co...................	5	45
Lewiston Journal Co.	10	00
Brunswick Pub. Co.	2	75
Frank A. Waugh..........................	38	12
Shaylor Ingraving Co......................	15	00
W. E. Leland	6	10
E. L. Lincoln	2	35
E. L. Lincoln	6	50
Dec. 31, E. L. Lincoln	25	00
E. L. Lincoln	5	00
Bertha Babb	2	00

26

H. H. Withwill	2	39
E. F. Hitchings	1	52
E. F. Hitchings	5	76
W. E. Leland	4	35
M. C. R. R. Co., freight	4	60
Wallace S. Ladd	1	32
H. P. Gould	36	00
Premiums	386	50
H. H. Whetzel	64	48
E. L. White	34	90
F. C. Sears	41	18
Wilfred Wheeler	35	49
Congress Sq. Hotel	170	11
James P. Porter	25	10
Transfer to permanent fund	90	00
E. L. White	150	00
Lewiston Journal Co.	10	00
F. R. Conant Co.	2	25
Mrs. L. B. Raynes	64	77
P. E. Simmons	3	64
F. H. Morse	10	05
Wilfrid Wheeler	15	00
F. C. Sears	15	00
W. W. Brown	8	00
Maine State Bookbinding Co.	15	35
E. L. White	8	06
H. L. Keyser	25	05
H. L. Keyser	6	00
Maine State Bookbinding Co.	13	40
	$1,521	58

Permanent fund for the year 1912	$1,980	00
Life fees for the year 1912	90	00
	$2,070	00

Permanent fund invested at follows:

4 shares stock, First Nat'l Bank, Farmington	$400	00
2 bonds Stockton Springs Water Co., "First mortgage"	970	00
Deposit in Savings Banks	700	00
	$2,070	00

Respectfully submitted,

ELLIS L. LINCOLN,

Treasurer.

The President then appointed the following committee to receive, sort and count votes: Mr. A. K. Gardiner, Mr. Clement, and Mr. Littlefield.

The following officers were elected for the ensuing year: H. L. Keyser, Greene, President; W. H. Conant, Buckfield, First Vice President; A. K. Gardiner, Augusta, Second Vice President; E. L. White, Bowdoinham, Secretary; E. L. Lincoln, Wayne, Treasurer; Member of the Executive Committee to serve for three years, Prof. E. F. Hitchings, Orono.

Member of Experiment Station Council for one year, Mr. Robert H. Gardiner of Gardiner.

Voted to leave the election of the trustees in the hands of the Executive Committee.

The following were elected as representatives to the Federation of Agricultural Societies of Maine: H. L. Keyser, Greene; W. H. Conant, Buckfield; E. L. White, Bowdoinham.

Representative from Maine to the New England Fruit Show, Homer N. Chase, Auburn.

Voted, that in the possibility of any vacancy in any office, the Executive Committee be instructed to fill the same.

The committee appointed at the last annual meeting of the Pomological Society to take under consideration the matter of the State Fruit Farm, reported as follows:

We find that the law passed for the purchase of the farm also put the management of the farm into the hands of the director of the experiment station and the receipts and expenditures are kept by the treasurer of the University of Maine, which are open for inspection. Every item goes on, everything sold from the farm and everything that is paid for. We think that those figures would be useful if they were published. We understand an appropriation is to be asked for in the next legislature and when that matter is brought up any amendments to the original law will be in order.

Respectfully submitted,

JOHN W. TRUE,

For the Committee.

Voted to accept the report.

Dr. Twitchell reported for the Committee on Resolutions as follows:—

Resolved, That this State Pomological Society, recognizing the marked results obtained at our State Fruit Farm, and realizing the necessity for direct knowledge of the methods and cost of storage of fruit, would urge upon the legislature the importance of an appropriation for the erection of natural and artificial cold storage plants at Highmoor, said construction and future maintenance to be conducted in such manner as to furnish an object lesson in different methods, and a full knowledge of cost to the apple growers of the State. The increasing crop of fruit renders this step necessary, while the necessities of individual growers make imperative the solution of economic and permanent construction upon a basis within the reach of the small farmer.

The question of choice of system is one the State may well determine without further delay for the future good and profit of the growers, as well as the proper handling of the fruit at Highmoor.

Resolved, That the sincere thanks of this Society are due the City of Portland, the Board of Trade and business men, the press of the State, the railroads and all co-operating agents to the complete success of this great exhibition and the thirty-ninth annual session of this Society.

Resolved, That it is with just pride we view the marked improvements in uniform grade fruit exhibited here, and would recommend that hereafter, all boxes, barrels and plates of defective fruit be excluded from display at our annual exhibitions.

Resolved, That we affirm our belief in the importance of offering liberal prizes at future exhibitions for small packages, where fruit and package may compete together and the public be educated to the worth of this method of disposal of our fruit.

Resolved, That the time has come for a reclassification of our premium list, the dropping of varieties having no positive hold upon the market, and the centering of effort on the thorough testing of new varieties with special reference to adaptability to Maine conditions and to insuring a quality superior to the best standard winter apple of today.

Resolved, That we endorse the action of the Committee on Legislation to insure the growers all items of expense attending the growing and marketing of crops and products at our State Fruit Farm.

Resolved, That we urge upon the farmers of the State hearty co-operation in the extended demonstration work now being organized by the University of Maine.

Resolved, That as interested growers of fruit we would express our appreciation of the services of our State Horticulturist and his cordial spirit of co-operation with the society at all times and under all conditions.

Resolved, That we heartily endorse the recommendation of President Keyser, that an effort be made to increase the state appropriation for the further extension of the work of this Society, and to promote the growth and further development of our pomological and horticultural interests.

Resolved, That in the death of the Honorable Z. A. Gilbert, the Maine State Pomological Society has met with an irreparable loss. In view of this loss and his long and faithful service as president of this Society, we recommend that Dr. George M. Twitchell, a long time associate and intimate friend of Mr. Gilbert, be invited to prepare an appropriate memorial and sketch of his services to the Society for publication in the next annual report of the Society.

Resolved, That it has been a great pleasure to our Society to greet and welcome the representatives of the fruit and horticultural societies of other New England States. Their presence and assistance have contributed largely to the success of our meeting. May they be with us often in the future.

D. H. KNOWLTON,

G. M. TWITCHELL,

CHARLES S. POPE,

Committee.

Voted, to accept the report as a whole.

Prof. E. F. Hitchings presented the following:

Owing to the great and increasing volume of summer visitors; to the natural adaptability of our soil and climate to the growing of choice vegetables and flowers as well as fruit; and recognizing the fact that there is a great and growing demand for first class vegetables throughout our State; and realizing that horticulture is fast becoming an important industry; and believing that the three divisions of fruit, vegetables and flowers should be given due recognition:

Therefore, be it resolved that we request the next legislature of Maine to change the name "Maine State Pomological Society" to "Maine State Horticultural Society."

Voted to lay the matter on the table.

Prof. E. F. Hitchings also recommended that the date of the Annual Meeting be one week later in November.

This matter was referred to the next annual meeting.

Mr. Clement of Winthrop presented the following:

No state institution which receives state aid shall compete for prizes against individuals or associations.

Voted to adopt the same.

CO-OPERATION IN THE CONTROL OF FRUIT DIS-EASES IN NEW YORK.

H. H. WHETZEL, Professor of Plant Pathology, Cornell
University.

IMPORTANCE OF FRUIT DISEASES IN NEW YORK.

While the total value of the fruit crops in New York is
surpassed by that of hay, grain, potatoes, etc., it is nevertheless
a total of sufficiently large proportions to warrant extensive
investigations of those diseases which tend annually to reduce
it. New York is justly noted for the importance of her fruit
industry and the intelligence and enthusiasm of her fruit growers. She has always led in educational efforts for the upbuild-
ing of horticulture. A pioneer in the nursery business, she
still remains the greatest producer of nursery stock in the United
States. She supports today two of the largest fruit growers'
associations of this country and her nurserymen stand high in
the councils of the National Nurserymen's Association. In the
production of small fruits she has few equals. She is par excellence, the deciduous fruit State of the union. True to their
conservative natures her growers do not make the noise of their
western competitors, but they have continued to furnish the
great bulk of the staple fruits for eastern markets.

For many years the leader, both in extent and variety of her
fruit industries, it is not surprising that the fruit plantings of
New York should suffer from a greater variety of diseases than
those of most other states, and while New York has led in the
development and application of means for their control, the
total annual losses to the fruit crops of the State are still
enormous.

Wallace estimated the loss from apple diseases in the State
of New York at about three and one-half million dollars. Our

recent work on the fire blight in nursery stock indicates that a large percentage of the apple, pear and quince trees are lost each year, while the injury from this disease in pear and apple orchards is often appalling in certain sections. On account of the difficulties of getting accurate records of losses in a sufficiently large number of cases, no satisfactory estimate of the total loss to the State from diseases affecting fruit can be made. This loss, however, is annually a heavy drain on the fruit industry of the State and represents one of the most serious leaks in the fruit business; serious because of its proportions and the difficulties of reducing it.

The control of the diseases of plants calls for the application of highly technical scientific principles and demands of the grower an exceptional degree of intelligence and interest. These problems demand in addition to intelligence and education on the part of the grower, the service of highly trained specialists in this field of science, namely plant pathologists or, as we call them, plant doctors. The growers of the State of New York have been especially fortunate in having at their service for the past fifteen years so noted a pathologist as my friend and colleague, Mr. C. F. Stewart of the State Experiment Station at Geneva. Mr. Stewart's studies and investigations have covered an exceptionally wide range of crop diseases but to none has he made greater contributions than to those of fruit. There is scarcely a disease of our fruits which he has not at some time studied and toward the control of which he or the men working under him have not contributed suggestions or experiments of marked value to our growers.

But the diseases of fruit are far too numerous and the problem to be solved too complicated to be met and solved by one or even several men, however well trained or experienced. There yet remains endless work to be done before this leak in the fruit business will be entirely stopped.

USUAL RELATION OF THE STATE TO THE GROWERS IN THE CONTROL
OF CROP DISEASES.

When the speaker came to the work in the New York State College of Agriculture in 1906 he found in operation there the three usual provisions for the investigation and control of plant diseases. One or more of these are to be found in operation in most states at present I believe. They are:

1. The maintenance by the State, through state appropriations at the college of agriculture and the experiment station, of an expert plant pathologist or botanist, together with one or two assistants in each case and the necessary equipment for laboratory work.

2. Provision, also by state funds, to the college of agriculture, for extension work among the farmers of the State. A very small part of this fund was in our case available for purposes of disseminating knowledge in regard to plant diseases and their control. This work was mainly in the nature of short talks or lectures here and there about the State. In addition to this some opportunity was afforded for similar extension work in the farmers' institutes on funds appropriated to the State Department of Agriculture.

3. Provision for the inspection of fruit trees, chiefly nursery stock, and the destruction of such as show serious infection by certain insects or fungi. This work in New York is also supported by state appropriations to the State Department of Agriculture.

Your attention is directed to the fact that these different means of attacking the problems of plant diseases and their control are supported solely on state or federal appropriations.

SOME OF THE PROBLEMS BEFORE US IN 1907 TO WHICH THE GROWERS WERE DEMANDING INSTANT ATTENTION.

1. The black rot of grapes. In 1906 an epidemic of black rot had resulted in an almost total loss of the crop in many sections of the grape regions. The industry was threatened and the discouraged growers cried loudly for help.

2. Apple Scab and Bordeaux Injury. Ever since bordeaux came into general use in the State for the control of apple scab more or less injury to foliage and fruit had been reported. So serious had the matter become that in 1907 Professor Hedrick, Horticulturist of the State Experiment Station, issued an extensive bulletin (No. 287) giving a summary of the known facts and the results of his observations on this problem. No satisfactory solution of the difficulty, however, was offered and by

1909 the growers were demanding some substitute for the bordeaux as the most satisfactory way out of the difficulty.

3. Serious epidemics of fire blight in several nursery sections of the State had broken out and the nurserymen desired to know what measures might be taken to reduce the losses. The spraying of nursery stock for the control of leaf blights, etc., which were often destructive, was rarely practiced though the need was evident in most nurseries.

4. The ravages of the fire blight especially in the pear orchards along Lake Ontario were becoming increasingly alarming and threatened the destruction of the industry in certain sections, while its appearance in the twig blight form on apples in many localities was causing marked apprehension on the part of the apple growers.

5. The increasing interest in apple growing was directing attention to the neglected orchards of the State and information on the nature and control of the apple tree canker was constantly being called for.

The above were but a few of the fruit disease problems demanding our attention. The resources available for meeting the situation were pitifully inadequate. Each problem called for the undivided attention of one or more men for a period of from two to several years. With only one assistant and $800 in 1907 with which to meet these demands and with a large number of students to be taught in addition, the prospect of getting results of any great or immediate value to the growers was most discouraging.

A NEW POINT OF VIEW.

For a year or two I lived, like my colleagues, in the hope that increasing appropriations by the state legislature would afford means for meeting the problems which in increasing numbers pressed for solution. Material increases in the annual budget for our work came but these were so inadequate for the work demanded of us that I soon began to realize that we could not hope to receive sufficient support from the State to meet the situation, certainly not within the period of our ambitious youth. What our growers needed and demanded of us was some immediate assistance in the solutions of their difficulties.

Finally in the winter of 1909 the demand for a substitute for bordeaux in the spraying of apples reached an acute stage. Aroused by the glowing reports of success with lime-sulphur in the Pacific coast apple regions and the appearance on the market of commercial concentrated lime-sulphur solutions for summer spraying for which unsubstantiated claims were made, our growers insisted on definite data as to the efficiency of this new fungicide under our eastern conditions. Loaded to our full capacity with problems already under way and with no prospect of adequate increases in our department budget to meet this new problem, I began to cast about for some means of meeting this legitimate demand of our growers.

In the midst of this dilemma there came to my hands in one of our scientific journals the description of a new type of coöperation which was being effectively worked between the department of chemistry of a western university and certain commercial concerns having problems of a chemical nature. So effective did this coöperation appear to be, not only in solving these problems, but also in training young investigators for further service along these lines, that I thought I saw here a solution of the difficulties in which we found ourselves relative to the problems in plant disease work.

After careful consideration of this scheme and full discussion of the problem with Director Bailey, we worked out a similar plan for coöperation with our constituency. The purpose of our first coöperation of this type was to get definite data on the question of the substitution of lime-sulphur for bordeaux in the spraying of apples. Care was taken in entering into the coöperation that no strings should be attached by which the commercial concern supplying the funds could make undue capital out of its relations with the University, and the contract received the full approval of the Director of the College and the Board of Trustees. The fundamental feature of this coöperation was the financial consideration, the Niagara Sprayer Company depositing with the Treasurer of the University the sum of $1500 per year for two years to provide salary and traveling expenses for a young plant pathologist to undertake a careful investigation of the problem. His appointment and all expenditures of the money deposited were to be under the complete control of the Director of the College with provision for cancelling the contract by the Director at his discretion. The College on its part agreed to provide the necessary laboratory equipment for the work and the necessary time of the head of the department of plant pathology to oversee and direct it. This coöperative arrangement was known as an Industrial Fellowship. The young investigator was to be at the same time a graduate student in Cornell University, receiving training for his advanced degree along the lines of plant pathology. It was further provided that this work should be conducted in a field laboratory in an orchard section in some part of the State during the growing season.

About the same time a similar arrangement was entered into with the Stuart Nursery Company of Newark. N. Y., for the investigation and control of the fire blight and other diseases in nursery stock. Since that time no less than twelve industrial fellowships have been established in the department of plant pathology in Cornell University, supporting the work of 20 men and representing a total of thirty-five thousand dollars including the sums being expended this year. In addition to this we have had during every growing season since 1908 coöperative arrangements with growers or commercial concerns for the season only (about three months) by which one of these young investigators is stationed in orchard, field or vineyard for the purpose of trying out his efficiency in meeting some special plant disease problem. This is usually understood to be preliminary to the establishment of a two year industrial fellowship and in most cases has so worked out. The young man has made good.

Last season we had in the field under this or similar arrangements no less than twenty-five men in seventeen field laboratories in different counties of the State.

This method of attacking the plant disease problems of the State was a radical departure for a state institution. It was the outcome of a pressing necessity and called for a new point of view in state college work. This point of view may be expressed in the following propositions:

1. It is the business of the State through its college of agriculture to provide the means in the form of a staff of experts and equipment by which the constituency of the college may be assisted in the solution of their problems.

2. The people on their part should provide means to meet the State (through the college) at least half way, in the solution of these problems.

3. Financial support by those most vitally interested in the solution of the problem is the surest means of enlisting their interest and in establishing practical methods for disease control.

4. With the financial support of those who have problems to be solved we are enabled to meet the demands of a much larger number of our constituency than under the old plan.

5. If it is worth nothing to the grower in dollars and cents of his own money to have these problems investigated, then it is not proper for the college to spend the State's money for that purpose. And if it is worth something to the grower in dollars and cents then he should be expected to put money into it.

6. During the growing season the field where the problem lies rather than the college is the important place for the prosecution of these investigations.

Many other sound reasons for such a coöperation will occur to you if you will give the matter some thought. The hearty support which our growers have given the scheme and the marked results we have obtained in a short time are ample justification of this new type of coöperation. I hasten to a consideration of some of the results which we have to offer.

ŧ

RESULTS.

At the winter meeting of our State Fruit Growers' Association in 1909, at which there were at least 500 growers present, in presenting a summary of the then known data on lime-sulphur as a summer spray, I asked those who expected to use lime-sulphur the following season instead of bordeaux for summer spraying of their apples, to stand. Only one or two arose and that with some hesitation. During that season and the next our investigations on the use of lime-sulphur as a summer spray were carried out by Mr. Wallace on the Niagara Sprayer Company Fellowship. At the winter meeting in 1911, after two seasons' evidence on the use of lime-sulphur, I called on those who still proposed to use bordeaux to stand up. Of the one thousand odd growers present only two or three arose. Thus completely had the practice of our growers as regards these two fungicides been changed and I believe I am just in attributing this in no small degree to the results we had shown at the summer meeting of the State Fruit Growers in our experimental plats at Sodus, N. Y. (1910). Over 1500 growers saw these results. With this evidence many of you are doubtless familiar from our publications on the subject. Lime-sulphur continues to be practically the only summer fungicide used by our growers for their apples. In fact bordeaux as a spray mixture for most fruit diseases has largely gone out of use.

In 1910 the apple scab appeared in epidemic form throughout the Genessee Valley just before the blossoms opened, with the result that the set of fruit was almost completely destroyed. The farmers of Genessee County, while not primarily apple growers, expect considerable returns from their small farm orchards. Aroused to interest in their orchards by the growing incomes of their apple growing neighbors to the north and filled with exceptional anticipation by the heavy blossom of 1910, they saw with chagrin the failure of their fruit to set and called upon the college for information and assistance to prevent a repetition of such a catastrophe in the future. At a meeting of Genessee farmers in the summer of 1910 we proposed the organization of a local fruit growers' association and the establishment by them of an industrial fellowship to provide for one or more field laboratories and the location of a young plant doctor or entomologist in each. Two organizations were effected, which were afterward merged into one, and three young men (two plant pathologists and one entomologist) were stationed in the county the next season to advise with the growers, direct their spraying operations and conduct experiments on the control of diseases and pests of their fruit.

So satisfactory was the arrangement that. at the end of the first year the growers united in an incorporated county association and the second year not only maintained their three experts but also through the association purchased their spray materials at a marked reduction and marketed over fifty thousand barrels of choice fruit. Their industrial fellowships are largely responsible for having put Genessee County within two years on the fruit map of New York State.

. For several years we have had reports of a destructive disease of peach trees in the peach sections of Niagara County. It is commonly known among the growers there as the European Canker, affecting the larger limbs of the trees and eventually killing them. The Newfane Peach Growers' Association was formed for the purpose of providing an industrial fellowship for the investigation of this and other diseases of the peach. In less than two years we have been able to demonstrate the cause of the disease and to locate the chief points for attack in its control.

The past season four nursery companies have united in providing a fellowship fund of $2,600 per year for two years for the maintenance of a fellow and four assistants in the work of studying the diseases of their crops.

Arrangements are now being completed for a fellowship and field laboratory in Orleans County and also in Clinton County for the investigation and control of apple diseases.

Under a fellowship established by the Union Sulphur Company in New York City and in coöperation with certain growers who have provided orchards, etc., we have been able to undertake extensive experiments in the investigation of dusting vs. spraying for the control of certain fruit diseases, especially the brown rot of peaches and the apple scab. While neither of these diseases have been abundant since these experiments began, still we have indications of interesting results to be obtained by dusting with sulphur.

Under a fellowship with the American Steel & Wire Company we have been enabled to make investigations on the use of iron sulphate for the control of certain diseases, especially the raspberry anthracnose. These investigations are not sufficiently advanced to warrant conclusions as yet but ample funds are available for settling the question of the fungicidal value of iron sulphate, so generally recommended in Europe for certain fruit diseases, especially of the grape.

These coöperations have not been confined to fruit growers alone. By means of an industrial fellowship and coöperation of local associations of growers we have been able to meet the demand for information and assistance in the control of the hop mildew which broke out three years ago in the hop yards of the State and threatened the industry. We have met with complete success and I believe I am safe in saying that we this season saved the greater part of the hop crop of the State from complete destruction by our advice and assistance to growers through the fellows in field laboratories in two of the largest hop growing regions of the State.

In addition to these we have, under industrial fellowships or similar financial coöperation, investigations in progress on diseases of truck crops, ginseng, florists' crops, potato diseases. etc. We are meeting to a far greater extent the demands of our growers for plant disease investigations than we could ever have hoped to do with state funds alone.

THE OUTLOOK.

We look forward to great growth and development of this type of coöperation not only in New York but in other states as well; not only along lines of plant disease control but also along other lines of agricultural investigation. Already evidences of this are beginning to come to our notice. We have at Cornell in horticulture, soils, and plant breeding, similar coöperative work under way. In Wisconsin the pea growers are supporting an expert at the college of agriculture for the study of diseases of field peas. This new type of coöperation, financial in nature, sound from a business point of view and most effective from an economic standpoint, has come to stay. It appeals to the live up-to-date director of investigations, it opens an unlimited field of operation and research for trained, ambitious young scientists, it provides a means by which growers with problems of pressing importance may secure prompt and effective assistance, it opens opportunities to commercial concerns with agricultural products, to extend the knowledge and use of these products to the mutual benefit of growers and manufacturer. It in no wise degrades or deteriorates scientific investigation; it stimulates, vitalizes, dignifies it. It brings to the grower fuller appreciation of the value of science in agriculture, it educates him. It brings to science the hearty espousal of its cause by the grower and the unlimited financial support which it deserves.

Gentlemen, the day will come and you will live to see it when we will have in the State of New York more than a hundred plant pathologists working on the problems of plant diseases and their control. Already we have a fourth of that number. We propose to train these young men, our growers propose to assist in their training and to provide the financial support to retain them for service in the State of New York. We cannot afford to train them as we have in the past and then send them West or East to work for our competitors. We propose to keep them.

If you care to have further information as to our methods of conducting these coöperative investigations or to know more of the results we have obtained I shall be glad to answer your questions if I can. I thank you for the interest and consideration you have shown in listening to what I have had to offer you on this subject.

Question: I had the pleasure of hearing Professor Whetzel two years ago in New York when he discussed the question of apple scab in a most lucid manner, and I wish he would take just a few moments to take up direct treatment of the apple scab, its original cause and manner of control. It is a little digression from the subject and yet it is almost germane to it.

Prof. Whetzel: I shall be very glad of course to tell you what little I know about apple scab and its control. The apple scab is a fungous disease. A fungus is a plant which lives on dead or living plants or animals. Now this fungus plant passes the winter in old leaves of the apple on the ground. It produces what we call winter spores. They are produced in bags, eight in a sack, and in the spring they are shot from those leaves into the air. They are shot only during moist, rainy weather, and their ripening is so timed that they are ripe just at the time that the blossoms are about to open. That is to say, if the blossoms open a week earlier in a given year, the spores are ripe a week earlier, and if the blossoms open a week later the spores are ripe a week later. The same weather conditions which bring open the blossoms also ripen and bring about the distribution of the spores. There is no object whatever in spraying the trees when they are dormant for the control of apple scab. The spores are not ripe or distributed at that period. If they were distributed then there would be no place for them to find an effective lodging, because they germinate after they lodge, on the young leaves or young fruit. The first period at which the spores are matured and bring about infection, is when the buds which contain blossoms and leaves, begin to show pink. That is the stage, just before the blossoms open, when you usually have the first infection from apple scab. The spores on the ground are shot into the air, and carried by the breeze through the orchard. Some of them falling on these leaves or blossom stalks infect the tissue, form a scab spot and bring about the injury.

Now the ideal time to make the first application for scab— you have already made the dormant spray for other things— is just when those blossom buds are beginning to spread apart; the leaves will all be turned back and the blossoms will have just pulled apart; the middle blossom at least will show pink, the others usually do. Now the ideal period does not last more than a day or two at most, so that to spray effectively, most effectively, you should be able to spray your entire orchard, or at least all the varieties that are in that condition within one or two days' time. There are very few orchardists who have orchards of any size, who are prepared to do this. We have figured that no orchardist should expect to effectively spray his trees with less than one power machine for ten acres of orchard.

Question: Why not spray the ground.

Prof. Whetzel: Because the spores are inside of the leaves and the spray mixture will not reach the spores. The water will go through the leaf but the poisons that kill the spores will be left on the outside, filter out, and the spore case in which these spores are contained will open up and shoot the spores into the air just the same. We have found that you may soak a bunch of diseased grapes in strong blue vitriol, and it will yet continue to produce active spores. There is nothing to be gained by spraying the ground. Your first spray should be thorough and effective. It should be put on as a fine spray with at least 200 lbs. pressure. It should be put on ahead of the rain periods that come at that time, not after the rains. You should spray against the wind when you put it on. I won't stop to explain that now because it would take too long, but the most efficient way to spray is against the wind. The next application should be made just after the blossoms fall. When two-thirds of the blossoms are off the trees the average grower should begin to spray, and if he is fortunate he may have three or four days in which to do this spraying. He may have only a day or two. He should spray the varieties that are ready to spray and not start at the north side of the orchard and spray across. If these two sprayings are thoroughly and effectively done, in most seasons only one more spraying will be required to control the apple scab, and that will be a spraying about the last of July or the first of August to catch the late infection which we sometimes have in seasons that are wet at the end,—such a season as you had this year. In some cases it might be desirable to spray ten days or two weeks after the second spraying, that is, after the spraying following the falling of the blossoms, but in New York, at least, this is not necessary. Spray with lime-sulphur 1-40, arsenate of lead 2 lbs. to 50 gals. Use high pressure angle nozzles, and high tower so as to get above the trees. You can't spray effectively and stand on the ground. We don't know anything about spraying in this country. Some of us do a fairly good job at squirting some seasons, occasionally a man has sufficient equipment to really do good work if he knew how, and a few growers really do fairly good spraying, but before we grow those fancy apples we will have to do a good deal better spraying.

Question: Wouldn't it be desirable to burn those leaves as they lay on the ground?

Prof. Whetzel: Any method of getting rid of those leaves of course in the fall would be desirable, but as a general proposition the leaves fall rather late from apple trees, they are seldom dry enough in the fall to burn and burn them all up. Any method of putting straw or similar material over the orchard and burning them is apt to injure the trees, so we have never found it desirable to undertake to control the scab in this fashion. However, growers who plough in the fall usually have much less trouble from the scab in the State of New York than those who do not plough until late in the spring. You can't depend on those things absolutely. On the other hand, there is a great deal more to be learned in the way of sanitation in the control of these diseases than we have yet discovered. Any way to get rid of these leaves is a good thing.

GROWTH AND NUTRITION OF THE APPLE TREE.

Dr. W. J. Morse, Orono.

What I shall say with regard to the growth and nutrition of the apple tree will probably contain little which is new to those orchardists who have thoroughly studied the subject. However, my observations of the way that apple orchards are usually handled, in several different states, frequently by men of considerable experience, leads me to believe that there is much need of a more intimate acquaintance with certain fundamental principles of plant nutrition and their application to orchard practices.

A man who would hitch a cow in a wooden stanchion and then pile her rations on her back because they would thus be nearer her stomach would be considered a fit candidate for a lunatic asylum. If he should then give a flock of sheep the free range of the stable, even though he placed the fodder in reach of the cows, and expect the sheep to get their living upon the same food supply and the cows to remain in good condition and give a full flow of milk we would place him in the incurable ward. Yet he differs but little from the man who places his fertilizer only around the bases of the tree trunks or from the man who expects his trees to grow strong and vigorous and produce an abundance of large apples, and at the same time is not satisfied unless he yearly secures a full crop of hay from these same orchards. In the first instance he should not be too severely censured. He shows an honest desire to give the tree something in return for what it gives him and is placing this food material where he thinks it is most needed, therefore the comparison is to a certain extent unfair. It does not take a very bright man to discover the business end of a hungry animal but to the uninitiated it is not so easy to locate the millions of tiny feeding organs of a hungry plant. On the other hand I maintain that the man who expects his orchards to produce paying crops of both apples and hay upon the food supply and care which should be given for one crop alone, is on a par with the man who expects to maintain his herd of cows and flock of sheep upon the rations of one.

These statements should not be taken as implying that good crops of apples cannot and are not often obtained in New England on well fertilized and otherwise well cared for orchards in sod. It is also admitted that some of the most highly colored fruit is obtained in this way. However, carefully conducted experiments go to show that to secure the most profitable returns year after year the orchardist should not rob his bearing trees of food materials by trying to produce other crops, especially hay, on the same land at the same time.

Before I attempt to discuss the more fundamental questions of how the tree takes up the crude food materials from the soil, transports them to the leaves to be manufuctured into plant food, and then transports this elaborated or manufactured food to the various organs of the plant to nourish and build up the tissues, I wish to call your attention to some practical results which we have obtained at Highmoor Farm from cultivation, fertilization, pruning and spraying, and I hope to make clear, before I finish, that all of these have a more or less direct bearing upon questions of nutrition and growth.

Highmoor Farm was purchased by the State in 1909 and came under the management of the Maine Agricultural Experiment Station that summer too late to do much that year. Originally there had been 5000 trees but for various reasons, chiefly through neglect by certain of the previous owners, the number had been reduced to about 3100. Many of the remainder had been badly injured by borers and winter killing, and fires started by railroad locomotives had been allowed to run through a part of the orchards at various times. All of the trees were in a semi-starved condition, sadly in need of pruning, and there was little evidence of previous cultivation. After determining which trees were in a hopeless condition the number was reduced to 2300 in 1910. The trees were about 20-25 years old in 1909.

I cannot take the time to go into the details of the treatment which these orchards have received since the Station assumed control. Briefly, in 1909 they were sprayed once in late spring,

just as soon as the purchase of the farm was assured, largely
to control leaf-eating insects which were present in great numbers. The purchase was completed too late to begin cultivation
that year, but 300 pounds of commercial fertilizer was applied
per acre as a top-dressing and pruning was begun as soon as
possible. Since then all of the orchards except certain plots
left for comparison have been brought under cultivation and
each year sown to a cover crop after mid-summer. They have
been liberally dressed with commercial fertilizer. In the spring
of 1910 one thousand pounds of lime per acre was worked into
the soil to correct acidity. Pruning has gone on each year to
remove surplus, dead and diseased wood, and to open up the
tops to admit the sunshine. By repeated examinations borers
have been hunted out and destroyed. Since 1909 the main
orchards have been sprayed at least three times each spring. In
1909 and 1910 bordeaux mixture and arsenate of lead were used
in the main orchards but lime-sulphur and arsenate of lead have
since been used and will continue to be used unless something
better is obtained. While bordeaux mixture is a very efficient
fungicide, the Ben Davis and Baldwin, which varieties constitute
the major portion of the orchards at Highmoor Farm, are very
susceptible to injury from this spray.

Unless one has had experience in similar work in orchard
renovation the results obtained are a little short of marvelous.
Many here have seen these orchards the present season and
before the Station took control. Others have been in the orchard this summer and have seen the plots which have been fertilized, sprayed, and pruned but not cultivated and along side
the plots which, in addition to this, have been thoroughly cultivated. In one case the fruit was scanty and undersized and the
leaves were light green and small, while in the other the fruit
was good sized and abundant and the leaves were large, vigorous and of rich deep green. To one who has not seen the
orchards the annual yield of fruit since the Station assumed
control of the farm tells the most convincing story.

In 1909 thirty-one hundred trees produced two hundred barrels of fruit, of which only ninety were merchantable. In
1910 twenty-three hundred trees produced 350 barrels of which
275 barrels were merchantable. In 1911 twenty-three hundred
trees gave a total yield of 2,450 barrels of which only 114 bar-

rels were classed as culls. The season of 1912 gave the greatest surprise of all, for no one connected with the farm anticipated that trees which were in the condition these were in 1909 and which gave a large crop in 1911 would show a still farther increase in yield of 750 barrels. The figures just obtained for 1912 show a total yield of 3,200 barrels of which 2,950 were merchantable. The percentage of merchantable apples would have been greater this season if continued rainy weather had not prevented the application of the lime-sulphur spray on a part of the orchards before the blossoms opened. Experimental work conducted this year showed that for the present season this application was probably more effective in preventing scab than all the others combined. It also may be remarked in passing that the use of lime-sulphur in place of bordeaux mixture in 1909 and 1910 would doubtless have given a slightly greater percentage of merchantable apples, but this would not have influenced the total yield materially, which depended to a large extent on the nutrition of the trees.

Before leaving the discussion of the practical results obtained at Highmoor I wish to state that the growth of the trees has more than kept pace with the increase in production of the fruit. This is particularly evident in the Baldwin orchard where the trees were especially unhealthy looking and stunted when the Station took control. Some of these trees appear to have nearly twice the spread of limbs that they had three years ago. This may be illustrated by the life history of two small branches taken at random in this orchard a few days ago. The first was put forth from the main branch in 1905. In 1906 it grew two and three-quarters inches, in 1907 four and one-fourth inches, 1908 four and three-fourths inches, 1909 five inches, 1910 three inches. In 1911 came the real response to the new method of treatment when it elongated and matured seventeen and one-fourth inches of new wood. The present season it has done nearly as well and although weather conditions have not been so favorable, the growth has amounted to sixteen inches in length. In other words in 1911 and 1912 this limb gave an average annual growth which was more than three-fourths of that of the five preceding years taken together. The other limb is two years younger. In the three years 1908 to 1910 inclusive, the entire growth in length was only eight and one-half inches. In 1911 it was twenty and three-fourths inches and in 1912 nineteen and one-half inches, or an average annual increase of two and one-half times that of the three preceding years combined. It should be remembered that, as has been previously stated, these trees have produced in succession two fair crops of apples while making this growth. It should also be remembered that during the last three years they have not been competing with a hay crop which would eat up the food materials and make great demands on the water supply just at the time that the trees needed it the most. The only thing which has been grown in the orchards aside from apples has been a fall cover crop which has been plowed under the following spring.

It is the common practice to speak of the ordinary natural and artificial fertilizers as plant food. Strictly speaking this is incorrect. Fertilizers furnish some of the crude food materials which the plant takes in along with water and certain other materials dissolved in water. From these and with the carbon dioxide gas from the air and through energy obtained from the sun's rays it builds up food substances suitable for the nourishment and growth of its various tissues. There are certain chemical elements such as calcium, magnesium, sulphur, iron, nitrogen, phosphorus, and potassium which must be present in the soil to properly nourish the plant. The most of these are present in ordinary soils in sufficient quantity but the supply of nitrogen, phosphorus and potassium is not usually sufficiently abundant to withstand repeated cropping so that they must be replaced by some means or other. All complete artificial fertilizers contain each of these elements in some form. The active, living part of the plant cell in which the work of food manufacture goes on is a nitrogenous compound. Potassium is presumably active in assimilation or the absorption of carbon from the air and in the formation of this living substance, while phosphorus and sulphur rank with nitrogen as important constituents of it. Until quite recently it has been taught that sulphur was present in ordinary soils in sufficient quantity for plant growth. The work of Hart and his associates at the Wisconsin Experiment Station and that of certain German investigators raises a question as to the soundness of this teaching and it is possible that in the near future the use of sulphur as a fertilizer may become a common agricultural practice. As a matter of fact sulphur is a constituent of certain of the compounds ordinarily used in commercial fertilizers such as potassium and ammonium sulphates.

We are apt to regard the soil simply as a storehouse for plant food materials but we lose sight of the fact that much of this food material is not in condition for the plant to take hold of it. It is, as we say, unavailable. How does it become available? Through the activities of millions upon millions of minute living organisms. What do these organisms do? Under favorable conditions they are constantly at work tearing down the more complex organic substances such as those which make up the tissues of the cover crop which is plowed under in the spring, or the stable dressing which is applied, or any other animal or vegetable substance in the soil, and converting what otherwise would be absolutely useless to the plant into more simple chemical compounds which it may readily absorb through its roots. What are favorable conditions for their work? The presence of an adequate supply of moisture, food, air and warmth and an alkaline condition of the soil. How are these conditions best supplied? By cultivation and increasing the humus content of the soil by plowing under cover crops and the application of stable dressing or other fertilizer and liming where necessary.

Thus we have seen that the soil of the orchard is not only a storehouse for plant food materials but that it is a vast manufactory filled with tiny machines, each working day and night when conditions are favorable, turning out a product which the tree can use to build up into food for its tissues. These processes go on most actively in the spring and early summer. The cover crop which served its purpose the fall before in checking too long continued growth and the production of immature wood, prevented washing by fall rains, and helped to protect the roots from the rigors of winter. It also stored up in its tissues some of the available food materials of the season before which would have been washed away and lost. When turned under in the spring it at once furnishes food for these beneficial soil bacteria to grow upon and multiply and to convert into substances which may be used by the trees. It tends to lighted the soil, and to admit the air which is also essential

to their activities. From its nature it increases the water holding capacity of the soil, which not only benefits the soil bacteria
but also is of the greatest importance to the trees when the dry
summer months come on and large demands are being made
upon the soil for water to develop the growing leaves, wood
and fruit.

So much for the cover crop—now wherein are the benefits of
cultivation? It is well known that a heavy soil is cold and
that the lighter and more porous it is the warmer it is. A soil
that is frequently stirred is better aerated. Frequent cultivation
tends to break up capillarity and consequently helps to prevent
losses of water from the soil by evaporation. Cultivation
also makes the particles of soil finer and thus allows more ready
access to the materials it contains. Hence we see that cultivation does much to produce the right conditions under which
these beneficial soil bacteria are able to do their work.

The higher plants with green coloring matter, to which
class the apple tree belongs, differ from animals in that they
are able to build up from comparatively simple chemical compounds, with the aid of this green coloring matter and the
energy obtained from sunlight, the quite complex food substances necessary for the repairing and building up of tissues
and the carrying on of various other vital processes within the
plant. Before we can intelligently discuss how the apple tree
does this and what bearing it has on a rational system of orchard management we must know something of the structure of
the various organs of the tree.

All plants are built up of cells and these are of different kinds
and shapes and they are variously modified according to their
functions. The essential parts of a plant cell of the class to
which the apple tree belongs consist first of a cell wall made
up largely of a substance called cellulose which is readily per-
meable to water. It contains identically the same chemical substances and in the same proportions as starch but differs from
it in the way these substances are combined. Filter paper or
raw cotton are almost pure cellulose. In woody tissues and
bark the cell walls have become much altered through the depo-
sition of other substances. Within the cell wall is the living substance called the cytoplasm or protoplasm. This is a nitrogenous or albuminous substance more closely resembling the

white of an egg than anything else we meet with in every day life. Except in the youngest cells this cytoplasm forms a thin layer just within and in close contact with the cell wall, and in it the different processes of food manufacture, transforma- tion and nutrition go on. Imbedded in it are various small bodies called plastids. Some of these are known to perform certain definite work in the cell. Two classes of these which are very much alike in many ways are of especial interest to us. The green ones or chloroplasts which are so abundant in the cells of the leaves as to give them their green color are the bodies which are concerned in the manufacture of starch. Other colorless ones in cells in other parts of the tree or in portions of the trunk and roots are the agents which store up the starch in those cells for a future food supply. The cavity within the cell is filled with the cell sap which consists largely of water with other substances in solu- tion. Somewhere within the cell, sometimes suspended in the cavity or often at one side, but always connected with the layer of cytoplasm within the cell wall, is a very definite body called the nucleus. While this in many respects is by far the most .important of all the parts that go to make up the cell, in that it is considered by many to be the controlling factor in the various vital activities of the cell and plays a very important role in the transmission of hereditary characters, it is not neces- sary for our present purpose to discuss it farther.

The cells which go to make up the root hairs are long and slender and are very thin walled. Those which go to make up the tissues of the root, trunk and branches are variously modi- fied. Many of the wood cells are long and slender with pointed ends which overlap each other, breaking joints, and thus giving strength. In other cases the end walls of larger cells in the woody tissues disappear along with their living contents. To all intents and purposes much of the interior of the trunk is dead tissue, but it is by no means functionless. The disappearance of the end walls of the large cells leads to the formation of large tubes or ducts, running up and down the stem, and these serve a most useful purpose in helping to provide a passage for the food materials in solution from the roots below to the leaves above. They may be roughly compared to a system of pipe lines. Some of them are curiously pitted while others are strengthened by a spiral arrangement which reminds one of the metal reinforcement used on lines of rubber hose designed to withstand great pressure, only the spirals are on the inside rather than on the outside of the tube. It must not be assumed that the tissues of trees are not subjected to considerable pressure from this upward flow of sap. On a steam gauge attached to a maple tree I have obtained a pressure amounting to twenty-five pounds to the square inch.

Running radially out from the center of the trunk are rows of short cells whose shape and arrangement may be likened to a brick wall. These cells remain alive much longer than many of the woody cells which adjoin them, and they serve to unite all the separate living tissues of the stem. They are active in transporting food materials from the outside inward and are connected with the water conducting elements and serve as storehouses for starch, etc. They form the so-called medullary rays which are quite prominent in cross sections of the trunks of certain kinds of trees. Just within the bark is the cambium ring composed of a layer of cells which are in active division as long as growth is taking place rapidly, especially in the spring. It is here that growth in thickness takes place. This explains why in grafting it is absolutely essential in order to secure a perfect union that the inner line of the bark of the scion should exactly coincide with that of the stock. In budding the little ring of exposed cambium tissues is seated in direct contact with the outer layers of the same tissue of the stock. Hence ideal conditions for a union is thus povided.

In the leaves the shape of the cells and their arrangement may be compared to the stones of a loosely piled stone wall, but there is a certain amount of order and purpose to it. The upper and lower surfaces of the leaves are covered with a definite protective layer of cells, called the epidermis. Scattered through this are many little mouth-like openings called breathing pores or stomata. These openings are surrounded by two peculiarly shaped guard cells which remind one of lips. These guard cells are so constructed that they automatically open apart when the leaf is turgid with water and close together when the reverse is the case. The breathing pores not only serve as avenues for the escape of watery vapors from the interior tissues of the leaf but also for the escape of oxygen gas which is a by-product in the manufacture of starch and allow for the entrance of carbon. dioxide gas from the air which is absolutely essential for the manufacture and production of starch, sugar and other carbonaceous compounds used in the nutrition and growth of the tree. It will be seen that the loose, spongy nature of the leaf tissue is adapted to these processes also.

We are now ready to start with the simple food materials in the soil which have been supplied by means of chemicals or which have been produced by the breaking down of organic matter in the soil and its conversion into available form by the soil bacteria. and follow their course till they are built up into the tissues of the tree. In the first place they must be in solution. This requires the presence of an adequate supply of soil water which may not be present during the diest summer months unless evaporation has been retarded by means of frequent cultivation. The root hairs give off an acid secretion and it is generally thought that this assists in dissolving and bringing into solution certain mineral food substances.

Now having the plant food materials in available condition and in solution, how does the apple tree take them up? The natural answer is, by means of the roots, but if you press the question farther and ask if all of the roots or only certain parts of each root function in this matter I venture to state that the average individual has rather hazy ideas on the subject. As a matter of fact the entire process of absorption of these food materials in solution takes place in a very limited portion of the roots and is confined largely to the root hairs. Root hairs occur in only one narrow zone and this is just back of the growing point at the end of each and every tiny rootlet. Knowing this fact we can appreciate how very important it is in transplanting trees that these small rootlets are not broken off and are disturbed as little as possible if the tree is to go on growing without a serious setback. And knowing this fact also it is not at all surprising that so many young orchards come to grief the first year, and infant-tree mortality is so large. Another important lesson which this fact teaches is that the man who distributes his fertilizer only closely around the tree trunks could not place it in a more inaccessible place so far as the majority of the organs of absorption are concerned if he sat up nights and worked over time trying to devise a means of so doing. Hence to place the food materials where they will do the most good they should be distributed all over the ground shaded by the foliage and particularly upon the outer portions of this area.

Ater the solutions of food materials are absorbed they pass along to the cells adjoining the root hairs and then upward through the roots and trunk and branches in the wood inside the cambium zone, and then outward into smaller and smaller branches till they reach the leaves. These are the laboratories of the tree where the actual manufacture of the food for the nourishment and building up of the tissues takes place. In these leaf laboratories the more simple chemical compounds brought up in solution from the soil are combined with some of the water itself and with the carbon dioxide of the air into the much more complex food substances. Sunlight is the ultimate source of energy for this process and it cannot take place without it.

Thus we readily see the necessity for pruning. While pruning is of great advantage in removing dead, diseased and surplus wood and in providing opportunity for the better coloring of the fruit, it is absolutely essential to ensure the most efficient and maximum production of food substances. In a thick topped apple tree only the outer leaves receive the full rays of the active summer sunlight. Those within are so shaded that they fall far short of working to their full capacity and almost may be classed as non-producers in this great leaf community of plant-food manufacturers. Moreover such leaves must of necessity be weaklings for their own tissues are dependent for nourishment upon the food which they manufacture. The apple scab fungus which is one of the greatest enemies of the apple tree in Maine finds among them the ideal conditions under which to gain a foothold. This fungus loves shade and moisture, while free access of sunlight and the free circulation of air through the tree-tops are of great assistance in keeping it in check. It more readily attacks the leaves that are in a weakened condition and a leaf so attacked rapidly loses its food manufacturing ability. Hence the attacks of apple scab indirectly deprive the tree of its tissue building materials.

A well pruned, well shaped, open-topped apple tree allows the admission of sunlight to all of the interior portions. The limbs are so arranged that the maximum number of leaves are exposed to the source of energy and they are thus worked to their full capacity. This same arrangement also provides less favorable conditions for the development of scab and it also facilitates the application of protective sprays to the interior portions of the top.

Starch is of almost universal occurrence in green plants and is an important plant food. That it is manufactured in the green leaves and only in the presence of certain active rays of a beam of sunlight is a fact easily demonstrated by any school boy. While starch is constantly being formed when the sun is shining on a green leaf it is in the form of grains and not in solution. By other agencies it is constantly being converted into closely related soluble substances like sugar and transported to other parts of the plant. There it is either used at once or converted into starch again and stored till future needs require it. The potato gives a familiar illustration of this. Here the food material manufactured by the parent plant the season before is stored up in the tuber ready to be used as a source of nourishment for the young plant till it has developed a root system of its own and is able to shift for itself. This transformation and removal of manufactured starch goes on throughout the night. Hence the leaf that at the close of a sunny day was gorged with starch begins the new day with a clean slate ready to repeat the process of manufacture.

The plant manufactures starch from the elements supplied by carbon dioxide and water alone and releases oxygen in the process, which escapes through the breathing pores of the leaves. The albuminous substances which go to make up the living cytoplasm of the cell contain in addition to the chemical elements found in starch, nitrogen, sulphur and phosphorus. In the formation of albuminous substances it is generally held that a part of the starch is first converted into some other form of carbohydrate and that this is in some way combined with the other elements mentioned.

The course of the long distance transport of the elaborated albuminous food substances in passing back down the branches and trunk differs from that of the upward current of crude materials in that it is carried down in the innermost but living portions of the bark just inside of and in contact with the cambium zone or region of growth. When we know the path of the upward passage of crude materials and the downward course of the elaborated food we are able to explain many common observations in the orchard. Thus we can readily understand why, if the wood is sound, a tree may go on growing for some time or sometimes recover after it has been nearly or partially girdled. However, if not enough manufactured food can be sent back down to nourish the roots they will gradually lose their power to take up crude food substances from the soil and the death of the tree will result. When we resort to bridge grafting we are simply putting in what may be called an artificial pipe line to bridge the gap and in this way convey manufactured food down to the roots that they may be suitably nourished and thus be able to perform their proper function.

Before closing I wish to call attention to one more practical point. In pruning fruit and shade trees it is practically impossible to get the majority of people to make the cut at the proper place. From what we have learned regarding the course of the downward movement of the elaborated food materials, the region of growth and consequently the region in which new tissues must be formed for covering wounds, it is perfectly evident that the cut must be made parallel with and as close to the main trunk or branch as it can possibly be made. The surface must be smooth and no projecting edges of wood left at the margins of the wound to prevent the new tissues from closing over it. Such a wound will completely heal in due time, provided the exposed wood is properly protected with a coating of pure white lead and linseed oil. A cut made farther away from the main trunk or branch makes a much smaller wound but such a wound either never heals at all or if it does heal it takes much longer than when the cut is properly made. Frequently the bark extending out beyond the line of the trunk dies away, leaving an unsightly stub which later decays, and the decay thus started is communicated to the interior of the trunk, leading finally to the decay and death of the tree. Many orchards have been converted into graveyards through the lack of observation and the ignorance of fundamental principles of growth and nutrition, as applied to apple trees, on the part of men who pruned them or failed to prune them.

THURSDAY AFTERNOON.

GREGORY ORCHARDS.

THEIR SOURCE AND AIM.

By A. K. GARDNER, Augusta.

As a result of the New England Fruit Show held in Boston in October, 1909, Mr. James J. H. Gregory of Marblehead, Mass., gave to the State of Maine a $1000 first mortgage bond, with the provision that at intervals of five years $200 of the interest should be paid to the orchardist who could show to a committee of three the most excellent orchard of one acre or more grown on his own land, of trees of his own selection (the Ben Davis excepted) five years from setting; the first planting to be in the spring of 1910 and judged in 1915. This most generous offer of Mr. Gregory's induced others to offer like premiums as follows:—

Premium by a friend	$150
Bowker Company	100
B. G. Pratt Company	100
Douglas Pump Company	100
Deming Pump Co., Salem, Ohio	50
Charles J. Jager Co., Boston, Mass.......	50
Portland Farmers' Club	50

This great movement received the hearty support of many of our leading orchard men throughout the State, with the result that a large number entered for the contest, and names were being booked for the acre or more of standard apple trees. Information regarding this contest was published and distributed as follows:—

"Although we do not wish to issue cast-iron rules or provide for a whole lot of red tape, we do believe that if we are in the forward movement for better fruit for Maine, and if we would place our fruit on a par with that of our western neighbors, we must adopt the best methods known to the fruit industry. We must gain the confidence of our commission men and the consuming public before we can hope to make a success with our apples. Our first duty is to thoroughly renovate our present orchards and then enter this contest to show that we believe in the possibilities of our Maine grown apples. We have the best of soil, as good a climate as can be found, for many choice varieties, and one of the best markets of the world at our very doors. Why should not Maine lead in this important industry that means so much to the health as well as profit of our people?

We will outline some of the essential points to be considered in entering this contest.

SELECTING STOCK.

It is left with each contestant to make his own selection of any standard varieties, the Ben Davis excepted. Of course much depends upon the right selection. If one wishes for a home orchard alone, he wants to select those varieties that appeal to him or his family, for we do not all have the same taste in this regard; but one should use his best judgment and select those that would give fruit for the table from early fall to late summer. This would require but few varieties, providing they were well selected. If a commercial orchard is planned, and that is what is most desired in this campaign, we would recommend but one variety, providing it be a strong polenizer; if not, it would be well to set every fifth row to some variety that blossomed at the same time and was rich in pollen. Those who enter this contest should plan to make this acre the nucleus of an extensive commercial orchard and start where additions could be made from year to year as desired.

This stock should be of the first quality, preferably two years old, straight, of good top formation and with plenty of roots. It is very essential that stock be selected at the earliest possible moment, as there is a great scarcity of standard apple trees in the market."

28

At the end of the season, report sheets were sent to each contestant calling for name, address, location of orchard, slope, soil, previous soil management, variety or varieties, use,—commercial or home—distance apart of trees, fertilizer, amount and cost, crop raised, cost of production, amount of crop, value of same, cost of trees, expense of setting, expense of care and amount of growth.

It was believed that by covering the ground thoroughly, definite and valuable data could be obtained regarding adaptability of variety, best methods of pruning and management and the necessary costs in setting an orchard and bringing it into bearing.

The orchards were visited by a member of the Department and advice as to pruning, etc., given to each grower. Unfortunately, this advice was not followed as carefully as it should have been, in a great many cases. When the returns came in, it was found that one hundred seventy-eight (178) growers had entered the contest. Most of the questions were fully and comprehensively answered, but those relating to costs were disappointing and showed lack of business methods in the management. Some of the compilations regarding the reports have been made up and are given below.

The orchards are located in Counties as follows:—Androscoggin, 26; Cumberland, 9; Franklin, 13; Hancock, 9; Kennebec, 16; Knox, 8; Lincoln, 9; Oxford, 19; Penobscot, 15; Piscataquis, 10; Sagadahoc, 6; Somerset, 9; Waldo, 17; Washington, 7; York, 5; Aroostook being the only county not represented.

As regards variety, Stark leads slightly over the McIntosh in number of times planted. Stark, 50; McIntosh, 49; Baldwin, 31; Wealthy, 23; Wolf River, 18; Spy, 17; Tallman Sweet, 13; Arctic, Gravenstein and King, 8; Delicious, Dudley Winter and Gano, 7; Banana, King David and Rhode Island Greening, 6; Senator, 5; Longfield and Rolfe, 3; Alexander, Baxter, Bellflower, Hubbardston, Jonathan, Maiden Blush, Milding, Opalescent, Paragon, Red Astrachan, Wagener and Wismer, 2; America, American Blush, Arkansas Red, Beitegheimer, Black Ben Davis, Dutchess, Fall Pippin, Ohio Nonpareil, Pewaukee, Stayman, Spitzenburg, Walbridge and York Imperial, 1. The large

number of varieties planted may be accounted for in that many
of the orchards are for family use.

The distance apart varied somewhat, the popular distance
being two rods each way.

```
48 were set ................................ 33 x 33
33  "    "   ................................ 30 x 30
30  '        ................................ 40 x 40
16  '        ................................ 35 x 35
 6  '·   ··  ................................ 30 x 40
 4  '        ................................ 35 x 40
 4  '·   ··  ................................ 36 x 36
 2  ·'·      ................................ 27 x 27
 2  '·   ··  ................................ 30 x 35
 2  '        ................................ 25 x 25
 2  "    "   ................................  6 x  6†
 1 was set ................................. 20 x 20
 1  "    "   ................................ 30 x 33
             ................................ 34 x 34
             ................................ 25 x 35
 1  ··   ··  ................................ 28 x 28
 ı  ··   ··  ................................ 33 x 40
```

As regards method of handling:

    87 were cropped
    20 were in sod
    15 were in grain
     6 were in pasture
     4 were clean cut with cover crop
     2 were in clover
     2 were mulched
     1 was pastured to hogs

†Transplanted later.

	Cost of Trees.		Cost of Setting.	
	Average per A.	Average per tree.	Average per A.	Average per tree.
Androscoggin	$14 48	$.407	$2 95	$.09
Cumberland	11 35	.249	3 14	.068
Franklin	14 22	.335	2 94	.063
Hancock	16 77	.418	5 07	.112
Kennebec	15 06	.372	2 57	.059
Knox	15 06	.415	3 35	.092
Lincoln	26 37	.608	2 53	.058
Oxford	16 23	.354	4 62	.093
Penobscot	11 89	.392	3 49	.115
Piscataquis	15 79	.370	3 88	.100
Sagadahoc	18 41	.447	3 83	.093
Somerset	15 11	.386	3 33	.085
Waldo	11 40	.284	3 03	.065
Washington	17 07	.591	5 16	.153
York	13 05	.390	3 77	.090

Highest cost of one tree.............................. $1.94

Lowest cost of one tree............................... .10

Average cost of one tree.............................. .387

Highest cost of setting one tree...................... .25

Lowest cost of setting one tree....................... .015

Average cost of setting one tree...................... .085

Average cost of one acre of trees.................... $15.24

Average cost of setting one acre..................... 3.44

Largest number of trees per acre.................... 109

Smallest number of trees per acre................... 27

Last fall, the reports were sent out again, asking many of the former questions and in addition, spray materials, trees re-set and the cause of death.

Twenty-four of the original contestants failed to send in any data and have been dropped from the list.

The second year reports proved very interesting and in general were satisfactory. The cost of handling again furnishing the disappointing feature.

Four hundred sixty-nine (469) were killed during the first year; 110 by mice, 132 by winter-killing and canker, 38 by failure to start, 25 because of poor stock, 12 by poor root systems, 35 by unknown causes, 37 by snow and ice, 16 by deer, 50 because of the extremely dry season, 4 by carelessness in driving, 1 by scale, 1 by borers, 1 by rabbits, 4 by tarred paper and 3 because of woolly aphis.

This loss must comprise nearly 1-12 of the total number of trees and plainly indicates that the locations were either very unfavorable or that the method of handling was at fault.

The cultivation methods were very similar to the first year; most of the orchards being cropped to garden truck, corn and potatoes.

There were not as many who practiced spraying as had been anticipated, especially the sprays for aphis. These lice were prevalent in nearly all the orchards and were damaging the growing tips to a great extent. As the spray is simple to make and easy to apply, the fact that it was not used is the more surprising.

Sixty-nine (69) of the orchards received no spraying whatsoever. Bug death was used in two, Paris green in two, lime-sulphur in thirty-eight, whale oil soap in six, arsenate of lead in thirty-four, kerosene emulsion in nine, tobacco infusion in eleven, Pyrox in twelve, Bordeaux Mixture in sixteen and Bordo Lead in one.

THE OUTLOOK.

The inspections this season have shown that only a comparatively small number of the orchards will offer keen competition for the prizes.

What are the reasons for this? They are many. That it is not due to climate conditions is demonstrated by the fact that many of the best orchards are widely scattered, or to soil by the fact that orchards in the same neighborhood under similar soil conditions vary greatly.

It would appear then that the variations are due, first, to poor stock, and second, to lack of care. As the majority of the original stock averaged over forty cents per tree, the cause of this variation would seem to be elsewhere.

Lack of proper care is the important fault with these orchards.

1. Lack of time.

2. Nonappreciation of the advantage of proper pruning, spraying and growth.

Unfortunately for our fruit industry, the majority of our growers relegate the orchard to the background and allow it to play second fiddle to the other crops on the farm. The expression, "I didn't have time as other work interfered," is so common that it has become monotonous.

If we are to put our orchards to the front where they rightfully belong, we can't allow other work to interfere. The trees must be of paramount importance if we are to successfully compete with the growers of other sections.

PRUNING.

A sturdy tree that is capable of supporting fruit is the tree we desire in the orchard and to get this tree we must prune the young tree carefully and systematically. A certain amount of heading must be carried on both at the time of planting and later, removng branches that are not desirable and prevent a well balanced top.

We need a tree here that has at least a moderately open top, as the short season and lack of sunshine tend to produce poorly colored fruit. The impression that a low head interferes with cultivation, weakens the tree by starting it high and having the branches come out too near together.

Many varieties, unless headed back, produce long, weak branches with little bearing surface, which are not desirable.

Inspectors have dwelt upon these points each year, but there seems to be little inclination to carry them out on the part of some of the growers.

It is an established fact that a certain amount of spraying aids materially in the development of the young tree. Scale insects sap the strength from the growing tissue in the main limbs and trunk; aphis check the terminal growth and curl the leaves by sucking the juices from them. Scab and fruit spot cause the leaves to fall prematurely before they have thoroughly completed their function and leaf-eating insects often defoliate the trees leaving them without what we may term their lungs.

No young tree can do what it is capable of, if these pests are allowed free rein and the extra expense incurred in their suppression will be more than offset in the more rapid development of the tree itself.

Many trees have been driven too fast, resulting often in winter-killing; others have not had sufficient food, resulting often in canker, which they are too weak to resist.

Where nitrogen has been used extensively, especially as nitrate of soda, the wood has not sufficiently ripened in the fall to withstand the severe cold during the winter and the trees have killed back badly.

Just how fast a tree should grow must be judged mainly by its appearance and not by a set fertilizer formula. Early forcing hardly ever pays in the long run. In general the orchards that are receiving cultivation, either through garden crops or cover crops, are doing better than those in sod, even though the latter are receiving applications of commercial fertilizer.

The orchards in grain suffered more than the others, especially a year ago when the soil became so dry. Oats especially should be planted elsewhere.

As regards growth, I would say, prune out the branches that are unnecessary to the framework and weaken it; spray so that the tree may be healthy and capable of doing its best; keep down invading grass and weeds during the growing season; feed the tree carefully and see that the growth is checked so as to allow the maturing of the wood before the cold weather comes.

In many of the Gregory orchards this management has been carried on and the results are clearly manifested.

Let us hope that in 1915 when the second orchards are set, more men will enter the contest and go in with the firm determination that theirs shall be the best, not necessarily the most expensive, for the question of economy enters the competition, and that other crops will not interfere with that work which is the most pleasant and profitable if rightly carried on.

RESULTS IN 1912 AT HIGHMOOR FARM.

By G. A. YEATON.

Mr. President, Brothers and Sisters of the State Pomological Society:

You have been talked almost to death. Everybody has talked to you. They talk to you downstairs. They talk to you up-stairs. They have played the organ, they have done almost everything, and the only hopes that I have of your staying here is that the door is going to be locked so that you can't dodge. But I will tell you another thing, that I am not going to make any long talk at all, for I realize the fact that you are very tired indeed and that it has been a strenuous week for us all. Unfortunately I have not written out any of the talk that I am going to make. It is simply facts as they have been presented to us through the orchard that I am going to talk to you about.

In the first place Dr. Morse reviewed the situation very thoroughly this morning. The very best that I can do is practically to give you a repetition of what he said. I am going to tell you some of the things that have been accomplished.

When the State took over the farm three or four years ago the orchard was in a very serious condition indeed. It was on the verge of collapse. The trees had been neglected. Many of them had made but a trifling growth for a number of years previous. The roots were just barely holding the life in the tops and not making any growth whatever, just simply existing, lingering at this poor dying rate. The State took them over and commenced to fertilize, prune, spray, and cultivate, and did a work of regeneration. To prove that that was the right thing to do,—the first crop was less than 200 barrels and of that only ninety barrels were merchantable. The next year we got a little better crop. The only note that I have made was the number of barrels, and that is so very important, illustrating thoroughly the value of cultivation, pruning and spraying, the treatment that the orchard has had, that I am going to read from my notes. In 1909 there were 200 barrels of which 90 were marketable apples. In 1910, 350 barrels were produced, of which 275 barrels were put into the market. In 1911, 2400 barrels were raised, and 2300 were put into the market. In 1912 the grand total was 3217, of which 2750 were fancy No. 1 apples, packed so that the members of the Pomological Society would be proud to have any one inspect them as he would see a pack that was a credit to all, and the whole State of Maine, because it is an object lesson, and we say the main feature that we are endeavoring to bring out at Highmoor Farm is the value of an object lesson, to induce others to go and do likewise. Now to bring these results about we have used systematic spraying, fertilizing, pruning and cultivation. We found this year that in order to cultivate more economically than we had in the past, it was advisable to get a traction engine or a motor plow. The trees are set in rows twenty-five feet apart each way. You will understand that that is so close together that the limbs come very near together in the center, making it almost impossible to cultivate with a team; especially if you are using 1600 lb. horses. So the Station bought a traction engine or motor plow and the plowing between the rows as far forth as we could was done with that, and then a disc harrow was attached to the corner of this auto plow which allowed us to cultivate close to the trees. That has been done a great deal more economically than could possibly be done by the horses with the old fashioned method. One can run the engine, one taking care of the harrow, either the disc or the spring tooth, and guiding it up close to the trees. It saved a great deal of expense and the result has been phenomenal. The trees, without any more fertilizer than has been used in years past, have made a wonderful growth, the leaves are in a better, more healthy color than they have been in the past, and the or. chard is really coming along very nicely indeed.

Now when the Station took this farm over, the mice had worked there a good deal and many of the trunks of the trees were girdled part way round, some of them more than three-quarters of the distance. This past season in one of the orchards we have been doing some tree surgery. We have cut out the diseased wood so as to get down to the clean wood in order to make a good healing, and then have filled those with cement. We are intending, and probably it will be carried out next spring, to bridge graft below, starting in below where the mice have girdled and inserting the scion below. While it is of course going to be a great deal of injury, as it has set back the tree in its productivity quite a good deal by the loss of the flow of the sap, yet we believe that by bridging that over we can induce that tree to bear the normal crop again. Those are some of the few things that we are trying to demonstrate to the people that it is feasible to do.

Now in almost all of the orchards we have given absolutely thorough cultivation from the early spring until about the middle of August. In one of the orchards we have left, partly from necessity and partly for an experiment, a piece around the tree four feet. We plowed up to four feet each way. There is an eight foot space, four feet from either side, and where it has been plowed both ways there is really a circle of eight feet around the tree that has not been cultivated, and where the trees have had a thorough, clean cultivation in the rows adjoining those with the eight foot space, we can see by the new growth this year that it has made quite a good deal of difference. Where there was clean cultivation there has been from two to five inches more growth. Now that may seem to you a small thing, two to five inches, but when you consider that the average growth of our orchards throughout the State is only about eight inches, you will see it is really a phenomenal growth. And that has been accomplished more through cultivation than it has from the fertilization.

The fertilizer experiments have been as follows: In No. 1 orchard, the first four rows this year had no fertilizer whatever; the next four rows, 500 lbs. of the commercial fertilizer which analyzes 4-8-6,—nitrogen 4, phosphoric acid 8, potash 6; and the next four rows had a half a ton of that same grade. That is the grade of phosphate used this year in all of our orchard work. This year with the cultivation that we have given the orchard, it has not shown in new growth or the size of the apples where the fertilizer was applied. Whether there was no fertilizer applied this spring, 500 lbs. or a thousand pounds, we practically got the same results. Now that does not prove one single thing to us because since the Station took over this farm the trees have had thorough cultivation all the time. But in time to come, it will show us whether we have got to fertilize more, or whether we can curtail the expense by cutting out a part of the fertilizer, or whether we have got to increase our fertilizer to get the best results.

Now for the practical orchard man we have got to have the results. Those of you that were in to hear Bro. Hale last night heard him tell us that we had got to figure it so fine, if we were going to have the balance on the right side of the sheet, that we had got to cut out an eighth of a cent here, a quarter there, two cents on the package—we must cut our expenses down if we are going to have our profit on the right side of the sheet. If we can run our orchards and produce equally as good results with a small, medium or minimum amount of fertilizer, we are going to save some of the expense. Now I don't believe it is advisable for us to favor simply a growth of apples, or to get a great big, coarse, ill-flavored, uncolored apple, thinking that because we produce more bushels we are going to get more dollars. The people are coming to distinguish more clearly quality from quantity. Quality is that which will tell in our orchard work in the near future. If we produce a barrel of apples and put them out onto the market, and you or any one gets one of our apples, and that apple is a choice, well colored and good flavored apple, you are going to call for more of that kind. That is what the Experiment Station is trying to demonstrate to the people,—that we must produce quality. Unfortunately nine-tenths of the trees that are set on Highmoor Farm are Ben Davis, but even with that poor quality of apples we can demonstrate to you that you can improve them. The Governor of South Carolina said that almost everything had been improved, even the Irish potato had been improved and educated. Now I believe that we can in a measure improve the Ben Davis apple. It is rather a hard proposition, but I believe it can be done. Instead of bringing out a great coarse-grained one, produce the best type that we can, one that is well colored, and then it will sell fairly well at a fair price.

Along the line of work that we are doing, besides demonstrating the effect of fertilizing and cultivating, we are endeavoring to produce other varieties of apples and determine the adaptability of those apples to our Maine conditions. We have a small nursery that is below the orchard. There are about three thousand trees. The original stock was French crab seedlings, set a year ago this last spring. This year in July and August we budded those over, to the apples which appealed to us as being desirable to grow in this section of the State. Of course it takes a long time, it is a slow process, this picking out, selecting, sorting and grading up to get a new variety of an apple that will take the place of the Baldwin as a commercial apple and at the same time bring out the color, and one that will stand up and ship across the water or to any other section of the country,—and stand up as well as the Baldwin and will have as fine a flavor as the McIntosh.

The pruning is another thing. We have done what we could to demonstrate the different methods of pruning. We have allowed some of the trees to grow as they naturally would. The Ben Davis is naturally inclined to a close-growing top. We have taken this out to allow the sun to come in and ripen up and color the fruit. It has had a wonderful effect. We have found where we have opened the top up that we have got larger apples and very much better colored apples; and the fungous diseases which attacked those which were closer growing, where the sun did not have a chance to come in and assist in killing out the spores, have troubled us less. We have had fewer scabby apples and less trouble from the fungous diseases. This demonstrates the advisability, in our section especially, of opening up the top, not trying to have them too dense or to allow them to run into the air too high, but to keep them down low and open them up so as to allow the sun and air to come in. Those are some of the things accomplished this year at Highmoor.

Now after the crop was grown the problem that confronted us was that of packing and taking care of it. When there were

only three hundred barrels it was a very easy thing to take
those apples and bring them to the barn and pick them over,
but when it had multiplied itself by ten and we were going to
have three thousand barrels instead of three hundred it was a
different thing. We had to go to work then and put up a
packing shed large enough to accommodate us. The Director,
by permission and consent of the Board of Trustees or Council
as it is called, went ahead and built a packing shed 40x80 feet.
We made a mistake in not putting it up 100 feet, because it
would have been considerably more economical to handle the
apples with the larger sorting space. We shouldn't have had to
handle the barrels over so often. We needed that shed very
much indeed and in the short time that we had this year to
handle the crop it facilitated it very greatly and allowed us to
handle it a great deal more economically.

It may be interesting to all to know what effect our spraying
has had in controlling the insects and fungous diseases which
have attacked the orchards—not simply our orchard there at
Highmoor but all over the State. We found that we had got to
get rid of the insects which were bothering us. In order to
control them we have tried different methods of spraying, different spraying materials, different strengths, different methods of
applying them. The commercial orchards were practically all
sprayed with the lime sulphur of the commercial strength, that
tested out 33, or 32 to 33, degrees. The dormant spray was
given 1 to 10, the spray just before the buds were opening,
when they showed the pink, 1 to 20, the summer spray after the
leaves were all open, 1 to 40. Where we gave those three
sprays we practically controlled all of the scab and other fungous diseases. In the experimental plots in the No. 2 orchard
there were different strengths, and different materials used. For
instance, the lime-sulphur alone without any other insecticide
put in. Then there was arsenate of lead, just simply the insecticide and no fungicide, applied, and all of those different
applications, which Dr. Morse told us about this morning, in
different strengths. I will say right here that with lime-sulphur,
the combination of the lime-sulphur with the three pounds of
arsenate of lead at the commercial strength, gave us the best
result of any. Those apples were free from worms. In all of

our packing this year we have only found two codling moths in Highmoor orchard—from three thousand barrels only two codling moths have been found this year. That is a record, I think, we certainly all ought to feel proud of. We had but very little russeting under those methods. On the plot where we used the Bordeaux mixture, the 3-3-50 formula, with the three pounds of arsenate of lead added, there was a good deal of russeting. It may be interesting to you to know that the foliage of the Ben Davis is more susceptible to spray injury than any other apple we have. The fruit is also susceptible of russeting. They show it quite a good deal, and the spray did not control the fungous diseases, the sooty blotch and the apple scab, enough better than the lime-sulphur so that I would feel justified in recommending that to any one else.

I might say though, that we have done some cross pollenating and hybridizing of the apples. For instance, we have seedlings which we started, the Tallman Sweet for the male parent and the Spy for the female. We have got about twenty or thirty of the different crosses, the Baldwin and Tallman, the Spy and Tallman, the McIntosh with the Grevenstein. We have got, of those small seedlings that are anywhere from six to ten or eleven inches high, 1007 which are going to be tested out the next year. Where there are three or more of the same seedlings we are going to fruit one on its own root, the next one we are going to fruit on one that has been worked to a Tallman Sweet and the third one on a French Crab, to see whether the stalk has any influence over the scion, and whether we will gain anything by rebudding and re-working; whether on its own root it would produce apples sooner than it would if we budded it on to one of the other varieties; and to see whether by cross-working it a second time on to the Tallman Sweet it would be improved in quality.

Those are the experiments that we have tried out this year, and we have succeeded in controlling the scab where we have fought it out as we know we should, we have done away with practically all the insect pests except the green aphis, and that is a continual warfare. As the Bible says about the poor,—we always have them with us. The only way you can kill them is by spraying early and often with something that will strike against them, and with force enough so it will be driven right on to the insect. They don't eat, but do their mischief by sucking. Aside from them, we have controlled the diseases of the trees and our insect pests there on the farm.

PRACTICAL FRUIT GROWING.

By W. H. CONANT.

It s a well known fact that a large per cent of the fruit produced in Maine is grown by farmers who carry on a system of diversified farming, and, in many cases, the orchard is a second or third consideration.

But I am glad to say a great many are waking up to the possibilities in orcharding, and today fruit growing is a live question in many Maine counties. Yet there is a lack of system in orchard management, and the question is often asked, "What shall I do for my orchard?" and so I wish to speak just a few moments on the management of bearing orchards from the standpoint of a grower. There are various systems of orchard culture, all of which are good under favorable conditions, but I believe that tillage with cover crops is best adapted to our conditions and our short seasons in Maine.

There is a balance between fruit and wood growth and this can be maintained much easier under the tillage system. The question is asked, "How and what shall I feed my orchard?" In the first place we should realize that tillage in a measure is fertilization, that working the soil liberates plant food that otherwise would not become available.

There are three principal elements of plant food with which we must supply our trees if we wish to derive best results. They are nitrogen, phosphorus and potash.

On account of varying soil conditions there can be no set formula for feeding the orchard, yet many Maine orchardists have used the following formula with excellent results; three to four per cent nitrogen, seven to eight phosphoric acid, and ten per cent potash, used at the rate of five hundred pounds per acre.

Tree feeding should be done as early in the spring as the conditions of the soil will permit, whether farm dressing is used or commercial fertilizer. Supplying available plant food at this season tends to force a wood growth in June. I make a practice of plowing my orchard early in the spring and sowing the fertilizer broadcast. This is harrowed in well and I continue to harrow at least once a week until July 1st, when I believe cultivation should cease except in extremely dry seasons when cultivation should be continued through July to conserve moisture by aid of a dust mulch.

In many orchards after cultivation has stopped wild grasses and weeds come up which form a substitute for a cover crop; if not, a light cover crop should be sown. This tends to check wood growth so the new growth may ripen up early to prevent winter-killing.

The orchard should be well pruned, and the early spring seems to be the most favorable time for the average grower to do this work. The ever-increasing orchard pests make spraying a necessity, and this should be carefully and thoroughly done.

I have a one-acre orchard containing fifty-eight mature trees that under this system of culture has yielded in the last three years as follows:

1910	125 bbls.
1911	250 "
1912	160

making a total of 535

which I consider a good yield for a shy-bearing variety like the Northern Spy.

In closing, I want to add just a word of caution: *Do not try to force the orchard too hard with nitrogen.* Learn to control this element of plant food and feed as near a balanced feed as possible, otherwise you will get quantity at the expense of quality.

I earnestly believe the Maine orchardist who adopts this, or some similar system of orchard management, will in a comparatively short time be harvesting annual yields of fruit, the quality of which would be second to none in the world.

IN MEMORIAM.

HON. Z. A. GILBERT.

1833—1912.

Without detracting in the least from the valuable service rendered by the loyal workers in fruit culture, from the earliest period to the year just closed, it is but just to claim that Maine is indebted to Mr. Z. A. Gilbert for its progress in fruit problems more than to any other man.

Instinctively a farmer, naturally a close thinker and reasoner, conservative in methods and habits, and yet with an earnest spirit for investigation, he combined those rare qualities which, from the first, made him a safe leader, a wise counsellor, a progressive worker, a successful farmer and a reliable neighbor, friend and co-worker. A close intimacy extending over many years has strengthened first impressions of his powers of leadership. Granted a long life of service for his beloved State and its fundamental industry, his faith never wavered and there was little patience with those who doubted the certain outcome of the years. To think as he worked was ever his motto, and thus wherever he spoke, ripe, well digested thoughts, clearly expressed, carried conviction.

His term of public office for the advancement of the agriculture of the State covered that period when service was rendered for the good of the cause and with little thought of compensation, but throughout the years that service was as cheerfully and unstintingly rendered as though the salary had been liberal. Thousands of young men found the way to a happy, prosperous farm life through contact with this loyal friend of the rural home.

As one of the founders of the Maine State Pomological Society, as its president at different times for a long period, he
aided in laying the foundation deep and strong for what today is
an organization of power and influence. We who labor under
more favorable conditions must not lose sight of the long years
of thought and effort necessary to give this society a secure
position with the State and insure that aid without which it
could not exist. Carrying into his study of pomology the same
spirit of investigation manifest elsewhere, backed as it was
with a high conception of the possible value of the fruit industry, he labored incessantly for a wise discrimination in selection of location and varieties, and for that care necessary to
insure fruit of highest quality. Perhaps his most enduring
work on fruit problems has been to strengthen desire for the
few varieties best suited to the State of Maine. In knowledge
of these he was an authority recognized throughout New England. How much of the later growth and prosperity of this
society, and the industry, is due to his wise counsels, earnest
words and faithful work cannot be estimated, but those whose
good fortune it has been to labor with him in his field willingly
bear testimony to his leadership. His was the type of sturdy
American manhood which saves, equalizes and promotes the
better conception of rural life. He was a loyal son of Maine.
He believed in the agricultural possibilities of the State. He
loved rural life. He delighted in good crops, well bred and
selected stock, and an abundant harvest of fruit. He had little
use for the light and trivial but every movement looking to the
betterment of the town, the school, the church, the home,
found in him a warm advocate, a loyal defender, a persistent
worker. His wise counsels in our grange gatherings, institutes
and fruit sessions have been treasured by thousands who have
caught from him a new vision of life, and been lifted to a higher
level of attainments. His devotion was manifest in attendance
upon the Field Day at Highmoor only a few days before his
death. On that occasion he said to the writer, "I am not good
for anything but I could not stay away. I wanted to see what
is being done for better fruit and shake hands with old friends."
Maine waits the coming of the man to take up the work with
his spirit, carry it forward with his determination, and protect

every rural interest with the same devotion to the farm home as characterized his every act.

For more than forty years he was the recognized agricultural leader of Maine, always true to the best interests of the every-day, practical worker in field, barn, orchard, dairy and home.

The sincerest tribute we can offer will be the evident purpose of doing our work with the same devotion, intelligence and loyalty that dominated his life.

G. M. TWITCHELL.

INDEX TO AGRICULTURE REPORT.

INDEX TO POMOLOGIAL REPORT.

Lightning Source UK Ltd.
Milton Keynes UK
UKHW010957030119
334850UK00007B/730/P